UNDERTANDING LOWER PLANTS

By

Dr. Pooja

Deptt. of Botany
R.C.C. College
Ghaziabad (U.P.)
(India)

DISCOVERY PUBLISHING HOUSE PVT. LTD.
NEW DELHI-110 002

Published by:
Tilak Wasan

DISCOVERY PUBLISHING HOUSE PVT. LTD.
4831/24, Ansari Road, Prahlad Street
Darya Ganj, New Delhi-110002 (India)
Phone: +91-11-23279245, 43764432
Fax: +91-11-23253475
E-mail: parul.wasan@gmail.com
info@discoverypublishinggroup.com
discoverypublishinghouse@gmail.com
web: www.discoverypublishinggroup.com

First Edition: **2011**
ISBN: 978-81-8356-859-3

Understanding Lower Plants

Printed at:
Shree Balaji Art Press
Delhi

PREFACE

The present title *"Understanding Lower Plants"* provides a structured approach to learning by covering all the important topics in a uniform, systematic format. The book has been comprehensively designed incorporating recent advances in this fast moving field. It is written to provide accessible information on lower plants in compact form for undergraduate students in biology and related life sciences. It will be useful for both beginning students and those who are more advanced. In addition, busy lecturers who require a quick reference compendium will find it useful, particularly for tutional planning. Simple, yet hopefully clear figures and tables are provided throughout the book.

The over-riding goal of this book, and indeed of the whole *Understanding series,* is to present the essential information concering microbiology in a compact, readily accessible form which leads itself to student learning and revision. The convergence of various approaches has generated a rich panorama of detail, the significance of which we are still attempting to unraval. The present text has been written as an introduction to this rapidly growing field.

To make the work more comprehensive and informative, the author has consulted many authoritative books, research journals, abstracts, monographs etc., so there can be no claim to originality except in the manner of treatment.

The author expresses his thanks to his friends and colleagues whose continue inspirations have initiated him to bring out this book.

The author expresses his gratitude to Mr. Wasan and staff of M/s Discovery Publishing House Pvt. Ltd. for their whole hearted co-operation in the publication of this book.

In the mean time, the author will remain sincerely responsible for any shortcomings of the book and be grateful to the readers for their suggestions and constructive criticism for the continuous betterment of the book. He takes this opportunity to appeal to the readers to send their suggestions straightaway to his Publisher.

Author

CONTENTS

Chapter 1 **1—7**

PLANT SCIENCE

Chapter 2 **8—14**

THE PARTS OF PLANTS

Length of Vegetative Period

Chapter 3 **15—23**

LEARNING TO NAME PLANTS

The Parts of a Leaf, The Veins, Simple and Compound Leaves, Leaf Form, Arrangement of Leaves on Stems, Other stem characters, Species and Genus

Chapter 4 **24—37**

SEASONAL ASPECTS OF PLANTS

The Autumnal Aspect, Colours and Pigments, Pigments and the Colours of Leaves, Pigments not Limited to Leaves, Pigment Formation, Environment and Chlorophyll, Environmental Effects on Carotenoids, Anthocyanins and the Environment, Deciduous and Evergreen Habits, Dormancy and Periodicity, Winter Aspect, Spring Aspect, Summer Aspect

Chapter 5 **38—47**

CELLS AS BIOLOGICAL UNITS

Cells, Solutions, Colloidal Systems, Cytoplasm, The Nucleus, The Vacuole, The Cell Wall

Chapter 6 48—55

THE TISSUE SYSTEM OF LEAVES

Cells and Tissues, Leaf Bud Development, Leaf Development, Leaf Tissues, The Stomata

Chapter7 56—64

NON-GREEN PLANTS

Parasitic Plants, Autophytes, Saprophytic Plants

Chapter 8 65—82

THE BIOLOGY OF BACTERIA

External Factors and Bacteria, Light, Water, Oxygen, Temperature, Bacteria and Sanitation, Bacteria and Disease, Diseases of Plants, Bacteria in Milk, The Science of Bacteriology, Spontaneous Generation, Speculation, Early Experimentation, Sterilization by Heat and Chemicals, The Chemical Theory of Fermentation, Louis Pasteur, Modern Bacteriology, Methods of Killing and Controlling Bacteria

Chapter 9 83—92

BACTERIA OF THE SOIL

Distribution, Nitrogen Sources of Green Plants, Ammonifying and Nitrifying Bacteria, Ammonification, Denitrification, Nitrogen-fixation, The Nitrogen Cycle, Sulfur Bacteria, Bacteria and Phosphates, Iron Bacteria

Chaptrer 10 93—114

THE FUNGI

Vegetative Parts of a Fungus, Bread Mold, Yeasts, Water Molds, Blue and Green Molds, Mildews, Cup Fungi, Morels, and Truffles, Mushrooms, Toadstools, and Puffballs, Fairy Rings, Smuts, Rusts, Slime Molds, Lichens, Fungi and Research

Chapter 11 115—133

PLANT DISEASES

Economic Aspects of Plant Diseases, Symptoms of Plant

Diseases, Control of Plant Diseases, Damping-off, Downy Mildew of Grapes, The Powdery Mildews, Brown Rot of Stone Fruits, Peach Leaf Curl, Wood Rots, The Smuts, Plant Diseases caused by Bacterial, Fire Blight, Fire Blight is Difficult to Control, Clubroot of Cabbage, Galls, Nematode Galls, Virus-diseases of Plants

Chapter 12 134—154

UNDER-WATER ENVIRONMENTS

The Land Habitat, The Water Habitat, The Fresh-Water Environ-ment, Lakes and Ponds, Light, Photosynthesis, Oxygen, Nitrogen, Inorganic Salts, Seasonal Stratification of Water, Plant Population, Rivers and Streams, Marshes, Swamps, and Bogs, The Salt-Water Environment, Plants and Animals in the Ocean, Artificial Environments

Chapter 13 155—186

THE ALGAE

What are algae?, The Kinds of Algae, Economic Aspects of the Algae, Algal Periodicity, The Green Algae: Chlorophyceae, Protococcus, Chlamydomonas, Ulothrix, Oedogonium, The Stone-worts, The Blue-Green Algae: Myxophyceae, The Diatoms: Bacillariophyceae, The Yellow-Green Algae: Xanthophyceae, The Brown Algae: Phaeophyceae, Kelps, The Red Algae: Rhodo-phyceae, Nemalion, Batrachospermum and Lemanea

Chapter 14 187—238

ORGAIZATION AND LIFE CYCLE OF ALGAE

Habitat, Organization of the Plant Body, Classification of Algae, Division Chlorophycophyta, General Features, Motile Unicellular and Colonial Orgaisms, Unicellular Organisms, Carteria, Colonial Organisms, Nonmotile Unicellular and Colonial Organisms, Unicellular Organisms, Zoospore Producers, Azoosporic Organisms, Colonial Types, Azoosporic Organisms, Filamentous Organisms, Zoospore Producers, Azoosporic Organisms, Memberanous Organisms, Coenocytic and Tubular Organisms

Chapter 15 239—254

MOSSES AND LIVERWORTS (BRYOPHYTES)

The Sporophyte and Asexual Reproduction, Classification of Mosses, The Liverwort Plant, The Hornworts

Chapter 16 255—273

FERNS, CLUB MOSSES AND EQUISETUMS (PTERIDOPHYTES)

The Ferns, The Fern Plant, The Sporophyte, The Gametophyte, Fertilization, Embryo of the Sporophyte, Chromosome Numbers, The Aquatic Ferns, The Lycopods or Club Mosses, The Sporophyte, Seeds, The Quillworts, The Equisetums, The Sporophyte, The Gametophyte

Chapter 17 274—285

EUGLENOPHYCOPHYTA AND CHAROPHYTA

Division Euglenophycophyta, Division Charophyta

Chapter 18 286—301

PHAEOPHYCOPHYTA

Ectocarpus, The Kelps, Other Kelps, The Rockweeds: Fucus and Sargassum

Chapter 19 302—324

CHRYSOPHYCOPHYTA AND PYRRHOPHYCOPHYTA

Class 1. Xanthophyceae, Botrydiopsis, Tribonema, Botrydium, Vaucheria, Class 2. Chrysophyceae, General Features, Ochromonas, Synura, Dinobryon, Class 3. Bacillariophyceae, Classification of Diatoms, Division Pyrrhophycophyta, Classification of Pyrrhophycophyta

Chapter 20 325—341

RHODOPHYCOPHYTA

Class 1. Rhodophyceae, Subclass 2. Florideophycidae, Callit-ham-nion, Polysiphonia, Griffithsia

INDEX 342—353

CHAPTER 1

PLANT SCIENCE

Every animal is in some way dependent upon plants every moment of its life. One may well begin the study of botany by inquiring into the ways in which man and other animals of his own community are dependent upon plants and plant products, or are otherwise influenced by plants.

This local survey may be extended into other communities and geographic regions. If the inquiry is also projected into historic and prehistoric records one may learn how plants and a knowledge of plants have played a significant and at times a decisive role in the advance and decline of civilizations in many parts of the world. Everywhere man and other animals use plants directly as food, or eat other animals that feed on plants.

Directly or indirectly all animals are dependent upon plants as the source of food. During the growth of the animal a part of this food is transformed by physiological processes into the substances of which the body is composed. A larger part of it is oxidized within the tissues of the animal, and energy is liberated.

As a result of this liberated energy the temperature of the body of the animal is often maintained above that of its surroundings, and the animal is also able to move about and to do other kinds of work. Through the burning of such plant derivatives as wood, coal, petroleum and gas in furnaces or engines man secures light, heat, electricity, and mechanical energy by which he has been able to modify his immediate environment, supplement his own ability to move about, and transport materials and supplies wherever they are needed or desired. These two products of green plants-food substa-nces and chemically bound energy—are indispensable to all living organisms.

There are also certain substances derived from plants which are essential to the health and well-being of all animals-for example, the vitamins and the mineral elements chemically bound in organic compounds.

With the progress of civilization many other plant products have become indispensable or at least highly desirable. From plants we obtain the materials of which most of our houses are built, finished, and furnished. Much of our clothing is made from plant fibers. Paper and rubber made from plant products have increased our means of communication and transportation.

Many of our beverages and some of our important medicines contain plant derivatives. A large part of the population earns a living by supplying itself and the rest of society with plant parts or plant products. Certain of the larger plants are used to beautify our homes, to decorate the landscape, and in other ways to add to the enjoyment of living.

We use trees to protect us from intense heat and light. Forested areas have become the centers of many forms of sport and recreation. They are also continuous sources of cover and food to countless animals both large and small.

Plants not only hold the soil against erosion by wind and water, but they improve its texture and composition; and myriad microscopic plants contribute to its fertility. But the relation of plants to animals is not wholly beneficent.

Weeds, for example, decrease the yield of crops and greatly increase the labor of cultivating them. Many plants contain toxic and irritating substances that cause suffering, illness, or the death of human beings and other animals. Certain microscopic plants may invade the tissues of the animal body and lead to disease and death.

Others cause diseases and destruction of the larger plants, and still others grow on commercial food products in shipment and storage and lessen their value or destroy them. Such plants test the ingenuity of every generation of human beings to devise means of avoiding, controlling, or eradicating them. The value of plant science to society has been increasingly appreciated as knowledge of plants has advanced.

The farmer who plants a field; the orchardist who attempts to secure a crop of fruits; the florist who seeks the production of ornamental plants and flowers; the forester who tries to obtain a profitable yield of timber on a tract of land; the gardener who supplies our markets with edible and succulent leaves, stems, and roots; industrialists who seek to find new sources and new forms of plant products to meet our social needs; and the conservationists who strive to preserve our soils from wind and water erosion and to rescue our disappearing fish and game animals—all these find themselves confronted by an often bewildering array of problems that lie within the field of *plant science*, or *botany.*

Many of these problems have been solved by a study of the structures, the chemical composition, the physiological processes, the heredity, and the life histories of plants; or by a study of plants in relation to soil and climatic conditions.

Other problems have been solved through the discovery of facts about the growth and chemical diversity of bacteria and fungi, their various effects on the growth of other organisms, and the means of controlling their development.

Numerous unsolved problems remain. That society recognizes the need of continued and far-reaching research with plants is attested by its maintenance of forest and agricultural research stations in every country and in nearly every state and province throughout the world.

Through the years these institutions have provided an increasingly important addition to research by teachers and graduate students in colleges and universities. As a result of these investigations each generation has an increased wealth of botanical knowledge available for both personal and social needs.

Through instruction one may readily learn how to select and apply a portion of this accumulated knowledge. Thus far we have stressed the importance of plants and of the science of plants mainly in relation to human economics, occupations, health, and the survival of all animals.

The general desire of man to know and interpret his environment and to speculate about himself and his environment must also be emphasized here. Plants are a conspicuous and important part of that environment.

In addition to the interrelations of plants and animals there are many important relations among plants themselves, between plants and their physical environments, and between the parts of each individual plant.

These interrelations have been and still are interpreted on the basis of several diverse assumptions ranging from magic to science. Throughout the ages some of these interpretations, whether obtained in the classroom or elsewhere, whether correct or incorrect, have become a part of the general outlook and culture of everyone.

A study of plants as part of a general education would be quite inadequate unless it included interpretations of these interrelations based on present scientific knowledge and method.

In the chapters that follow we shall find that an understanding of these interrelations on the basis of evidence is not only a matter of personal interest, but one that is both desirable and necessary for the welfare of society.

What is a plant? When we pull weeds in a garden, mow the grass on a lawn, enjoy the shrubs and trees in parks and forests, we readily recognize these living organisms as *plants.* Stale bread and fruit may be covered with *mold.* We have all seen other *fungi* in the form of mushrooms in fields and woods.

The surfaces of ponds and moist soil at times become green with "pond scums"-microscopic plants that may be distinguished as *algae.* Those who have visited the seashore are familiar with "seaweeds," which are other and larger kinds of algae.

Tree trunks and rocks that have long been exposed to the weather are often partially covered by gray-green or highly coloured patches of *lichens.* Everyone who even occasionally strolls on forest trails distinguishes some of the *mosses* and *ferns.*

Much of the decay of plant and animal products, and many of the diseases of both plants and animals are due to the presence of *bacteria. All these organisms are plants.*

On first thought it may seem rather easy to answer the question: What is a plant?

But we may be thinking only of such plants as trees, shrubs, and herbs, and of such animals as(men, dogs, and birds. When we include in our survey mosses, algae, fungi, bacteria, and numerous kinds of one-celled animals, the observable differences among plants are often far more striking than those between certain plants and certain animals.

This fact makes it surprisingly difficult to list any group of qualities that are characteristic of plants alone. Similarity of plants and animals. The larger plants differ from the larger animals in so many ways that they not only are readily distinguished but are commonly thought to be quite unrelated.

To suggest that horses and trees have certain characteristics in common may seem absurd. But students of living organisms have found that many of the processes in plants and animals are either identical or essentially similar if the basis of comparison is *limited to certain fundamental features.*

Among the microscopic organisms are many that resemble animals quite as much as they resemble plants; and except for the many things one may learn about plants and animals in trying to do so, it would be futile to try to classify them strictly in either category. The reader may be content to call a certain object a plant because it looks like a plant. One's concept of what looks like a plant, however, is dependent upon the various kinds of plants he has seen and recognized as such.

Concepts versus definitions. Perhaps you will be amazed to learn that even botanists cannot give you an acceptable definition of the term *plants. How* much disturbed should you be? Since you are an animal, would it he reasonable to expect you to know what an animal is?

Can you give an acceptable definition of the term *animals?* Even if definitions can be given when a new subject in botany is opened up for discussion, it may be well to postpone them, for there are almost always excellent opportunities for you to discover for yourself certain things about the phenomenon in question.

Shortly you may discover that, although you have not learned to make an acceptable definition, you have acquired usable concepts which you can continue to enlarge as your knowledge and understanding increase. In this way you will become able to help formulate, evaluate, and apply definitions rather than merely memorize them. A definition may be faulty. Moreover, there are many plant phenomena about which we must be content with reasonable concepts-for example, growth-as well as plant and animal.

The biological sciences. Knowledge that pertains to plants or animals or to both is called biological science. The range of biological information that has accumulated through the centuries-but more especially during the last hundred years-is now so extensive that no one person is entitled to be called a biologist in the sense that he is a master of the whole field.

The facts and principles that have been or may be derived from the study of plants are called botany, and the knowledge similarly gained from the study of animals constitutes zoology. Because of the great diversity of structures and life relations among the many species of both plants and animals, botanists and zoologists have difficulty in viewing their subjects as wholes.

Most botanists have become especially interested in some one or only a few of the many phases of the subject, such as the classification of plants, their physiology, their structure, life histories, diseases, heredity, geography, or geological history. This specialization has certain advantages in research and in practice.

But the behaviour of plants, in the broadest sense, results from interactions among processes characteristic of many special fields of study. Thus in the interpretation of plant phenomena we are forced to seek an ever-widening background of biological, physical, and chemical knowledge. In a general study of plants we shall be concerned not with the special phases of the subject, but with that general background which experience seems to indicate is most worth while to anyone.

We may begin our study as indicated at the beginning of this chapter, or we may prefer to go into the field and learn to distinguish plants from other objects in our environment.

The plants growing all about us are just as important objects of study where they grow as are the materials carried to the laboratory, and they may be studied much more frequently and leisurely. These are two possible methods of approach for beginners. In other chapters of this book several other approaches to the study of plants are suggested; any of them may be preferred to the ones suggested in this chapter.

CHAPTER 2

THE PARTS OF PLANTS

The principal parts, or organs, of the more familiar seed-bearing plants may be distinguished in a bean plant as it develops from the seed that is planted to the seeds that are harvested. This life cycle from seed to seed includes part of two life histories, or generations, of beans; for like a human being each bean plant begins its existence as a single cell.

The young plant, or embryo, already visible in the seed developed from a fertilized egg. After the germination of the embryo in the seed the rest of the life history of the bean plant as well as the development of the embryos of the next generation may be completed in a few weeks.

Some of the structural changes that occur in a growing bean plant may be visualized by studying figures elsewhere in this chapter, but much more can be learned by planting several bean seeds and watching the changes that occur in the plants from day to day.

Within the seed coat is an embryo consisting of a short stalk (the hypocotyl) and a pair of very large, thick, leaf-like structures (the cotyledons) which are at the first node. At the apex of the hypocotyl is a terminal bud (the plumule), and at the other end is a root tip from which the primary root develops.

Two or three days after the seed is planted, the primary root begins to elongate. It breaks through the seed coat and penetrates into the soil. From the primary root lateral roots grow more or less horizontally. The young plant is now firmly anchored, and the rapid growth of the hypocotyl lifts the cotyledons well above

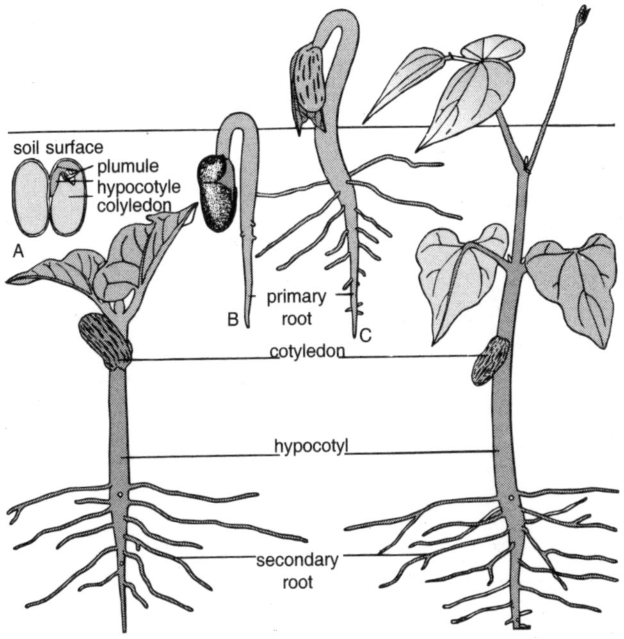

Figure 2.1: Early stages in the development of a bean plant.

the soil surface. As the cotyledons increase slightly in size the broken seed coats fall away. From the plumule a stem bearing leaves begins to develop. A lateral bud soon becomes visible in the axil of each leaf. Each bud consists of a stem tip bearing embryonic leaves.

The first true leaves that develop at the second node of this stem are simple, opposite, and heartshaped. From the terminal bud another stem segment (internode + 3rd node) grows, and from this third node only one leaf forms-this time a leaf of three leaflets.

Growth in height continues by the development of additional stem internodes and new leaves at the nodes until 5 or 6 leaves are formed. In the meantime, leaf-bearing branches may also be developing from the lower lateral buds.

These four distinct parts—the *roots*, the *hypocotyl*, the *stems*, and the leaves—constitute the vegetative organs of the plant. Intern-ally they are all interconnected by veins, or vascular

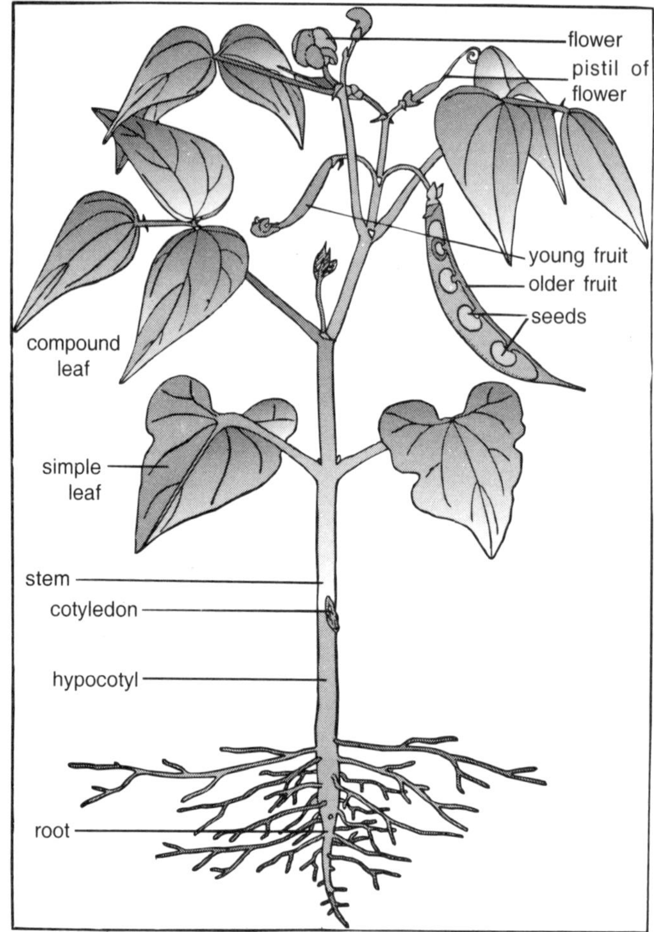

Figure 2.2: Diagram of older bean plant: stem with leaves and flowers, and with fruits (pods) of various ages from the pistil. The seeds are borne within the fruits.

bundles. Usually after the formation of leaf-bearing branches, another type of branch that bears flowers appears. Within a few days a pod, or fruit, begins to develop from the pistil of the flower. As the pod increases in size, seeds develop in it and soon enlarge to the size of the seed that was planted. When the seeds are mature the life cycle of the bean plant is complete. The *flowers*, *fruits*, and *seeds* are often spoken of as the reproductive organs of the

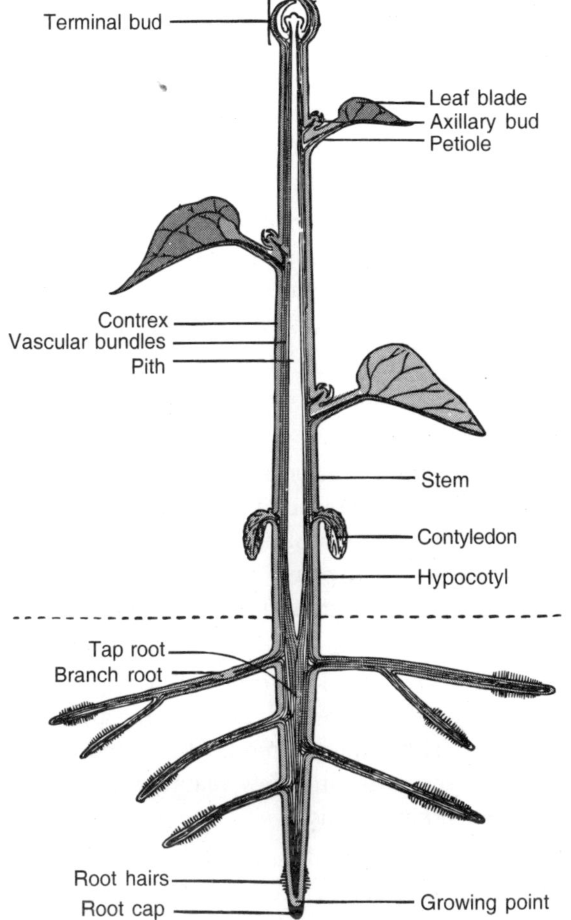

Figure 2.3: Diagram of some external acid internal structures of a seed plant.

plant in contrast to the vegetative body made up of roots, hypocotyl, stems, and leaves.

The major part of the various food-making processes occur in the vegetative organs. Other processes in reproductive structures result in the formation of seeds. Growth and the utilization of food occur in all organs of a plant.

Every generation of a seed plant is in general a repetition of the same orderly sequence of vegetative structures followed by reproductive structures. From past experience you probably have formed general ideas of these several parts of plants.

But if these ideas are vague they will not be useful in either reading or discussion. To regard a leaf merely as the part that is green, a root as the part in the ground, and a seed as what one plants is quite inadequate.

If enough plants are examined it will be discovered that any of these organs may be green, any of them may be found underground, and all of them are planted by man.

A stroll on the campus or in nearby gardens and conservatories for the purpose of learning to distinguish the parts of plants will be much more profitable than a search for technical book definitions.

Roots, for example, are usually thought of as cylindrical, more or less tapering, underground structures. From observations of tropical plants in conservatories, of mature vines growing on walls, and of mature corn plants in a field one will learn that roots are not always underground. Stems are still more variable in form.

They usually are aerial cylindrical structures, but some develop below the soil surface and may become greatly thickened like the tuber of Irish potato. Among the lateral outgrowths of stems are the leaves. Only in a few plants will leaves be found originating from other organs.

There are myriad forms of leaves, but generally they are flat organs with a very large surface compared with their weight. Leaves above the surface of the soil are usually green during at least part of the year. Beginning with such general ideas, one may readily build more accurate and usable concepts of these organs through further personal observations.

Flowers are of every size from a twentieth of an inch to three feet in diameter, and of every colour, often of superb and startling mixtures of colours. Usually flowers are easily recognized, but careful observation is needed to decide what is the flower in the flowering dogwood, Indian paintbrush, calla lilly, jack-in-the-pulpit, snowball, poinsettia, and hydrangea.

Brightly coloured parts are not found exclusively in flowers.

Nor are flowers always brightly coloured, as may be discovered by examining flowers of grasses, sedges, and several kinds of trees.

Fruits usually develop from the pistils or from the pistils and adjoining parts of flowers. The name fruit is applied to a great variety of structures, such as the dry fruits of the grasses, and "sticktights," as well as the succulent berries of the grape and tomato, the fleshy apples and pears, the pumpkins and melons, the firm green fruits of the walnut and of osage orange.

To obtain some notion of the remarkable variety of fruits it is best to observe the transition from flowers to fruits on many

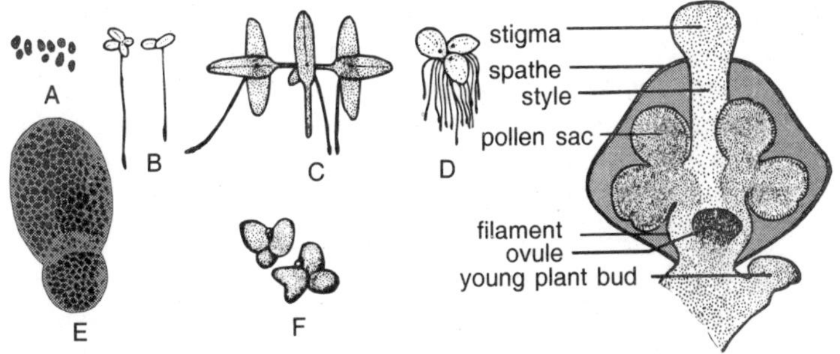

Figure 2.4: The duckweeds are the smallest of the flowering plants: A, Wolffia Columbiana; B, Lemna minor; C, L. trisulca, and D, Spirodela polyrhiza, natural size; E, Wolfa, enlarged; F, flowers of L. trisulca on floating plants, natural size; G, a flower of L. minor, much enlarged. F and G drawn from photographs by W. H. Camp and L. E. Hicks.

kinds of plants at any time such observations can be made in the field or greenhouse.

Seeds develop from certain structures in the pistil of the flower and are borne inside the fruit. They may be very minute; they rarely exceed a few inches in length. Their most general characteristic is the presence of a firm coat or shell surrounding an embryo plant from which an adult plant may develop more or less like the plant on which the seed was borne.

Length of Vegetative Period

The bean plant matures in a few weeks; that is, the formation of reproductive organs takes place after a relatively short vegetative period. The vegetative period of plants may be either long or short; it depends both on the kind of plant and on the environment. Some of the autumn flowering plants start from seeds in the spring.

Some grasses, clovers, primroses, and carrots start from seeds in late summer and remain in the vegetative condition until the second summer. The so-called century plant grows vegetatively 20 to 30 years before it bears flowers, fruits, and seeds. Woody plants grow vegetatively from a few to many years, and tlwn for many succeeding years reproduce during each growing season.

In later chapters it will be shown how the vegetative period of a plant may be lengthened or shortened by such external factors as light, temperature, moisture, and soil salts.

We have referred thus far only to the more familiar seed-bearing plants, most of which have the seven principal plant organs in one form or another. Some seed plants lack one or more of these organs. Some of the duckweeds have a small globose body with no distinction of root, stem, or leaf; others have a flattened body with a well-formed simple root; all of them have flowers, fruits, and seeds.

The wellknown Spanish "moss" of the South has no roots. Many cacti are notable for the absence of leaves. In some plants, such as the dandelion and the common plantain, the stem is merely a small flattened cone at the top of the root.

The tropical parasitic plant *Rafesia* has neither roots nor leaves-just a short stem, a flower, a fruit, and seeds. Ferns have roots, stems, and leaves but no flowers, fruits, or seeds. The pond scums and seaweeds (algae) have none of these organs, and certainly there are no organs closely resembling them among the fungi.

It is evident that none of these organs is essential to all plants, but they are generally present in seed-bearing plants. As we shall see later, certain fundamental processes are usually associated with each of them but are not necessarily limited to them.

CHAPTER 3

Learning to Name Plants

We shall not get very far in the study of plants without studying them in the field and greenhouse. In order to observe and discuss plants intelligently, we must have appropriate names for them. Many common plants have local names which may suffice for ordinary conversation. But the names applied in one community may be different from those in another.

Furthermore, the same name is often used for quite different plants in other localities. Many other plants lack common names. To overcome these difficulties scientific names have been given to all the known *species* of plants, and by agreement these names are used and understood by botanists everywhere.

Botanists have recognized and named more than a quarter of a million species of plants. As a beginning it will be sufficient to know some of the local seed-bearing plants. Many plants can be recognized readily by their leaf and stem characters.

For the recognition of others, flowers, fruits, and seeds may have to be observed. Names of plants may be obtained from others who know them or from published "keys." To make the simplest keys or to use those made by others, it is necessary to examine the external features of leaves and stems and become acquainted with the terms that are applied to their parts, forms, and arrangements.

The Parts of a Leaf

If one examines a leaf, such as that of Japanese quince, it is evident that it consists of a broad, thin *blade,* a narrow cylindrical

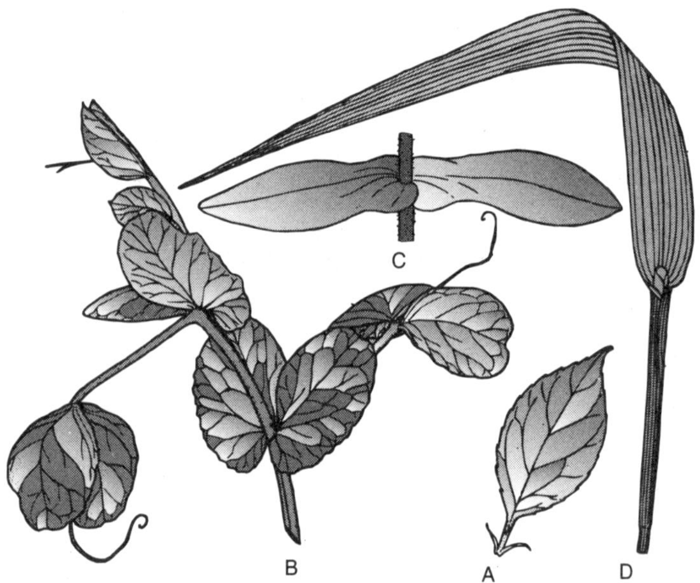

Figure 3.1: Diagrams of some parts of leaves. A, blade, petiole, and stipules of apple leaf; B, stem of pea bearing leaves composed of two large stipules, leaflets, and a terminal tendril; C, sessile leaves of zinnia; D, blade, ligule, and sheath of a grass leaf.

petiole, and at the base of the petiole a pair of small appendages, the *stipules.* A leaf consisting of these three parts is frequently called a *complete leaf.*

The primary parts of a complete leaf, then, are the blade, petiole, and stipules. The stipules are usually small structures; but some of them, such as those of pansy, Japanese quince, and garden pea, are large and bladelike.

Those of buckwheat and smartweed are *sheaths* surrounding the stem for some distance above the point of attachment. Stipules of the greenbrier are *tendrils,* and those of the black locust are *spines.* Some leaves have no apparent petioles and are described as *sessile.*

The leaves of many grasses, such as those of oats, wheat, and bluegrass, have neither petioles nor stipules; the blades are attached to the stem by *a sheath* which may be long or short. At the top of the sheath is a collarlike extension called the *ligule.*

The ligule of the bamboo and certain other grasses may consist merely of several long bristles. The needle leaves of such trees as pines and spruces appear superficially to be quite unlike those of broad-leaved trees. The leaves of pines and larches are in clusters, or *fascicles,* at the end of short *dwarf branches.* Spruce, fir, and hemlock' have solitary leaves. The leaves of arbor vitae are small *scales* oppositely arranged on the stem.

The Veins

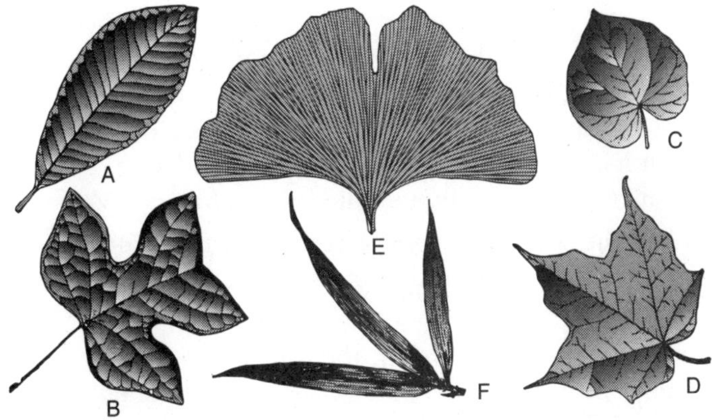

Figure 3.2: Arrangement of the larger veins. The leaves of magnolia (A) and tuliptree (B) exemplify pinnate venation; red bud (C) and black maple (D), palmate venation. Veins may also be parallel as in the bamboo (F) or dichotomous as in the ginkgo (E).

The most conspicuous structures of an elm leaf are the veins. The large vein near the middle of the blade is the *midrib.* In a maple leaf there are several prominent veins which are called the *principal veins.*

In general, the smaller veins form a network and unite with larger veins, which in turn connect with the midrib or the principal veins. These larger veins are smallest at the apex and margin of the leaf and gradually become larger toward the middle and base of the blade.

The arrangement of the veins of a leaf is termed *venation.* There are four general arrangements of the *principal veins* in leaves that are easily recognized. Leaves of oats and other grasses have *parallel venation,* the veins extending more or less parallel

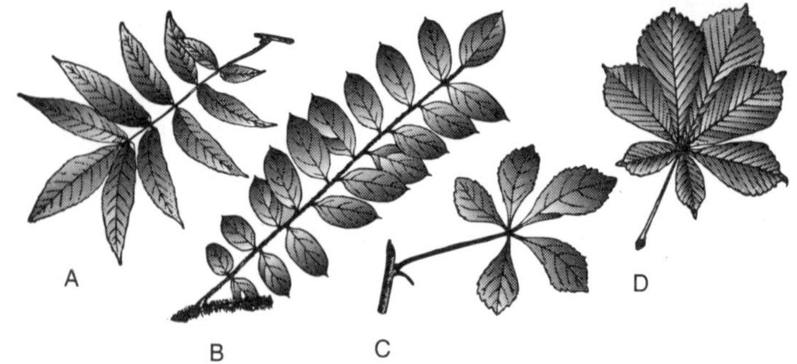

Figure 3.3: The leaves of bitternut hickory and clammy locust are pinnately compound (A-B). Those of Aralia and horse chestnut are palmately compound (C-D).

from base to apex. Many ferns and the curious ginkgo tree have leaves with *forked* or *dichotomous venation;* that is, each vein divides at intervals into two smaller veins of equal size.

When the secondary veins extend from the midrib like the divisions of a feather, as in the leaves of elm, the venation is said to be *pinnate.*

In the maple leaf, however, the principal veins extend from the petiole near the base of the blade, roughly simulating the bones in our hands. This type of venation is *palmate.*

Simple and Compound Leaves

Every leaf consisting of one continuous blade only is known as *a simple* leaf. A *compound* leaf such as that of the rose consists of several leaflets. If the leaflets are joined to the end of the petiole, as are those of the horse chestnut, the leaf is described as *palmately compound.*

When a compound leaf is composed of leaflets joined to the sides of the central axis of the leaf (the *rachis),* it is termed *pinnately compound.* The leaflets in a compound leaf may be odd or even in number.

Compound and simple leaves are usually readily distinguished, but some divided simple leaves closely resemble those commonly described as compound. Such leaves as those of tomato and potato which have deeply divided blades can scarcely be distinguished from compound leaves.

In fact, there is apparently every gradation between simple undivided leaves and distinctly compound leaves. A bud may be found in the axil of each leaf of broad-leaved trees and shrubs, but there are no buds in the axils of leaflets.

Leaf Form

The shape of a leaf is usually characteristic of a species, and the form of the *apex* and the *base* of the blade may be distinctive. Leaves may also have characteristic edges, or *margins.* Some of the common terms used to describe leaves are illustrated in Figure elsewhere in this chapter.

Arrangement of Leaves on Stems

Leaves usually have definite arrangements on the stem. On willow twigs the leaves are *alternately* and *spirally* arranged. There is a single leaf at each node, and a line drawn through the successive points of attachment forms a spiral about the stem.

The leaves of maple occur two at a node on opposite sides of the stem and exemplify the *opposite* arrangement. The plane of attachment of each successive pair of leaves is at right angles to that of the leaves immediately above and below.

The catalpa twigs have three leaves at a node arranged radially. This arrangement is termed *whorled* or *cyclic.* There are several types of spiral arrangement of alternate leaves. If the spiral runs halfway round the stem in passing from one node to the next, as in elm or corn, the arrangement is described as 1/2 alternate. This arrangement is called two-ranked because the points of attachment of the leaves ppear in two ranks, one on either side of the stem when the stem is viewed endwise.

If leaves are attached at angles of 120° that is, the spiral passes through 3 nodes before completing a cycle and the fourth leaf-base is directly over the first-they are said to have the 1/3 alternate arrangement. These'leaves occur in three ranks on the stem. This arrangement is best seen in the sedges.

Many trees have a more complicated leaf alignment. A spiral drawn around the stem from one bud to another directly below it passes through 5 nodes and twice around the stem; the sixth bud is directly below the first bud.

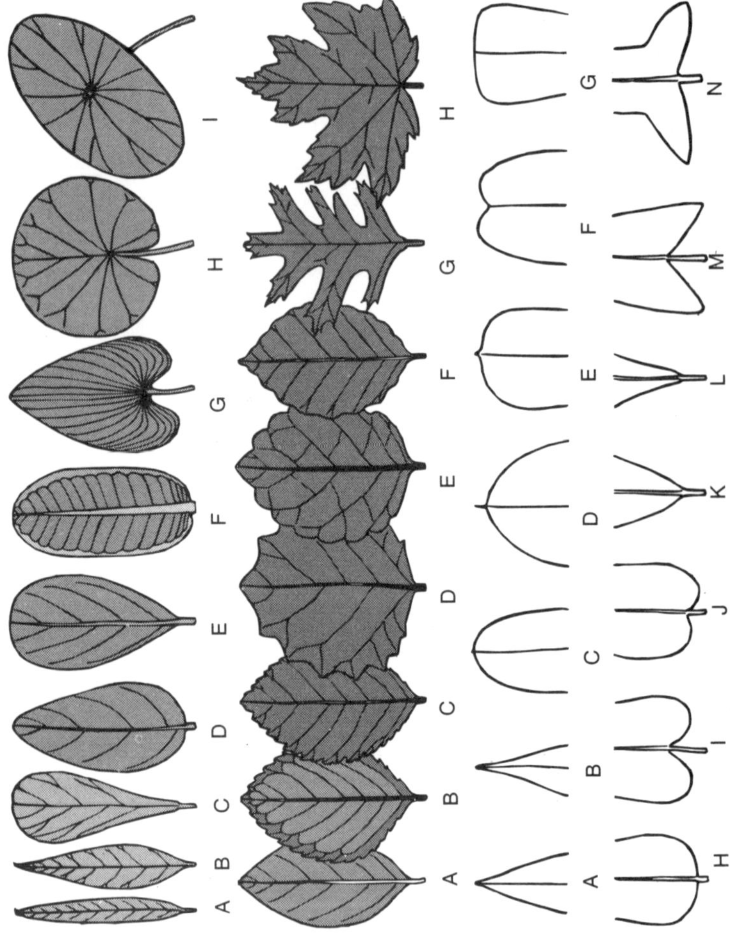

Figure 3.4: Forms of leaves. Upper row-forms of leaf blades: A, linear; B, lanceolate; C, spatulate; D, ovate; E, obovate; F, oblong; G, cordate; H, orbiculate; I, peltate.
Second row-forms of leaf margins: A, entire; B, serrate; C, doubly serrate; D, dentate; E, crenate; F, undulate; G, pinnately lobed; H, palmately lobed.
Third row-forms of apexes of blades: A, acute; B, acuminate; C, obtuse; D, aristate; E, mucronate; F, retuse; G, truncate.
Lower row-forms of bases of blades: H, rounded; I, equally lobed; J, obliquely lobed; K, acute; L, acuminate; M, sagittate; N, hastate.

Figure 3.5: Diagram of leaf arrangement on stems, as seen from above and from the side. A, oppositely arranged leaves; B-D, alternately arranged leaves. B, the onehalf, or two-ranked, arrangement; C, the one-third, or three-ranked, arrangement; D, the two-fifths, or five-ranked, arrangement.

This arrangement is called the 2/5 alternate type. Still other leaf and scale arrangements may be found, such as 3/8, 5/13, 8/21. The numerator of any fraction in the series is equal to the sum of the two preceding numerators.

The same relationship holds for the denominators. These arrangements of leaves are not invariable. Owing to the influence of light on the growth of stems and leaves that are not equally illuminated on all sides, the stems become twisted and the arrangements are altered.

Other stem characters

Certain other stem characters are often used to identify trees and shrubs. Since a *bud* is present in the axil of each leaf of most deciduous trees and shrubs, bud arangement is a useful character in the dormant season when there are no leaves on the stems. Buds differ in size and form in different species.

Their outer *scales* may be smooth or hairy. *Leaf scars,* which are left when the leaves have fallen, also have rather definite shapes and patterns. The outer covering or bark of a twig may be green or gray or brown, and various other descriptive terms are applied to its surface, such as smooth or rough, ridged or warty.

In a few instances the colour and form of the *pith* may be distinctive. Keys to plants based on vegetative characters. If we examine a maple tree we notice that its leaves are simple, lobed, palmately veined, and oppositely arranged on the stem. No other trees in North America have all four of these characters.

The eastern hemlocks have short-petioled, needle-like flattened leaves with white lines on the under surface. When characters such as these are definitely assorted and grouped so that by careful reading and comparison with the specimen in hand we may find the name of the plant, we have what is known as a *key.*

Many keys have been published for the plants of local, state, and national regions. Local keys are usually more convenient because the number of plants included is smaller. For the beginner those based on such external characters of leaves and stems as are outlined above are most useful; moreover, they are quite adequate for the identification of most trees and shrubs.

Keys are often based on the forms and detailed structures of flowers, fruits, and seeds; such keys are necessary to identify , many of the common herbs. Keys based on both vegetative and reproductive characters are more difficult to use since they imply considerable knowledge of structures and terminology.

Species and Genus

No one expects anything but an oak tree to develop from an acorn, or anything but a hickory tree from a hickory nut. To go a step farther, when white-oak acorns are planted the individual trees that develop are normally all white oaks like the parent trees. These individual white oaks all belong to a single *species.*

Similarly black oaks develop from the acorns of black-oak trees, and only yellow oaks grow from yellow-oak acorns. Species that have many fundamental characters in common are grouped together as a *genus* (plural *genera*).

We do this in common speech when we speak of the "oaks," and we identify the *species* when we say this is a white oak or a black oak. Botanists long ago began the use of Latin names in order to avoid the confusion arising from the fact that common names applied to the same plant in different localities differ widely, and the impossibility of learning these common names in several hundred languages.

The Roman name of the oak is *Quercus* and the Latin word for white *is alba;* hence the name chosen for white oak *is Quercus alba. All* oaks belong to the genus *Quercus,* and for each species a second name is chosen by the author who first describes the species; by agreement subsequent authors use this same name.

This is a great convenience, for students of all countries can use the same language when referring to the names of plants. These names have come into such general acceptance in all scientific writings that they are often spoken of as "scientific names" in contrast to the "common names" which may vary in every locality and country.

CHAPTER 4

Seasonal Aspects of Plants

The succession of the seasons and the changes in plants and landscapes associated with them are familiar to everyone who has lived in the temperate zone. Even in the tropics there are but few localities in which seasonal changes in weather and in plants do not occur.

Changes in plants during the year have always attracted attention, even of primitive men. They have inspired much prose and poetry, as well as scientific study and description. Explanations for their occurrence were proposed so far back in the history of the human race that they became an important part of mythology and folklore.

Even today newspapers and magazines frequently contain stories that are merely new versions of these ancient myths which ascribed supernatural and mysterious powers of foresight to plants and animals alike. The changes that occur in the form and appearance and in the relative abundance of different species from season to season may be seen in the lawns, pastures, cultivated fields, and forests of your own community.

An accurate account-a diary-of such observations over a period of a few years would include many valuable botanical data. This is another way in which the study of plants may be approached. Many seasonal phenomena may be studied best as individual problems during appropriate seasons when the material is abundant and observations may be made over extended periods of time.

As an aid to such preliminary observations, certain facts about seasonal aspects of plants have been brought together in this chapter. Data helpful in further observations and interpretations are included in many of the subsequent chapters.

There are such great differences in the behaviour of individual species that few generalizations apply equally to all kinds of plants. Some of the questions and problems that are sure to arise from your own preliminary observations may be solved by further study or by well-planned simple experiments.

Let us begin with plants in autumn when most courses in botany begin, and, by following the cycle of the seasons, consider some of the most apparent changes that occur in plant processes and plant organs.

THE AUTUMNAL ASPECT

The summer with its long days, high temperatures, and intense light is waning. The effects of cooler weather and of the shorter period of daylight upon certain chemical processes in plants soon become evident in the leaves of our deciduous trees and shrubs.

The green colour of chlorophyll gradually disappears, and the yellow pigments with which the green pigment had been associated in the cells of the leaves now become conspicuous. In many leaves there is an additional formation of other pigments which range in colour from red to purple and which are called collectively the anthocyanins.

As the season advances both the yellow pigments and the anthocyanins break down; and brown substances, especially tannins, increase and modify the leaf colour. When the autumn is characterized by bright sunshine and moderately cool weather colouration is at its best.

When frost occurs early or when the weather is wet and cloudy, the anthocyanins are formed to only a slight extent and the yellow and brown pigments are dominant in the landscape.

These autumn colour changes in the leaves of many deciduous trees contrast sharply with the persistent green colour of both the needle-leaved and broad-leaved evergreens. Many herbs likewise remain green through the winter months, at least in parts near the soil. Furthermore, the leaves of some trees and shrubs remain green until after they have fallen to the ground.

Colours and Pigments

The colour we ascribe to an object or substance depends upon the kinds of light rays that pass from it to the retinas of our eyes. When a beam of "white" light passes through a clear glass prism the rays of different wave length are separated by refraction and appear as bands of colour.

Similarly we see a rainbow when the different rays of ordinary daylight are reflected to our eyes in separate bands by drops of water in the atmosphere. On the one side of the bow we perceive the longer waves of light as red, on the other side the short waves as violet.

Between these extremes the bands of orange, yellow, green, blue, and indigo represent in order colour perceptions resulting from the effects of rays of successively shorter wave lengths. The colours of objects are also partly dependent upon the relative sensitiveness of our eyes to the different rays of light.

They are especially sensitive to the rays we perceive as green and yellow. The various chemical compounds in plants absorb certain light rays and reflect others. We receive our colour impressions from the reflected rays. As a matter of convenience we call these compounds pigments and we ascribe to them the colours perceived through the eye when light is reflected from them.

Thus we speak of green pigments, yellow pigments, and various others from red to violet. Among the most important pigments in plants are *chlorophylls* (leaf green) ; the *carotenoids* (including carotenes and xanthophylls), varying from pale yellow to orangered; and the *ant hocyanins*, varying from red through blue to violet.

Pigments and the Colours of Leaves

The colours of certain leaves-for example, the purple-leaved coleus and canna-may result from a combination of all these pigments. The anthocyanins may occur in the outer cell layers of the leaf, the chlorophylls and carotenoids in the inner cell layers.

When a red leaf is placed in hot water the anthocyanins disappear from the cells into the water and the green colour of the chlorophyll within becomes evident. The chlorophylls and carotenoids may be dissolved from the leaves by alcohol, and then separated from each other by appropriate chemical means.

Carotenoids are always present in green leaves, but their presence is obscured by the chlorophylls until the latter disintegrate. Surprising as it may seem, the carotenoids may be present in as large amounts in the leaves of midsummer as in the yellow autumn leaves.

In many common trees and shrubs the anthocyanins are formed mainly in the autumn; in others, such as certain varieties of maple, the young leaves also may be red. The anthocyanin in purple varieties of beech, plum, hazel, and barberry is evident throughout the growing season. Many other examples of leaf pigmentation may be found in every community.

Pigments not Limited to Leaves

Of course these pigments are not limited to the leaves of plants. The presence of chlorophyll in most herbaceous stems and the young stems and twigs of woody species is familiar to all. Likewise, certain parts of flowers are usually green, and the term "green fruits" has come to be a synonym of young fruits in common speech.

Many varieties of fruits remain green when ripe, while in others the chlorophyll disintegrates and the associated yellow pigments become more evident. In still others anthocyanins partially or wholly mask the yellow. Some seeds, such as those of certain varieties of peas and beans, are green.

Chlorophyll is formed in the aerial roots of many orchids and in the roots of many other plants when they are exposed to light. The carotenoids seem always to be present wherever chlorophyll occurs. They may also occur in the absence of chlorophyll.

Carotenoids are the underlying cause of the yellow and orange colours of the flowers of zinnias, sunflowers, and goldenrods; of the fruits of oranges, lemons, and tomatoes; and of the seeds of corn, peas, and clover.

The anthocyanins are most conspicuous in red, purple, and blue flowers and fruits; but purple cabbage, potatoes, popcorn, and beets exemplify their common occurrence in other plant parts. Among the fungi (molds, lichens, mushrooms) other pigments may be as brilliant and varied as are those in our common green plants.

Pigment Formation

Among the common plants one may find some species that lack anthocyanins, while others are without chlorophyll and carotenoids. The absence of a pigment from a plant, or a part of a plant, may be due to its heredity, its stage of development, or some condition in the environment of the plant.

Chlorophyll is not formed in the cells of toadstools or in "Indian pipe" in any environment. Neither is it formed in some parts of variegated leaves under any circumstances.

The other pigments also may be absent from certain plants regardless of the conditions under which they develop. The absence of pigments in these plants must be due to the hereditary constitution of the plant.

Environment and Chlorophyll

Any condition that is necessary for the maintenance of the plant is indirectly essential to the formation of plant pigments. There are, however, certain conditions that are more directly related to it. In most plants light seems to be necessary for the making of chlorophyll. We are all familiar with blanched celery in which the part deprived of light lacks chlorophyll, or with the white and yellow potato sprouts that develop in a dark cellar.

During the warm nights of early spring bluegrass grows rapidly, and in the early morning the base of the blade that grew during the night is disclosed by its lack of chlorophyll. But in some plants light is not necessary for the formation of the green pigments.

Green seedlings of spruce, pine, and other conifers may develop in the dark. Grapefruit and lemon seedlings, certain algae, and the sporelings of mosses and ferns may synthesize chlorophyll in darkness if they are supplied with sugar.

Sugar is one of the substances from which the chlorophylls are made, and from the formulas of chlorophyll it is evident that compounds of nitrogen and magnesium are also utilized. Experiments have shown that manganese and iron are essential to the formation of chlorophyll, but they do not constitute a part of the chlorophyll molecule.

The seedlings of some green plants growing at temperatures below 50° F. may fail to form chlorophyll, and unless the temperature is raised they ultimately die.

Environmental Effects on Carotenoids

The formation of the yellow pigments is also dependent upon certain environmental conditions. The seedlings of some varieties of corn and other plants are conspicuously yellow when growing in darkness; others, such as oats, are colourless under the same conditions and become yellow only when exposed to light.

Perhaps there are certain factors that might be substituted for light in these cases, but they have not been discovered. Seedlings in which chlorophyll is made in the dark also contain carotenoids.

Anthocyanins and the Environment

The roots of some plants, such as beets and radish, become red or purple in darkness; but light is necessary for the formation of anthocyanins in most leaves and fruits. In some instances the blue and violet rays are necessary.

In both leaves and fruits intensity of colour is increased by abundance of light, relatively low temperature, and a low supply of nitrates and certain other inorganic ions in the soil.

Apparently these environmental conditions influence the formation of anthocyanins partly through their influence on the sugar content of the cells, but many other conditions within the cells are necessary for the formation of anthocyanins. Leaves and fruits on the same tree or on the same variety of tree in different local situations may differ widely in the amount of anthocyanin they contain.

Peaches in the top of the tree, and apples fully exposed to the sunlight are redder than those inside the crown and shaded by the outer foliage. The more intense colouring of fruits from the Northwestern States as compared with those from the Eastern States exemplifies this same principle.

Low night temperatures also are very important in the accumulation of sugar and the formation of bright colours in apples. At low temperatures anthocyanin formation increases in many evergreen plants; for example, the leaves of certain varieties of juniper and arbor vitae become copper-coloured in autumn, and similar changes occur in many heaths, of which the cranberry is an example.

The intensity of anthocyanin colours of flowers may vary with light intensity. The red colour in some flowers is associated with an acid condition, and blue with an alkaline condition.

If a red geranium petal is crushed on a blotter and held alternately near ammonia and acetic acid, one may see these colour changes. Similar colour changes may also be seen in the uncrushed petals. This change in colour does not occur in all anthocyanins because of the presence of certain ions, such as potassium.

The flowers of the cobaea vine change from green to red, and finally to violet, as they fade. Some rose flowers are pink when the buds unfold and bluish when they fall. Flowers of the French hydrangea are blue when the plants grow in acid soils containing salts of aluminum.

They are rose coloured when the plants grow in alkaline limestone soils where the aluminum salts are insoluble. It must be remembered that the anthocyanins form a very large group of chemical compounds, and the behaviour of the pigments of any particular plant may be explained only by the properties of the particular pigments present in that plant.

Deciduous and Evergreen Habits

Another striking autumn phenomenon is the falling of the leaves from many species of plants. This has been shown to be definitely related to the shortening daily period of light. During the summer a specialized layer of cells, called the *absciss layer*, forms at the base of petioles and leaflets.

The subsequent disintegration of this layer may be started by conditions within the leaf brought about by a variety of external conditions such as drought, change in length of day, low temperatures, or leaf injuries. Hence any one, or all, of these conditions may bring about leaf fall. Trees and shrubs that lose all or nearly all of their full-grown leaves annually are said to be *deciduous*.

In contrast to deciduous plants are those in which the life of any one leaf extends through several years. These plants may have either broad or needle leaves and their appearance varies but little from season to season; the most familiar examples are the *evergreen* trees and shrubs.

Many herbaceous plants also have green leaves during the winter, as for example, the common dandelion, evening primrose, teasel, and chickweed. These also might be classed as evergreens.

Dormancy and Periodicity

The gradual lowering of the temperature and decrease in the length of the daily light period lead not only to pigment changes and leaf fall, but to the death of many plants that started from seed the preceding spring. Some part of the plant, however, remains alive and dormant throughout the late summer, autumn, or winter.

The part or parts that remain alive and dormant vary greatly with the kind of plant. If the plants have completed one life cycle-including germination of the seed, vegetative development, flowering, fruiting, seed formation, and death—within a single warm season, they are called *annuals.* The dormant organ of such plants is the seed.

The seeds of some annuals, however, may germinate in the autumn; the plants pass the winter in the vegetative condition and bear seed the following spring.

When the life cycle from seed germination to seed formation covers a part of two warm seasons the plant is called a *biennial.* Shepherd's-purse may grow as an annual or as a biennial in certain climates, and wheat is cultivated both as "winter wheat" and as "spring wheat."

Varieties of wheat have been selected for each of these growth regimes. During the life cycle of many biennials the first season of growth ends with the formation of a thickened root, a short stem, and a rosette of leaves near the soil surface.

These young plants remain dormant during the winter and in the second growing season their life cycle is completed by the development of upright stems, flowers, fruits, and seeds. Then the plant dies.

Whether certain plants grow as annuals, biennials, or perennials depends upon the temperature, length of day, and length of the growing season to which they are exposed.

The *perennial herbs* are like annuals and biennials in having a vegetative stage previous to the formation of flowers and fruits, but differ from them in having continuous vegetative growth and seed formation for many successive seasons.

The annual active period of growth of perennial herbs is followed by a dormant one when most of the living plant is underground, with no parts extending much above the soil surface. Some of these plants have "winter rosettes" of leaves, others have very short lateral branches with small leaves, and still others have large buds above ground.

Some of the perennial herbs may continue living indefinitely. Perhaps some have been living in their present localities for centuries; but since a part of the underground roots, or stems, dies each year and new parts are added each year, the age of the oldest part of the plant body is rarely more than 3 to 10 years.

Trees and shrubs are *woody perennials;* they may live 5 to 10 years or longer before they begin to bear flowers, fruits, and seeds. Any horticulturist or forester will tell you that there is great variation in the abundance of reproductive structures in trees from year to year and that certain trees bear fruits and seeds only once in several years. This periodicity is dependent in part on weather and soil conditions, and in part on heredity.

Winter Aspect

The most distinctive feature of plants in winter is the dormancy of most plant organs. The internal causes of dormancy characteristic of late summer and autumn usually disappear during the winter months, but owing to low temperatures no growth occurs.

Many plants will start developing at this time if they are moved into a greenhouse. Nevertheless, some processes continue within plants that have every appearance of being dormant. Roots develop slowly in unfrozen soil, and there may be some movement of materials within the plant body.

In plants with green parts (winter wheat, bluegrass, and evergreen trees and shrubs) food manufacture may occur when daytime temperatures are above the freezing point. Witch hazel and alders may flower during winter thaws, as well as during late autumn and early spring.

Winter and early spring are the best periods in which to study the characteristic buds, twigs, and bark of the woody perennials. By means of these characteristics one may readily learn to identify trees in winter.

The leaves of temperate evergreens vary in their endurance of freezing temperatures. A sudden exposure to low winter temperatures during midsummer kills them. Most of them, however, withstand temperatures well below the freezing point after they have become "hardened" by exposure to the gradual changes in temperature during autumn.

Figure 4.1: Diagram of winter rosette of leaves of teasel (A), and of evening primrose (B).

But they do have limits below which injury or death results from low temperatures. In some species injury results only when the low temperatures continue for several days. Others are killed by exposure to temperatures below freezing for a few hours. Twigs and parts of larger stems also may he killed by low temperature.

In any part of the temperate zone trees and shrubs may be "killed back" by extremely low temperatures. The amount of "winter injury" varies from year to year, and many interesting problems occur to the careful observer.

Winter injury may result from low temperature alone; but in many instances it results from a drying up of the plant during sudden thaws in late winter or in early spring while the soil is still frozen.

The roots of winter wheat and other grasses are often broken or pulled from the soil as it is heaved by the formation of layers of ice beneath the surface of the soil. When subzero temperatures occur, the water in the buds, twigs, and smaller branches is frozen. Still lower temperatures may even freeze the water in the trunks of large trees.

A sudden drop to a very low temperature may result in the splitting of the wood and bark. There is another effect of winter that is quite beneficial, or even necessary, to many plants. Many sedds and buds do not germinate readily unless they have been exposed to temperatures near the freezing point for several weeks.

Many plants, such as blueberries, unless exposed to a low temperature in the dormant period, do not grow well during the following season. Neither of these cases of "winter conditioning" depends upon actual freezing; indeed, many plants grow best after an exposure to a temperature of 5° to 10° above the freezing point for a few months.

Tulip, hyacinth, and narcissus bulbs that are to be "forced" into early blooming are planted out-of-doors; after several weeks of winter temperatures they are brought indoors. Without this low-temperature treatment of the bulbs, the new plants will develop poorly and bear malformed flowers or none.

Inquiry among local nurserymen will probably disclose other practical problems connected with the winter season.

Spring Aspect

The lengthening of the daylight period and increase in temperature bring to an end the dormant period of plants. Lawns and fields begin to green through renewed growth of dormant leaves and buds. Buds on many trees and shrubs enlarge and a new set of twigs and leaves develops.

This is the best time of year to see that the buds of woody plants are stem tips bearing either leaves or rudicmentary flowers, or both, usually with an outer covering of scales. Examination of trees and shrubs at this time will disclose not only these three types of buds, but also several ways in which buds "open" and enlarge. This is the time of year when you can learn by your own observations: which buds on different plants open first and from what buds the current year's branches develop, whether the extension of the main stem or branch always develops from the terminal bud, and if the branches from all lateral buds grow equally.

You can also ascertain whether leaves and flowers develop on twigs from the same or from separate buds, which of our common trees blossom before the development of leaves, and whether these flowers are borne on twigs of the previous year or only on new twigs.

These are but a few of the questions that may be answered by a study of woody plants in the field. With the coming of spring countless millions of seedlings appear in every unoccupied plot of ground. New branches develop on perennials and biennials, and leaves are followed soon after by masses of flowers of every imaginable hue.

Spring is the period of most rapid development in most plants, partly because the overwintering parts have been "conditioned" by the low temperature and partly because of increased light, increased length of day, and an abundance of available water in the soil.

After growth has started it may be retarded either by drought or by low temperatures. On the other hand, elongation of the stems and expansion of the leaves of most trees and shrubs stop within a few weeks, even if temperature and moisture conditions continue unchanged. The growth of new stem segments is definitely limited by internal conditions and their elongation usually ceases by late May or June in northern latitudes.

Sprouts from stumps and pollarded trees continue to elongate for several weeks more. This is the period when many of the flowering plants of densely shaded woods have their annual development, flower, fruit and return to dormancy. In the open there are many plants in which the period of development continues into the summer and autumn before flower, fruit, and seed formation closes the annual cycle.

Spring, then, is the period of most active growth of roots and shoots of woody plants. It is the period of most active utilization of food, and the period of rapid respiration and food synthesis. The high rates of these processes stand in sharp contrast to their much lower rates during the winter season.

Summer Aspect

With the coming of the longest days temperatures are high, and available soil water on the average begins to decline. Growth of plants, as a whole also declines, but many of the flowers of springtime are now being followed by fruits and seeds.

The development of branches and the enlargement of trunks of trees and shrubs are greatly reduced. Soil water declines to the point where many plants with shallow root systems wilt, and summer leaf fall may take place. Some plants or plant parts may become dormant as a result of high temperature and the long daylight period.

There are fewer plants in bloom in midsummer than in spring of autumn. The smaller grasses have attained maturity and completed their life cycles. The larger grasses, such as corn, continue development and bloom in summer.

Summer is the period of greatest food accumulation in the stems and roots of biennials and perennials. It is also the period when fungi and bacteria cause numerous plant diseases and rapid decay of organic matter.

Insects also have reached maximal abundance, and their

injuries to leaves and stems and fruits become most apparent. Some plants bloom only when the days are long and the nights are short. As a result the summer season is the time of flowering of corn, clover, mallows, cotton, and many other plants.

As the days become shorter at the close of summer and the temperatures decline, increased water is available in many parts of the United States because less of the rainfall is lost by evaporation. The water relations of plants are improved over those of the summer and the growth of many herbaceous plants increases.

Not infrequently a second wave of flowering occurs in some plants, such as violets, that bloom abundantly during the spring months. But the further decline in temperature brings the conditions of autumn, and we have completed our very brief view of the more noticeable seasonal phenomena.

We have observed that certain vegetational aspects are character-istic of each season; that some phases of growth belong to one season rather than to another; and that dormancy, growth, maturity, and death of plants form a regularly recurring cycle.

The problems of plant science are all about us and each season brings its own challenges to investigation and understanding. We need not confine our outdoor study of botany to a single environment, to one season of the year, or to any one locality.

CHAPTER 5 Cells as Biological Units

The development of every science is invigorated and its aims are redirected from time to time as the result of some important invention. A striking example in the field of biology is the invention of the microscope in the seventeenth century. Superficial observation and study of plants had been going on for untold centuries.

The origin of many of our most important cultivated and medicinal plants antedates the oldest archeological discoveries. In Europe and Asia several thousand plants had been described by the time that the invention of the microscope made it possible to examine their more minute structure and to discover that many plants consist only of single cells.

CELLS

The early microscopists were so fascinated with the world of minute plants and animals previously unseen and unsuspected that they studied and described them in preference to the finer structures of the larger plants.

Cells were seen and recognized as structural parts of plants, but for a hundred years observations were limited mainly to cell walls. In the latter part of the 18th century various microscopists began to study "cell contents."

By the middle of the 19th century it became evident to a number of eminent biologists that the properties which we associate with life are the properties of that part of the cell contents which had come to be called *protoplasm.*

Moreover, its organization into *cytoplasm* and *nucleus,* and the enclosed *vacuole* had been recognized.

Many biologists had by this time accepted three general principles:

(1) that the bodies of all living organisms are composed of cells, or products of cells;

(2) that in certain features the cells of plants and animals are essentially alike; and

(3) that protoplasm is the physical basis of life phenomena. To these principles we may add

(4) that when plants are similar it is because their protoplasms are similar,

(5) that when plants develop or behave differently in the same environment it is because their protoplasms are unlike, and

(6) that life is a recognized property of a very complex physical -chemical (colloidal) system.

Parts of the cell. As shown in figure elsewhere in this chapter, the essential parts of the usual enlarged plant cell may be outlined as follows:

1. The protoplasm, differentiated into cytoplasm, nucleus, and plastids.
2. The vacuole—a cavity within the cytoplasm filled with water containing sugars, salts, acids, and other substances largely in solution.
3. The cell wall—a more or less complete covering around the protoplasm. Fine strands of protoplasm sometimes extend through the wall from one cell to another.

In order to appreciate protoplasm as the medium in which the numerous chemical and physical processes of the cell occur, it will be neces-, sary to digress for a moment and consider some of the properties of different states of matter.

You have seen solid crystals of sugar and salt disappear as they dissolved in water. You are also familiar with gelatin and fruit jellies in which organic matter is dispersed in water without being dissolved. Protoplasm seen through the microscope

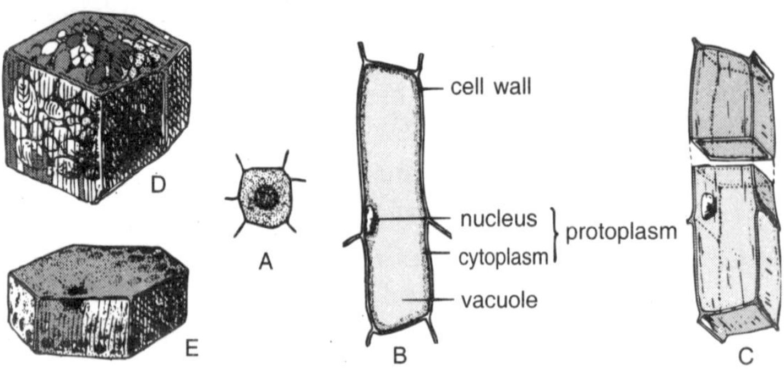

Figure 5.1: Plant cells as seen through a microscope: A, a meristematic cell composed of a nucleus and cytoplasm surrounded by a cell wall; B, an older cell which has become enlarged by growth of the cell wall and the formation of a large central vacuole; C, cell B as seen in perspective; D, starch grains formed in plastids in a cell of a potato tuber; E, chloroplasts in a cell of a moss leaf.

resembles a jelly more than a solution.

The solid, liquid, and gaseous states of matter are familiar to every. one. But when matter is dissolved in water or when, as in jelly, it is dispersed in water without dissolving, such strikingly new properties become evident that we must recognize two additional states of matter: *solutions* and *colloids.*

Solutions

When a substance dissolves in water its particles become subdivided and separated as molecules. The molecules of salts, acids, and bases are to some extent further separated into ions.

The resulting solutions are either colorless or colored homogen-eous liquids, and the particles remain equally dispersed throughout the solution because of their constant motion. For example, if a gram of table salt (sodium chloride) dissolves in a glass of water the solution remains colorless, but if a similar amount of copper sulfate dissolves in the water the solution is blue.

When salts, acids, and bases have dispersed in water as ions, each ion has a characteristic positive or negative electric charge. Many of the reactions which occur in solution are the result of these electric charges: particles with unlike charges attract each other and unite, and those with similar charges repel each other.

For instance, if one pours the above solution of copper sulfate into the solution of sodium chloride, the resultant solution will contain temporary molecules, or compounds, of NaCl, Na_2SO_4, $CuCl_2$, and $CUSO_4$; and also the free ions: Na^+, Cl^-, Cu^{++}, SO_4^{--} . . ., etc.

A solution is a stable system in which one or more substances become so finely divided in the form of molecules and ions that they become dispersed among the molecules of the water throughout the system.

COLLOIDAL SYSTEMS

When substances are almost completely insoluble in water it is possible by various means to subdivide them into very small particles which when dispersed in water continue to remain separated and distributed throughout the water for a long time.

If grains of sand or pellets of clay are dropped into a beaker of water, they immediately fall through the water to the bottom of the beaker. If the pellets are crushed and the beaker is vigorously shaken for a moment, the smaller particles of clay are held in suspension in the water and it may remain turbid for an indefinite time.

Streams and ponds that do not become clear on long standing are excellent examples of turbid suspensions. Some of the suspended particles in a drop of turbid water may be seen through a microscope.

Turbid water due to fine clay therefore illustrates a suspension in which solid particles are dispersed in water. Each particle is a cluster of molecules and has a definite surface which is electrically charged.

In very fine suspensions the particles may not settle out for months or years, because of the constant bombardment of the water molecules and because the particles have similar electric charges.

Suspensions differ from solutions in that the water and the particles dispersed in it form a twophase system. The one phase is the solid particle, the other is the water, and between each particle and the surrounding water is a definite surface of contact.

When a mass is broken up into fine particles, the aggregate surface of the particles is enormous. For example, a onecentimeter cube has a surface of 6 sq. cm., but when disintegrated into particles of colloidal size the combined surfaces of all the resulting particles are equal to about 1.5 acres. Another type of colloid is exemplified by milk, in which proteins and fat-like compounds (lipoids) are dispersed in water which contains other proteins, salts, and sugar in solution.

Dispersed throughout this liquid phase of milk are numerous visible globules composed largely of fat. These globules slowly rise to the surface and form a layer of cream.

In butter the phases are reversed; fine droplets of water are dispersed in fatty material. White of egg is a typical protein-in-water colloidal system; the yolk is a colloidal system of many phases, with fats, proteins, pigments, and other substances dispersed in water.

When white of egg is heated or treated with alcohol, vinegar, or strong salt solutions it *coagulates.* When meat, which is largely protein, is boiled it also coagulates. Gelatin desserts and fruit jellies are familiar examples of colloids.

When a gram of gelatin is dispersed in 50 grams of hot water a highly fluid colloid, called *a sol,* is formed. When it cools and stands for a few hours it becomes a semi-solid jelly, or *gel.* The gelatin becomes finely divided and dispersed in the water but does not dissolve. Its particles are much larger than molecules.

Owing to the elasticity and certain other properties of this type of colloid, the dispersed particles are thought to be fiber-like and arranged like twigs in a loose brush heap.

When a gelatin-water gel is heated it becomes highly fluid, but after it cools and stands for a time it again becomes organized into a more or less rigid gel. Thus the gel and sol states of a colloid may be reversible, and the change from the one to the other may be brought about by changes in temperature, water content, acidity, or any one of several other conditions.

Drastic changes in the internal organization of a colloid may result in coagulation. Protoplasm is a very complex colloidal system with protein, carbohydrate, fat, and lipoid phases dispersed in water, in which are various salts, sugars, acids, and other soluble compounds.

Many of these substances are chemically unstable and react with extreme readiness. All masses of protoplasm have a surface film rich in lipoids which prevents unlimited dispersion and keeps the mass intact.

The highly reactive character of the protoplasmic system at ordinary temperatures is one of its most important properties. Since it is a colloidal system there are very large surfaces between the water and the other phases, and here surface energy may bring about reactions not possible in a solution. These surfaces also accumulate electrical charges which may be significant in reactions.

Because it is a many-phase system, a change of one phase may result in the alteration of other interlocking phases and the modification of the whole protoplasmic system. Like gelatin and jelly, protoplasm is more or less elastic, and some of its constituents may have a brush-heap structure.

Furthermore, protoplasm is a self-perpetuating system, in that it can combine foods (carbohydrates, fats, and proteins) into the system and enlarge its mass. It is evident, therefore, that the jelly-like part of the cell which was named protoplasm is not a single chemical substance.

Life, like all the other distinctive properties of protoplasm, is a result of the chemical components and their complex organization in a colloidal system. When the system is disorganized the distinctive properties disappear, for the materials or compounds are not alive.

CYTOPLASM

The protoplasm in most plant cells is organized into cytoplasm, plastids, and nucleus. In young cells these parts completely occupy the space within the cell wall. As the cell enlarges, microscopic droplets of liquid become visible in the cytoplasm, the colloidal matrix is drawn together, and the droplets coalesce, forming larger water-filled cavities called vacuoles.

In most plant cells the coalescence of small vacuoles results finally in the formation of a single vacuole, and the cytoplasm with its embedded plastids and nucleus becomes relegated to a thin layer lining the cell wall.

In other cells the nucleus may retain its central position, supported by cytoplasmic strands which are the remnants of the cytoplasm separating the several vacuoles before they coalesced into the single large one. Cytoplasm is usually granular in appearance because of the presence of particles of various foods and other substances. Cytoplasmic movements (streaming) may be seen in the cells of some plants.

Table 5.1: Names of Plastids and their characteristic contents.

Names of Plastids	*Characteristic Contents*
Green plastids or chloroplasts.	Chlorophylls, carotenes, and xanthophyll, sometimes minute starch grains.
Starch plastids or amyloplasts.	Starch grains.
Fat plastids or elaioplasts.	Oils and fats.
Color plastids or chromoplasts.	Pigments found in chloroplasts, also red, yellow, and other pigments.

Plastids are protoplasmic bodies in the cytoplasm. Special reactions take place in them, often resulting in the accumulation of particular substances, such as starch and chlorophyll.

There are usually several to many plastids in each cell; and as the cells multiply by division, the plastids also increase in number by division. They are named on the basis of certain substances that accumulate in them, as shown in Table anywhere else in this chapter.

In very young cells there are small colorless plastids (leucoplasts) that apparently may develop into these more specialized types, depending upon environmental conditions.

The Nucleus

The nucleus is usually more refractive to light than the cytoplasm and under the microscope appears brighter. Often its protoplasm is denser and forms a more rigid gel, but sometimes it is a fluid sol surrounded by a membrane. Chemically it differs from the cytoplasm in that the proportion of proteins is less and its proteins are far more complex.

They are relatively high in phosphorus and possibly on this account more reactive. There seems to be good reason to regard the nucleus as the center of many cell activities; as we shall see in a later chapter, it contains certain very minute bodies (chromosomes) that are the carriers of many of the hereditary factors of the plant.

The Vacuole

At maturity the vacuole occupies most of the space inside the cell walls; it is filled with "cell sap," a solution of sugars, salts, acids, and other soluble compounds. It may also contain colloidally dispersed proteins, carbohydrates, and other less soluble substances.

Some of the substances in solution readily pass from the vacuole into the surrounding cytoplasm or from the cytoplasm to the vacuole; others do not. Sometimes crystals of salts accumulate in the vacuole, or the cell sap may become colored with pigments as in the cells of many flowers, fruits, and red autumn leaves.

The Cell Wall

The outermost part of a plant cell is the cell wall, formed at the surface of the enclosed protoplasm. During cell division the first wall between the daughter cells is composed of pectic material, and on the inside of this pectic wall (middle lamella) successive layers composed of cellulose or of cellulose and pectic compounds are deposited.

Sometimes other substances, such as cutin and lignin, accumulate in cell walls and thereby change their properties. Most cells on the outer surface of plants contain cutin in the outer wall. The cells in wood exemplify walls that started as pectic compounds and cellulose and became lignified.

Cell walls also possess colloidal properties and swell in water. They are composed of small submicroscopic particles between which molecules of water may penetrate and be held tenaciously.

The cell as a whole

From this description of the parts of the cell and the study of cells with a microscope, it should be possible to picture the cell as a structural unit, and at the same time as a dynamic unit, displaying those properties and processes commonly associated with living organisms. Some of these structures and processes may be briefly summarized.

1. All plants consist of one or more cells.
2. Cells are formed by the division of previously existing cells, and less frequently by the fusion of cells.
3. The properties associated with life reside in the protop-lasm, which is a complex colloidal system of proteins, carbohyd-rates, fats, and lipoids permeated by a water solution of acids, bases, and salts, many of which are highly reactive. Owing to the enormous surfaces between the water and the colloidal particles the protoplasmic system contains surface energy and electrical energy not characteristic of solutions.
4. The protoplasm therefore is a chemical and physical system, no one constituent of which is living; the qualities that distinguish protoplasm from non-living systems result from the unique organization of atoms, ions, molecules, and colloidal particles with their associated chemical, electrical, and surface energies.
5. The protoplasmic system sustains itself in the presence of food, and can combine food substances into its own structure and thereby increase its mass. In other words, it *grows.*
6. In the development of the plant cell, vacuolation occurs and the cytoplasm at maturity becomes a sack-like layer surrounding a solution of sugars, salts, acids, and very dilute colloidal dispersions in the water of the vacuole.
7. During its development, the usual plant cell also becomes surrounded by a cell wall-at first primarily of pectic material, later of cellulose layers-which may be altered in several ways. The cell wall has a high water content during the active life of the cell.

8. The large proportion of water pervading all parts of the cell constitutes a medium in which the movement of materials and the chemical and physical changes within the cell readily occur.
9. As a result of the chemical changes constantly going on in the cell, electrical energy is released as in a battery, and one end of the cell usually has a higher electric potential than the other. Consequently most cells are polarized, and their opposite ends may behave differently.
10. In cell masses of the larger plants electric potentials also develop, and the apex of a plant organ may become electri-cally negative or positive to the base.
11. Since the living part of the cell is protoplasm, it is the protoplasm that dies when a cell or any group of cells dies.

With these principles in mind, one has a basis necessary for interpreting the various extraordinary reactions of living plants. Today we know only a minor part of the energy and material relations within plant cells, but our present knowledge is certainly sufficient to lead us to doubt the necessity of assuming the presence of mysterious forces to account for the behavior of organisms.

CHAPTER 6 The Tissue System of Leaves

In the preceding chapter, cells are described as unit structures embodying several interrelated physical and chemical systems. Cells are considered as the physiological units of plants because they are the smallest bits of protoplasm known to be capable both of independent existence and of reproduction through division.

In later chapters less highly organized cells of bacteria and certain algae are described. There are several thousand species of plants that live as single cells. In other thousands the cells are aggregated in colonies in which the individuals cells are more or less independent.

In the larger and more familiar plants the millions and billions of cells of which they are composed remain not only firmly attached but are to some extent mutually dependent. During the development of these plants, systems of cells called *tissues* are formed by cell enlargement and differentiation.

CELLS AND TISSUES

The cells of a given tissue may have a common origin; all of them may be similar in position, shape, texture, or color; or several different kinds may form a distinct structural complex. Nevertheless, the tissues of many common plants may be distinguished readily.

In this chapter we shall try to picture the tissues of a leaf, emphas-izing the fact that the leaf, or foliage organ, like other organs of a plant, is a system of tissues, the cells of which are differentiated, but intimately related, structurally and physiologically.

Leaf Bud Development

Leaves develop from buds; they first become visible through the microscope as small protuberances (primordia) in the meristematicl region near the growing apex of the stem. The cells of the primordium divide and continue to produce new cellsall

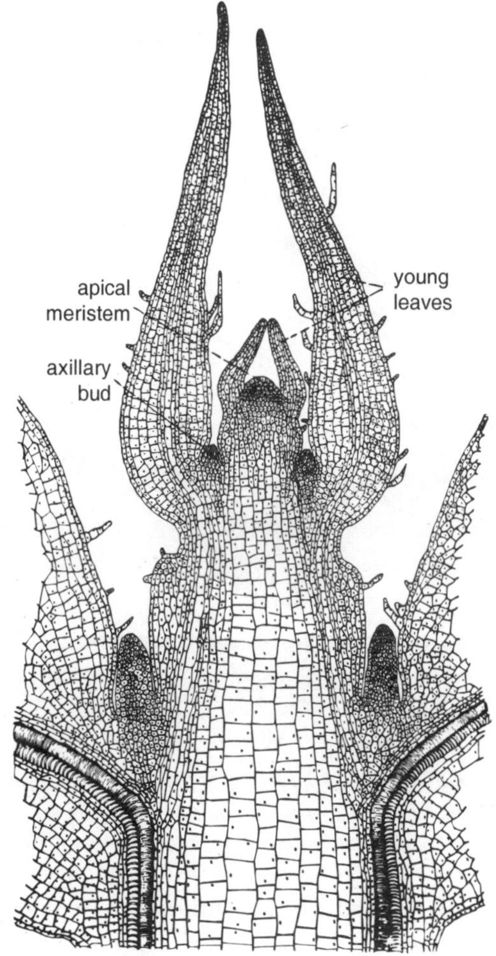

Figure 6.1: Diagram of vertical section of a vegetative bud of coleus.

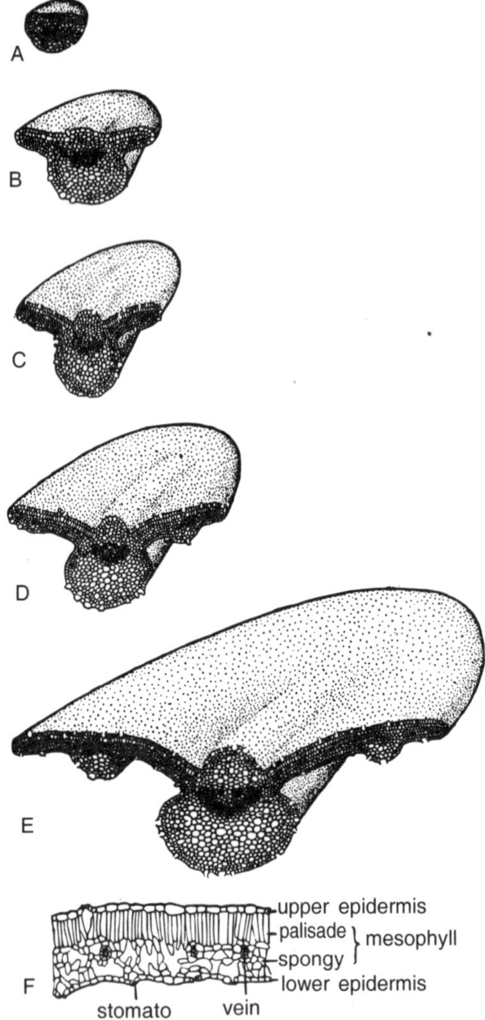

Figure 6.2: Cross sections of leaves. A-E, sections of embryonic leaves from the terminal bud of a tobacco plant in the order of relative age. The oldest leaf (E) in the series was less than one centimeter in length. F, cross section of a small portion of a blade of a mature leaf of tobacco.

very similar in size and shape. The uniform brick-like cells of the leaf primordium are completely filled with protoplasm and become stratified in several (5-8) layers. As this protuberance expands farther-becoming more leaf-like, but still very small-cells in the middle layers divide irregularly and form groups of cells from which the vascular tissues of veins develop.

In the leaves of many of our trees, to which the above descrip-tion particularly applies, this entire development proceeds slowly through the spring, summer, and autumn months within the buds. By the end of winter some of the leaves in the bud have attained their characteristic pattern in miniature.

The cells of the prospective future veins are slightly different-iated, whereas the remaining ones are still similar. Thus far *cell division* has been the dominating process of development. All cells remain in complete contact and there are no intercellular spaces.

LEAF DEVELOPMENT

With the warmer weather of the following spring, growth is renewed. The stem tip and young leaves expand and press the bud scales apart. During the rapid increase in size, *cell enlargement* and *cell differentiation* dominate the growth process, leading to the formation of the distinctly different tissues as seen in microscopic sections.

Cell division usually stops first in the *epidermis,* next in the *spongy mesophyll,* and last in the *palisade mesophyll.* Cell enlargement, however, continues longest in the epidermis; as a consequence, the cells of the spongy tissue are pulled into an open meshwork, and the palisade cells become separated laterally.

Meanwhile the veins have increased in diameter. Expansion of the leaves follows rapidly after the opening of the buds; they often double their size within twelve hours. In some plants with small leaves the whole development from leaf primordium to mature leaf may occur at a rather uniform rate during ten days to two weeks. In large-leaved plants, such as tobacco, the leaves grow for a month or more before becoming mature.

Leaf Tissues

When we look at the surface of a magnified leaf we can see that the epidermis is composed of a layer of angular or interlocking cells. The outer cell wall contains a deposit of cutin, a fat like substance. This cutinized layer is often called the cuticle.

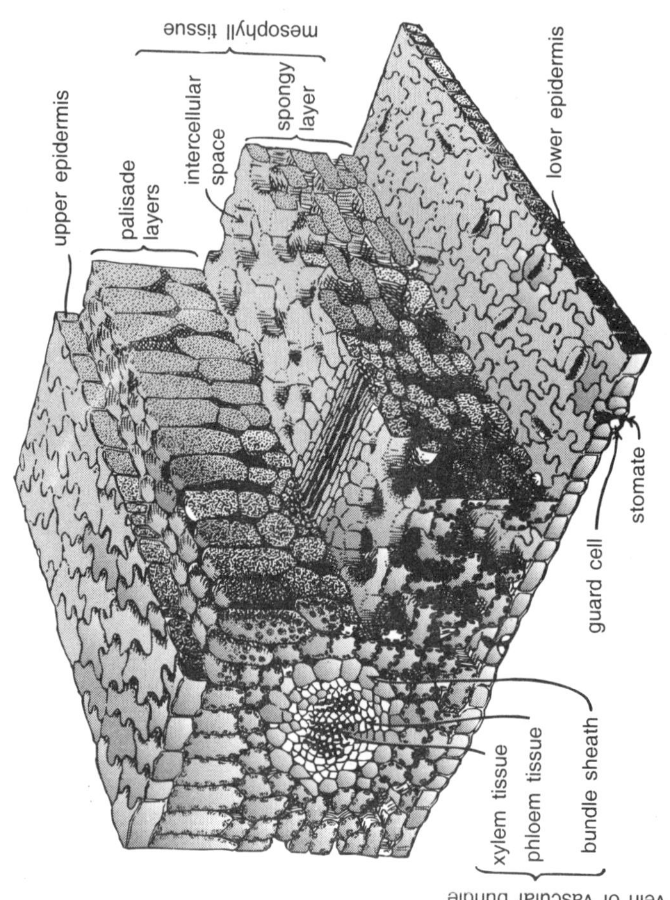

Figure 6.3: Arrangement of tissues in a leaf of the common periwinkle (Vinca).

It may be very thin, or it may be so thick that the outer wall is the most conspicuous part of the epidermal cell. In the lower epidermis, and sometimes among the upper epidermal cells, paired specialized guard calls partially separate and form a pore or stomate.

When open, the stomates are passages connecting the air within the intercellular spaces of the leaf with the external atmosphere. Between the upper and lower epidermis there are several layers of cells constituting the *mesophyll.*

The upper layers usually have elongated bundles of the stem. Near the junction of the petiole and stem there is a short region in which the sclerenchyma is either less or absent, and in which parenchyma cells rich in cytoplasm form a disk-shaped layer several cells thick across the petiole, except in the bundles.

This is the absciss layer. It is formed during leaf development. Later as the cell walls of this layer disintegrate many of the cells become separated. The middle lamella and sometimes other layers of the cell walls become jelly-like or are dissolved, and the petiole

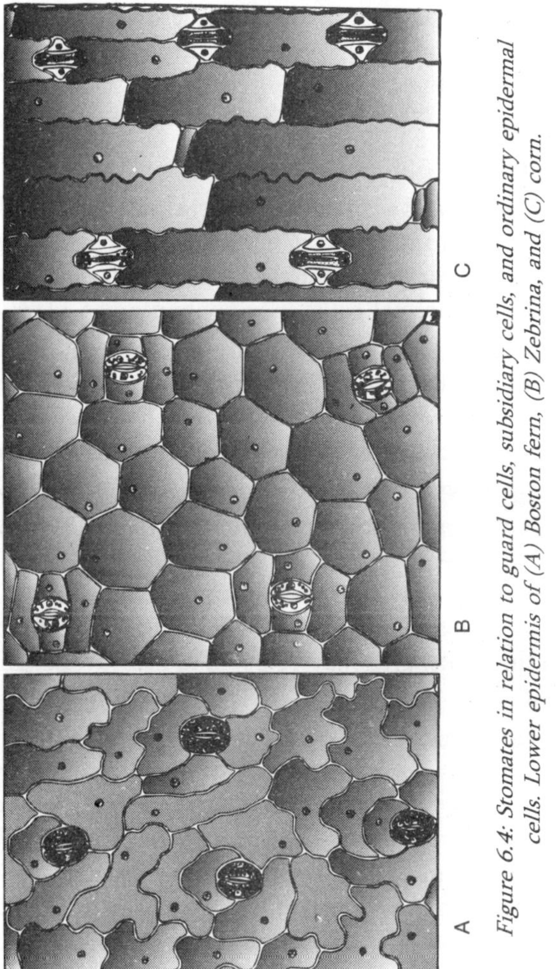

Figure 6.4: Stomates in relation to guard cells, subsidiary cells, and ordinary epidermal cells. Lower epidermis of (A) Boston fern, (B) Zebrina, and (C) corn.

is separated from the stem. The leaves of deciduous trees may be supported for a time by the vascular strands, but these are ultimately broken.

The breakdown of the absciss layer in the petiole of some herbaceous plants may take place and the leaf abscise within 48 hours. This process is retarded by hormones from the blade and hastened by such conditions as drought, injury to the blade, low and high temperatures.

Abscission is usually preceded or followed by changes in the cells attached to the stem below the absciss layer. These changes result in the closure of the vessels and the development of scar tissue evident in the *leaf scar.* Abscission is not limited to absciss layers.

The Stomata

In describing the epidermis the paired guard cells which surround the stomate were mentioned. These are highly specialized cells formed by subdivision of epidermal cells; unlike the ordinary epidermal cells, they contain green plastids.

In tree leaves the guard cells do not separate until the leaf has attained a fourth or a third of its size. In many leaves they are found exclusively, or mostly, in the lower epidermis. Less frequently they are most abundant on the upper surface; they rarely occur in equal numbers on both sides of the leaf.

Stomatal openings are so minute that the area of an average pinhole may be equivalent to that of 2000 to 2500 stomates. On many common leaves, however, there are from 100 to 600 stomates per square; millimeter of leaf surface, and when they are open their total area may be equal to nearly 1 per cent of the lower leaf surface.

The most remarkable thing about stomates is that they are opened by, the swelling and arching of the guard cells, and closed by the shrinking and straightening of these cells. When a plant is moved from darkness to light, the guard cells are affected by light and their internal pressure increases, causing them to separate and open the stomate. On a warm day this opening may take place in about 15 to 30 minutes.

Thus in the summertime stomates open after sunrise and

remain open for two or more hours, depending on conditions discussed in other chapter of this book. The closing of the stomates depends on a number of factors, mostly internal.

Here it need be emphasized only that external factors-light, water, and a warm temperature—are the most important prerequisites for their opening.

CHAPTER 7

Non-Green Plants

The term "non-green plants" is ordinarily used by botanists to refer to all species of plants that lack the inherent potentiality of synthesizing chlorophyll. It is a hereditary characteristic of species. For example, no chlorophyll is synthesized in any individual plant of the meadow mushroom, or of the common bread mold, under any environmental conditions.

On the other hand, chlorophyll is synthesized in most corn plants in the light, but not in the dark. The meadow mushroom is a species of the non-green plants. Corn is a species of the green plants, even though some individual corn plants are albinos.

These albinos cannot survive and reproduce in nature as non-green plants. Likewise coleus is a species of the green plants, though certain varieties of it contain so much anthocyan that the plants appear purple. Green-colored molds are not species of green plants because the pigment in them is not chlorophyll.

The green color of frogs, snakes, insects, and birds is due to other kinds of pigments or to the refraction of light. Some of the flatworms and smaller animals are green because green algae live within their bodies. The terms chlorophyllous plants and non-chlorophyllous plants may be used in preference to green plants and non-green plants.

Nearly 80 per cent of the known species of plants are green, but there are fewer individual green plants on the earth than non-green ones. Most non-green plants are small and inconspicuous. Many of them are onecelled plants which cannot be seen unless they are magnified by means of a microscope.

Among the larger fungi are the familiar molds, puffballs, mushrooms, toadstools, and bracket fungi. Most non-green plants are either fungi or bacteria, but there are also a few species of non-green algae and several dozen species of non-green seed plants.

Among them are Indian pipe, dodder, beechdrop, snow plant, squaw-root, "pine sap" and broom-rape. Certain species of algae can live in the light as green plants, and also in the dark as non-green plants if an external supply of sugar or of some of its derivatives is available.

Non-green plants live in all sorts of habitats in water and soil, and also within and on the bodies of plants and animals. Those that grow within or on the living tissues of plants and animals and obtain food from them are *parasites.*

Those that obtain food from the dead bodies of plants and animals, from their products, or from their non-living parts, such as the dead bark and heartwood of trees, are *saprophytes.* If they can grow only within living tissues they are called *obligate parasites.* If they cannot grow within living tissues, they are said to be *obligate saprophytes.*

But if they can grow either as parasites or as saprophytes, they are referred to as *facultative species.* There are all sorts of gradations between saprophytic and parasitic plants. With the exception of a few special groups of bacteria, non-green plants cannot synthesize sugar.

Some of them, such as yeast, when supplied with an external source of sugar, inorganic salts, and water, can make the rest of the foods necessary for growth and reproduction. Others are dependent upon an external source of amino acids, or of proteins also.

Plants that can synthesize sugar are sometimes called *autophytes* in contrast to parasites and saprophytes. In addition to food, nongreen plants may also be dependent upon an external supply of certain vitamins and hormones, as well as inorganic salts.

We may apply at once all that we know about the physiology and heredity of green plants toward an understanding of non-green plants, for the living part of a non-green plant is protoplasm and there are definite species of them just as there are of green plants.

The principal differences between these two types of plants lie in the processes by which they obtain food and in the consequences of these processes. Some of these consequences are beneficial to other plants and to animals, and some of them are harmful and destructive.

PARASITIC PLANTS

Figure 7.1: An epiphytic orchid the roots of which merely hold the plant on the branch of the tree.

When a plant grows within or on, and also subsists upon food from the living parts of another organism, it is a parasite. The parasitized organism is the *host.* It may or may not be injured by the parasite. If it is injured, it is said to be diseased. Some parasitic plants are beneficial to the host.

The nitrogen-fixing bacteria in the roots of clover, for example, are beneficial to their host, since upon their death their chemically bound nitrogen becomes available to the clover plant. All sorts of gradations may be found from extreme parasitism to a total lack of it.

Some parasites grow only within certain organs of one kind of host. Others grow within or on numerous kinds of hosts. Still others are but partial parasites. Sometimes both host and parasite are benefited rather than harmed by their relationship.

Some plants are merely perched upon or attached to others, but obtain no food from them. These plants are known as *epiphytes,* in contrast to parasites. Examples of epiphytes are Spanish moss hanging on the branches of a tree, and the mosses and lichens attached to the bark of trees wherever trees grow.

In deciding whether a plant is a parasite, it is necessary to consider both its position and its source of food. It may be even more difficult to decide when an animal is a parasite. A protozoan may live within the cells of a plant.

Roundworms burrow into roots and survive on the food within the root. Aphids obtain food by sucking the "juice" from living plants. A grasshopper climbs upon a plant and eats its young leaves, while a cow roams over the pasture and eats the live leaves of grasses.

A mistletoe which grows on a variety of trees in the southern half of the United States is a good example of a partial parasite. Its sticky seeds adhere to the branches of trees; and when one of them germinates, a root-like haustorium grows through the bark to the conductive tissues of the host.

The stems and leaves of this mistletoe contain chlorophyll,

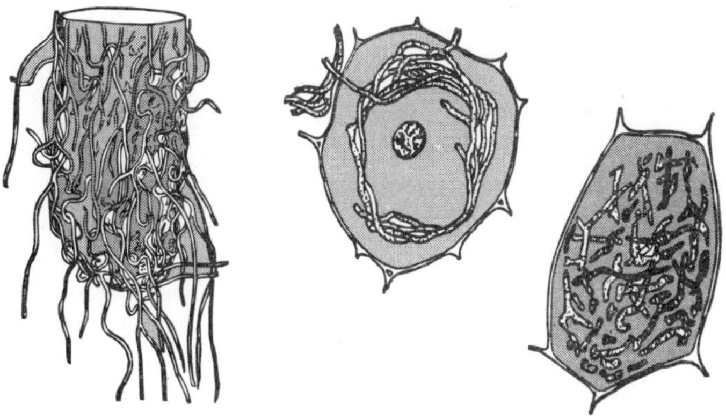

Figure 7.2: External and internal mycorhizal fungi.

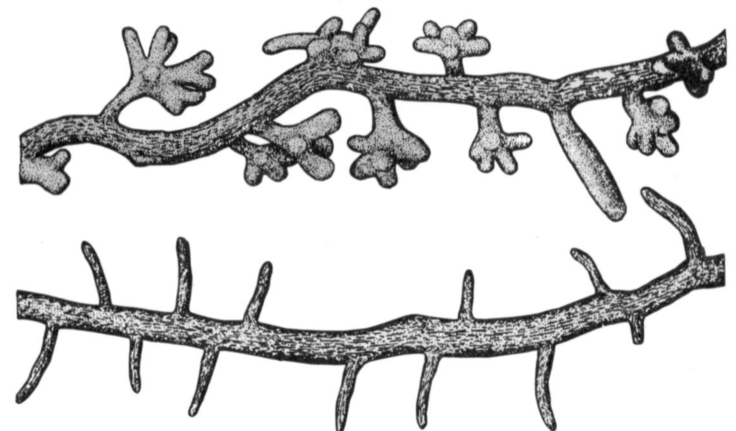

Figure 7.3: Eastern white pine mycorhiza (A), and root (B) not infected by fungi.

and some sugar is synthesized in them. Water and salts are of course obtained from the soil through the host. No one knows at present what percentage of the food of the mistletoe is obtained from the host, or whether it can develop under experimental conditions in the absence of a host.

The relation of such plants as the mistletoe to their hosts is similar to that of a grafted scion to the stock. An analogous partial parasitism occurs when the root tips of green plants penetrate the roots of other green plants and become haustoria. How frequently this process occurs is unknown.

The roots of some plants, such as those of bastard toad flax of the eastern states, and of the desert shrub, *Kram.eria,* of the southwestern states, habitually form haustorial unions with the roots of many other plants.

It is well known that unions occur among the roots of adjoining forest trees. Whether they are of any value to the trees is not known. Some non-green seed plants, such as the small purple beechdrops attached to the roots of beech trees and the slender climbing dodder which becomes attached by haustoria to the stems of a great variety of hosts, obtain food directly from green plants.

The Indian pipe, when casually observed, appears to be a

saprophyte living on the litter of decaying leaves on the forest floor, but it apparently obtains all its food from fungi which digest the fallen leaves, and also live in and on its roots.

Several layers of fungal filaments completely invest each of its many short roots, and numerous branching filaments of the fungus permeate the surrounding layer of decaying leaves and humus.

Owing to the surrounding sheath of fungal filaments, the cells of the roots of Indian pipe are not in direct contact with the soil. Fungi that live in such intimate relation with the roots of plants are called *mycorhizal fungi.*

They may live wholly external to the root, merely forming a sheath around it; the fungal filaments may grow into the cells of the root; or the entire fungus may grow within the cells of the root. Such mycorhizal fungi are habitually present on the roots of most green plants in forests. Some of them have been reported as harmful to certain trees, others as beneficial, or even essential to them.

Under natural conditions, pines, heath plants, and beeches are apparently dependent upon mycorhizal fungi, for their seedlings live but a few years if deprived of them under experimental conditions.

Diversity among the Non-green Plants

There are all sorts of gradations between saprophytes and parasites, and also between these two groups and the autophytes. Many terms have been proposed to designate these intergr-adations. Some of this diversity is related to (1) the kinds of substances the organism can digest and utilize as food, (2) the method of securing food, and (3) the kind of substance oxidized during respiration.

In the cells of all animals, of all green plants, and of most non-green plants also, respiration involves the oxidation of reduced carbon atoms in sugar, or in organic compounds derived from sugar. When this oxidation is complete, one of the end products is carbon dioxide.

A few groups of bacteria, however, are unique in that they oxidize reduced nitrogen, reduced sulfur, or reduced iron. Consequently nitrates, sulfates, and oxidized iron in the soil are among the end products of respiration of these bacteria.

The oxidized compounds are essential tc, green plants, which are therefore partly dependent upon the activities of these bacteria. The bacteria in turn are partly dependent upon the activities of green plants for reduced nitrogen, and upon both green plants and other kinds of bacteria for reduced sulfur and iron.

These special groups of bacteria are unique in one other way. Although they are non-green and are underground, they synthesize sugar from carbon dioxide and water. The energy necessary for this synthesis is obtained from the oxidation of reduced nitrogen, sulfur, and iron. They are as truly autophytes as the green plants.

The synthesis of sugar in these bacteria in the absence of light is often referred to as *chemosynthesis* in contrast to photosynthesis. Similarly, certain bacteria may oxidize reduced manganese and synthesize sugar.

The green and some purple bacteria contain pigments similar to chlorophyll; and when they are exposed to light, photosynthesis occurs within them.

Autophytes

All plants, whether green or non-green, in which sugar is synthesized from carbon dioxide and water are called autophytes in contrast to parasites and saprophytes.,Perhaps the term should be limited to those in which the synthesis of amino acids and proteins also occurs.

Most autophytes, however, are *not* independent plants. They could not continue to live in a world devoid of all non-green plants. The non-green plants are dependent upon certain reduced compounds made in the green plants.

The green plants in turn are dependent upon certain oxidized compounds from the non-green plants. Dependent relations between green and non-green plants briefly outlined above are indicated in figures anywhere else in this chapter.

Others will be indicated in later chapters. [n the absence of adequate data we have assumed that the first food made from carbon dioxide by autophytic bacteria is some kind of sugar, as it is in green plants.

Saprophytic Plants

These are the organisms that cause most of the decay of organic matter. They live upon and obtain food from the dead bodies of plants and animals, and also from the products of all living organisms. Some of them have enzymes that digest cellulose, pectic compounds, and even kerosene and coal.

Digestion of these substances occurs outside the body of the plant. Their enzymes, therefore, must diffuse from the living cells where they are synthesized into the surrounding media.

External digestion and the digestion of substances that cannot be digested by most other organisms are outstanding features of this group of plants. Among the animals there are a few protozoans, such as those in the alimentary tract of termites, that can digest cellulose.

External digestion, however, is a common characteristic of animals, for the food within the alimentary tract is still outside the cells of the body. The processes that occur in the digestion of bread in the alimentary tract of an animal are no different fundamentally from those that occur when bread is decomposed by mold.

The plant may digest certain substances the animal cannot, but saprophytic plants are present in the alimentary tracts of animals and they may digest certain substances there. Some woodboring beetles can chew the wood, but their internal fungi digest it.

Without the saprophytic plants the surface of the earth would soon become encumbered with the undigested remains of plants and animals. Except in bogs where the growth of saprophytes is comparatively slow, only a thin surface layer of humus has accumulated in all of geological time.

Moreover, without a comparatively rapid digestion of cellulose and the subsequent oxidation of the products of digestion, the supply of carbon dioxide in the air would gradually become depleted.

During decay not only is carbon dioxide formed and liberated to the air, but inorganic ions are liberated from their organic union and are again available to green plants. Some saprophytic plants are valued in industry because they do not completely oxidize certain compounds, but leave a residue which man values for certain purposes. These residues are often referred to as products of fermentation.

The complete oxidation of a substance in saprophytic plants usually consists of a series of steps, each of which is the result of the activity of successively different organisms. Sugar is oxidized to alcohol by yeast. Acetic acid bacteria oxidize the alcohol to acetic acid.

Other organisms then oxidize the acetic acid to simpler compounds and finally all are oxidized to carbon dioxide and water. After insoluble substances are digested, many intermediate and successively simpler compounds may be formed before oxidation is complete.

Moreover, the kinds of intermediate products formed vary with the species of organism that oxidizes each of them. The industries producing beer, wine, vinegar, glycerin, alcohol, and cheese all depend upon the fermentation products of carefully cultivated species of saprophytes.

The quantity and quality of the products vary with the kinds of fungi and bacteria present. The unpleasant odors of decaying matter likewise are due to the intermediate products of oxidation-reduction which are formed during the growth of certain bacteria and fungi. Saprophytes are ever-present agents of destruction, and are the organisms that make cold storage and refrigeration necessary in our modern civilization.

The freezing, canning, drying, and preserving industries are based on methods of eliminating saprophytes. Buildings and other wood structures are protected from them by means of metal, paint, tar, and creosote. As agents of decay they dissipate more of the energy chemically bound in sugar during photosynthesis than all other living organisms combined.

On the other hand their very destructiveness is valued as a means of removing sewage and other undesired organic products. Saprophytes, then, are as intimately associated with our daily lives as are the green plants and parasites.

CHAPTER 8

The Biology of Bacteria

Of all the groups of non-green plants, the ever-present bacteria and their effects are most often discussed among educated people everywhere. Although the great majority of the human race has never seen bacteria, every individual has had both direct and indirect contacts with them.

Characteristics of some bacteria are indicated in figures elsewhere in this chapter. They are the causes of many diseases and of much of the decay of organic substances. Certain pleasant and unpleasant flavors of foods such as cheese, milk, butter, and eggs result from bacterial action, and bacteria influence our lives in many other ways.

As a matter of fact, household sanitation, sewage disposal, refrige-ration, quarantine, vaccination, aseptic surgery, personal hygiene, and all of our splendidly organized and vitally necessary methods of guarding and purifying water have developed as we have learned how and where bacteria live and how they affect plants and animals, including ourselves.

Some bacteria manufacture their own food; others obtain it from living or non-living sources. A few species are unique in that they can synthesize sugar and other foods from water, carbon dioxide, and inorganic salts.

Most species, however, depend upon an external source of sugar, and sometimes of protein also. At one end of the scale are the bacteria that derive energy from light, or from compounds containing reduced nitrogen, iron or sulfur, and synthesize sugars and other foods. Such organisms are independent of other living plants except for the sources of reduced nitrogen and sulfur. At the other extreme is the obligate parasite that grows only in the living tissues of another organism.

Between these two extremes are the various kinds of saprophytes that live and multiply upon the dead tissues and products of other organisms. The autophytes among bacteria include the nitrifying bacteria that oxidize ammonia to nitrates and nitrites; the iron bacteria which oxidize ferrous to ferric salts; and some sulfur bacteria that oxidize reduced sulfur.

These are extremely important in soil development and will be discussed in more detail in the following chapter. The energy released by these oxidations is utilized in the synthesis of sugar and other foods.

The other autophytes are the green and purple sulfur bacteria, the first of which utilize the energy of light and the second the energy of reduced sulfur in making sugar.'

Most species of bacteria are obligate saprophytes or parasites, but some of them may grow either as parasites or as saprophytes.

External Factors and Bacteria

The environments in which bacteria and their allied organisms live and reproduce are so different from those of larger plants that some of the effects of environmental factors need to be considered, especially those of light, water, oxygen, and temperature.

Light

Most bacteria, because of their location in soil, in foods, in decaying matter, and within other living organisms are rarely exposed to the direct rays of light. Most species live only a few hours when exposed to full sunlight.

Sunlight, therefore, is a destructive factor in the development of most bacteria and of great importance in the purification of rivers polluted with sewage, and in the elimination of bacteria from all exposed surfaces.

The rapidity with which certain bacteria are killed by direct light depends upon the intensity and quality of the light. Although the evidence is extremely difficult to obtain and the results are often conflicting, it appears that the rays of the blue and violet end of the visible spectrum are most injurious to bacteria, particularly the pathogenic species.

The intensity of the light used must always be kept in mind in comparing the destructive effects of various radiations. Near infra-red rays through their heating and drying effects may be germicidal. The ultra-violet rays are very destructive and have proved to be very important in hospitals and in water purification.

Bacteria are destroyed by short rays of light apparently through the coagulation of the protoplasm, or the formation of some toxic substance in the medium.

Water

Bacteria cannot grow and multiply in the absence of water, although some may remain alive for months or years in an arid environment. About 85 per cent of the weight of active bacteria is water. Spores are supposed to contain much less water than the vegetative cells.

Diffusion of foods and other materials into the bacterial cell is impossible unless the cell is surrounded by at least a film of water. Current statements that living bacteria have persisted inside rocks since the time of their formation a million years ago have not been generally accepted, because of the almost insurmountable difficulties in proving that these microorganisms may not have been carried into the minute pores of the rocks with the movements of underground water and gases.

The solution or substrate in which bacteria grow is commonly called the *medium.* The properties of a medium are determined by the substances it contains. For example, sugar and salts may be in solution in the medium, thus determining its concentration.

When the concentration of water in the medium is less than in the bacterial cells, water diffuses out of the cells and the bacteria may become inactive. Consequently jellies keep more readily than preserves, preserves more readily than canned fruits, and canned fruits more readily than fruit juices to which no sugar has been added.

Jellies have a high concentration of sugar and a comparatively low concentration of water. In the fruit juices the converse is true. In the laboratory bacteria are often placed in gelatin or agar media. When the water content of gelatin falls below 50 per cent, bacteria develop very slowly.

When the gelatin dries out, the vegetative cells become inactive and eventually die. As noted above, however, many bacteria, especially those found in the soil, may live-but not grow-for months or years in a desiccated state.

Since most of the bacteria that are causes of disease cannot survive desiccation, there is little danger of living ones being carried long distances by air currents.

Oxygen

Molecular oxygen is essential to nearly all living organisms. A few kinds of bacteria, however, can live without it. Most organisms use free oxygen in the respiratory processes and are known as *aerobes.*

Some bacteria, such as those that are the causative agents of lockjaw and those that cause butter to become rancid, grow only when the free oxygen content of the medium is extremely low, and when organic substances containing combined oxygen are available. These bacteria are known as *anaerobes.*

Anaerobic bacteria occur especially in poorly drained soils, in deep waters of lakes and seas, and in all sorts of media from which oxygen has been removed or excluded.

Bacteria are exposed only to the oxygen that is dissolved in the medium surrounding them. At room temperature this is ordinarily a very dilute solution equivalent to dissolving 1 cc. of free oxygen in 100 liters of water.

If the oxygen content of the medium is increased to 30 times this amount, most bacteria die. In other words, oxygen at such concentrations has the same effect on bacteria as a solution of formaldehyde, or bichloride of mercury, two of our commonly used antiseptics.

Even pronouncedly aerobic bacteria cannot withstand very high concentrations of oxygen. If the oxygen content of the air above the nutrient medium is increased to 4 times the usual amount, the growth of some strains of *Streptococcus* is stopped.

Even the same strain of bacteria differs in its susceptibility to oxygen according to the medium in which it is growing. Anaerobic bacteria grow better within liquid media or below the surface of agar media because of the decreased oxygen content. Among the bacteria there is a marked diversity in their endurance of molecular oxygen.

Hydrogen peroxide (H_2O_2) is toxic to bacteria because it changes readily to water and atomic oxygen which is very active chemically. In the presence of molecular oxygen, hydrogen peroxide may be formed in the medium in which the bacteria are growing. The hydrogen peroxide may in turn be toxic to the bacteria.

Temperature

When compared with other plants, bacteria as a group can live under a very wide range of temperature conditions. In this respect they are perhaps equaled only by the blue-green algae. The temperature of the bacteria is of course the same as that of the media in which they grow.

Within a limited range, high temperatures accelerate life processes and low temperatures retard them. Food is used less rapidly at lower temperatures, and bacteria with a limited food supply live longer under such conditions.

Some of the bacteria that thrive in hay infusions multiply at temperatures as low as 40° F. or as high as 110° F. The minimum temperature at which some species can grow may be higher than the maximum temperature at which others can survive.

The optimum temperature for most bacteria lies between 70° and 100° F. Few species continue vegetative development at temperatures higher than 115° F. Some bacteria, however, that bring about the rapid decay of organic matter, such as silage, may live at temperatures as high as 175° F.

Living bacteria have also been found in hot springs at temperatures but little below this figure. This endurance of high temperature is remarkable in view of the fact that many proteins begin to coagulate and some fats begin to liquefy and separate at 145° F.

Although bacteria are often distinguished as aerobes and

anaerobes as noted above, certain species may grow as aerobes at one temperature and as anaerobes at another. Many of the high-temperature bacteria, for example, will not grow at temperatures below 110° F. when exposed to air, but will grow under anaerobic conditions at 95° F.

At temperatures near the freezing point bacteria grow very slowly, but may survive for weeks or even months. When freezing occurs and the medium becomes solid, diffusion is extremely slow and life processes are reduced to a minimum.

Typhoid bacteria are known to have lived four months in ice cream and for about five years when kept frozen. Streptococcus bacteria that cause sore throat may also live in ice cream. Certain pathogenic bacteria and some of the common microorganisms of the soil are known to survive for a few days when exposed to the temperature of liquid air (about -310° F.).

Cultures of certain bacteria have been exposed to the temperature of liquid hydrogen (about -425° F. or about 35° above absolute zero) for short intervals with no apparent harm to the organisms.

What are bacteria? Bacteria are at once the simplest in structure, the smallest in size, the most abundant, and the most generally distributed of all plants, both green and non-green. Only the blue-green algae are comparable in these respects. Although one-celled organisms, bacteria often cohere in distinct groups more or less heritable in form.

The cells have gelatinous sheaths; and when many of the sheaths coalesce, the bacterial scums often seen on water and on damp objects are formed.

The cells of bacteria are so small that their exact structure is difficult to ascertain. Definite cell walls exist in most bacteria, but relatively little is known about their chemical composition.

Nucleo-proteins containing nucleic acids characteristic of those present in chromosomes have been obtained from some bacteria by chemical analyses. Nuclei, chromosomes, and mitotic-like figures have been noted in a few bacteria after special treatments of the cells.

Whether or not nuclei and chromosomes are present in all

bacteria, the occurrence of species and races of bacteria is good evidence that the hereditary mechanism in them is as definite as it is in other organisms.

One would expect genes in bacteria to mutate as they do in other organisms, and there is evidence that new races of bacteria originate in this way. Certain observations are interpreted by some investigators as evidence of sexuality in bacteria, but this interpretation is regarded as inconclusive by others.

A few bacteria move about by a gliding movement not understood at present. Many species are not motile at all; but in others protoplasmic threads known as *flagella* (sing., *flagellum)* extend through the cell wall and are organs of locomotion. A

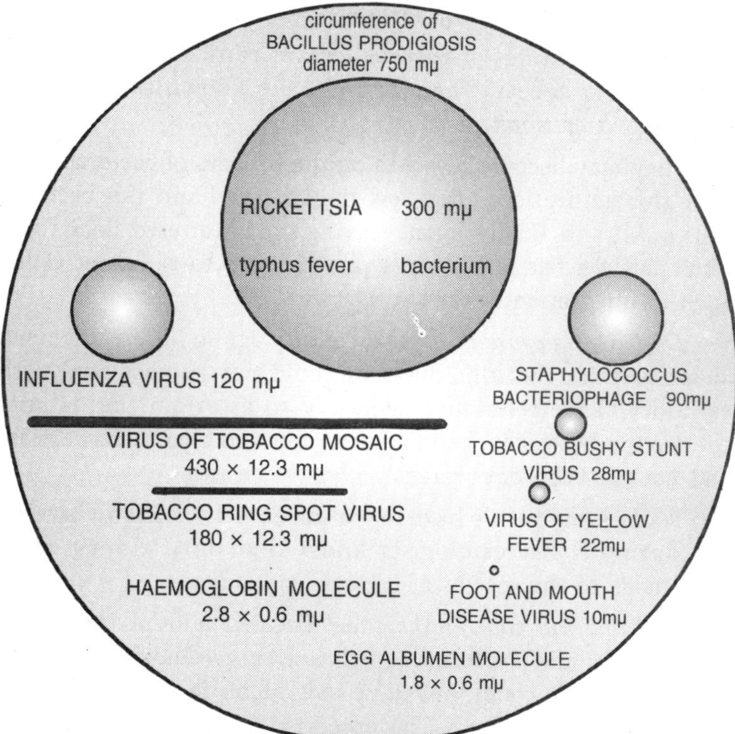

Figure 8.1: Diagram of the relative sizes of several viruses compared with those of certain bacteria, bacteriophage, and protein molecules. On the same scale the diameter of a human red blood corpuscle would be 3.5 feet.

single flagellum may be several times the length of the cell. Locomotion results from a rotary or whip-like movement of the flagella.

The flagellate forms are active for a time but later become stationary and lose their flagella. Brownian movement of both living and dead bacteria is a common phenomenon.

Bacterial cells are slightly heavier than water (sp. gr. 1.038 to 1.065). The largest bacillus studied is from 3 to 6 microns in diameter and 40-60 μ in length.

The coccus forms may vary from 0.15 μ to more than 1 micron in diameter. It requires several billions of such cells to weigh a milligram.

Destruction of Bacteria by Viruses

In some cultures of bacteria certain particles much smaller than bacteria appear. These particles are known as *viruses,* or virus-like *bacteriophages.*

They may become adsorbed on the surfaces of bacteria. Soon after this adsorption, often less than a half-hour, the bacterial cells swell and finally burst, leaving only scattered debris and virus particles, or remains that are referred to as "ghost cells." Such disintegration is known as *lysis.*

Do bacteria cause disease? A century ago so little was known about bacteria that this question could not be answered with certainty. The techniques necessary to ascertain the definite connection between a certain bacterium and a particular disease had not yet been discovered.

Today some people have the mistaken notion that all bacteria are harmful. Bacteriologists know that only a very small percentage of the species of bacteria cause disease.

Cell division and reproduction. Bacteria multiply by simple cell division, and the resulting halves form two new individuals. Under favorable conditions these individuals in turn divide, and there are four individuals. This process may continue indefinitely.

At suitable temperatures divisions may occur as often as every 20 minutes, which is the same as saying that an individual may exist but 20 minutes. A little computation will show that within a day the number of such rapidly dividing bacteria becomes enormous.

If division occurred every 30 minutes, starting with one bacterium, we would have: At the end of 24 hours, 281 million million bacteria = 1 pint in volume. At the end of 48 hours, 281 million million pints = about 32 cubic miles of bacteria. Such rapid increases of bacteria are limited to very short periods of time. Toxic substances that inhibit growth of bacteria often appear in the medium. Their food, water, oxygen, and salt supply is limited to the film immediately surrounding them.

Colonies of bacteria cannot become very large because the movements of substances through the mass is limited by the rate of diffusion. In nature other environmental factors such as light, moisture, and temperature rarely remain favorable for long periods. Bacteria are also consumed by many microscopic animals.

The protoplasm of a bacterial cell may contract into a rounded mass at one end, or in the middle, with the formation of a secondary wall; this mass is termed a *spore.*

It contains less water, is less likely to be injured by drying, and will endure greater extremes of temperature and greater concentrations of poisons than the ordinary bacterial cell.

It is because the spores of certain bacteria can withstand a temperature of boiling water that steam pressure is used in sterilizing cans of corn, beans, peas, and other vegetables. Most of the bacteria that cause diseases do not form spores. Those that cause botulism and tetanus are exceptions.

Bacteria and Sanitation

We often go to considerable trouble to prevent decay; but we owe our continued existence on the earth to the fact that bacteria (and fungi) remove the dead bodies of plants and animals that would otherwise have accumulated on the earth.

Together with the fungi they secrete enzymes which digest the highly complex organic substances composing the bodies of plants and animals into simpler substances. By repeated oxidations these substances are ultimately changed into carbon dioxide, water, and inorganic salts. These are again available to green plants.

The sewage that is drained into rivers is digested and oxidized by bacteria to simple harmless compounds. Our great cities, where thousands and sometimes millions of people are crowded into a small area, must have enormous sewage-disposal works in which aeration and other conditions are made favorable for a more rapid growth of the bacteria of decay, and the quick destruction of the sewage. This prevents the pollution of streams, lakes, and harbors into which the sewage would otherwise be carried.

The modern processes of filtering and purifying the water supplies of cities not only remove sediment, but also eliminate the bacteria of disease.

The processes include adding minute quantities of alum and chloride of lime to the water, and then filtering it through sand.

For many years the water-borne organism causing typhoid fever took a large annual toll in human lives. Cities are now practically free of this disease; most typhoid cases originate from polluted well water in rural communities.

To eliminate the contamination of surface wells requires merely careful location and construction of the wells with reference to surface drainage which often contains large numbers of bacteria.

Sanitary practices, such as quarantine, disinfection, admitting direct sunlight into living rooms, cleanliness, cooking foods, pasteurizing milk, and keeping foods in refrigerators, are all related to the elimination or the reduction of the number and kinds of bacteria with which we come into contact.

BACTERIA AND DISEASE

While most bacteria are not causes of disease, some are, and these are known as pathogenic bacteria. The invasion of the body tissues by bacteria is known as *infection.* The severity of the disease depends upon the ability of the organisms to invade the tissues, multiply rapidly, and cause injury.

The injury to the body is due to the destruction of tissues and the formation by the bacteria of certain poisonous substances called *toxins.*

When the body is invaded, *antitoxins,* or *antibodies,* are formed that neutralize the effects of the toxins either by combining with them chemically, or otherwise rendering the cells immune.

In this way the body is protected until the bacteria are destroyed by the colorless blood cells (leucocytes), or until the bacteria are made harmless by other means.

The term *immunity* denotes the qualities of a plant or animal by which the invasion or growth of pathogenic organisms is prevented, or their products are rendered harmless.

A plant or animal is *susceptible* to an infectious disease when such qualities are absent, or inadequately developed. Not all persons are equally susceptible to certain diseases, and susceptibility may vary in the same individual from time to time.

A person is usually immune to a disease if his blood contains the corresponding antibody, or is able to produce it. Some of the more common bacterial diseases of the human body are tuberculosis, pneumonia, diphtheria, typhoid fever, and tetanus.

DISEASES OF PLANTS

Although most of the diseases of plants are caused by fungi, the destruction of plants by bacteria is often sufficient to present a serious economic problem. Bacteria may be present in the healthy tissues of some plants.

They may, however, penetrate the host through wounds or natural openings and then spread throughout the plant or remain localized within certain tissues.

They are carried from plant to plant by insects, by man, and by other animals. Bacteria are less frequently dispersed by rain and wind.

Bacteria in Milk

Among the natural media in which bacteria grow, milk is ideal for most bacteria of decay and some pathogenic organisms (patho-gens). Milk, then, must be handled carefully if it is to be used as food.

The cows, the stable, the vessels in which the milk is placed, the persons who handle it are all possible sources of bacterial contamination.

It is of paramount importance that attention be paid to cleanliness and to the retardation of bacterial growth by immediate refrigeration. In spite of all precautions, bacteria do occur in milk. To check their multiplication, particularly after shipment from the dairy farm to the cities, the milk is heated.

This process, which is known as *pasteurization,* destroys nearly all the active pathogens. Such heating, however, does not kill spores; but if the milk is kept cool, their subsequent germination and growth are largely prevented.

Milk may be heated to 165-175° F., held a few seconds, and immediately cooled again.

The Science of Bacteriology

The study of bacteria has made great strides since Leeuwenhoek in 1676 first saw through his crude magnifier the "animalcules" from his teeth. Many years elapsed and many investigations were made before the biological significance of these microorganisms was established.

Even now a large portion of the world's population has never heard of bacteria, a larger number is indifferent to their importance, and too many people still like to believe that disease results from mysterious influences rather than from bacterial infection.

Spontaneous Generation

Since earliest times man has probably been interested in the question of the origin of living organisms on the earth, and has tried to formulate answers on the basis of what he imagined or what he observed. Some of these observations, and also the inferences drawn from them, we now know were erroneous.

It was believed, for example, that mice came from rags and meal, that mud produced frogs, that putrid meat changed to bees and flies, and that water in some manner gave rise suddenly to all sorts, of *fully formed* aquatic organisms.

Although many people ardently subscribed to a special creation of each kind of plant and animal, they at the same time accepted the idea of the spontaneous production of such organisms from inorganic matter.

It required, of course, only simple experiments to show that screened meats produce no maggots, that rags and meal inside stoppered bottles never give rise to mice, and that frogs develop from frog eggs and not from mud.

Although a few individuals as early as the 17th century definitely expressed the opinion that organisms arise only from preexisting organisms, it was not until after the middle of the 19th century that the theory of spontaneous generation was shown to be utterly false as an explanation of the origin of fully formed plants and animals.

Speculation

Early Greek philosophers, including Aristotle (384-322 B.C.), all subscribed in their writings to the idea of spontaneous development of living organisms. Their statements were copied and enlarged upon by nearly all the medieval scholars of Europe.

For example, there was then a widespread belief in the "goose tree" and the "vegetable lamb." Geese and ducks were thought to be formed either directly from the fruit of certain trees, or from sea shells borne by these trees.

Current also were the so-called observations that certain trees bore melon-like fruits containing fully formed lambs. Such incredible accounts as these were widely accepted until early in the 18th century.

Early Experimentation

During the 16th century a few investigators with a desire to experi-ment for themselves showed that spontaneous generation of some organisms was clearly erroneous. Van Helmont (1577-1644), although he thought his experiment proved that mice came from wheat grains, was troubled because these mice were just like those borne by a female mouse.

The Italian physician Redi (1626-1697) proved experimentally that "worms" in meat are fly larvae. He further showed that if the flies are kept from depositing eggs on meat, no larvae develop in it. Redi did not, however, draw the inference that this experiment disproved spontaneous generation.

Indeed, he suspected that "worms" in plant galls arose spont-aneously from plant juices. Vallisneri (1661-1730) soon afterward proved that these "worms" likewise developed from the eggs of insects.

Leeuwenhoek and his Microscopes

The early Dutch student of microscopy, Leeuwenhoek (1632-1723), looking through his simple magnifiers, saw organisms invisible to the unaided eye. He examined all sorts of infusions containing microorga-nisms, and left accurate descriptions, and many remarkable figures of bacteria, yeasts, algae, and many other organisms.

Leeuwenhoek did not subscribe to the theory of spontaneous generation, but insisted that the tiny organisms he saw grew from similar organisms that got into his infusions from the air.

Sterilization by Heat and Chemicals

In 1776 Spallanzani (1729-1799), an Italian, proved that if meat broth is heated for an hour or two in hermetically sealed flasks, no microorganisms develop in the broth.

The methods employed in this simple experiment were used by Appert in 1810 to exclude bacteria and molds from foods, and are the basis of our canning industry.

The objection was immediately made, in the case of Spallanzani's experiment, that the heating had spoiled the air inside the flask so that no organism could live there, and therefore that spontaneous generation had not been disproved.

Upon exposure to air the broth was soon teeming with organisms. For this objection Spallanzani's experiments provided no explanation.

Schultze in 1836 obtained similar results, although he admitted air to his previously heated flasks of broth through tubes containing strong acids and other chemical compounds.

Schwann (1810-1882) the same year allowed the air to enter the flasks through intensely heated tubes. It was argued by opponents that both the heat and the chemicals had altered the air.

Von Schroeder and von Dusch in 1854 filtered air entering the flasks through cotton or wool plugs, and no organisms developed in the flasks of broth.

These experiments are the forerunners of the modern use of cotton plugs in culture flasks in all pathology and bacteriology laboratories.

The Chemical Theory of Fermentation

Owing to poor techniques, other investigators often failed to confirm the results of these experiments or to secure consistent results, and the belief in spontaneous generation continued. About this time the so-called *chemical theory of fermentation* was current, and this indirectly gave comfort to the proponents of spontaneous generation.

This theory, supported by Liebig (1803-1873) and others, assumed that in decay, or in fermentation, large molecules simply disintegrated into smaller ones, and that fresh meat spoiled because it came into contact with other spoiled meat which initiated the breaking up of the molecules.

In other words, this theory would imply that microorganisms, though they may accompany decay and fermentation, are not the causes of these putrefactive processes.

Louis Pasteur

A few people had suggested as early as the 18th century that bacteria, or certain microscopic agents, are the causes of fermentation and disease. But it was not until the latter half of the 19th century that Louis Pasteur (1822-1895) with a series of brilliantly planned and expertly conducted experiments finally eliminated the idea of spontaneous generation as a correct explanation for these phenomena.

Pasteur's first conviction that microorganisms are the *cause* and not the *result* of fermentation came when he was investigating the troubles in the beet-sugar distilleries at Lille, France.

Besides the normal fermentation resulting in alcohol, the vats frequently contained lactic acid, a product for which there was no market.

Pasteur found that when yeasts were present alone in the vats, alcohol was formed. When certain rod-shaped bacteria were present, however, lactic acid appeared also. By properly transferring the two organisms to sugar solutions he was able to secure either alcohol or lactic acid at will, depending upon whether the yeast or the bacterium was present in the solutions.

The proponents of spontaneous generation were still not convinced and demanded more proof. Pasteur felt certain that bacteria are present in the air and set about to verify his conviction.

He prepared numerous flasks of various sterilized media, sealed the sterilized flasks, and later opened them at various places, such as in rural districts, on busy street corners, and on mountain tops.

The results indicated clearly that bacteria are much more abundant in some areas, such as dusty streets, than in quiet countrysides or mountain tops.

Even then the skeptics were unconvinced: they insisted that the sealing of the flasks had brought about an unnatural condition.

Pasteur soon afterward utilized an experimental idea that did away with the necessity of sealing the flask. Sterile media were placed in sterile flasks the necks of which had been drawn out into long, narrow S-shaped tubes having very small openings at the outer ends.

In this experiment the flasks were not sealed, and the culture media were given free access to the air. No matter where the flasks were placed or how long they were kept, bacteria did not develop in the media.

But when the flasks were opened so that the media became exposed to air in the usual way, they soon became contaminated.

The results of these experiments were clear, but there was a lack of unanimity in the inferences drawn from them. Pasteur was so sure of the completeness of his demonstration that in a public lecture at the Sorbonne in 1864 he closed his address with these prophetic words: "Never will the doctrine of spontaneous generation recover from the mortal blow of this simple experiment."

Nearly all thinking people now accept the fact that organisms arise only from preexisting organisms and not by spontaneous generation.

Some of the flasks prepared by Pasteur have been kept to the present time, and no living organisms have appeared in them.

Two centuries earlier, Redi had proved experimentally that worms do not arise spontaneously from meat. From the time of Redi to that of Pasteur many critical experiments were performed. One result of these experiments was the gradual abandonment of the idea that plants and animals like those on the earth today arise by spontaneous generation.

Progress in understanding the origin of living organisms, and in following certain practices, such as those of sanitation, personal hygiene, aseptic surgery, and the preservation of food, was seen to depend upon other ideas and upon further discoveries.

Even more impressive than all these early experiments are the facts known today about the composition, organization, and correlations of the parts of living cells, and of multicellular organisms.

That such highly organized structures could arise suddenly from either inorganic or organic masses of matter appears quite untenable.

Even if non-living colloidal masses of organic matter ever attain the state of being alive, escape destruction, and multiply, a very long geological period of time would elapse before highly organized cells capable of exact duplication by reproduction could evolve.

After considering pertinent data from all fields of science for 25 years, Oparin came to certain conclusions about the probable origin of living organisms on the earth, and clearly summarized the data and conclusions in a small book which is cited at the end of this chapter.

Pasteur's experiments were not limited to the question of spontaneous generation. He studied vinegar-making, silkworm diseases, rabies, and diseases of sheep and cattle.

He not only showed that bacteria and other microorganisms cause diseases, but he developed methods of vaccination that made man and other animals immune or at least less susceptible to certain diseases.

Perhaps one of the most touching stories in all biology is

that of Pasteur's treatment of the little boy who was bitten by a mad dog.

Modern Bacteriology

Out of the experiments of Pasteur and equally significant ones by Koch (1843-1910), Lister (1827-1912), and many others, the modern techniques used in the control of pathogenic organisms have developed.

Bacteriology is now an important biological science with many specialized phases of research in medicine, dentistry, veterinary medicine, agriculture, dairy technique, plant pathology, and many industrial processes.

Methods of Killing and Controlling Bacteria

It was known long before bacteria were discovered that certain practices are valuable in the preservation of foods, caring for wounds, and the prevention of disease.

Most of these methods were found out accidentally because the true nature of putrefaction and diseases was unknown for many centuries, and these methods are consequently crude and often not dissociated from magic. There is now a great body of experimentally established facts about the control of bacteria.

In the references below, further information may be secured about the effectiveness and uses of the following means of controlling bacteria: cleanliness, ventilation, sunlight, drying, refrigeration, antiseptics, brine and sugar solutions, sterilization, fumigation, pasteurization, canning, precipitation by chemicals isolation, vaccination, antitoxins, and serum treatment.

CHAPTER 9

Bacteria of the Soil

Bacteria of many kinds-both harmful and beneficial-live and grow in the soil. They are often incredibly numerous, sometimes numbering as high as a billion individuals in a gram of fertile garden soil. Some of the relations of bacteria to decay and disease were described in the preceding chapter.

We shall now consider the importance of soil bacteria to cultivated plants and soil formation. Many soil bacteria are important in the maintenance and improvement of fertility; some have quite the opposite effect.

Distribution

Most soil bacteria occur in the upper two to ten inches of the soil where the supply of organic compounds is usually greater. In the surface inch of soil, bacteria are not so numerous because of the destructive effects of light and of frequent desiccation.

Relatively few bacteria are found below a depth of two or three feet in humid regions. In well-aerated soils, such as those of irrigated semi-deserts, bacteria grow at greater depths. They are probably always present as far down as the roots of plants extend.

Nitrogen Sources of Green Plants

Since nitrogen makes up such a large part of the atmosphere of the earth, it was early assumed that green plants obtain nitrogen from the air. The noted chemist, Liebig, was convinced that this must be so, for he believed that the ammonia of the air was a sufficient source of nitrogen for plants. A long time and many experiments were needed to show that nitrates and ammonium salts in the soil are the usual sources of nitrogen in plants.

Although this fact was surmised in 1838 by Boussingault of France, and in 1847 by Lawes and Gilbert of the Rothamsted Experimental Farms in England, nearly a half century elapsed before final proof was obtained.

The various methods by which atmospheric nitrogen is combined in compounds which green plants can utilize began to be understood just before the beginning of the present century.

The occurrence of nitrogen compounds usable by green plants is due almost entirely to the action of certain bacteria. Such bacteria may be referred to as *nitrogen bacteria,* and several groups are known to play an important part in the nitrogen cycle in nature.

The importance of such microorganisms is recognized when we recall that every time a crop is harvested, the nitrogen within the plant is removed from the field. In the course of a few years this practice, along with the natural leaching by water, would seriously deplete the nitrogen content of the soil.

To maintain soil fertility the nitrogen compounds lost in this way must be constantly renewed. The nitrogen bacteria are very important in this renewal. The three groups of bacteria that form nitrogen compounds usable by green plants are the *ammoni f ying bacteria,* the *nitrifying bacteria,* and the *nitrogen-fixing bacteria.*

A fourth group, the *denitrifying bacteria,* by releasing nitrogen from these compounds, have the opposite effect and decrease the nitrogen content of soils.

Ammonifying and Nitrifying Bacteria

Although millions of dollars are spent every year in adding commercial fertilizers containing nitrogen compounds to soils, our immediate interest is how the combined nitrogen in natural organic compounds is again made usable to green plants.

These compounds include the undecayed remains of plants and animals. The ammonifying and nitrifying bacteria bring about a chain of chemical and physical processes by which the nitrogenous substances are transformed into simpler and more soluble compounds. These are really processes of decay, and the nitrogen bacteria are among the saprophytes that bring this about.

Ammonification

The disintegration and digestion of the large protein molecules of organic bodies in the soil are activated *by proteolytic* (protein-dissolving) enzymes. The resulting products, largely urea, peptones, and amino acids, undergo additional chemical changes by which ammonia (NH_3) is released.

In so far as nitrogen is involved, this is a reduction process known as *ammoni fication,* and it takes place only through the agency of microorganisms. Some of the chemical reactions may be represented as follows:

Urea + Water → Ammonium carbonate

$$CO(NH_2)_2 + 2H_2O \rightarrow (NH_4)_2CO_3$$

Nitrification. Ammonia in turn becomes the compound transformed in nitrate formation. Only a few species of soil bacteria activate this process; they may be classified into two groups. The first group oxidizes ammonia to nitrous acid.

Ammonia + oxygen → Nitrous acid + Water

$$2NH_3 + 3O_2 \rightarrow 2HNO_2 + 2H_2O$$

The nitrous acid may form salts with basic ions in the soil.

Nitrous acid	+	Potassium carbonate	→	Potassium nitrite	+	Carbon dioxide	+	Water
$2HNO_2$	+	K_2CO_3	→	$2KNO_2$	+	CO_2	+	H_2O

The formation of nitrous acid and nitrites from ammonia occurs in soils in America and Australia primarily in the presence of species of *Nitrosococcus;* in the soils of Europe, Asia and Africa species of *Nitrosomonas* are the nitrite formers.

The last stage in nitrification is the oxidation of nitrous acid and nitrites to nitric acid and nitrates.

Nitrous acid	+	Oxygen	→	Nitric acid
$2HNO_3$	+	K_2CO_3	→	$2HNO_3$

The nitric acid may form salts with basic ions in the soil.

Nitric acid	+	Potassium carbonate	→	Potassium nitrate	+	Carbon dioxide	+	Water
$2HNO_3$	+	K_2CO_3	→	$2KNO_3$	+	CO_2	+	H_2O

Nitrous acid and nitrites seldom accumulate in soils, for as rapidly as they are formed other nitrifying bacteria of the genus *Nitrobacter* oxidize them to nitrates. Thus the process of nitrification includes the oxidation of ammonia to nitrites, and the further oxidation of nitrites to nitrates.

Each step in the process from proteins to ammonia, from ammonia to nitrites, nitrites to nitrates, is dependent upon the presence of appropriate bacteria.

Nitrification is an oxidation process and the energy released is used by the bacteria in the synthesis of sugar from carbon dioxide and water, and also in the further elaboration of sugar and certain inorganic salts into proteins and other cell compounds of the bacteria.

These microorganisms, then, are autophytes. The conditions necessary for natural nitrification include moderate moisture, warm temperatures of the soil, good aeration, and fairly neutral reaction, in addition to the raw materials necessary for certain food syntheses in the bacteria.

The bacteria involved in ammonification are common and widespread in most soils, but the nitrifying bacteria are largely restricted to well-aerated, moist, nearly neutral soils.

Denitrification

The nitrates accumulated in soils through the agency of bacteria may disappear in several ways. They may be used by green plants, carried away by water, or changed into insoluble substances. They may also be reduced by other organisms to nitrous acid and ammonia, or to molecular nitrogen.

This reduction of nitrates to gaseous nitrogen is referred to as *denitrification.* It occurs under certain conditions and decreases the nitrogen content of the soil. Some of the chemical reactions involved in the reduction of nitrates may be indicated as follows:

Nitric acid	→	Nitrous acid	+	Oxygen
$2HNO_3$	→	$2HNO_2$	+	O_2

$$\text{Nitrous acid} \rightarrow \text{Water} + \text{Nitrogen} + \text{Oxygen}$$
$$4HNO_3 \rightarrow H_2O + 2N_2 + 3O_2$$

The organisms that bring about the reduction of nitrates are principally anaerobic bacteria, known collectively as *denitrifying bacteria.* Since denitrification is a reduction process and may occur in the absence of light, the organisms must obtain energy by oxidizing carbohydrates and other organic compounds.

Denitrification is likely to occur in any soil containing nitrates under anaerobic conditions. It is characteristic of poorly drained soils, and of soils periodically flooded, as in rice fields. In certain regions denitrification may so deplete the soil of available nitrogen compounds that plant growth is restricted.

Nitrogen-fixation

Nitrogen constitutes nearly 80 per cent of the earth's atmosphere; the combined nitrogen in all plants is relatively so small that if plants could directly use the free nitrogen of the air the supply would be inexhaustible. Over every acre of land surface the air contains nearly 300 million pounds of nitrogen.

It has been calculated that the earth's atmosphere contains the prodigious total of over 5000 million million tons of nitrogen. In spite of this, nitrogen is the most expensive component of fertilizers.

Certain bacteria together with a few other organisms directly utilize the free nitrogen of the air. These bacteria transform this free nitrogen into compounds usable by all plants. The chain of processes in this transformation is termed *nitrogen-fixation.*

It has been known for more than 20 centuries that certain legumes, such as clover, beans, and peas, enrich the soil. For this reason legumes have long been used in crop rotations because farmers have known that other crop plants grow better and yield more following the plowing under of legumes.

It was not definitely known that nitrogen compounds accumulate in legumes through the agency of nitrogen-fixing bacteria until 1886-1888. Since that time the life cycles of these organisms have been thoroughly studied. These bacteria occur as microscopic motile rods free in the soil.

When legumes are planted and roots form, the bacteria invade the cells of the roots by way of the root hairs. The root becomes infected and enlarges locally in the form of *nodules.* These nodules contain millions of bacteria, which become somewhat enlarged and branched.

The bacteria are dependent on the carbohydrates in the legume roots. Unless there is an abundance of sugar in the roots of the host plant, few or no nodules develop, because the bacteria do not invade the root hairs.

Although several species of bacteria infect legumes, there may be considerable specificity in their relations to the host. Some investigators have classified legumes on the basis of the bacteria to which they are most susceptible.

The red, white, and alsike clovers, for example, constitute one group; alfalfa, sweet clover, and yellow trefoil another group; certain peas a third group; and cowpeas, peanuts, lima beans, and Japan clover still another group.

Recent experiments indicate that the specificity of the nitrogen-fixing bacteria may not be as pronounced as earlier experiments seemed to show. Although the series of events in "fixing" nitrogen are not well known, the important process is the combining of free nitrogen with other elements, resulting in a nitrogenous compound, perhaps an amino compound.

The formation of these complex compounds is a reduction process and requires the energy made available through the oxidation of sugars made by the leguminous plant.

The bacteria multiply, mature, and die within the nodules, and the nitrogen compounds are used or accumulate within the legume. At the death of any part of the roots of the legume these compounds enter the soil.

Still another group of bacteria fix nitrogen without being associ-ated with higher green plants. These organisms are saprophytes and make possible a series of processes sometimes called *non-symbiotic nitrogenfixation,* in contrast to the nitrogen-fixation in legumes, which is called *symbiotic.*

They live especially in humous soils and derive their energy by the oxidation of such organic compounds as carbohydrates, organic acids, and other products of fermentation. In addition to energy, the fixation of nitrogen by the bacteria is affected by many other conditions in the soil.

Dark prairie soils are ideal media for these bacteria and under natural conditions have the highest nitrogen content. Non-symbiotic nitrogen-fixing bacteria may be classified into two groups : those using free oxygen *(aerobic),* largely species of the genus *Azotobacter;* and *anaerobic* species belonging to the genus *Clostr-idium.* The species of *Azotobacter* are coccus forms and non-motile; those of *Clostridium* are rod-shaped and spore-forming.

The Nitrogen Cycle

We have now discussed the origin of nitrogenous compounds in soils through the agency of bacteria. Neither nitrification nor nitrogen-fixation in soils occurs in the absence of certain micro-organisms, chiefly bacteria. We may now summarize the complete cycle of events in the origin and transformation of nitrogen compounds.

In the green plants, amino acids are made from carbohydrates and nitrogen salts and are used by both plants and animals in the synthesis of proteins. The death of plants and animals results in a residue of substances, some of which are proteins.

Through the agency of bacteria the proteins are digested to simpler compounds such as amino acids. Then through further chemical change qmmonia is formed from water and the NH_2 ions. *Ammonification is* the name applied to this series of processes.

Ammonia is then oxidized to nitrites and to nitrates through the agency of nitrifying bacteria. These processes are *nitrification.* The nitrates may be used by green plants and by most non-green plants in the synthesis of proteins, and we are back where we started. Certain other groups of bacteria may reduce the nitrates and nitrites to gaseous nitrogen. This is *denitrification.*

Other groups of bacteria bring about the transformation of free nitrogen of the air to amino compounds which accumulate in the organisms. This is known as *nitrogen-fixation.* Nitrogen-fixing bacteria are of two kinds: those living symbiotically in legume roots, and those living free in the soil. Upon their death the nitrogen compounds become available.

All the processes having to do with nitrogen in its relation to green plants may be grouped together into what has generally been known as the *nitrogen cycle*.

Sulfur Bacteria

We have seen earlier that sulfur is a part of the molecule of some amino acids and proteins. Green plants in general obtain sulfur from sulfates of the soil. Upon the death of the plant the proteins containing sulfur are acted upon by bacteria, with the formation of hydrogen sulfide.

The hydrogen sulfide is oxidized through the agency of *sulfur bacteria* to elemental sulfur and sulfur dioxide. The latter is further oxidized to sulfuric acid which may react with a salt, such as calcium carbonate, and form calcium sulfate.

This formation of sulfates is known as *sulfofication,* and takes place through the agency of the bacteria. The sulfates are then available to green plants and the cycle is complete.

Sulfates in the soil may be depleted through the action of another group of bacteria, forming hydrogen sulfide. Reduction of elemental sulfur may also result in the formation of sulfides. This reduction process is known as *desulfofication.*

Sulfofication is an oxidation process through which sulfofying bacteria obtain energy that is used by them in the synthesis of sugar and other foods. Such microorganisms are thus autophytes, and in this respect resemble the nitrifying bacteria.

Bacteria and Phosphates

Organic compounds of phosphorus are present in plant and animal residues. Before the phosphorus is usable by green plants, these complex compounds must be resolved by soil microorganisms. Such decomposition involves a number of reactions; phosphoric acid is finally formed, it accumulates in the soil as phosphates of calcium, magnesium, iron, and aluminum.

Iron Bacteria

Bacteria are associated with the transformation of iron compounds in the soil through oxidation-reduction reactions. Certain iron bacteria are able to bring about the oxidation of ferrous to ferric iron, thereby obtaining energy by which they synthesize their sugars and other foods; thus they are autophytes.

Under anaerobic conditions ferric iron may be reduced to ferrous iron by other iron bacteria. Although it is rarely necessary to add iron to soils, iron deficiencies sometimes occur in alkaline regions owing to the formation of insoluble compounds of iron both by colloidal aggregation and by bacterial action.

Compounds toxic to some bacteria have been isolated from certain species of soil bacteria. It had been known for many years that pathogenic organisms are rapidly destroyed when added to the soil, and it had been early suggested that products of certain soil bacteria might indeed be toxic to others.

Scientific research in recent years on microorganisms of the soil has resulted in the isolation of antibiotic substances, such as gramicidin and tyrocidine from *Bacillus brevis.* Numerous bacteria are now known to inhibit the growth of other bacteria.

If we could review all the activities of the many kinds of bacteria we would appreciate still more their fundamental importance in our biological world. Parasitic bacteria may cause the death of living organisms. Numerous saprophytic bacteria in turn digest the organic compounds in the dead bodies, and oxidize the carbon compounds in respiration.

Through these disintegrative processes the inorganic ions, such as those of phosphorus, iron, and magnesium, that are chemically bound in the compounds of living cells are liberated; and ammonia and carbon dioxide are formed.

A few special groups of bacteria through these unique respiratory processes oxidize the reduced nitrogen and sulfur of body compounds to nitrates and sulfates, which may again be reduced by bacteria or by green plants.

Thus by numerous activities of groups of bacteria following each other in definite succession the body compounds indigestible by animals and green plants become converted into simpler compounds that are usable by green plants.

In the grand "passing show" of nature, green plants and the larger animals play the easily visible roles; but their action would soon cease were it not for the bacteria and their associates, the fungi, most of whose activities are off-stage, unseen, and even unsuspected a century ago.

CHAPTER 10

The Fungi

Slightly moist bread in a warm room soon becomes covered with filamentous molds. Clothing, leather, and books left in moist rooms are soon "musty" because of the development of other kinds of molds. The flavors of some kinds of cheese are due to the growth of blue and green molds.

Around old stumps in meadows, and within forests where organic matter is abundant, puff balls, mushrooms, and toadstools may be found. From decaying logs and even from standing trees bracket mushrooms often protrude.

Field and garden crops are often infected with *mildews, rusts,* and *smuts.* In the process of bread-making yeast causes the dough to "rise." Many animals, including man, suffer discomfort through skin invasions of molds which cause, among other diseases, "ringworm" and "athlete's foot."

Certain molds are the sources of chemicals having great medicinal and industrial value. Some of these plants are saprophytes, some are parasites, and some live as both saprophytes and parasites. All these plants collectively are called *fungi* (sing. fungus).

The name fungus is the old Latin word for mushroom. Just as it is hard to tell whether some organisms are plants or animals, the great diversity among fungi makes it equally difficult to distinguish clearly certain fungi from certain bacteria and algae.

The most common characteristic of fungi is a vegetative body of either a loose web or a compact mass of filaments none of which contains chlorophyll. The fruiting and reproductive bodies of numerous fungi are readily recognized, but the reproductive bodies of many common fungi are seldom found; hence some fungi must be recognized without them.

Vegetative Parts of a Fungus

A toadstool among the leaves on the forest floor, or a bracket fungus on a fallen tree trunk is but a small part of the fungous plant. The part not readily seen consists of a widely dispersed mass of filaments. In describing fungi these filaments are called *hyphae* (sing. *hypha).*

Hyphae are either continuous tubular structures, or divided by cross walls into cell-like segments containing one to many nuclei. Usually they are highly branched and form loose cottony masses, such as may be readily seen in the bread mold.

The common meadow mushroom has colorless hyphae that spread in all directions through a large mass of soil and are usually unseen unless one digs carefully around the fruiting bodies that appear above the soil.

The "mushroom" is formed by the growing together and coalescence of numerous hyphae into a compact characteristic structure.

The whole aggregate of hyphae growing on, or within, the substrate is called the *mycelium* (Greek for *fungus).* The undergr-

Figure 10.1: Stages in the development of the common edible pink-gilled mushroom (Agaricus camperstris).

ound hyphae of some species grow in small compact masses, forming tuber-like bodies.

Those of some other species form compact hard strands of many hyphae that grow as a collective unit and push their way through firm substrates. The cell walls of hyphae are composed of such substances as cellulose, pectose, callose, and chitin.

The foods found in fungi are carbohydrates (including sugars and glycogen), fats, and proteins. Various kinds of enzymes are synthesized in the fungi, and are important in transforming substances not only within the fungous cells, but outside in the host or in the substrate.

Fungous hyphae may grow into the tissues of the host or other substrate by mechanical pressure similar to that of growing roots, or the substrate may be digested by enzymes from the hyphae. Fungi may be found wherever the environment is not inimical to the establishment of a mycelium, and where there are substances they can digest and use as food.

They are found on land and in water, growing free as saprophytes or as parasites within, or upon, many different hosts. Aquatic fungi are not as numerous as terrestrial ones, and are far less abundant than the algae and bacteria. The aquatic species live as parasites on fresh-water and marine organisms, or as saprophytes on the dead bodies and residues of such organisms.

They are most numerous in well lighted and well-aerated water where there is the largest number of host plants and animals. Any aquatic organism may be invaded, injured, or destroyed by parasitic fungi at some stage of its life cycle. The growth of aquatic fungi may be checked by epidemics of bacteria.

Terrestrial fungi occur everywhere on, or in, most kinds of plants and mans animals, as well as on their dead bodies. It would be difficult to find a twig lying on the ground in a forest that is not being invaded and disintegrated by some fungus, and one may easily discover the cobuwehhv fungous hvphae among the fallen leaves on the forest floor.

Soil fungi are most abundant in the upper foot of soil. Fungi digest the woody tissue by enzyme action. They injure the living hosts largely through. the destruction of tissues, through the formation of toxic substances, through the consumption of food, and through interference with physiological processes.

There are some 100,000 species of fungi and thousands of chemically different substrates; hence some fungi grow where

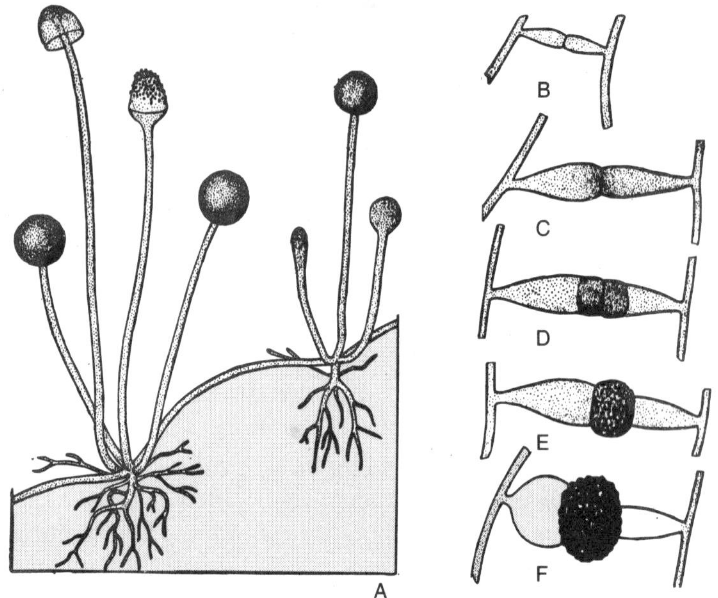

Figure 10.2: Bread mold (Rhizopus) : A, general habit of growth and reproduction by asexually formed spores; B, C, D, E, and F, stages in the fusion of hyphae of male and female mycelia and the formation of a zygote.

others cannot. Fungi are roost numerous and grow best in moist warm situations, but they rnav he found also on the desert, in refrigerators, and on the arctic tiindra.

Millions of bushels of fruits and vegetables in storage are destroyed each year by fungi. Most of the apples, for example, that spoil in storage are destroyed by a single fungus, a blue mold which causes a soft rot.

In northern states where snow covers the ground throughout the winter, much of the grass on golf greens is killed at the soil surface by another fungus. the so-called "snow mold." The spores and other dormant structures of fungi often survive the natural extremes of temperature and drought for long periods.

We shall now consider in more detail a few of the common species of fungi, in order to secure a better understanding of their structures, growth. and reproduction, and also of their biological significance.

Bread Mold

If a moist piece of bread is placed under a bell jar for a few days, a tangle of colorless hyphae may cover the bread and even fill the jar. This is the mycelium of the bread mold, *Rhizopus nigricans.*

Its hyphae are much branched and have no cross walls; some

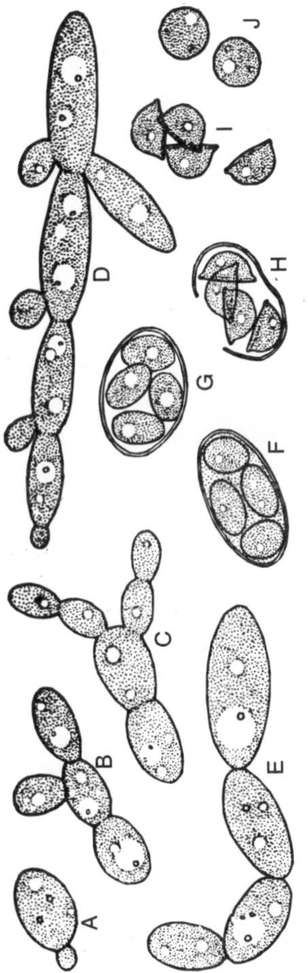

Figure 10.3: Yeast from fermenting sauerkraut, A-D, vegetative growth of diploid cells by budding. F-J, monoploid ascospores formed after reduction division of a diploid cell. A-G, Saccharomyces; H-J, Hansenula.

of them (rhizoids-root-like hvphae) penetrate the bread for short distances, while others form the visible web. Bread mold, of course, grows on many other substrates. Enzymes from the mold digest the bread.

The resulting soluble food diffuses into the hyphae of the mold. Decay is nothing more than the digestion and oxidation of organic substances.

Growth of the fungus may continue until the food is exhausted. The mycelium starts from a spore as a single hypha and spreads over the bread by terminal growth of its multitudinous branches. At node-like points on the spreading hyphae upright branches and several rhizoids develop.

These nodes also become new centers from which radiating horizontal hyphae extend and increase the complexity and density of the mycelium.

The tips of the upright hyphae enlarge and form globular spore cases, *sporangia,* which eventually contain many vegetative spores. Many sporangia usually develop at about the same time, and upon their rupture millions of black spores are liberated from them.

The spores are so light that they float in the air for long periods; hence it is easy to see why moist bread when exposed to the air for even a short time and then placed in a closed container soon becomes "moldy."

When spores come to rest on a moist organic substrate, they germinate almost immediately, and from them new mycelia originate. When bread is wrapped in waxed paper while still warm from the oven, mold spores are more likely to be kept out, and the bread keeps in good condition for a much longer period.

Sexual reproduction can be observed between mycelia of bread mold started from different spores on the same culture plate. Where hyphae of the two mycelia come in contact, the adjoining walls dissolve and the contents of the two "cells" fuse.

The union of the two protoplasts, or gametes, results in a heavy-walled black zygote. Upon germination of a zygote, a short hypha develops which terminates in a globular sporangium containing spores.

From these spores branching hyphae grow, and the development of a new mycelium begins.

Yeasts

In the discussion of respiration it was noted that the formation of alcohol and carbon dioxide from a sugar solution may be brought about in oxygen-free containers if certain yeasts are

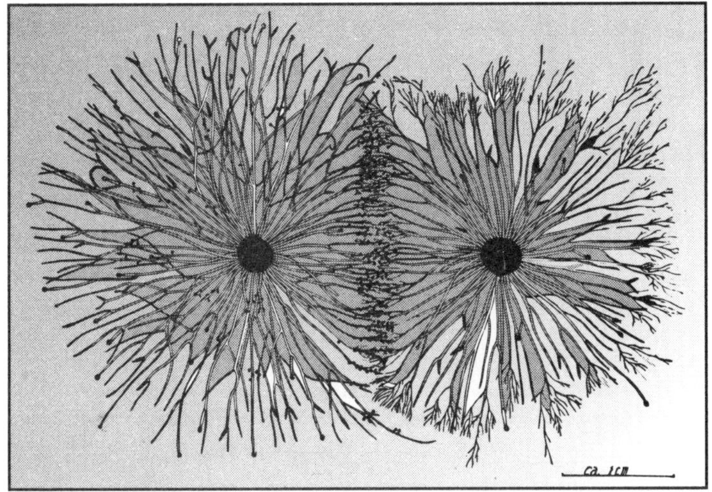

Figure 10.4: Diagrammatic representation of zygotes formed in the water mold, Achlya, when hyphae of a female mycelium (left) come in contact with those of a male mycelium (right).

present. When yeasts are thoroughly mixed with flour and water, their activities bring about the "rising" of bread dough.

The carbon dioxide resulting from the oxidation of sugar accumulates in bubbles throughout the dough and makes it porous. While the bread is baking, the alcohol vaporizes and with the carbon dioxide passes from the bread into the air.

The yeasts are generally microscopic one-celled plants more or less ellipsoid in form. Although a single yeast cell is microscopic, the enormous numbers that develop in a sugar solution soon make it cloudy, and eventually sediment collects at the bottom of the vessel. The yeast cakes sold by commercial firms consist of starch grains and yeast cells pressed together into a compact mass.

New cells develop vegetatively in yeasts either by simple

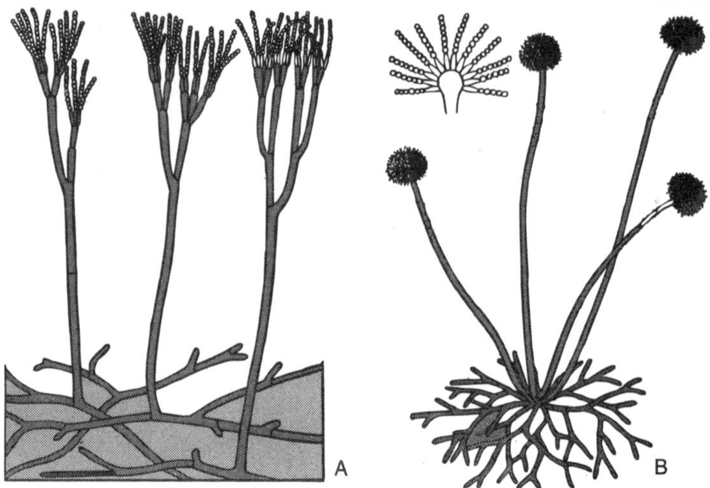

Figure 10.5: A, blue mold (Penicillium); B, green mold (Aspergillus). The spores (conidia) are formed by successive abstrictions of the tips of the upright hyphae (conidiophores) that develop from a felt-like meshwork of mycelium on the substrate. These one-celled vegetative spores develop in enormous numbers and are readily carried everywhere by air currents or by rain water, especially in the summer months.

division or by "budding" accompanied by the usual duplication of chromosomes. If there is not an immediate separation of the "bud" from the parent cell, short, fragile, branched or unbranched chains of cells develop.

Reduction division in diploid cells is followed by the development of monoploid *ascospores.* These spores may fuse in pairs forming diploid cells or they may "bud" and form monoploid vegetative cells which may increase,in number by budding and also fuse in pairs and form zygotes.

Thus the vegetative cells of yeasts may be diploid or monoploid. In some species of yeast, such as the pressed yeasts of commerce, most of the vegetative cells are diploid.

Water Molds

In temperate latitudes in early spring dead fish and other aquatic animals may be found in ponds and streams, completely covered with a colorless slimy mass of fungous hyphae. The same fungus, or other species of water molds, may also grow on living animals, and on decaying plant and animal remains.

They are at times very destructive to fish eggs and young fish. Water molds were so named before it was generally known that many species of them grow in moist soils. The vegetative phase consists of tubular branching hyphae within the host or the substrate.

The slimy mass of filaments on the outside of the animal is largely made up of hyphae that terminate in club-shaped sporangia, within which the protoplasts divide into many motile spores. After liberation from the sporangium, the motile spores may undergo various changes in appearance; from them new hyphae develop.

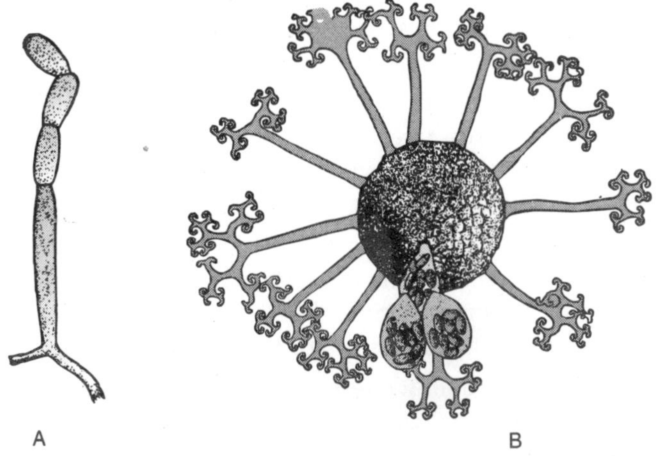

Figure 10.6: Reproductive structures of a powdery mildew: A, conidia formed during the summer months; B, an ascocarp, which lives through the winter and within which the asci and ascospores develop. They can be forced out of the ascocarp by a slight pressure as indicated in the drawing.

Sexual reproduction begins by the formation of egg cases, or *oogonia,* each containing from one to twenty egg cells, and by the development of *antheridia* containing sperm nuclei. The union of a sperm nucleus and an egg nucleus results in a *zygote.* Upon germination the zygote divides internally and motile spores result.

From these motile spores new hyphae may develop under favorable conditions. Hyphae may develop, however, from unfertilized eggs-another example of parthenogenesis in plants.

It has been discovered that at least four hormones are necessary in sexual reproduction in one of the water molds.

Blue and Green Molds

These molds were named on the basis of spore color in some common species. Some blue molds impart flavor and color to certain varieties of cheese, such as Camembert and Roquefort.

These fungi and others are the causes of the 'decay of vegetables, fruits, and meats both in storage and during transportation, and they occasion enormous monetary losses.

They are aerobic and during warm periods of high humidity may grow luxuriantly on many household articles. In tropical and semi-tropical climates electrical and optical equipment may be much damaged by these and other molds.

The main structural features of blue and green molds are shown in figure elsewhere in this chapter. Two species of blue mold (*Penicillium notatum* and *P. chrysogenum*) are sources of penicillin, a compound having definite bactericidal properties.

It is especially effective against certain pathogenic cocci, as well as one of the spirochaetes causing syphilis. Similar compounds synthesized in smaller mold fungi are streptomycin and chloromycetin. Such substances are known as *antibiotics.*

Aureomycin is another recently discovered antibiotic. The lethal effects of some of these antibiotics on the causal agents of prevalent human diseases are summarized in figure elsewhere in this chapter.

Mildews

During summer and early autumn cobwebby mycelia may be seen on the leaves of such plants as ragweed, knotweed, red clover, lilac, crimson rambler, sunflowers, and willows. The hyphae of these fungi also have cross walls.

When in contact with a leaf, some of the branches of the hyphae become haustoria or rhizoids which penetrate the epidermal cells of the host tissue.

The mycelia of these fungi are on the surface of the host. Other hyphae grow upright from the surface mycelium and bear at their tips chains of colorless conidia in a manner similar to

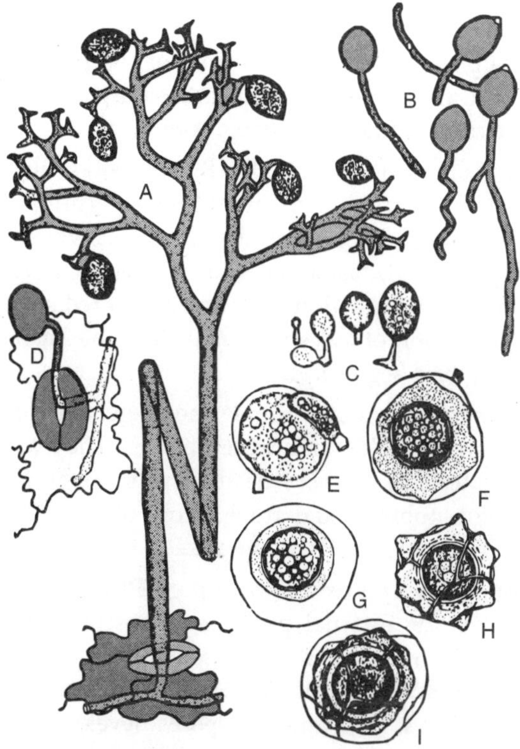

Figure 10.7: Enlarged drawings of the reproductive structures of a downy mildew parasitic within tobacco, tomato, eggplant, and pepper. The mycelium is intercellular. A, a branched conidia-bearing hypha protruding from a leaf through one of the stomates; B, germination of conidia; C, stages in the development of a conidium at the tip of a hypha; D, the hypha from a germinating conidium has grown into a leaf through a stomate; E-I, stages in the development of a zygote by sexual reproduction.

that of the blue molds noted above. The conidia, or summer spores, are carried about by air currents from leaf to leaf, and many plants thus become infected during the growing season. These fungi are called *powdery mildews* because of the appearance of the conidia.

In late summer small black dots may appear among the hyphae on the infected leaves. The dots are reproductive bodies and under the microscope are seen to be spherical and thick-walled, with curiously branched transparent appendages. These fruiting bodies, or *ascocarps,* are the result of the growth of coalescent hyphae, following the fusion of the protoplasts of an oogonium and an antheridium. Each ascocarp contains several sac-like structures termed *asci* (sing. *ascus*).

Within each ascus are usually 8 *ascospores,* although the number may vary from 2 to many. The germination of an ascospore the following spring results in a hypha which may grow upon other plants and start a new life cycle of the fungus. Sexual union preceding the formation of ascocarps and reduction division during the formation of ascospores make possible many kinds of hybrids and hybrid segregates.

The *downy mildews* have tubular non-septate hyphae similar to those of bread molds and water molds. They are internal obligate parasites that are very destructive to many plants, such as potato, onion, tobacco, and grape. More than 1000 such fungi belong in a group called *Phycomycetes.*

One especially interesting group of Phycomycetes is the *Entomoph-thorales,* internal parasites of insects. The powdery mildews, on the other hand, have septate hyphae and special reproductive structures (ascocarp, ascus, ascospore) not found in the downy mildews. Asci and ascospores develop in more than 12,000 species of fungi.

All of these fungi are called *Ascomycetes.* Other representatives of this group are yeast, blue and green molds, cup fungi, morels, and truffles. Numerous conidia develop on upright hyphae of some of the Ascomycetes during the growing season.

The life cycle of a downy mildew is so unlike that of a powdery mildew that different methods of eradication are needed. The mycelium of the downy mildew parasitic on potatoes may over-winter in the tuber and the next spring grow into the tissues of the new potato plant developing from that tuber.

Branched conidiophores grow outward through the stomates, and conidia are formed from the terminal branches. The conidia may be carried by wind or water to other parts of the plant or to other plants. Motile spores develop within each conidium.

When the leaves are wet, the motile spores emerge from the conidia and germinate almost immediately. The resulting hyphae penetrate the host, and new internal mycelia develop.

Sexual reproduction may take place when the fungus is growing in culture, but apparently does not occur when the fungus is growing in the potato plant. The reproductive structures of the downy mildew of tobacco are illustrated in Figure elsewhere in this chapter.

Cup Fungi, Morels, and Truffles

The cup fungi are usually found growing on soil and on decaying wood. The vegetative body, or mycelium, is largely underground or near the surface. The part usually visible, the fruiting body, is cup-shaped and lined with a layer of parallel asci and sterile hyphae.

Each ascus generally contains 8 ascospores. The morel, prized for its flavor, is related to the cup fungi, but has a hollow reproductive body covered above with a layer of asci. The fungus is not edible after the spores have matured and should be eaten only when immature.

A related group of fungi are the truffles, which are widespread in Europe and are also found in several places in the United States. Truffles are considered a delicacy and gathering them is an industry in France.

The plants, which generally grow from 3 to 12 inches below the surface of the soil, have a peculiar odor which is not evident to most people. Pigs and dogs have been trained to locate the plants.

The fruiting body of the truffle is a globose, warty structure enclosing the spore-bearing tissues. This fungus is disseminated by rodents that eat the truffles and scatter the undigested spores.

Mushrooms, Toadstools, and Puffballs

These are popular terms and do not correspond to any technical classification of fungi. To many people the term "mushroom" means an edible fungus while "toadstool" refers to a poisonous or inedible one. No such distinctions can be made on the basis of the form, color, structure, or place where they grow.

A few species may be safely eaten by some persons, but not by others. Beside the edible species, others are woody or unpalatable, and a number of species are deadly poisonous to all of us. The term "puffball" refers to a fungus that emits clouds of spores when stepped on.

Puffballs are inedible when mature, but many of them are edible when young. Perhaps the best advice to would-be mushroom hunters is to learn to identify positively a few of the common edible species and avoid all others.

The vegetative parts of all these fungi are in the soil, wood, or other substrate on which the reproductive bodies appear. These bodies, varying from a fraction of an inch to more than two feet in height or diameter, are compact masses of hyphae.

The vegetative hyphae of some toadstools are the cause of destructive wood-rots in timber and in wooden buildings. When mature, the reproductive structures may contain almost countless numbers of spores.

The common meadow mushroom often bears 2 billion spores, a polypore 10 billion, and a good-sized puffball may have 7000 billion spores. It has been estimated that only about one spore out of each trillion spores ever develops into a new plant.

The appearance of fruiting bodies is illustrated in Figures elsewhere in this chapter. Owing to the club-shaped hypha on which their spores are borne, such fungi as toadstools, puffballs, smuts, and rusts are called *Basidiomycetes.*

There are some 13,000 known species of basidiomycetes. Some mushrooms are basidiomycetes, but others are ascomycetes. The culture of the common meadow mushroom is an important industry in scattered localities, where it is carried on in specially constructed buildings with insulated walls, in caves, or in old mine tunnels where the temperature and humidity can be controlled.

Light is not harmful, but it is not necessary; and it increases the difficulty of controlling other conditions. After the beds of soil rich in organic matter are prepared and sterilized, they are inoculated with pieces of mycelia of pure races.

These mycelia develop from spores sown on boiled grain in sterilized culture bottles.

Fairy Rings

When growth conditions are favorable in lawns and pastures, the fruiting bodies of the common meadow mushroom often occur in so-called "*fairy rings*". The rings were thought in ancient times to represent the paths traversed by dancing fairies.

The circular appearance is due to the outward growth of the underground mycelium from the original center. The hyphae are perennial, and their radial extension is accompanied each year by the death of the older portions of the hyphae in the central areas.

The fruiting bodies thus appear in circles which increase in diameter from year to year. Nearly perfect rings of this mushroom 160 feet in diameter have been reported, but the diameter is usually less than 20 feet.

Similar rings are developed by many other fungi, including morels and puffballs. Some have attained diameters of nearly a quarter of a mile and could have resulted only after hundreds of years of outward extension of the mycelium from the original center of growth.

These largest rings are usually irregular, and occur in incomplete circles. An eruptive skin disease of man and other mammals, known as "ringworm," is caused by a fungus.

Pustules appear in irregular circles about the point of infection because of the radial growth of the hyphae in the skin. The lesions are caused by the fruiting bodies of the fungus as they break the skin, and thus appear as miniature fairy rings.

Smuts

Seed plants of many kinds, particularly many of the grasses, are infected by parasitic fungi that are unlike those just described. Owing to their appearance, some of them are referred to as *smuts,* others as *rusts.*

The vegetative and floral parts of oats, wheat, rye, corn, rice, and onions sometimes contain black or dark-brown masses of fungous spores. These masses are generally regarded as the smut plants, but they are merely the reproductive structures of an extensive mycelium in the host.

Several types of smuts may be exemplified by the loose and covered smuts of oats and barley, the loose and stinking smuts of wheat, and by the corn smut. At threshing time the mature spores of *bunt,* or the *stinking smut of wheat,* may stick to the surface of the wheat grains and remain there until the grains are planted!

At that time the spores germinate in the soil. The resulting short basidium-like hyphae bear basidiospore-like spores called "sporidia." These spores fuse in pairs and germinate, or they may germinate without fusion.

The resulting hyphae penetrate the young wheat seedling. The internal mycelium grows to the stem tip, keeps pace with the growing wheat plant, and finally enters the ovularies of the inflorescence. The floral parts are greatly distended by harvest time.

Masses of smut spores have replaced the embryo and endosperm of the seeds. During the threshing of the wheat these spores are released and scattered among the other grains of wheat. Unless these grains are disinfested before they are planted, another generation of bunt fungus will grow in the next crop of wheat.

The spores of the *loose smut of wheat,* appearing as dark-brown or black masses in the inflorescences at flowering time, may be blown to the stigmas of other wheat plants. There they germinate and the resulting hyphae penetrate the ovularies.

The mycelium remains dormant within the embryo until the seed is planted and starts to grow. It is not possible by superficial examination of the seed to ascertain the presence or absence of the internal mycelium.

Following the germination of these seeds the mycelium grows within the developing host plant, and masses of spores appear just before flowering time, replacing the destroyed flower parts. Thus the life cycle is complete.

The methods of control of this fungus must evidently be different from those used in the elimination of the stinking smut of wheat. The loose smut of barley is similar.

Masses of corn smut may also be seen on any part of an infected mature corn plant. The infection, however, always takes place when the tissue is young. The corn smut fungus does not spread throughout the host from the point of infection but remains more or less localized.

The smut galls and their masses of spores appear one to three weeks after infection. The spores may remain alive in the soil or in plant litter for many months, and consequently the fungus is difficult to eliminate.

Rusts

One of the most complex life cycles in the entire plant kingdom is that of the *black stem rust* of cereals and grasses. The *stem rust* of wheat is important commercially because during some years it decreases the yield of the American wheat crop by an estimated 120 million bushels.

The life cycle of this rust illustrates so well how difficult may be the problems encountered in attempting to control the fungi that cause diseases of economic plants, that it will be described in more detail than would otherwise be justified in this textbook.

During the summer the fungus is first apparent on the surface of stems and leaf sheaths as patches of innumerable red spores (*uredospores*). These spores are blown about by the wind and the hyphae from them infect other wheat plants. New mycelia develop, and the spores from them may be blown to other wheat plants.

This process may be repeated every week or ten days during the spring, thus spreading the fungus rapidly over large areas. These same internal mycelia a little later produce many two-celled, thick-walled black spores (*teliospores*).

These second spores in the life cycle begin to appear before the wheat plant is mature, and they live over the winter on the stubble and straw. After winter dormancy they germinate, and a short club-shaped hypha *(basidium)* develops from each of the two cells.

The basidium is four-celled, and from each of its cells a third kind of spore *(basidiospore)* forms. Reduction division occurs just previous to the formation of basidiospores; hence there will be genetic differences among the basidiospores and the mycelia that grow from them.

During the remainder of the life cycle of this rust certain

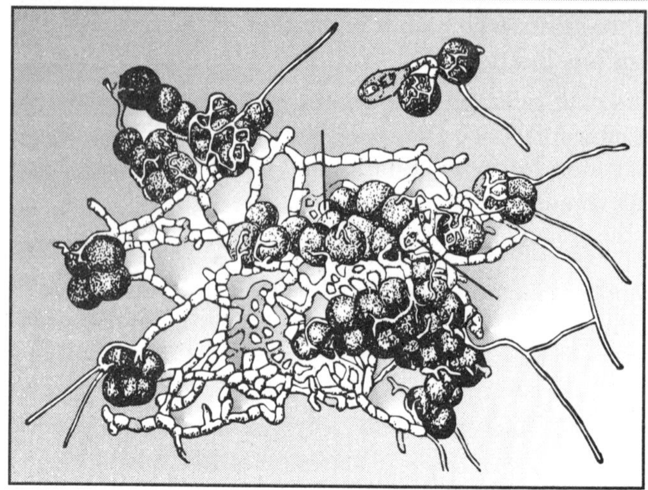

Figure 10.8: Early stages in the development of a lichen. The hyphae surround and penetrate the cells of the alga.

remarkable phenomena occur. The basidiospores are blown about by the wind. Hyphae from these spores do not infect wheat plants, but they do infect the common barberry plant and a few of its relatives.

The hyphae penetrate the leaves of barberry. In a short time there appear on the upper surfaces of the leaves pustules of flask-shaped masses of hyphae, *spermagonia,* which produce a fourth type of reproductive body, *spermatium.*

The spermatia may unite with receptive hyphae of the internal mycelium and result in binucleate hyphae. Since the different spermatia in a leaf may have originated from various races of the rust, such a union makes possible hybrids between different races.

Such hybrids and the resulting hybrid segregates still further complicate measures of control. Further growth of these binucleate hyphae within the barberry leaf results in a mycelium and pustules of cluster cups *(aecia,* sing. *aecium)* on the lower surface of the barberry leaf. Within these cups, a fifth reproductive body, the cluster cup spore, or *aeciospore,* develops.

Aeciospores in turn continue the life cycle only when they lodge and germinate on young wheat plants and a limited number of other grasses. The mycelium from them grows within the tissues of the wheat plant, and first the red spores, and later the black spores, develop-thus completing the life cycle.

Here, then, is a parasitic rust that lives successively on two totally unrelated host plants during a *complete* life cycle. It has several kinds of spores, which are morphologically and physiologically different from each other.

Curious as it may seem, the first definite proof that diseases may be caused by parasites was obtained when Anton de Bary discovered many of the facts of the life history of wheat rust in 1865.

It is interesting to note the possible variations in the life cycle of the stem rust of wheat, as given above. Red spores cannot survive the winters of the North Central States. They may, however, be blown many miles southward and there cause infection of growing wheat or other grasses in the fall.

Red spores borne in the South cannot survive the hot dry summers and so do not cause infection of the young wheat plants there in the following fall. In the early spring red spores from southern wheat are blown northward and successively lead to infection of the growing wheat of higher and higher latitudes.

This cycle of infection by means of red spores alone, makes possible widespread epidemics of wheat rust in the absence of barberry plants. Such a condition can be controlled only by procuring immune races of wheat. These general epidemics, however, occur more rarely than the local epidemics in regions in which the common barberry is growing.

The problem of crossing and selecting varieties of wheat immune to stem rust is further complicated by the fact that there are more than 180 races of the fungus which pass one stage of their life cycle in barberry.

A variety of wheat may be immune to most of these races, but a few races may infect and injure it so much that cultivation of it is unprofitable except in the limited areas where these particular races do not occur. It thus becomes evident that continuous research and experimentation will be necessary to combat the organisms causing the rusts.

Other interesting examples of two-host rusts are the white

pine blister rust (white pine stem, and currant or gooseberry leaves), and apple rust (apple leaves and fruits and red cedar shoots). However, not all rusts involve two host plants, and many of them do not infect crop plants.

Slime Molds

A rather curious group of non-green organisms are the slime molds. They are frequently classified as plants, sometimes as animals, and may be discussed in connection with the fungi. The vegetative part of the plant is a multinucleate mass of naked protoplasm with about the consistency of mayonnaise, called *a plasmodium.*

The plasmodium lives in moist places and streams through and over the substrate and finally comes to rest on the surface of plants and other objects. The different species of slime molds have characteristically colored plasmodia and variously shaped sporangia bearing many spores.

Lichens

Certain fungi and certain algae live together, forming the compound plant structures called *lichens.* These plants grow in a great diversity of habitats, such as on exposed rocks, on tree trunks, and on the ground.

They grow and survive in the most extreme habitats on the earth, from the mountains of the antarctic where the temperatures are rarely above freezing, to the deserts of southern California where midsummer temperatures of rocks on which they grow may be as high as 175° F.

Some kinds of lichens appear almost structureless, forming a thin coating on the rock surface and on soil (crustose); others are somewhat leaf-like in appearance (foliose); and still others are much branched and cushion-like (fruticose).

The latter are represented by the so-called "reindeer moss" (*Cladonia*) of north temperate and tundra regions. Lichens are usually grayish-green in color, but many species are bright yellow, red, brown, or black.

A lichen is sometimes considered to be merely a fungus that is parasitic on certain algae, just as fungi are parasites on wheat, corn, and potatoes. Experiments have shown that the lichen fungus, when growing alone on culture media, usually does not develop a body structure resembling that of the lichen; nor does the alga in pure culture.

Nevertheless, the form of the lichen is heritable and reproduced from one generation to another. For this reason it seems desirable to regard the lichens as distinct compound plants and to classify them as a separate group.

There can be no doubt that the fungus derives most of its food from the algae enclosed by it. The alga in turn may have a more constant water supply because of its covering of fungous hyphae. The algae have a much longer photosynthetic season inside the lichen than if they grew directly on the same substrate.

The species of fungi of the lichens usually belong to the group that bear asci and ascospores. A few species of basidiomycetes are also known to form a part of the lichen body. The alga is either a green or a blue-green; one of the commonest is *Protococcus.*

Vegetative propagation is exceedingly common among lichens, and takes place through the dissemination of minute isolated fragments containing both the fungous hyphae and the algae.

Groups of fungi. The four groups of fungi recognized by many botanists are the *Myxomycetes* (slime molds), *Phycomycetes, Ascomycetes,* and *Basidiomycetes.* The bacteria are often included with the fungi, certain slime molds may be associated with animal groups, and the lichens are a special problem because of their "dual" nature.

There are in addition many fungi in which zygotes, ascospores, or basidiospores either arc not formed or have not yet been discovered. Here belong, for example, fungi causing leaf spot of beets, "athlete's foot," and early blight of potato. These fungi are known as *Fungi Imperfecti.*

Fungi and Research

Research and experimentation with fungi have gone on for many years, resulting in a vast store of knowledge regarding their growth, life cycles, occurrence, and value as synthesizers of organic chemicals, as well as better methods of control.

In recent years some fungi have been used as experimental organisms in elucidating fundamental aspects of heredity and sex. We have already referred to *Achlya.* Certain vitamins and amino acids may be synthesized in some races of the pink bread mold *(Neurospora),* for example, but not in others.

Each failure in a synthesis is due to a single gene mutation. From this mold we get important information on chemical mechanisms by which certain gene actions result in the formation of known characteristics. Much fundamental research today deals with molds and other fungi, together with certain bacteria and algae.

CHAPTER 11 Plant Diseases

Among the earliest records of cultivated plants occur references to plant diseases, but for centuries the causes were thought to be mysterious and supernatural. The ancient Hebrew, Greek, and Roman writers frequently mentioned smuts and rusts, and diseases of the olive, the vine, and the fig.

From the fall of the Roman empire (476 A.D.) until the 19th century, however, little was added to the knowledge of plant diseases. Even in modern times explanations of the causes of diseases of plants were impossible as long as people subscribed to the doctrine of spontaneous generation of living organisms.

As late as the first quarter of the 19th century many fungi were regarded even by scientific men as merely transformations of the cellular structure of the plant upon which they grew. Plant diseases were thought to be due to internal disturbances resulting in the auto-degeneration of the tissues.

About the middle of the 19th century the recognition of fungi as causes of plant diseases came about through the researches of certain mycologists, the most famous of whom was Anton de Bary, who discovered the true nature of rusts in 1853 and published an account of the life history of stem rust of wheat in 1865.

The idea that some diseases are caused by parasites had often been expressed, but de Bary proved it beyond any doubt. About this time the researches of Louis Pasteur and others were forming the foundations of the science of bacteriology.

These investigations soon led to the rejection of the belief that fungi and bacteria, associated with diseased parts of plants, were produced in the lesions by the tissues of the diseased plants. That bacteria may cause diseases of plants was first proved definitely in 1880 when Burrill of Illinois discovered that bacteria cause fire blight of pears and apples.

Proof of infectious diseases in both plants and animals was established at about the same time. While the early contributions to our knowledge of plant diseases were mostly by European workers, the study of plant diseases and their control is now progressing most rapidly in America.

Figure 11.1: Head of rye in which two large black ergot sclerotia have developed.

Research in plant pathology is being carried forward not only by the universities and colleges but also by the United States Department of Agriculture and by every state agricultural experiment station, as well as by several privately endowed institutions and industrial laboratories.

Plant diseases are so diversified that no single statement satisfactorily defines them as a distinct group of phenomena. When parasites partially or wholly invade and infect a host, the resulting injuries or alterations in development, behavior, and well-being may be referred to as "infectious diseases."

Agents, such as fungi, bacteria, viruses, nematodes, and certain insects, which cause infectious diseases are called *pathogens.* Examples of easily observable symptoms of plant diseases are galls, blights, leaf spots, and wilts. These symptoms are just as "normal" to an infected plant as their absence is to an uninfected plant.

Indeed, a welltrained pathologist can often tell which pathogen is present in a host by the characteristic appearance of the symptom. One may wish to use the term "plant disease" to include physiological conditions that result from a deficiency of food, water, oxygen, light, or inorganic salts.

Such diseases have been called "deficiency diseases." The observable symptoms when such deficiencies exist are a characteristic, or "normal," development of the plant under such conditions. They are often sufficiently specific that by studying their appearance one may learn to decide correctly which particular condition is deficient.

Likewise, wounding results in plant development *peculiar* to wounding but unusual in an unwounded plant. Yet the effects of many kinds of wounds are not considered to be diseases. Gnawing insects and grazing animals, as well as lawn mowers and pruning knives used by man, injure plant tissues, but such wounds in themselves are not diseases.

Economic Aspects of Plant Diseases

One needs only to examine the records of modern history to realize the extent of human misery and distress, as well as the starvation of millions of other animals, brought about by plant diseases.

Table 11.1: Average Annual Reduction in Yield Due to Diseases, in the United States for the Years 1933 to 1937 Inclusive. Estimates by U. S. Dept. of Agriculture.

Crop	*Percentage Reduction in Yield*	*Actual Reduction in Yield*
Field corn	14.66	266, 947, 000 bu.
Wheat	12.64	89,227,000 bu.
Irish potato	18.12	58,031,000 bu.
Peach	10.82	7,639,000 bu.
Apple	13.62	18, 331, 000 bu.
Tomato (manufacture)	14.86	186,000 tons
Tomato (market)	19.64	2,687,000 bu.
Tobacco	23.20	379,249,0001b.
Cotton	15.46	1, 881, 000 bales

When rye is infected by the ergot fungus, large purple to black bodies replace many of the rye grains. These structures are poisonous to man and other animals. From the 17th to the 19th century there were about 45 epidemics of ergot poisoning in Germany and about 20 in France and Spain.

The Irish famine was brought about by the destruction of most of the potato crop by a blight fungus during the years 1843 to 1846. This blight resulted in the death of a quarter of a million people and the migration of a million and a half persons from Ireland to America.

The increasing occurrence of plant diseases is undoubtedly the result of increased concentration of crops, continuity of areas devoted to single crops, more rapid systems of transportation, and greater transfer of plants and plant products from one part of the world to another.

When a new plant is introduced into a country great care must be exercised to prevent the simultaneous introduction of its associated parasitic organisms. When certain plants of a given area are badly infected with pathogenic organisms, the government sometimes prohibits the transportation of such plants, or plant parts, into other sections of the country. This is known as "plant quarantine."

In spite of our ever-increasing knowledge about plant diseases, they continue to cause enormous losses every year throughout the world. Farmers, orchardists, and nurserymen frequently cultivate a crop at a loss instead of a profit because of diseases or unfavorable weather conditions.

Environmental conditions and plant diseases. We are aware that the existence of any plant depends upon its environment. Some of us have seen whole crops destroyed by unusual environmental conditions, such as flood, drought, tornadoes, and fires.

As might be expected, plant pathogens are influenced by the environmental factors of the soil and the atmosphere. Whatever affects the host, such as temperature, light, oxygen supply, and the water content of the soil, will also directly or indirectly influence the organism causing the disease.

Considerable information has been accumulated in recent years regarding the direct relationship between the prevalence or rarity of certain diseases and certain environmental factors. A few illustrations will be cited.

It should be noted also that environment alone may cause injuries, some of which, such as bitter pit of apples and blossom-end rot of tomatoes, have been referred to as "diseases".

The potato scab fungus causes more lesions on tubers growing in an alkaline soil, whereas the growth of the organism causing clubroot of cabbage is favored by an acid soil. The organism causing tobacco root rot is practically eliminated from soils of very high acidity.

The weather influences the abundance or scarcity of plant diseases largely through the effects of temperature and moisture either on the bosts or on the parasitic organisms.

Peach leaf curl is generally more widespread in years having cold wet spring seasons. Potato scab lesions are usually most abundant at a temperature of about 70° F.

The fusarium-wilt organism which infects tomatoes growing

in greenhouses makes little progress at soil temperatures of 63° F. and 95° F., but develops rapidly at temperatures midway between these extremes. When growing in soils of either low or high water content, the tomato plant is not affected much by the wilt organism.

A medium water supply results in a vigorous and succulent plant which is quite susceptible to wilt. Potato scab appears to be more severe on potato tubers growing in dry rather than in moist soil.

Apple scab develops rapidly in cool, moist weather. Rainy periods between the time of opening buds and petal fall increase the prevalence of the disease. Discharge of ascospores from the asci in fallen leaves occurs only when they are thoroughly wet.

The new leaves on the tree will become infected only when they are continuously wet for several hours. Variations in hosts, parasites, and plant diseases. It has been known for many years that the extent of infection and the susceptibility to plant pathogens vary from season to season, from host to host, and even among individuals of the same species of host.

Many of these phenomena cannot be accounted for by the effects of the environmental factors enumerated above. A better understanding is possible today because of increased knowledge of the genetic complexity both of host plants and of plant pathogens.

Varying degrees of infection and injury may occur even under apparently similar field environments. A species of fungus causing disease may be composed of several races, each differing from the others in its virulence on specific hosts. Owing to population shifts, some of these races may be more abundant or less abundant than others at various times on different hosts.

For example, it has been reported that the species of fungus *(Puccinia graminis)* which causes stem rust of wheat is a mixed population of at least 180 races, each of which can be distinguished by its relative virulence in different varieties of wheat.

Through a period of time the relative abundance of the different races in a given area fluctuates, with corresponding changes in infection and destructiveness of the disease. Both mutation and hybridization must be considered. They may occur in the host, or in the pathogen when it is growing either in pure culture or inside the host.

From a highly mutating pathogen several new mutant races, differing in virulence in various hosts, may appear within a few generations. These new races may remain constant or continue the variability of the species through further mutations.

In those fungi where nuclear fusions occur, recombinations of heritable factors due to hybridization of different races may result in hybrids varying in degree of virulence. For example, investigators at the University of Minnesota crossed two monoploid races of the corn smut species and from the resulting hybrid obtained nearly 40 segregates, no two of which were alike.

In 1928 "Race 56" made up only 0.5 per cent of all the varieties of the wheat stem rust fungus isolated from rusted wheat in the United States, and was found only in three states.

By 1938 this race was found in 66 per cent of the tests made and had extended over large areas in the United States, Mexico, and Canada.

Evidently wind was a very efficient agent in scattering spores of this new genetic race. Moreover, Race 56 was the primary cause of the elimination of Ceres wheat, which had been one of the least rust-susceptible wheat varieties in the country.

New races of such pathogens are possible at any time, and thus the fight against the causal agents of such diseases must be waged continually.

Newly introduced varieties of wheat less susceptible to wheat rust than varieties formerly harvested may also differ in characteristics important to millers and bakers.

Each new variety has to be tested for flour composition and quality, important factors in making bread, cake, and other well-standardized food products.

Symptoms of Plant Diseases

The external symptoms of plant diseases are of many kinds, and only a few of the commoner ones will be summarized here.

1. *Pustules* are fruiting bodies or spore masses of parasitic

fungi which have ruptured the outer tissues of the host. Rusts and smuts are common examples.

2. *Scabs and blotches* are surface lesions caused by local growth of fungi. Apple scab is a common example.
3. *Mycelia* may be prominent, such as the external mycelia of powdery mildew, the compact masses of mycelia of ergot of rye, and the black "tar-spots" on leaves of willow and maple.
4. *Overgrowths* of host tissues result in malformations of leaves, stems, and roots. Crown gall of apple, raspberry, and grape; black wart of potato; black knot of cherry and plum; clubroot of cabbage; root nodules of legumes; nematode galls on roots of tomato and cotton; insect galls on leaves and stems of various plants; and "witches' brooms" on hackberry are some common examples.
5. *Leaf spots* are dead spots caused by the local growth of parasites in the leaf tissues of the host. They occur frequently on leaves of cherry, tomato, rose, and many other plants.
6. *Wilts* include various diseases that are first noticeable by the sudden wilting of leaves or of the whole plant. Bacterial wilts of cucumber and cantaloupe are rather common. Damping-off of seedlings and cuttings is a type of wilt disease caused by local infection and weakening of stems near the surface of the soil.
7. *Rots* are the result of the decomposition of the cell walls of affected tissues, such as the soft rot of sweet potatoes, bitter rot of apples, and brown rot of stone fruits.
8. *Blight* is the term applied to the sudden dying of leaves, shoots, and blossoms. The fire blight of apple and pear is common wherever these trees grow in America.
9. *Cankers* are sunken dead areas on stems in which the bark is killed. Fire-blight cankers are caused by bacteria. The nailhead canker on stems of apple trees is caused by a fungus. Similar dead areas may be caused by low temperatures and by sun scald.
10. *Yellowing or chlorosis* of leaves is caused by viruses, by

some fungi and bacteria, by low temperatures, or by a deficiency of certain salts.

Control of Plant Diseases

In recent years it has become increasingly evident that really efficient measures for controlling plant diseases must depend on an accurate and detailed knowledge of the life cycle of the pathogen. The acquisition of this knowledge is sometimes a laborious and technical procedure.

Special training and well-equipped laboratories are essential to progress in acquiring the necessary facts. When the life cycle of the causal organism is known, experience has shown that there is usually some point in the cycle that is subject to attack by methods of control.

Spores or young hyphae outside the plant are often easily destroyed by chemicals or heat; but it may be impossible to eliminate an internal mycelium that develops from them without injuring the host. For example, a spore or hypha of the apple scab fungus may be destroyed by a suitable fungicide on an apple leaf before the first hypha has grown into the leaf.

After the hypha is once inside the leaf it is difficult to kill it without destroying the leaf. Similarly it is much more economical to try to eradicate the black stem rust of wheat by removing barberry plants than by attempting to spray the wheat.

Numerous plant diseases are known, and many control measures have been devised and applied with varying success. Even when a partially efficient control measure has been worked out, it has been found by bitter experience that the application is not a rule-of-thumb matter.

No single procedure will give the same results in all kinds of weather, with all varieties of plants, or at all times of the year. In other words, the successful application of such treatments as sprays, dusts, and hot water depends on the condition both of the host and of the parasite; and such measures must be used with keen discrimination if the results are to be effective.

With these general considerations in mind, representative diseases caused by fungi, bacteria, slime molds, nematodes, and viruses will now be considered. Apple scab. In the United States as a whole, scab is the most destructive of apple diseases.

The olive-brown areas of "scab" are quite noticeable on the leaves, fruits, and flower pedicels. These spots not only lessen the commercial value of the fruit, but also decrease photosynthesis, cause early abscission of fruits and leaves, and check the growth of the remaining apples.

The mature ascospores in the old dead leaves on the ground are projected into the air from the bursting asci during rainy weather in the spring and are blown about by the wind to the apple trees. The spores germinate almost immediately on the living tissues of opening buds, young leaves, and flowers if a film of water is present.

Sprays of lime sulfur, or wettable sulfur, must be applied before extended periods of rain to prevent infection by the hyphae from the germinated ascospores. After infection and growth of an internal mycelium, conidia develop and are distributed to other parts of the tree by rain water.

It is extremely desirable that all pre-blossom infections of apple scab be prevented, since conidia may be produced all summer long from hyphae of mycelia if the early infection by ascospores is allowed to occur. Sprays are applied often enough to protect all young growing parts from invasion.

This protection is generally secured by some such program as the following:

(1) a delayed dormant spray is applied as soon as the leaves which surround the young flowers have emerged about 1/4 inch;

(2) a pre-pink spray before the slightly emerged petals have become colored;

(3) the pink spray before the flowers are in full bloom;

(4) the calyx spray just after petal fall and before the blossom end of the fruit has been covered by the calyx;

(5) another spray ten days after the calyx spray; and

(6) later sprays applied when necessary.

A well-informed plant pathologist, with the aid of weather forecasts and information from orchardists concerning the condition of the buds, can intelligently modify the above spray program according to weather conditions.

In some states pertinent information concerning spray programs is broadcast daily by radio for all sections of the state during the spring months.

Damping-off

Seedlings of plants often are infected at the surface of the ground in such a way as to cause the killing of the stem and consequent death of the whole plant. Gardeners and nurserymen are especially troubled by this damping-off disease in seedbeds.

Several species of fungi cause damping-off, and they have been reported from all parts of the world. Practically all species of plants are susceptible to these fungi.

Sometimes the plant is destroyed before the seedling emerges from the ground; in other cases the disease may not be apparent until after the seedlings or cuttings are transplanted. The fungi may live for long periods of time in the soil as saprophytes. It is doubtful if highly organic soils are ever free from such organisms.

Abundant moisture on the plant or in the soil, and a fairly high temperature are favorable to the growth of these fungi and their invasion of green plants.

Control measures for damping-off lie largely in soil disinfection and the proper regulation of temperature and humidity. Hot water, steam, sulfuric acid, and formaldehyde have all been found effective means of disinfecting soils. Dusting seeds with copper or mercury compounds is also an efficient control.

Downy Mildew of Grapes

This disease is probably native to North America, having been reported in the United States in 1834. It was not known in Europe until 1875. The presence of the downy mildew on grapes in France led more or less accidentally to the discovery about 1881 of an important fungicide known as Bordeaux mixture.

A disease caused by the root louse *(Phylloxera)* had become a serious menace to the vineyards of France, and in order to combat this disease the French imported some American grapes which are immune to the root louse.

The American stock, however, was infected with the downy mildew fungus which then spread all over Europe. Apparently at least one vineyard-keeper customarily sprinkled a copper sulfate-lime mixture on the vines along the highways to discourage theft of the grapes.

The French pathologist, Millardet, observed that where such a mixture was sprinkled on the vines, the ravages of mildew were reduced. He began experiments which led to the general use of Bordeaux mixture as a spray for the successful control of this and other diseases.

The fungus invades all green parts of the grape plant and appears as whitish patches of mildew. The fungous hyphae enter the plant largely through the stomates. The presence of the mycelium within the plant may result in loss of leaves, dwarfing of young twigs, and destruction of fruit.

Since the fungus winters over as spores in fallen leaves, the disease may be combated by getting rid of the leaves (sanitation), and by spraying the plants with Bordeaux mixture before the young hyphae from the spores invade the young leaves and flowers.

The Powdery Mildews

The powdery mildews occur everywhere in temperate and tropical regions and on a large variety of hosts. These fungi are visible on the surface of the affected plant, and sometimes the parasitized tissues of the host become malformed.

They are either whitish to grayish, powdery or mealy depending upon whether the visible structure is the mycelium, the summer spores, or the blackish fruiting bodies. The powdery mildews are always superficial parasites and in this way differ sharply from the downy mildews considered above.

The methods recommended for the control of powdery mildews include removing the infected parts, or using an appropriate spray or a sulfur dust.

Brown Rot of Stone Fruits

This disease is important in the United States and Europe because it destroys the fruit of such orchard crops as peaches, plums, cherries, and apricots. Among the pome fruits the apple may also be affected. The disease is usually recognized by the rotting of fruits, blasting of flowers, and the killing of young stems.

A brown spot appears on the fruit and may enlarge until the whole fruit is decayed. In later stages the fruit dries and shrivels to a condition that has given rise to the term "mummified fruit." When the flowers are infected, "blossom blight" occurs and results in the death of the flowers.

The fungus may grow from the blossoms into the twigs, and there cause cankers and death of the twig. New infections may occur from the time of early flowering until the fruit is mature. Insects and winds are the principal means of spore dispersal. The fungus may overwinter in mummified fruits and in twig cankers.

Control of the disease may be accomplished by thorough pruning accompanied by removal of mummies and diseased twigs and the application of the appropriate sulfur sprays or dusts throughout the growing season.

Peach Leaf Curl

Typical symptoms of peach leaf curl are pinkish, puckered, and thickened leaves or parts of leaves. Infection of peach leaves is most frequent when a cold wet period follows the parting of the bud scales in spring. The mycelium invades the tissues and in a few weeks a layer of asci forms on the upper surface of the leaves.

This disease causes the early abscission of the leaves. Young shoots and flowers are also infected and killed. The disease is easily controlled by one application of a lime-sulfur or Bordeaux spray *during* the dormant period before the buds begin to swell.

Wood Rots

Trees, fence posts, telephone poles, railroad ties, and bridge timbers sooner or later decay, as the result of the activities of certain wood-rotting fungi. These fungi nearly all belong to the groups of "fleshy" fungi.

They may destroy the heartwood, the sapwood, or both. Changes in the color and texture of the wood usually accompany the growth of the fungi. The internal mycelium is of course the destructive agent through its formation of wood-digesting enzymes.

The external fruiting bodies, popularly known as "conks," produce numerous spores, which are carried to other trees primarily by wind. Living trees are infected through wounds, as well as by the direct growth of the fungus from infected stumps into the heartwood of trees in sprout forests.

It is practically impossible to control wood rot in forests. The infection of orchard trees may be avoided by careful treatment of wounded trees, and by the eradication of all infected ones.

Telephone poles, railroad ties, and other timbers in contact with soil may be protected for long periods of time by appropriate treatment with coal-tar creosote, tar, crude oil, or certain salts of zinc. When fox-fire is traced to its source it is usually found coming from saprophytic fungi living in partially decayed wood or bark. Some of the energy set free in respiration in these fungi is light energy.

The Smuts

The smuts described in the preceding chapter are destructive to cereals, but effective measures of controlling some species have been discovered. The importance of knowing exact life cycles of fungi that cause disease before one attempts to formulate methods of control is shown by a study of three kinds of smuts: corn smut, loose smut of oats, and loose smut of wheat and barley.

The spores from the black masses or lesions on the corn plant fall on the ground, remain there over the winter, and may be the source of infection of young plants if carried to wounds during the following spring. The most effective methods of control are selection of seed from healthy plants, selection of hybrids immune to the disease, and crop rotation.

The mycelium of the fungus which causes the disease known as loose smut of oats grows within the oat plant and produces millions of spores in the young flower panicle. These spores are blown about by the wind and some of them lodge in the flowers of healthy oat plants.

There they germinate; and the mycelium may grow among the glumes, or beneath the epidermis of the grain coat. Some spores may not germinate but remain attached to the outer portion of the glumes.

The fungus overwinters in either of these three places, and when the oats are sowed may cause infection of the seedling and eventually a smutted head at or before harvest time. The fungus is killed by treating the seed with formaldehyde or with ethyl mercury phosphate before planting.

The fungi causing loose smut of wheat and barley live through the winter as mycelia inside the grain. Spores may also survive the winter on the seed. The spores on the surface are easily killed, but it is difficult to kill the hyphae inside the seed without injuring the embryo.

The fungous hyphae in the wheat seed are killed when the seeds are immersed in water at a temperature of 129° F. for ten minutes; the hyphae in barley seeds may be killed by similar treatment at 127° F. Neither the wheat nor the barley embryos are injured if these directions are accurately followed.

Plant Diseases caused by Bacteria

It is sometimes difficult to discover whether a disease is caused by bacteria or by fungi since both are often present in the same lesion.

It is of course necessary that this discovery be made before effective remedial measures can be worked out. Most bacterial diseases of plants are very difficult to control.

Among the better measures of control are: rotation of crops, use of disinfected seed, prompt and complete destruction of diseased plants or parts of plants, proper care of wounds made by storms and pruning, seed sterilization, and the planting of less susceptible varieties.

The fire blight of pear is probably the best known of these diseases, and the methods suggested for its control will be discussed.

Fire Blight

Fire blight is one of the most destructive of the diseases of pome fruits. Its most frequent symptoms appear as blighted twigs, flowers, and leaves. Infection takes place in the flowers, young shoots, and leaves.

Any diseased part of the plant may exude a sticky fluid containing the bacteria. Rain may distribute the bacteria to other parts of the plant. Insects, however, are the most important carriers of the bacteria from one plant to others.

Fire Blight is Difficult to Control

To decrease the possibilities of infection of apple and pear trees, tender sprouts should be kept removed from the trunk and larger branches during the early part of the growing season.

In addition, all blighted twigs should be removed from the

Figure 11.2: Fifteen different galls on hickory leaves caused by as many different species of insects.

pear orchard at least twice weekly during the active blight season.

Blighted branches found in the fall of the year should also be removed. Other suggested methods of control include the application of sprays at blossoming time and the planting of varieties of pears and apples less susceptible to the disease.

Clubroot of Cabbage

The organism which causes this disease in certain members of the mustard family, such as cabbage, turnips, and radishes, is a very primitive mold. Deformed, and club-shaped roots are evidence of the progress of the disease.

The organism enters through root hairs or through wounds, and digests the tissues of the host as the plasmodium grows. If the cambium is invaded, further development of the tissues of the root is very irregular. The disease is most prevalent in warm, wet, acid soils.

Control methods recommended are: use of disease-free plants, application of hydrated lime (from one to two tons per acre), planting of less susceptible varieties, avoidance of planting cabbage in infected fields.

Galls

The development of galls on leaves, stems, and other parts of plants is induced by insects, bacteria, and fungi. The greater variety of galls are caused by insects. Galls may be formed on many kinds of plants and are readily seen on oaks, hackberries, willows, goldenrods, asters, and roses.

In some way, perhaps primarily by means of hormones. the organisms living in these plants initiate peculiar overgrowths of certain local tissues, with the ultimate formation of a gall having a specific form and pattern.

Leaves and young twigs are the parts usually affected. The different forms and patterns of galls are correlated with the causal insects, rather than with the plants on which they occur. In many instances the insects can be identified from the characteristics of the galls.

Nematode Galls

The nematodes, sometimes called roundworms, may live either as parasites or free in moist soil containing organic matter. They eat their way into the roots of many plants, feeding upon the juices, and cause the overgrowth of the infested organs.

They infest the roots of tomato, tobacco, cucumber, lettuce, peony, strawberry, cotton, and many other cultivated and wild plants.

The so-called nematode disease of wheat affects the flowering parts, transforming the grains into galls. Stems and leaves of rye, clover, alfalfa, begonia, and many bulbous plants become distorted, swollen, and variously colored because of infestation by leaf and stem nematodes. An excessive development of fibrous roots of sugar beet is also caused by nematodes. The chief methods of control are soil disinfestation and crop rotation.

Virus-diseases of Plants

Among the diseases recognized in relatively recent times as being caused by viruses are tobacco mosaic, curly top of sugar beet, peach yellows, yellow dwarfing of onions, tomato streak, leaf roll of potatoes, virus gall of sugar cane, and witches' broom of sandalwood tree.

Viruses also affect animals and cause such diseases as infantile paralysis, smallpox, influenza, common colds, measles, and rabies. There are many viruses, each of which has characteristic effects on a plant. Some viruses have been found to cause diseases in many more varieties of plants than have others.

Viruses have been detected in more than a thousand species of plants growing in all parts of the world. The tobacco mosaic virus has been shown to he a protein of a high molecular weight, which may be purified by repeated recrystallization without losing its property of causing the disease.

This causal agent increases in number in contact with the protoplasm of the plant. It cannot be cultivated in any known non-living culture medium.

One kind of virus is lethal only to certain species of plants. Even these plants may survive for a long time if the concentration of the virus in their cells remains low. They may, however, fail to grow as well or yield as much as plants free of viruses.

Viruses are usually not localized in certain tissues and organs, but permeate all living parts of the plant. Herbaceous plants are apparently more susceptible to viruses than woody species, although lethal virus diseases of elm, plum, and peach are well known.

Viruses are transmitted from diseased to healthy plants by insects, such as leaf hoppers, aphids, and flea beetles, and sometimes on the tools used in cultivating, pruning, and grafting. Certain viruses are transmitted through the seed, while others are not.

Some viruses may be carried over from one season to the next in other plants such as weeds and wild plants which grow nearby. Control has been accomplished by the removal of such additional plants.

Other control measures include the eradication of diseased plants, control of the insects that transmit viruses, use of virus-free seeds, the avoidance of inoculating wounded parts of plants in grafting and vegetative propagation, and the selection of less susceptible varieties.

CHAPTER 12

Under-Water Environments

Numerous kinds of plants live continuously under water. Many epiphytes, on the other hand, grow in a medium of air and are in contact with water only during rains or when covered with dew. Even a rooted plant in dry uplands grows almost entirely in the atmosphere which surrounds its tops and fills the spaces between the particles of the soil.

Except for short intervals after rains, its root system in summer is in contact only with thin films of water held by the soil particles, and much of it is exposed to the soil air.

Other species of plants live partially submerged in the shallow water of marshes and swamps between uplands and near the borders of oceans, lakes, and streams. Some of them are limited to areas in which the water level fluctuates with the rains and tides.

Many plants can endure partial submergence for limited periods of time, and many others thrive with their roots and rhizomes in soil continuously below the water surface.

The erect stems of such plants extend above the water surface, or because of long petioles their leaf blades are exposed to the air above the water.

Among the plants of the world there appear to be all gradations between those limited to land and those limited to water habitats. Those on land can endure varying degrees of exposure to the air and to water loss by exaporation.

Those below the water surface can endure low concentrations of oxygen. Some submerged plants live wholly suspended in water.

Others have roots in the underlying substrate. The general processes of nutrition and growth in submerged plants are the same as those in land plants, and they are dependent upon the same external factors.

These factors, however, are not similarly distributed or equally available in air and in water media. A few of the conditions in land habitats and in water habitats are compared in the accompanying summary.

The Land Habitat

Plants and animals with high water content living in a medium of air.

The medium: the atmosphere above soil always in motion, and its molecules always in rapid motion; rarely saturated with water vapor; compressible, hence rarely destructive when in motion; air and water movement in soil restricted by soil particles.

Carbon dioxide: always available above and below soil surface.

Oxygen: always available above soil surface, not always available below soil surface.

Temperature: large daily and seasonal fluctuations of air temperature; smaller variations of soil temperature, except where relatively dry soil surface is exposed to the sun, where the daily and seasonal extremes commonly exceed those of the air.

Soil: stability, penetrability, porosity, gas content, and water content important in root development. Inorganic salts in soil and dust available when in solution or in direct contact; concentration sometimes very low; in arid regions more concentrated and sometimes toxic.

Light: usually abundant at upper vegetation surface; decreased at lower levels by taller plants.

The Water Habitat

Plants and animals with high water content living in a medium of water.

The medium: the hydrosphere relatively quiescent, except surface layers of large bodies of water and rapid streams; molecular motion comparatively slow; incompressible, hence offers great resistance to movement within it, and when in rapid motion very destructive.

Carbon dioxide: in solution, both free and bound in bicarbonates; concentration variable, often high in water containing organic matter and in soil beneath water.

Oxygen: in solution; concentration highest in surface layer, often deficient in deep water and in soil beneath water.

Temperature: smaller daily and seasonal fluctuations even in upper layers; temperature very constant in deeper water; temperatures of water and underlying soil not very different.

Soil: stability, porosity important. Inorganic salts obtained from medium by suspended plants, from soil by rooted plants; salt concentration sometimes very low; usually higher in oceans than in moist soils; in closed basins salts may accumulate to toxic concentrations.

Light: abundant at water surface except for clouds, fogs, and shade of plants above surface; rapidly decreases below surface. Rough surfaces and turbidity increase reflection, decrease light penetration.

It is evident that an aquatic environment includes most of the factors of a land environment, but the intensity or quantity of any factor is very different. Certain conditions essential to green plants, such as light, carbon dioxide, and oxygen, are more often at a minimum in water than in air.

Rates of diffusion also are so much slower in water that, in the absence of currents, the movement of dissolved gases to plants may be so slow that both photosynthesis and respiration are limited. On land transpiration often becomes destructive.

Because of these effects of the medium, some kinds of plants survive only in certain places on land, others only in certain places in water.

Plants that can live both in water and on land are either microscopic plants or those larger plants which have emergent leaves when growing in water.

The vertical spread of plants on the earth is diagrammatically represented in Figure elsewhere in this chapter. Under-water habitats are roughly of two kinds: fresh water, including lakes and ponds, rivers and streams; and marine, such as oceans, seas, gulfs, and bays. There are also inland bodies of water of high salt content in the plains, semi-deserts, and deserts.

THE FRESH-WATER ENVIRONMENT

The fresh-water environment includes all non-saline lakes and ponds, rivers and smaller streams, swamps, marshes, and bogs. Each of these types of habitat is considered separately.

LAKES AND PONDS

Lakes and ponds differ from each other chiefly in area, depth of water, permanence, effects of winds and temperature changes, and depth of light penetration. They represent the so-called standing water, in contrast to the flowing water of streams, although there may be surface movements due to winds, changes in temperature, and deep springs.

Light

The intensity of light at the surface of a lake is dependent primarily on the latitude and the time of day. It may be modified locally by clouds, fog, smoke, dust, and marginal shade. It is not, however, the intensity of the light at the surface that is of importance in the growth of submerged plants, but the light that actually penetrates the water to the depth at which they live.

The amount of direct sunlight that is reflected from a smooth water surface ranges from 2 per cent when the sun is directly overhead to nearly 100 per cent when the sun is near the horizon. Of the total radiation from the sun and sky during a day, 7 per cent is reflected from a smooth water surface; but when the water surface is rough, as much as 25 per cent may be reflected.

The light below the water surface is thus always less than that above. Natural bodies of water are usually colored or turbid with suspended colloidal particles and microorganisms. These minute objects reflect and refract the light in all directions.

They also absorb it and are highly effective in reducing light intensity in the water below them. About 40 per cent of the light that enters the water is usually absorbed in the first meter. Not more than 5 to 10 per cent of the visible rays penetrate to a depth of 10 meters; and at depths of 50 meters the light is negligible and consists only of certain green, blue, and violet rays. As a result of the reflection and absorption of light at the surface of the water, the length of the daylight period in deep water is relatively short and is limited to the middle of the day, when the sun's rays are near the vertical. Radiation from the sky is insufficient to illuminate the depths.

Photosynthesis

In clear-water lakes the layer of water in which effective photosy-nthesis occurs rarely exceeds a depth of 10 meters. In turbid or colored water it is much less.

It is therefore readily seen why the bulk of the suspended and rooted plant populations of lakes is confined to the upper layers of open water and shallow margins.

Only in the extremely clear water of high mountain lakes is photosynthesis adequate at greater depths. There are a few very slow-growing green plants that exist at depths of 15 and even 30 meters, where photosynthesis in them is evidently just above the compensation point.

The maximum depth of most rooted aquatics in the lakes of the United States is 6 to 7 meters. At this depth the plants are exposed to about 2 per cent of total sunlight.

Oxygen

Oxygen enters lake and pond water primarily from the atmosphere. It diffuses into the water more rapidly when the surface is agitated and increased by wind.

Additional dissolved oxygen is brought into lakes from the atmosphere by rain water and by rapid tributary streams, particularly if they flow over falls and riffles.

Oxygen is also added during the daylight period by photosynthesis in submerged green plants. The oxygen concentration is decreased through the respiration of both plants and animals. It is also dissipated by high temperature of the water.

Indeed, in shallow ponds containing an abundance of both plants and animals, the oxygen content may become so reduced during hot weather that fish and other submerged animals suffocate.

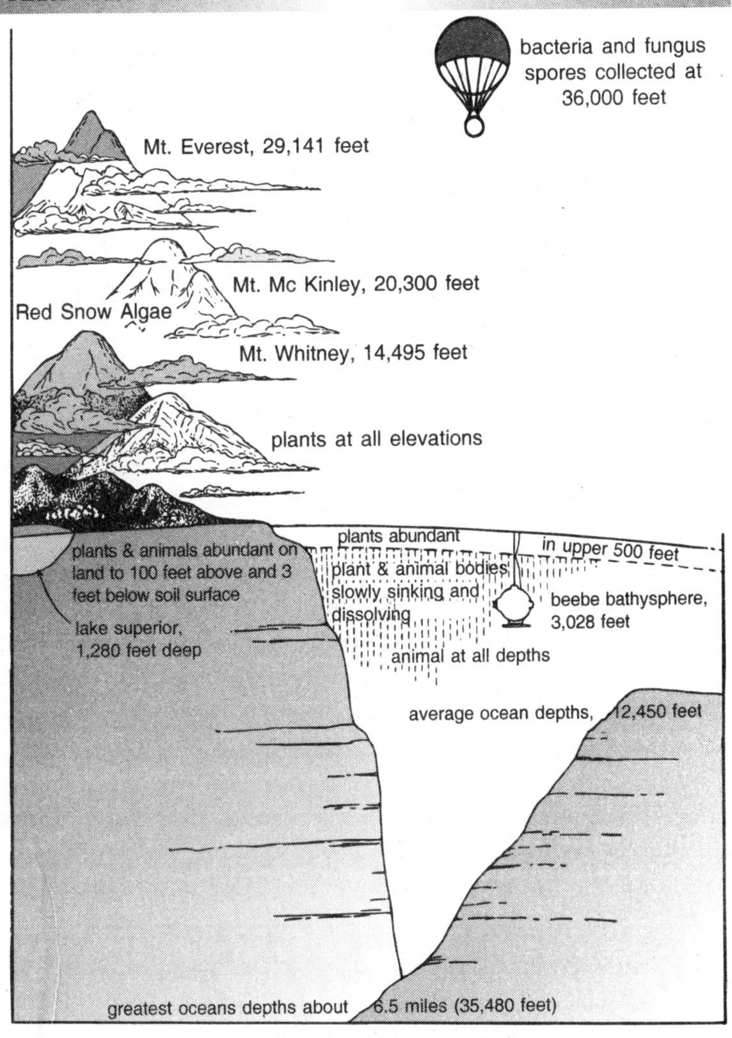

Figure 12.1: The vertical distribution of living plants on the earth.

The death of submerged plants in shallow water may likewise occur from suffocation.

Carbon dioxide. The sources of CO_2 in the water of ponds and lakes are diffusion from the atmosphere, oxidation of organic matter by bacteria and also the respiration of all other organisms, inflowing streams, and the release of CO_2 when the soluble bicarbonates of calcium and magnesium are changed to insoluble carbonates and accumulate as marl.

When carbon dioxide dissolves in natural bodies of water, more than half of it combines with the water, forming carbonic acid: $CO_2 + H_2O \rightarrow H_2CO_3$. The remainder exists as free carbon dioxide. Submerged green plants utilize in photosynthesis not only the free CO_2 but also the CO_2 in carbonic acid and the so-called "bound" CO_2 in bicarbonates, such as those of calcium, magnesium, sodium, and iron.'

There is about one-third of a cubic centimeter of CO_2 in a liter of air, and it is constantly available at the surface of land plants because of continuous air currents. In lakes the CO_2 concentration is highly variable.

It may be unavailable at times, particularly in bog lakes, and at other times it may accumulate to the equivalent of 20 cubic centimeters per liter of water.

Apparently the death of submerged vegetation in warm shallow water in midsummer may result from starvation, from suffocation, or from some other indirect effect of high temperature.

In spring and autumn carbon dioxide is quite uniformly distributed from the top to the bottom of deep lakes, but in summer and winter it may be either abundant or nearly absent at different depths.

Nitrogen

The nitrogen (N_2) in solution in water is no more usable in aquatic plants than is the nitrogen of the atmosphere in land plants. However, as on land, nitrogen may be combined by microorganisms into such usable substances as ammonia, nitrates, and organic nitrogen compounds.

Since so small a portion of it is transformed in biological processes in lakes, its concentration is rather constant and uniform.

Inorganic Salts

The chemical elements essential to fresh-water plants are the same as those essential to land plants. Rooted aquatics obtain the salts containing these elements primarily from the underlying soil.

A much smaller amount enters the plants from the water surrounding their green shoots. Suspended and floating plants are dependent on the salts in solution in the water.

The concentration of these inorganic salts in lake water is lower on the average than in soil water. Extensive sand areas in lakes may be as barren of rooted vegetation as similar areas on land, even though the lake water contains sufficient salts for the growth of large numbers of suspended and floating plants.

Seasonal Stratification of Water

For a period of time in spring and autumn the temperature of the water at different depths in lakes becomes nearly uniform (about 4° C.). This is the temperature at which water reaches its greatest density. It becomes lighter whether cooled below or warmed above 4°C.

As these uniform temperatures develop, convection currents are formed by the lighter water moving upward and the heavier water moving downward. Wind storms at these seasons result in mixing and stirring the water to great depths.

These are the spring and autumn "overturns." During the summer the surface water becomes warmer and lighter, with the result that layers of warm water float on the colder and denser water beneath. Winds then usually disturb only these upper layers of warm water, and there is little vertical mixing of water.

This condition prevails until autumn. As the water at the surface is cooled to 4° C. (39.2° F.) convection currents carry the water downward until the lake becomes uniformly dense and the autumnal overturn occurs.

With the coming of winter the density of the surface water is decreased again as it is cooled below 4°C. These upper layers of colder and lighter water float on the denser water below. If ice is formed it also floats, because its density is about nine-tenths that of water. Under these conditions the water is quite stagnant, and there is little or no mixing.

During both summer and winter the water in deep lakes may

become stratified. In summer, when there are the greatest differences in temperature between the upper and lower layers of water, there is an intermediate layer in which the records of temperature on a thermometer change as much as 3° to 5° C. per foot as the thermometer is raised or lowered through the water.

This layer in which differences in temperature are comparatively abrupt is known as the *thermocline.* Since many organisms, both plant and animal, move about only within certain temperature limits, and since their growth is also limited by the available CO_2 and O_2, it must be evident that these organisms in deep lakes are distributed in strata in summer, and to a less extent in winter.

During an exceptionally warm winter in a mild temperate climate the surface water may not be cooled below 4° C.; no spring overturn occurs, and there is no renewal of oxygen in the lower layers of water. During the following summer those fish that can live only in layers of cold water may suffocate. Similar consequences may also follow whenever there is insufficient wind to cause the spring overturn.

The data given in Figure elsewhere in this chapter should help one to understand:

(1) why in some lakes the thermocline in summer is a potent barrier between the many organisms that live above and below it;

(2) why the densest population of plankton, both plant and animal, occurs in the spring and autumn;

(3) why certain fishes in the summer time live only in deep water and others only in shallow water.

Violent winds may at any time cause the mixing of water to considerable depths. When the mixing results in carrying oxygen to greater depths, it may be followed by an enormous increase of certain species.

Violent winds may also increase wave action and destroy the plants in shallow water or wash them up on land. Wave action may also stirup mud; and with the increased turbidity of the water resulting in decreased light penetration, the algal population may decrease.

Plant Population

Most flowering plants cannot survive complete submergence, and only a limited number can thrive with their roots and lower stems permanently covered with water. Besides the rooted seed plants along the shore, the aquatic plant population includes the countless numbers of minute floating and submerged algae which are described in the next chapter.

All bodies of fresh water contain bacteria and lesser numbers of parasitic and saprophytic fungi. Bacteria are known to occur in the open water of lakes and ponds at all depths, and are often exceedingly abundant on the bottom deposits.

They are usually not harmful to man. There are bacteria of decay, of nitrification, and of nitrogen-fixation as well as those truly parasitic within other plants and animals. Their abundance is influenced by light, by sudden changes in temperature, by the amount of sedimentation, and by certain animals, such as the protozoa and rotifers, that feed on them.

Direct counts have shown that there may be from a few thousand to several million bacteria in a cubic centimeter of lake water. By way of comparison, a cubic centimeter of a moist, fertile soil may contain several billion bacteria.

RIVERS AND STREAMS

The temperature of the water in rivers and streams is fairly uniform from top to bottom. The greatest extremes of turbidity occur, varying from the muddy Missouri and Yangtze rivers to the nearly transparent water of "spring-fed" mountain brooks. Light penetration is diminished greatly in muddy waters.

Suspended silt may decrease the light in the first inch of water to 10 per cent of that at the surface. Oxygen deficiency does not usually limit the growth of aquatic plants in unobstructed streams. The oxygen content varies between day and night and may at times even exceed the saturation point in streams with abundant, submerged plants.

Stream water is usually moderately alkaline or neutral; only rarely is it as acid as the water in bog lakes, unless there is seepage from coal mines or other mineral deposits. Free carbon dioxide does not accumulate in running water but may increase in deep quiet stream pools.

In swift streams seed plants are not conspicuous, except for a few well-rooted species on the margins. Sluggish waters may, however, become completely choked by the luxuriant growth of submerged and floating plants, such as elodea, eel grass, pond weeds, water hyacinth, water cress, and willow herb.

The margins of rivers rarely have permanent plant communities because of deposition or erosion and everchanging water levels. The flora and fauna most characteristic of streams and rivers are the suspended microscopic or near-microscopic organisms known as plankton.

The plant constituents of the plankton are largely diatoms and other minute algae. The plankton "harvest" of rivers and streams is surprisingly large.

The total mass of plankton organisms of the Illinois River at Havana, Illinois-where it flows slowly-amounted in one year to 200,000 tons live weight, or about 10,000 tons of dry matter.

In other parts of the same river the tonnage may be greater or much less. Plankton develops in the more sluggish and deeper pools of streams, and these areas become the feeding grounds of innumerable animals. Plankton is not to be looked upon as a mass of living organisms floating downstream as fast as the stream flows.

It is decidedly localized. Neither is it true that plankton increases in variety and abundance downsteam. Flash floods in small tributaries may increase the plankton in the master stream. Great floods temporarily decrease the plankton in the whole stream system.

Compared with lakes, running water is a distinctly different environmental complex. Temperatures are more uniform, and no periods of winter and summer stagnation occur. In general the concentration of inorganic salts is higher in streams than in most lakes.

Effects of pollution with manufacturing and municipal wastes may be much more evident and destructive. Spores and seeds are less likely to lodge on stream bottoms; hence the establishment of new plants by this means is less frequent in streams than in still water.

MARSHES, SWAMPS, AND BOGS

As lakes and ponds are gradually filled by partially decayed organic matter and by silt washed from the uplands, rooted vegetation encroaches upon the area. This filling gradually brings about changes in the nature of the environment.

The effects of winds become less, and there is no overturn of water caused by winds in spring and fall. Shading by rooted aquatics becomes important, and organic matter accumulates rapidly.

In fact, all stages of transition from a typically acquatic habitat to a land environment may occur as lakes and ponds become bogs, marshes, or swamps through increased drought, through drainage, or through the accumulation of organic matter and soil.

A marsh is dominated by cattails, grasses, sedges, and rushes, and may be found in either temperate or tropical regions. A swamp is usually regarded as an area where the water never covers the soil deeply but is never far below the surface, and where the vegetation is dominated by shrubs and trees, such as buttonbush, low willows, alders, and swamp trees.

Bogs differ from marshes and swamps in that mosses form an important part of the vegetation; they and the other aquatic plants become enmeshed in a floating substrate which rises and falls with the water level and upon which sedges, grasses, low and tall shrubs, and even trees may subsequently grow.

Many northern lakes have open areas of water surrounded by floating marginal mats of herbs, bog mosses, and shrubs. As peat accumulates below the mat the bog may become more or less solid and support a forest of conifers, such as black spruce, tamarack, and arbor vitae.

Bogs may be either acid or alkaline. If alkaline, the water is generally clear, and shrubby cinquefoil occurs among the shrubs; if acid, the water may be brown in color, and sphagnum moss is usually present in the substrate.

Bog water is usually lower in dissolved oxygen, free carbon dioxide, and the salts of potassium and nitrogen than that of the more open type of lake. Likewise, the plant and animal population in bog lakes is comparatively low, and there are fewer species. In the Great Lakes region and northward, a peat substrate may accumulate on valley bottoms from bog plants that grew there.

The term "bog" is frequently applied in the Southern States to wet, acid sand flats on which many characteristic bog plants grow, as well as to areas having a peat and muck substrate.

Some typical bog plants associated with the grasses, sedges, and mosses of acid bogs are cranberry, blueberry, snowberry, leatherleaf, pitcher plant, sundew, and dwarf birch.

THE SALT-WATER ENVIRONMENT

The oceans, bays, gulfs, and a few inland bodies of salt water are also habitats of aquatic plants and animals. These marine habitats differ from the fresh-water environment principally in being saline. The salinity is due largely to chlorides and sulfates with smaller percentages of carbonates.

Few species of plants can grow both in the sea and in fresh water. The salinity is essential to the marine species and toxic to the fresh-water species.

Our largest bodies of water are the oceans, with a combined surface area of nearly 140 million square miles, or about 70 per cent of the earth's surface. In contrast to this, the surface of all bodies of fresh water taken together is scarcely one million square miles.

The vast expanse and diverse conditions of oceans constitute enormous possibilities of development of marine plant and animal populations. Ocean water is practically a continuous medium, in sharp contrast to the more isolated bodies of fresh water.

The oceans vary in depth from a few feet of water along the coasts to nearly 6 miles in the so-called "deeps." On the ocean floor are plains, hills, valleys, and mountain ranges.

Pressure varies from 15 pounds to the square inch at the surface to nearly 8 tons at the greatest depths. Such enormous pressures would seem to preclude the possibility of living organims, but the effects of this pressure are annulled by an equivalent pressure inside the body.

Equalization of pressure within the body, however, does not

take place rapidly; consequently, vertical migration of living plants and animals under these conditions is somewhat restricted. Except along the coast, the influence of the land on the ocean is much less than it is on bodies of fresh water.

The specific gravity of sea water with a salinity of 3.5 per cent is about 1.028 at 0° C. The density of the aerial environment of land plants is much less than that of their protoplasm, while the density of the living parts of marine organisms is about the same as that of the medium in which they live.

Most marine plants are slightly heavier than the water, but their small size and proportionally large surface areas, as well as occasional gas bladders and fat globules, contribute to their floating capacity. Dead bodies of marine plants and animals eventually sink to the bottom, unless devoured or dissolved, although the rate of sinking is extremely low.

Below depths of 5000 meters none of the parts of most of the smaller plants and animals can be found, for the whole body has gone into solution. The solar energy actually available to plants is decreased in the ocean by the same factors that decrease it in fresh water: absorption, reflection, suspended matter, wave action.

Where suspended matter and minute organisms are abundant, the water is apparently green because of the scattering of the short blue and violet rays and the absorption of the red and yellow. Blue water contains little or no suspended matter.

Photosynthesis in plants of the ocean generally occurs above a depth of 150 meters, although a few living green plants have been found at 300 meters. Beebe reports the disappearance of all but the blue and violet rays at depths of 250 meters in the clear water near the Bermuda Islands.

Below 500 meters almost complete darkness prevails, except for the feeble light emitted by certain deep-sea fishes and other animals. The gases of the air are absorbed directly from the atmosphere, although carbon dioxide and oxygen are subject to local variation because of photosynthesis and various oxidations.

Gases are carried to great depths through the action of storm waves and ocean currents. Sea water is a dilute solution of salts, with some dissolved gases and traces of many organic compounds,

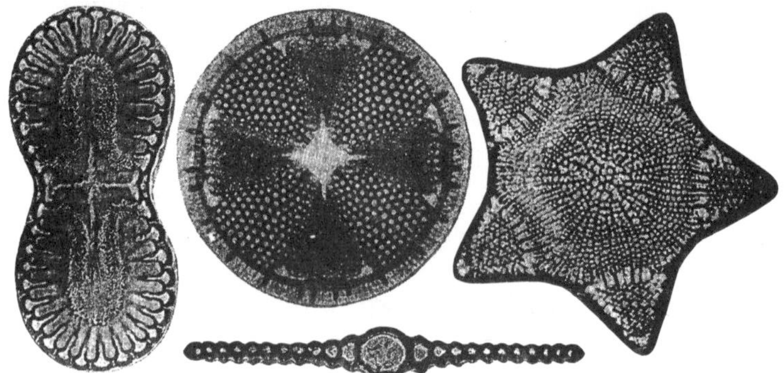

Figure 12.2: Diatoms.

containing more than half of the known elements. Some elements are in marine organisms but have not as yet been recognized in the water itself because of their extremely low concentrations. The relative amount of an element may be far greater in a plant or an animal than in the medium in which it lives.

Large quantities of potassium and small amounts of sodium, for example, accumulate in some marine plants, even though sodium salts are very abundant in the ocean and potassium salts relatively scarce.

The relative amount of any element that accumulates in the different species of plants may vary greatly even though the plants are growing in the same environment.

The relative proportions of salts in the main body of the ocean are fairly constant at all latitudes. The relative percentages of the different elements in the salt after the water has evaporated do not vary much from the following: chlorine, 54 per cent; sodium, 31 per cent; magnesium, 4 per cent; calcium, 1 per cent; bromine, 0.2 of 1 per cent; sulfate radicals, 8 per cent; and carbonate radicals, 0.2 of 1 per cent.

Surface temperatures of the ocean vary greatly with latitude and with the time of year. However, surface variations between winter and summer are much less than those encountered on land. Sea water becomes heavier as it is cooled until its freezing point is reached.

As a result, temperatures below 0°C. may occur, in contrast

to the rather constant 4°C. of most deep-lake bottoms. The bottom temperatures of the oceans in temperate regions are around 2°C. Seasonal variations in temperature are unusual below 500 feet. At depths of a mile or more the temperature is near the freezing point at all times.

The effects of temperature are so closely tied up with those of other factors that its influence has been frequently exaggerated. Temperature apparently often determines the range of plant distribution both vertically and latitudinally. Some species of plants grow and reproduce at or below the freezing point, such

Figure 12.3: Food relations of some aquatics. No matter how long the chain of animals is from algae to fish, the fundamental food organisms are the algae that transform inorganic materials into foods.

for example as the marine algae of arctic and antarctic regions.

The destructive effects of temperature, however, are much less in the ocean than on land because of the absence of extremes and rapid changes.

Indirectly temperature is important in another way since carbon dioxide is much more soluble in cold than in warm water; in the tropics the warm water may become almost depleted of this gas. Likewise the population of plant and animal plankton is less in the warmer water of tropical oceans than in the cooler water of temperate regions.

Other factors that reduce plankton population in the tropics are the increased rate of respiration, and deficiency in compounds of nitrogen and phosphorus.

PLANTS AND ANIMALS IN THE OCEAN

Water environments, both fresh and marine, are populated with great numbers and many kinds of plants and animals. The largest as well as the smallest known organisms live in the ocean. In the sea are whales, large fishes, crustaceans, and squids, as well as myriads of microscopic species.

The largest plants in the sea are the brown kelps some of which are 70 meters long. Among the smaller plants are the one-celled diatoms and the bacteria. Animals probably exist at all depths and over the entire ocean floor; but living green plants are rare below 300 meters because of inadequate light.

The plant population consists of both suspended and bottom species. It reaches its greatest density and has the greatest number of species in shallower water near shore where inorganic salts are more abundant and there is more adequate light from top to bottom.

Mud bottoms fairly teem with organisms, and many plants and animals are attached to rocky shores, whereas sand is a comparatively barren habitat.

The bacteria of the sea vary greatly in abundance depending upon depth of water, distance from shore, availability of suspended or dissolved organic matter, and the presence of other plants as

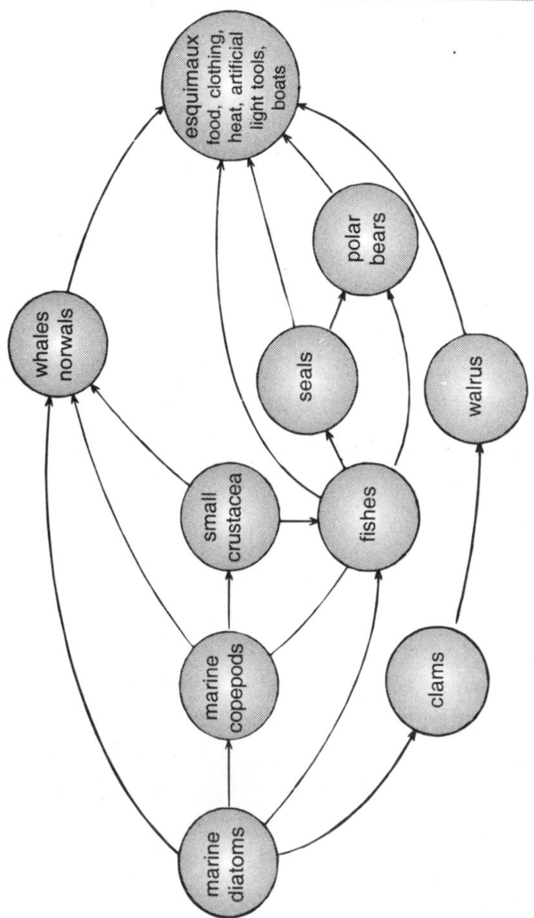

Figure 12.4: A diagrammatic representation of the dependence of Esquimaux on diatoms. Assume that each organism obtains only 10 per cent of the food consumed by the preceding one in the chain, and compute the amount of diatoms necessary for a gain in weight of 1 pound in an Esquimau boy.

well as animals. The sea water itself is not an especially good medium for the growth of most bacteria unless considerable organic matter is present.

As might be expected, bacteria are much more numerous near shore, and especially where the water is polluted by large centers of population. The number of surface bacteria, living and dead, may range from a few or none up to some 300 million individuals in one cubic centimeter of water.

In bodies of water less than 200 meters deep the bacteria are much more numerous in the mud bottoms than in the water above. These bacteria are largely anaerobic and spore-forming, as compared with the aerobic and non-spore-forming bacteria floating in the water. The bottom bacteria include the nitrifying, the nitrogen-fixing, and the humus decomposing types.

Certain bacteria of the sea are of interest because they obtain energy by the oxidation of such substances as hydrogen sulfide, sulfur, ammonia, nitrites, and methane, and use the energy in the synthesis of cell substances.

An accurate quantitative comparison between organisms on land and in the ocean is difficult to make. Krogh has estimated that the entire life zone on land is rarely more than 30 meters thick, from tree tops to root tips inclusive, in contrast to the 4000 meters of ocean in which animals live, and the 300 meters populated by green plants. For every tree in a forest there may be nearly a half million animals large enough to be seen by the naked eye. When the microscopic animals, bacteria, and algae are added to this, the total number is prodigious.

Under a square meter of ocean water near the equator, down to a depth of 200 meters, there may be a billion or more scarcely visible or microscopic plants and a million animals of various sizes, mostly microscopic. But the mass of these organisms is surprisingly small, perhaps aggregating only about 1/100 of a corresponding volume in a forest.

Forest trees stand for years, but many of the ocean plants are renewed several times a year. The total biological productivity in the ocean, however, probably never equals that in the forest, though locally it may be of comparable magnitude.

In sharp contrast to the land, no seed plants, no ferns, no mosses, no liverworts ever grow in the open sea. The plants characteristic of the ocean are limited to algae, bacteria, and a few fungi. The species of plants characteristic of the ocean rarely occur in fresh water. On the land the larger plants are the chief sources of food of the animal populations.

In the water microscopic plants are the initial links in the food chains of nearly all the animals. Enormous numbers of these plants grow every year, but directly they constitute only a small part of the food of the largest animals.

The food chain from green plants to the larger animals ("producer" to "consumer") may become greatly extended because the smallest animals, having consumed the plankton, may become the food of crustaceans and small fishes.

The latter in turn may be eaten by still larger fishes. It is evident that much of the energy value of the food originally made in green plants is never realized by the "ultimate consumer" because of the necessary respiratory and assimilatory processes of the often numerous "middlemen."

Each "middleman" may use in these processes up to 90 per cent of the initial energy value of the food. In spite of the small size of most marine organisms, a rapidly moving feeder can get large amounts of food in the sea. This is evident in the growth of the blue whale calf. At birth it is 7 meters long and weighs 2 tons, but may become 23 meters long and weigh up to 60 tons in two years.

Food of the blue whale consists entirely of plant and animal plankton which passes into the whale through the so-called "whale-bone sieve." As much as 2 tons of plankton have been found in the stomach of a mature blue whale at one time. If there are only three links in the food chain of the whale, the gain of 58 tons in weight implies consumption of food equivalent to 58,000 tons of algae in a two-year period.

Whalers often locate the places where whales may be found by the presence of large quantities of plankton on the surface of the water. Biologically algae and bacteria are the most important aquatic plants.

ARTIFICIAL ENVIRONMENTS

Many algae will grow and reproduce in artificial environments, called culture media, if these media are similar in composition to the environments in which the algae grow naturally.

The culture may contain a single species (pure culture); a single species of algae, although bacteria may be present (unialgal culture); or several species of algae (mixed culture). Such cultures of algae are of value in studying life cycles, in understanding physiological and genetic processes, in estimating possible maximal large-scale yields of "*algal crops*," and in doing controlled experiments with such environmental factors as light, temperature, salts, and gases. Such algae are available for further analyses for pigments, other cell constituents, and possible antibiotics.

CHAPTER 13

The Algae

Of all the plants in the biological communities of both fresh and salt water the *algae* (sing. *alga)* are the most important synthesizers of food. They are commonly called pond scums and seaweeds. Algae, however, are not confined to water habitats.

In the rainy tropics and subtropics they grow on moist surfaces everywhere, and even within the leaves of many plants. Some can grow in snow, as is often evident in the pink color of polar and high alpine snowfields.

The trunks of many woody plants of the moist temperate zone have green patches of algae, usually located on the shaded side. The algae of the soil are so numerous that one gram of earth from a heavily fertilized field may contain as many as a million individuals. A few algae grow in intimate association with certain fungi, forming compound plants known as *lichens.*

Algae grow within the aerial roots of cycads and in the hair follicles of the three-toed sloth. They are attached to the appendages of crustaceans and to the backs of turtles. They live within the bodies of many minute animals, and even in the intestines of some mammals, including man.

The algae, moreover, exhibit as much variation in color, in size, in form, and in method of reproduction as any of the other groups of plants. They may be red, orange, brown, yellow, yellow-green, green, blue-green, purple, and violet. Rarely are they colorless.

Some algae are so minute that their form is just discernible with a microscope. The giant kelps of the Pacific, on the other hand, attain lengths of more than 200 feet. In form algae may be globular, disk-shaped, thread-like, sheet-like, leaf-like, or large and paddle-shaped; branched or unbranched; attached or free-floating. The structures associated with sexual reproduction in some species are comparatively simple; in others, they are remarkably complex.

Among the various species of algae, vegetative propagation may result from the division and separation of cells, from the breaking of filaments, from specialized thick-walled dormant cells, or from motile spores that develop directly from vegetative cells. In one large group of algae no sexual reproduction occurs.

Algae are economically important both directly and indirectly. Commercial transactions involving the collection, processing, and sale of algae amount annually to several million dollars. The animals of the oceans, lakes, and streams are ultimately dependent upon various kinds of algae.

WHAT ARE ALGAE?

First of all, algae are plants. Some consist of only a single cell, a single filament, or branched filaments. Even the more complex ones have no organs exactly comparable to those of seed plants.

They contain chlorophyll, although other pigments may partly or entirely mask the green color. The presence of these pigments usually enables one to distinguish algae from fungi, bacteria, and small animals. Many of them are easily distinguished from other green plants by the number, size, and form of their chloroplasts.

Many species are capable of self-locomotion by twisting, bending, gliding, and swimming; and motile spores and gametes develop in many species.

The occurrence of motile algal plants and cells may require us to change one of our notions about plants if we have been accustomed to associate independent movement only with animals.

It should be remembered that the names "plants" and "animals" are very old and were used long before microscopes were made. It is easy to separate plants from animals when we are thinking of oaks and horses or corn and mice.

Now that the microscope has enabled us to see minute living organisms not even suspected before, it is not surprising to find that the criteria we are accustomed to use in separating plants and animals will not apply to many of these smaller organisms.

Among the many organisms having flagella some are more plant-like than others. When exposed to light, some of them are green and synthesize both sugar and amino acids; others remain colorless and obtain food only from external sources. Even within a single genus, such as *Euglena,* some species are more plant-like than others. For example, many species of *Euglena* are green and synthesize sugar when exposed to light.

Some of these green species can live in darkness as colorless saprophytes if supplied with sugar and protein foods, but others have failed to grow in continuous darkness.

They differ also in their ability to utilize nitrogen compounds. Some may utilize ammonia or nitrate salts, which means that they can synthesize amino acids from sugar and either ammonia or nitrate salts.

Still others cannot utilize either of these salts; consequently they cannot synthesize amino acids. Some can live only where peptones or other protein compounds are present in the external medium.

The Kinds of Algae

For many years algae were grouped on the basis of their color as red algae, brown algae, green algae, and blue-green algae. This classific-ation is still adequate for a general consideration of algae, though anyone unaware of other bases of classification would be confused on being told that some algae are colorless, that the red color of arctic snow is due to the presence of a red-colored green alga, and that the Red Sea was so named because of the abundance of a redcolored blue-green alga in it.

Most students of the algae now recognize 9 or more classes. This more critical classification is based in part on color, but also on other distinctive characters of (1) the structure of the vegetative cells and tissues, (2) the reproductive structures, (3) the successive stages in the life cycles, (4) the kinds of accumulated food, and (5) the forms of the chloroplasts or chromatophores.

The various colors of algae are due largely to the relative abundance of certain pigments in the cells. Chlorophyll is present in all algae except the colorless ones. Carotene and xanthophyll occur in most of them. The pigment fucoxanthin ($C_{40}H_{56}O_6$) is characteristic of the brown algae, and phycoerythrin and phycocyanin occur in the reds and blue-greens.

Economic Aspects of the Algae

To most people the algae of ponds and lakes, as well as those of the ocean deposited along shore after storms, are nuisances. Algae may accumulate in sufficient quantities to become an annoyance to bathers. Occasionally stock die after using water heavily populated with certain blue-green algae. Bad odors and tastes of drinking water are often attributed to the presence of decaying algae in reservoirs.

Tea and other subtropical plants are severely injured by algae which grow either on the surface of the leaves, interfering with photosynthesis, or within the leaves as parasites. Small fishes often become so entangled in algal mats that they die either there or subsequently from injuries received in extricating themselves.

Algae in fish hatchery ponds may so deplete the oxygen content of the water at night as to cause the death of the young fish through suffocation.

Algae are rather easily destroyed in small bodies of water by means of certain chemical compounds, particularly arsenites and copper sulfate. The latter is so effective that one part of it in a million parts of water is sufficient to kill most algae. Copper sulfate in such low concentrations is not harmful to fishes, nor is the water unfit for human consumption.

Although there are on the market numerous commercial products containing copper sulfate with adequate instructions for their use, a few crystals thrown into small pools will usually suffice. For larger ponds a quantity of the chemical may be placed in a sack, tied to the rear of a boat, and allowed gradually to dissolve in the water as the boat is moved over the surface.

Among other practical measures used for eradicating algae

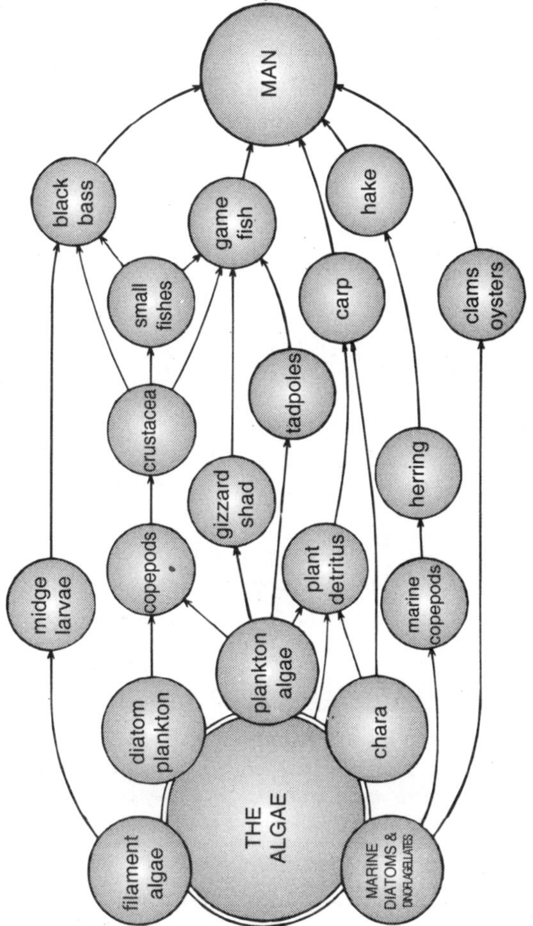

Figure 13.1: Diagram of representative food chains from algae to man.

from fish ponds are (1) the removal of the accumulating organic matter by draining the pond from the bottom instead of the surface, and (2) the maintenance of high turbidity.

Young crayfish are often added to the ponds because they increase the turbidity of the water, which in turn decreases the penetration of light and algae are unable to survive. Reservoirs may be kept free of algae by stirring up the muddy bottom with large propellers on boats.

Suppose we now examine the credit side of the ledger. As

has been noted before, the algae are the ultimate sources of food and energy of all strictly aquatic animals. The food chains of animals are numerous and varied.

Some fishes feed directly on the algae, while others obtain the *energy* bound up in the plants by eating animals that feed on algae. Some blue-greens, a few greens, and many species of red and brown algae are used directly as food by human beings in many parts of the world, particularly in the Orient.

Among algae, as among other plants, some species are much

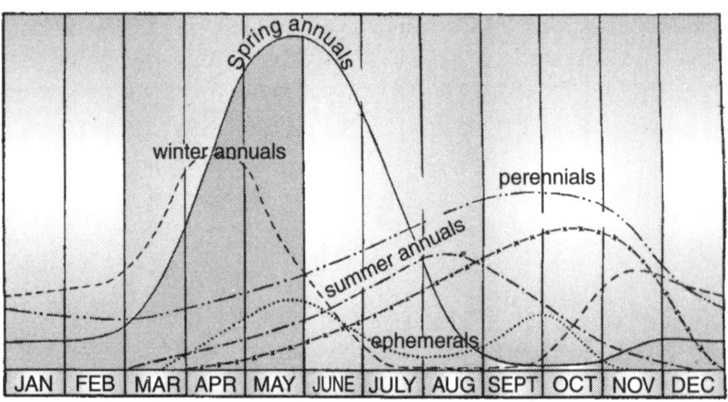

Figure 13.2: Estimated relative abundance of several seasonal assemblages of green algae in central Illinois. Seasonal assemblages would be very different farther north and farther south. Ephemerals include plankton species in which a life cycle is completed in a few days.

more important than others as sources of food, whether the consumer be man, fish, insect, or whale.

The giant kelps and other seaweeds are sources of iodine and potash. They have been used for many years by farmers along the coast as fertilizers because of their potassium content.

Dried and treated in various ways, they are used as stabilizers in making ice cream, candy, shaving cream, various other creams, jellies, salads, and emulsions; and also as the source of agar-agar, so important in the culture of bacteria and fungi.

The algae of the soil are very numerous, but the extent to which they contribute to soil fertility and aeration is only partly known. Soils have definite algal floras. Those living on the surface grow and multiply rapidly whenever the soil is moist.

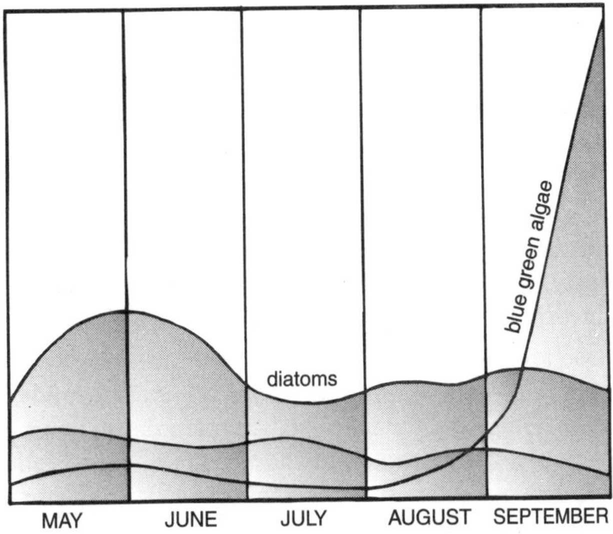

Figure 13.3: Relative abundance of some plankton algae in Lake Erie.

The algae below the surface grow very slowly; and since they live in darkness they are obviously living as saprophytes, using carbohydrates from the soil solution. Algae certainly contribute organic matter to soils, and it has been proved that certain nitrogen-fixing bacteria are much more effective when they grow in association with soil algae. The fungi and algae of lichens are the pioneer plants on certain kinds of exposed rock surfaces and are primary factors in the formation of the first layers of soil on such surfaces.

Algal Periodicity

Many fresh-water and marine algae have seasonal periods of germination of spores, vegetative growth, reproduction, and dormancy similar to those of flowering plants. Many species in temperate climates attain their greatest development in winter, in spring, in summer, or in the autumn; reproductive bodies mature and the vegetative structures disappear.

These algae are comparable to annual flowering plants. Their dormant period is passed as spores. There are also many perennial filamentous, or thick and leathery, species in which at least a part, usually the base of the vegetative plant, survives long periods of drought and cold. Each year new vegetative fronds develop. This group includes many seaweeds, certain red algae in fresh-water streams, and green algae such as *Cladophora* and *Vaucheria.* Plankton algae and some soil algae are very short-lived. A new population of these extremely abundant and important species may develop every few days.

They are the plants that form the so-called "water bloom" so common on ponds and lakes from midsummer to early autumn. Obviously, enormous numbers result from the accumulative reproduction of several generations in a few weeks.

Algae are more numerous in seasons when the water levels are high. They also reproduce most abundantly under these conditions. Their individual periodicity determines what species will be found associated at any time of the year. Ponds that regularly dry up in late summer appear to have a greater variety of species than permanent ponds.

The situation in large lakes is somewhat unlike that in ponds because great bodies of water neither warm up quickly in the spring nor cool rapidly in the autumn.

In Lake Erie, for example, the diatoms are likely to be abundant in May and June, the green algae in July and early August, the blue-greens in late August and September, and the diatoms again in October and November. A few species of diatoms are more abundant in winter than at any other season.

Water blooms are just as characteristic of large lakes as of ponds. At certain seasons of the year diatoms, blue-greens, or greens may within a few days become so abundant as literally to cover acres of water to the depth of an inch or two.

This colored soup-like layer may be objectionable to bathers, and it may be the source of offensive odors; but it contains an abundance of food available to the smallest aquatic animals. The life cycles of the algae composing the bloom are soon completed, and after several days the plants may disappear as suddenly as they appeared.

Most plankton algae are found within a few inches of the surface of the water, although one may usually find them in collections made at depths of 10 to 50 feet. We have discussed so

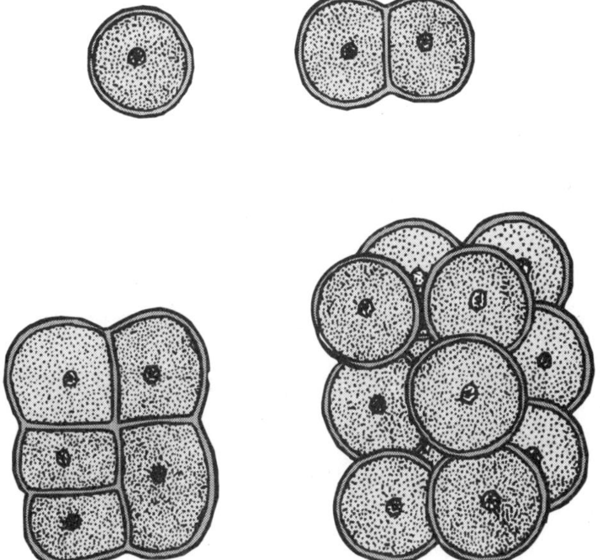

Figure 13.4: Forms of cells of a Protococcus.

far some of the general characteristics, distribution, and economic aspects of algae as a whole.

They constitute such a large and diversified assemblage of plants, however, that a better understanding of their growth and reproduction depends on a study of sonic of the commoner ones in more detail. We shall discuss in the next few pages some representatives of each of the important classes of algae.

THE GREEN ALGAE: CHLOROPHYCEAE

About 5000 species of green algae have been described and named. As a group of plants they are quite varied in structure, in appearance, and in several other ways. They are usually predominantly green in color during the vegetative phase, containing chlorophyll, xanthophyll, and carotene in about the proportion found in the seed plants.

They grow chiefly in water, both fresh and marine, but occur also on and in the soil and on many other kinds of moist substrates. Biologically they influence both the abundance and the distribution of certain other plants and of certain animals. Green algae are by far the most common ones in lichens.

They may be parasitized by animals and occur inside animals, such as hydras and rotifers. In size they vary from the microscopic forms to the filamentous, highly branched cladophoras, which may be several feet in length and are attached to rocks and stones of streams and lakes. A few common species are described below.

Protococcus

On the bark of trees and shrubs throughout the world there occur green-colored areas of *Protococcus,* sometimes several

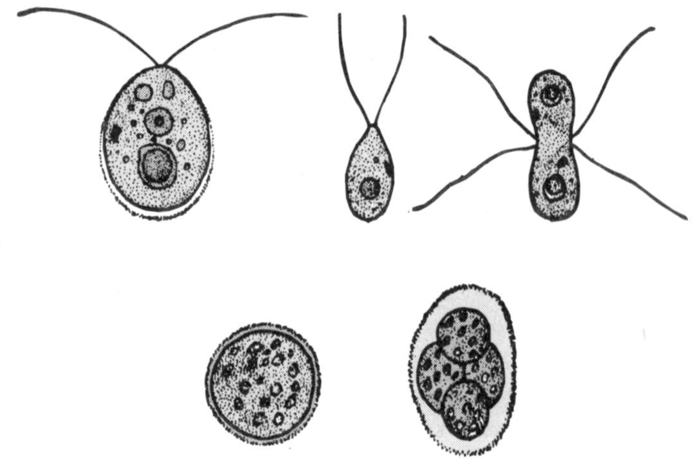

Figure 13.5: Forms of vegetative and reproductive cells of a Chlamydomonas.

square feet in extent. This alga grows most frequently on the shaded parts of the tree.

In drier regions it may be restricted to the lee side. Although most abundant near the ground, it may be found on the bark all the way to the tops of trees in moist open forests. No spores are formed and no sexual reproduction occurs in this alga.

Under the microscope the green areas of *Protococcus* are seen to consist of masses of rounded solitary cells or of groups of two to several cells. The chloroplast occupies most of the cell, and the cell walls are comparatively thick.

The plant may survive prolonged droughts and remain

dormant during long periods of low temperature, in spite of the fact that there are no apparent structural modifications that might prevent desiccation of the cells. When periods of rain and higher temperatures return, the cells again become active.

Propagation takes place only through the division and subsequent separation of the cells. No reduction division occurs; and, except for mutations, all the cells of *Protococcus* have the same chromosome complement. It is a nonmotile one-celled plant, though several plants may remain attached temporarily as an unorganized colony.

Chlamydomonas

In contrast to the one-celled non-motile *Protococcus* is the one-celled motile *Chlamydomonas.* It is often found as a part of the plankton, sometimes occurring in large numbers in small pools or even in indoor aquaria. The cell is spherical, ovoid, or elongate, and often flattened. Two flagella project from the anterior end. Both spore formation and sexual reproduction occur.

Cells with flagella similar to *Chlamydomonas* may remain attached and thus form definite colonies of several to many cells. Examples of such colonial algae are *Pandorina, Eudorina,* and *V olvox.* All of these algae are termed flagellate organisms.

Ulothrix

In the spring one may see bright green slimy filamentous growths of *Ulothrix* on the stones and rocks of the shores of streams, lakes, and ponds. Since the cylindrical cells of this alga are joined end to end and always divide in the same plane, the plant is a single unbranched filament.

Each plant is attached to rocks or other objects by a special holdfast cell. The chloroplast is a green band of cytoplasm open on one side. It appears to be pressed against the cell wall and is frequently confined to the middle section of the cylindrical cell. Its form in cross section resembles that of a horseshoe.

Starches and proteins accumulate in vegetative cells, but in the spores one finds mainly oils. The life cycle of a *Ulothrix is* far more complex than that of *Protococcus.*

After vegetative development the protoplast in each of many cells may become subdivided by a succession of mitotic divisions

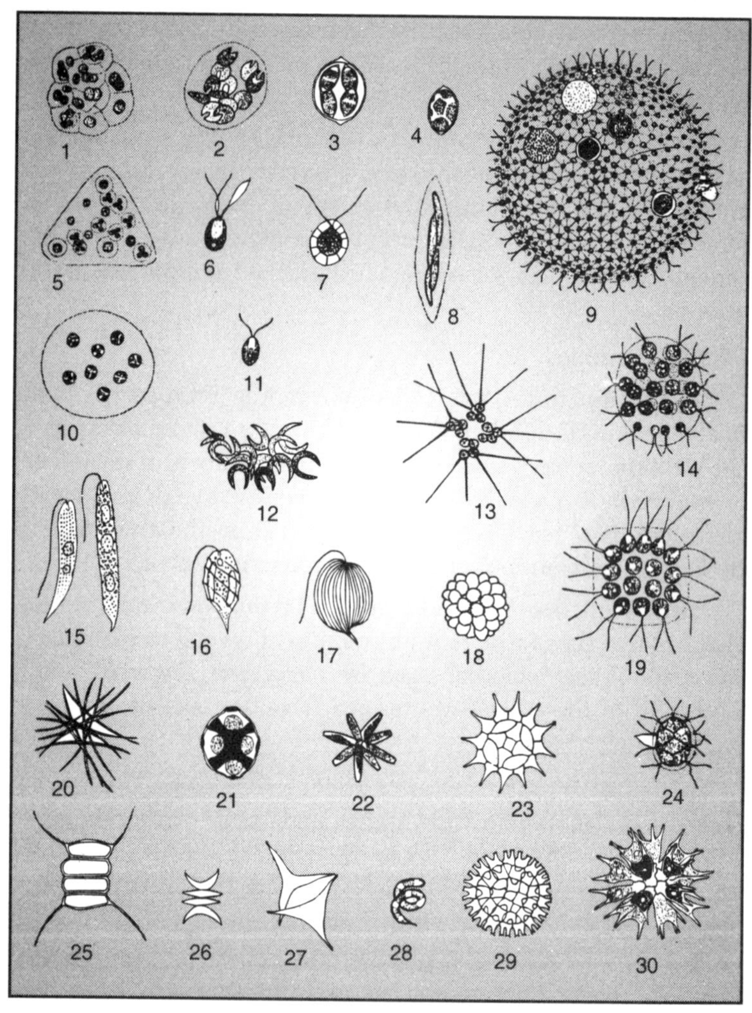

Figure 13.6: Forms of some unicellular and colonial algae. Genera represented: 1 and 5 Gloeocystis, 2 Kirchneriella, 3-4 Oocystis, 6 Carteria, 7 Sphaerella, 8 Quadrigula, 9 Volvox, 10 Asterococcus, 11 Chlamydomonas, 12 Selenastrum, 13 Micractinium, 14 Pleodorina, 15 Euglena, 16-17 Phacus, 18 Coelastrum, 19 Gonium, 20 Ankistrodesmus, 21 Gloeotaenium, 22 Actinastrum, 23 Pediastrum, 24 Pandorina, 25-26 Scenedesmus, 27 Tetraedron, 28 Ophiocytium, 29 Pediastrum, 30 Sorastrum.

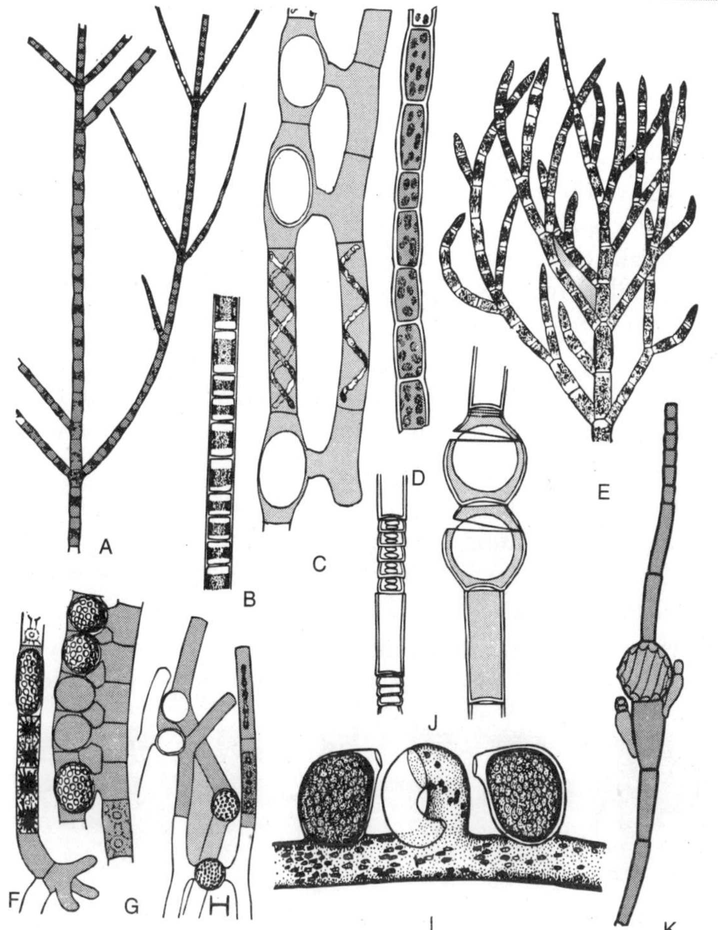

Figure 13.7: Common filamentous algae. Genera represented: A, Stigeoclonium; B, Ulothrix; C, Spirogyra; D, Tribonema; E, Chaetophora; F and G, Zygnema; H, Mougeotia; I, Vaucheria; J and K, Oedogonium.

into 2, 4, or 8 small protoplasts, each of which escapes through an opening in the wall of the parent cell and becomes a motile spore' with four flagella.

Both big and little motile spores may be formed in different cells of the same filament. The smaller ones are formed in groups of 16 or 32. After swimming about for a short period, a motile spore may become attached to some object and germinate by elongating and then dividing transversely.

Subsequent cell divisions all in the same plane result in a new filament. In still other filaments, or occasionally in some cells of the same filament, the protoplast may become subdivided by successive mitotic divisions into 8, 16, 32, 64, 128, or rarely more cells.

Each of these cells may pass through the wall of the parent cell in the same manner as the motile spore, which it resembles superficially except for its smaller size and its single pair of flagella. Such motile structures do not germinate, and new filaments do not develop from them.

They are termed *gametes.* The union of one gamete with another results in a zygote, which eventually becomes thick-walled and sinks into the mud at the bottom of the pond where it remains dormant for several months.

The union of the two gametes is termed *conjugation.* When the zygote germinates, its protoplast becomes subdivided into 4 to 16 parts, each of which becomes a motile spore from which a new filament grows.

The two gametes that unite appear to differ chemically and are referred to as + and – gametes, and they come from different

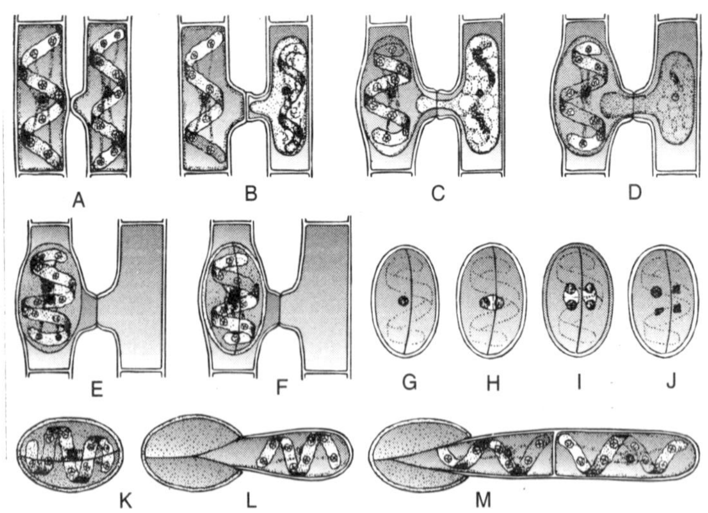

Figure 13.8: Reproduction in Spirogyra and inheritance of the chloroplast.

filaments. Since they are similar in appearance they are regarded as the simplest kind of sex cells. The special method of vegetative multiplication by means of either motile or non-motile spores which develop without previous union of gametes is often termed *asexual reproduction.*

The related series of processes including the formation of gametes, their subsequent union, and the development of the resulting zygote into motile spores from which new filaments develop are referred to as the *sexual reproduction* of the alga.

Reduction division occurs during the first nuclear division in the zygote. Hence each motile spore of *Ulothrix* and each cell of the filament has the monoploid number of chromosomes. The zygote alone has the diploid number of chromosomes.

Oedogonium

In fresh water throughout the world, attached to various objects during at least a part of their lifetime are several hundred species of *Oedogonium*. All of them are filamentous and unbranched, and each cell has a hollow cylindrical meshwork chloroplast.

The method of reproduction is in some respects similar to, but in others quite unlike, that of *Ulothrix.* Motile spores develop singly in the vegetative cells. Each spore has a ring of flagella at one end and escapes from the cell through a circular break in the wall.

Upon coming to rest, it germinates directly, and the new plant elongates by subsequent division of certain cells scattered at intervals in the filament. The first cell is the holdfast cell. The two kinds of gametes are quite distinct in appearance.

The male gametes, or *sperms,* formed singly or in pairs from the protoplast in special short cells known as *antheridia* (sing. *antheridium,* a sperm case), are quite similar in appearance to small motile spores. The female gamete, or *egg,* develops singly within a swollen vegetative cell, the *oogonium* (pl. *oogonia,* egg cases).

The egg is much larger than the sperm, never escapes from the egg case, is incapable of locomotion, and contains much food, chiefly oils. The sperms and eggs may develop in cells of the same filament or of separate filaments. That is, some species are bisexual, or monoecious; others consist of two kinds of unisexual filaments, one of which is a male filament, the other female.

They may or may not differ in size. In some species the male

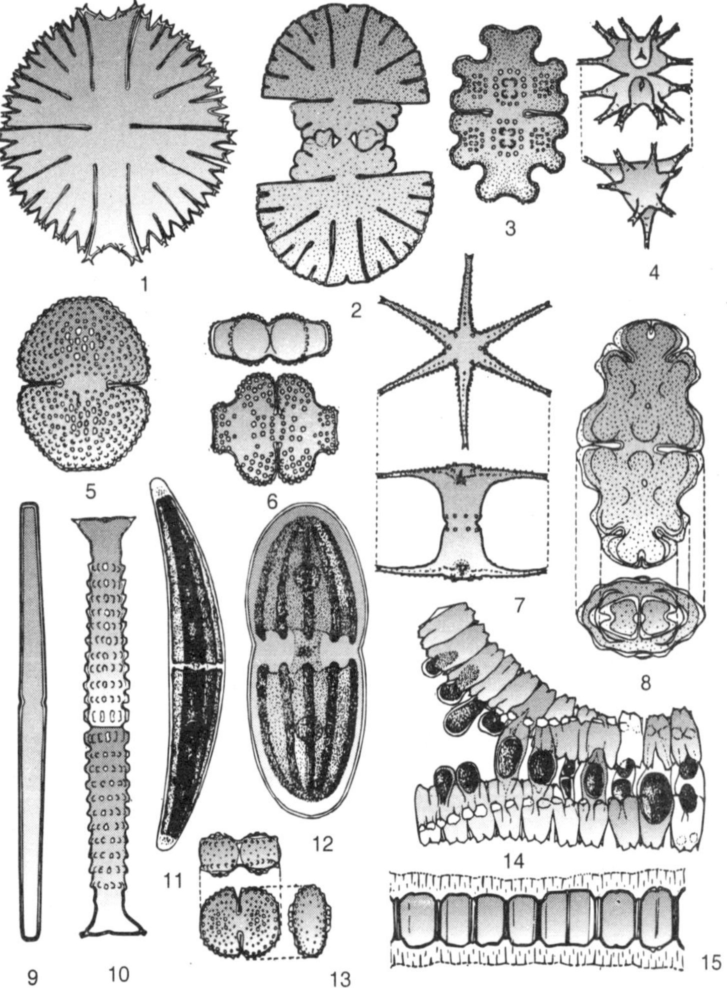

Figure 13.9: Various forms of desmids, and conjugation in Desmidium (14). Genera represented: 1-2 Micrasterias, 3 and 8 Euastrum, 4 and 7 Staurastrum, 5, 6 and 13 Cosmarium, 9 Pleurotaenium, 10 Triploceras, 11 Closterium, 12 Penium, 14-15 Desmidium.

filaments are very small and grow as epiphytes on the female filaments near the oogonium. These *dwarf males* develop from motile spores which germinate only when they become attached to an oogonium or adjacent cells. They usually consist of a holdfast cell and one or more antheridia. The sperm after liberation from the antheridium may swim to and enter an oogonium through a pore or slit, and fuse with the egg.

This fusion appears to occur mostly late at night or early morning. The resulting *zygote* is thick-walled, remains dormant for some months or even years, and upon germination four motile spores usually develop, each of which has the reduced number of chromosomes. A new filament develops directly from each motile

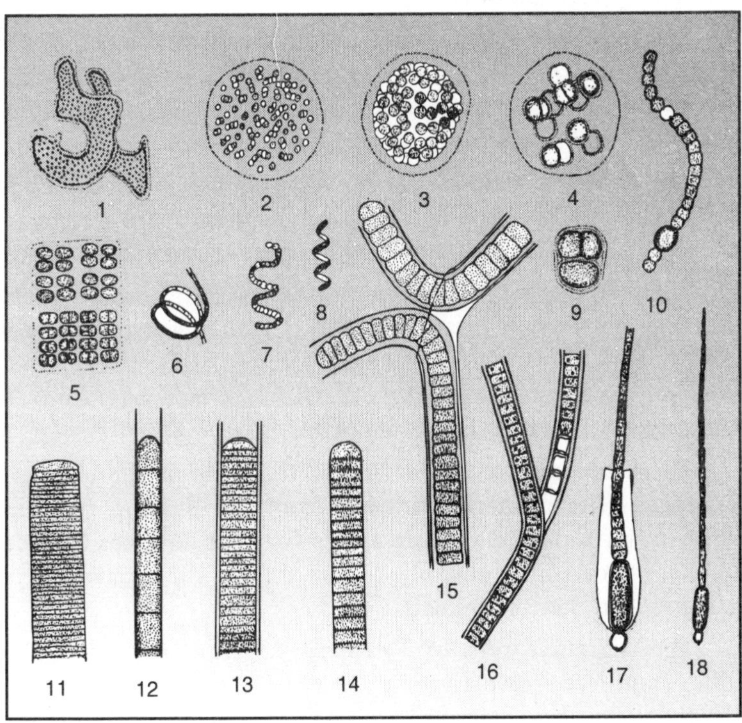

Figure 13.10: Forms of blue-green algae. Genera represented: 1 Microcystis, 2 Aphanocapsa, 3 Coelosphaerium, 4 Chroococcus, 5 Merismopedia, 6 and 13 Lyngbya, 7 and 10 Anabaena, 8 Spirulina, 9 Chroococcus, 11 and 14 Oscillatoria, 12 Phormidium, 15 Scytonema, 16 Tolypothrix, 17 Gloeotrichia, 18 Cylindrospermum.

spore, and each of its cells has the reduced number of chromosomes.

Other Common Filamentous Genera

Among the most widely distributed genera of pond algae is *Spirogyra,* with its usually spirally arranged, ribbon-like chloroplasts. *Zygnema* with stellate chloroplasts, and *Mougeotia* with a straight, ribbon-shaped chloroplast are almost as common.

In the large group of algae represented by these three genera, the cells are always cylindrical and there is a complete absence of flagellate spores. Sexual reproduction is effected by the union of gametes, one (or both) of which moves ameba-like to the other through *a conjugation tube.*

The zygotes resulting from the union of the gametes may remain dormant for several months or years. When they germinate, new filaments develop from them. Reduction division occurs at the first division of the zygote nucleus.

The green felt-like *Vaucheria* is very common in small streams and ditches. Cell division in it is unaccompanied by the formation of cross walls and thus the filaments are tubular and multinucleate.

The motile spores of *Vaucheria* are unusual in that a number of nuclei are present in a so-called "compound zoospore," from which a new filament develops almost immediately. Most species of *Vaucheria* have an oogonium with a single egg, and an antheridium containing several sperms.

These sex organs are formed at the ends of short lateral branches. The oospore resulting from fertilization remains dormant for some time before a new filament develops from it. Reduction division probably occurs during the formation of gametes as it does in animals.

The vegetative cells of *Vaucheria* have no starch and also differ from most green algae in the kinds of pigments present in the cells. The algae described above and many others are usually available in their natural habitats, and the details of their life cycles may be studied from living or preserved specimens.

The desmids are either unicellular or filamentous forms, a few of which are illustrated in Figure elsewhere in this chapter.

The Stoneworts

These plants are mentioned here largely because of their importance in the formation of marl deposits. The stoneworts *(Charales)* are rather widely distributed in both fresh and salt waters; a few species inhabit both.

They are attached to the soil beneath the water and often form extensive meadows several feet below the water surface. The plants become incrusted with calcium carbonate in limestone regions, and as the plants die, marl accumulates. About one hundred species have been described.

The plant body consists of a cylindrical axis bearing a whorl of branches at its several "nodes." The plants are nearly always erect and may vary in height from an inch to 3 or 4 feet. The stoneworts constitute a group very distinct from all other algae.

THE BLUE-GREEN ALGAE: MYXOPHYCEAE

The blue-greens differ from all the great groups of algae in that the nuclear substances of the cell are not organized in a well-defined structure in the cytoplasm as in other green plants.

Hereditary units of matter comparable to genes must be present, however, for the species are hereditarily different. Chlorophyll and other pigments are dispersed throughout the cell and not confined to plastids.

No motile spores are formed and no sexual reproduction occurs. Only about half the bluegreen algae are really blue-green in color. The others vary greatly in color owing to different amounts of blue, red, green, and yellow pigments.

Common to all blue-greens is the presence of a mucilaginous outer wall which may be so thick that the filaments appear to be embedded in a mass of mucilage.

Approximately 2500 species of blue-greens have been descr-ibed and named. Most of them grow in fresh water, but marine and other saltwater species are not uncommon.

They are able to grow in almost every conceivable habitat. They are important constituents of fresh-water plankton, and some of the water blooms of summer are due to their abundance.

The Red Sea was probably so named because of the presence in large numbers of one of these plants *(Trichodesmium),* which is predominantly red in color. Blue-greens that grow in hot springs live at temperatures between 1500 and 170° F.

Other species may remain frozen in ice for many months without injury. Blue-greens may become serious pests on soil in greenhouses by forming a gelatinous layer that prevents aeration of the soil beneath. They are very common in ponds in the far north.

The blue-greens constitute an important part of the algal population of soils, and their spores can withstand complete desiccation for many years.

They may grow as parasites within the bodies of man and other animals; as epiphytes on other algae and on the vegetative parts, particularly leaves, of many seed plants; and as hosts of fungi in a few kinds of lichens.

Species of blue-green algae regularly occur in the leaves of a water fern *(Azolla),* and on the scales of some liverworts. One bluegreen species grows in the aerial roots of some cycads, and many others may be found within the gelatinous envelopes of other algae.

In general, this group of algae may be considered as the characte-ristic plants in bodies of water high in organic matter, but not necessarily so.

When fresh-water streams are polluted by sewage, by poisonous wastes from various manufacturing processes, and by drainage from coal mines and oil wells, the blue-greens are the last to disappear.

In fact, in such habitats certain bacteria are about their only living associates. Blue-green algae are either unicellular, colonial, or multice-llular. Cells of the colonial species may be loosely or definitely aggregated into globular, saccate, plate-like, or irregular colonies with a few to many cells held together by mucilage.

The cells of some other species are joined end to end in definite regular or irregular filaments; the filaments may be branched or not. Division of the cells in only one plane results in a chain of cells; division in two planes, a plate-like colony; and division in three planes, a solid and often nearly cubical aggregate. The granules of food that accumulate in the vegetative cells are not definitely known chemically.

They undoubtedly are conversion products from sugar formed in photosynthesis; they are not starch. Glycogen, or possibly glycoproteins, and droplets of oil may accumulate, especially in the spores.

The plants increase in number by vegetative multiplication. Any vegetative cell in some plants, or only certain vegetative cells in other plants, may develop thick walls and become dormant.

After a period of time, new plants grow from these thick-walled cells. New filaments also result from the fragmentation of old filaments into small groups of cells, followed by repeated cell division.

THE DIATOMS: BACILLARIOPHYCEAE

The vegetative cell of a diatom has highly silicified walls (i.e., glass walls) composed of two overlapping parts *(valves)* that fit together like the halves of a petri dish. The wall is usually beautifully sculptured and ornamented.

The plant may be unicellular, filamentous, or joined in irregular colonies by gelatinous sheaths. Pectic compounds are present, but probably no cellulose. The chloroplasts are yellowish to brownish, and contain chlorophyll, xanthophyll, and carotene together with accessory pigments of unknown chemical composition.

Some 12,000 species have been described. Diatoms are distributed widely in both fresh and salt water. They are the important constituents of the plankton of the cooler waters of the sea, and at times are the principal algae of lakes and ponds, especially in early spring and in the autumn.

Owing to the mucilage from their cells, diatoms may become attached to other plants and to all sorts of unde water objects. Depending upon the amount and place of major formation of mucilage, the colonial species may form ribbon, chain, zigzag, or

Figure 13.11: Forms of brown algae (figures not drawn to scale). Genera represented: (A) Fucus, (B) Postelsia, (C) Ectocarpus, (D and G) Laminaria, (E) Chorda, and (F) Nereocystis.

branching aggregates. Although not as important as either greens or blue-greens in the soil, some species of diatoms are distinctly terrestrial and capable of withstanding desiccation for many years.

In regions of frequent rainfall diatoms may grow subaerially on tree trunks, on fences, and on rocky cliffs. As noted above, diatoms may occur in prodigious numbers in both sea and inland waters at certain times of the year.

They are probably the most important constituent of the ocean plankton. When the plants die, the cell walls remain unaltered after the death and decay of the rest of the cell. The empty "glass cases" may thus accumulate over a period of years in great quantities on the bottom of seas, bays, and lakes. Such deposits of fossil diatoms are known as diatomaceous earth and are found in many parts of the world.

One of the largest deposits is near Lompoc, California; it covers about 12 square miles with a stratum of commercially pure diatoms some 1400 feet thick, and in addition 3000 feet of diatoms mixed with silt, sand, and gravel.

Diatomaceous earth is quarried or mined, the annual output approaching 100,000 tons. Its largest use is in the filtration of liquids, especially those of sugar refineries. The powdered earth is added to the solution, collects on the cloth screens of the filter press, and prevents the suspended matter from passing through them.

Diatomaceous earth in the form of bricks is used in the insulation of boilers and smelting furnaces. At high temperatures it is more effective than asbestos or magnesia. Metal polishes, abrasive soaps, and toothpaste often contain diatom shells.

Living diatoms are of major importance as the food of fishes, oysters, and clams. Certain marine fishes feed almost entirely on them, or on the small animals that have consumed diatoms. The commercially important hake, for example, feeds upon herring; the herring subsist on copepods; and the copepods are dependent upon the diatoms for their food.

The accumulation and decay of diatoms in water reservoirs and ponds, on the other hand, may result in compounds that are extremely obnoxious to our senses of smell and taste. Some species are able to grow in waters highly polluted with organic matter. Diatom abundance is often associated with a plentiful supply of nitrates and silicates. Paucity of diatoms is sometimes directly due to the absence of soluble silicates in the pond.

Cell division in the diatoms is an almost unique phenomenon among plants. The new cell wall in the center of the dividing cell consists of two new valves. Each of the two resulting daughter cells then has one new valve, and one older valve that belonged to the parent cell.

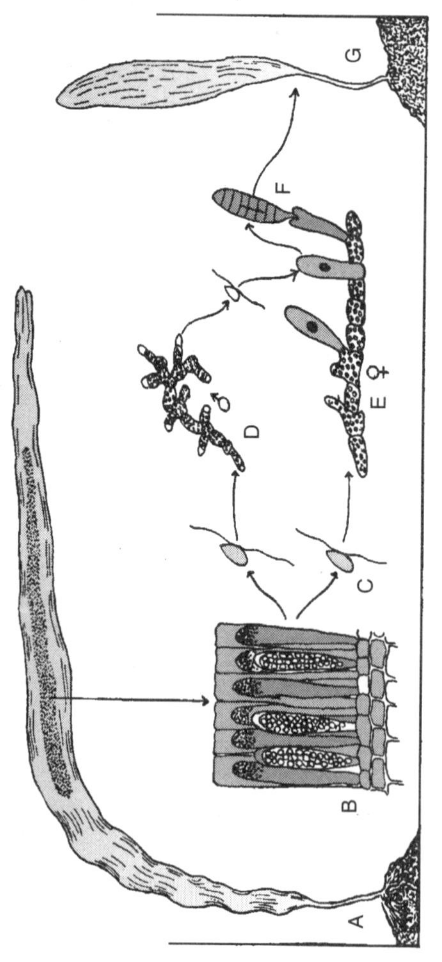

Figure 13.12: Diagram illustrating the life history of a Laminaria. On the mature thallus (A) an enlongated patch of sporogenous tissue develops, an enlarged portion of which is represented in (B) with three sporangia from which motile spores (C) later escape. Reduction division occurs during the formation of these spores, and from one half of them male gametophytes (D) develop, and from the other half female gametophytes. Sperms are liberated from the male gametophytes and after swimming in the water unite with the egg cells in the female gametophyte. From the zygote a young sporophyte grows at first attached to the oogonium wall (F), but later it is set free and ultimately becomes attached to some other substrate (G).

As a result, any given diatom cell may have a valve that has been a part of many ancestral cells. Spores are formed in the diatoms both asexually and sexually; and from them, after a period of dormancy, new plants develop directly.

The spores of diatoms have been indiscriminately called *auxospores* regardless of whether or not they are the result of sexual union. The prefix "auxo" refers to the increase in size of this cell. The cell formed from the auxospore is usually much larger than the cell, or cells, from which the auxospore originated.

Subsequent divisions of the cells, in vegetative multiplication of some species, lead to decrease in size of cells until auxospores again form. The diatom cell is diploid, the monoploid condition being represented only in the nuclei of the gametes, a condition not common among algae, but usual in animals.

THE YELLOW-GREEN ALGAE: XANTHOPHYCEAE

This comparatively small group of algae is almost entirely confined to fresh water and consists of about 400 species. The yellow-greens are similar to the greens in many respects, but are characterized by chloroplasts in which yellow pigments predominate over the green; by motile spores having two flagella of unequal length; by the presence of oils, but never starch; and by the rare occurrence of sexual reproduction.

Most of the yellow-greens occur free-floating in temporary ponds and pools, or as epiphytes upon other algae and upon the stems and leaves of submerged plants. A few species grow on small crustaceans. The aerial yellow-greens may be found on tree trunks or damp walls, or growing with liverworts and mosses.

A common yellow-green alga on prairie and bottom-land soils is the balloon-shaped *Botrydium.* The cells of the yellow-greens may be solitary, or united into colonies and filaments.

The cell walls are chiefly pectic compounds (pectose or pectic acid) often impregnated with silica, with carbonates, and sometimes with small amounts of cellulose.

The cells of several genera have walls made up of two overlapping halves that fit together like the two parts of a gelatine capsule used by druggists. Some of these characters of the yellow-greens resemble those of the diatoms.

Reproduction occurs through the formation and subsequent growth of motile and non-motile spores. Sexual reproduction has been observed only a few times, but seems to involve the union of motile gametes.

THE BROWN ALGAE: PHAEOPHYCEAE

The predominant color of brown algae is due to the presence of fucoxanthin, although green and yellow pigments are also present.

Brown algae are almost entirely marine, and the larger ones are often referred to as seaweeds. The largest ones, which are said to exceed 200 feet in length, are in the colder waters of temperate continental shores.

The motile spores and gametes have two laterally placed flagella, one of which extends forward and the other backward. The cells are uninucleate and have from one to many chloroplasts.

Oil, sugar, and complex polysaccharides accumulate in them. Some 1100 species are recognized. Most species of brown algae are found on rocky shores and do not ordinarily grow at much greater depths than 50 to 75 feet, although some of the kelps are attached to rocks at depths of 200 feet.

Many of the plants are completely submerged only at high tide, being exposed to the air at low tide. Waves, especially during storms, rupture the blades of the larger plants, and it is often difficult to find a perfect specimen.

The simplest brown algae structurally are filamentous and superficially resemble some of the greens. The majority, however, are large and parenchymatous with a rather high degree of differentiation in the plant body.

The leathery kelps, abundant in the colder temperate waters, have internal tissues that resemble the sieve tubes of seed plants. These algae consist of branching root-like holdfasts attached to rocks or other substrates, a long submerged stalk, and one or more conspicuously large, ribbon-like, or variously shaped floating

Figure 13.13: Forms of red algae (figures not drawn to scale). Genera represented (A) Chondrus, (B) Dasya, (C) Nemalion, (D) Grinnellia, and (E) Corallina.

blades. Some of the kelps are perennial, and the stalk increases in diameter by the formation of new rings of peripheral cells.

In the upper littoral zone along our coasts there grows in great abundance a branched, filamentous brown alga, known as *Ectocarpus.*

It is practically world-wide in distribution. Along the Atlantic coast it is common as an epiphyte on the rockweeds *(Fucus* and

Ascophyllum), and less common along the Pacific coast on certain kelps. Motile spores formed in some special cells may germinate and from them new plants develop.

Fusion of flagellate gametes from other filaments results in a zygote. The germination of the zygote results in a plant that is able to bear only motile spores. In general, one cannot distinguish the filaments that bear the motile spores from those that bear gametes until the reproductive structures actually appear.

There occurs then in *Ectocarpus* an alternation of asexual and sexual phases similar to those of seed plants, ferns, and mosses. Reduction division takes place during the formation of the motile spores.

Kelps

The body of a kelp consists of a holdfast, a stipe, and a very large blade. Kelps grow only in the colder waters of the oceans; they are absent from the warm waters of tropical and semitropical regions. Most species of kelp grow below low tide and are thus permanently in water.

The life cycle of the kelps may be indicated by a study of *Laminaria,* sometimes called devil's apron, found along both coasts of this continent. On the surface of the blade occur patches of sporangia, from which motile spores escape.

From these spores minute gamete-bearing filaments develop. These tiny plants may be few-celled or many-celled, and each one is unisexual, producing either only male gametes or only female gametes. The union of two gametes results in a zygote, from which the large plant we know as the kelp develops.

We thus have a pair of microscopic gametophytes (gamete-bearing plants) alternating with a large sporophyte (spore-bearing plant). The large blade-like kelp is the diploid plant. Reduction division occurs in it during the formation of the motile spores, which are the forerunners of the small unisexual gametophytes.

It is interesting to recall that in nearly all green algae the conspicuous plant is the one bearing gametes. In *Laminaria,* and a few other algae as well, the gamete-bearing plant is microscopic; the spore-bearing plant is the conspicuous structure, as it is in the seed plants.

Moreover, the conspicuous phase of *Laminaria* is diploid, and the microscopic gametophytes are monoploid. The conspicuous phase of green algae usually has the reduced number of chromosomes, and spore formation (except zygotes) results only in vegetative multiplication of the gamete-bearing phase of the life cycle of the plant.

Covering the rocks in the intertidal zones are the widely distributed "rockweeds" or "bladder wracks," represented on our coasts by *Fucus*. They occur in tropical, temperate, and arctic seas, but the species or genera are usually characteristic in each zone.

Most of the genera grow permanently attached to the rocks, although certain species of *Sargassum* are free-floating. *Fucus* is a dichotomously branched plant, attached by holdfasts and kept afloat at high tide by bladder-like structures filled with air.

It has no asexual propagation except by fragmentation, and has no alternation of spore-bearing and gamete-bearing phases. The reproductive cycle is similar to that of animals. Sperms and eggs are formed by the first cell division immediately following reduction division, and all other cells of the plant have the diploid number of chromosomes.

The reproductive organs develop only in special branches. Swollen conical structures *(receptacles)* at the tips of the branches contain rounded cavities *(conceptacles)* in which antheridia and oogonia develop. Usually 8 eggs are formed in a single oogonium, and 64 sperms in a single antheridium.

Upon release from the oogonium and conceptacle, the non-flagellate egg may be fertilized by a motile sperm. A new plant grows directly from the zygote. Reduction division occurs in the mother cell (oocyte) of the 8 eggs and in the mother cell (spermatocyte) of the 64 sperms.

THE RED ALGAE: RHODOPHYCEAE

The red algae are by far the most beautiful of all macroscopic submerged plants. They are most abundant in salt water, but are not infrequent in fresh water. Of the approximately 3500 known species, 200 grow in fresh water. They attain their greatest development in subtropical seas. Five different pigments are known to occur in the cells, with the red usually predominating, although various shades of blue and purple are common.

The red algae have definite nuclei and chloroplasts, and the chief accumulated food is a starch-like carbohydrate. They attain greater size on the whole than either the greens, blue-greens, diatoms, or yellow-greens, but none attains the size of the brown kelps.

The red algae grow attached to rocks near shore, but considerable numbers may be found at depths of 50 to 100 feet, and a few live 200 feet or more below the surface. Some species are epiphytes upon other algae.

The smallest species are little more than one-celled structures, but the majority are colonial aggregates, or filamentous and much branched, or blade-like and leathery. The larger species branch profusely, may attain lengths of several feet, and often have considerable differentiation of tissues.

A single filament, for example, may have a row of axial cells ensheathed by a cortical layer several cells in thickness. The red algae superficially resemble other modern algae, but their genealogical relations are very remote.

Some of the red algae in tropical waters take part in the formation of coral reefs, and are known as coralline algae (Fig. *291).* Corals are colonial animals; but always associated with them are red algae in which calcium carbonate accumulates, resulting in the massive reefs.

Fossil algal and coral reefs are found in the limestone rocks formed during the Paleozoic Era. Asexual reproduction among the red algae occurs through fragmentation, or the formation of non-motile spores. Strange as it may seem, no flagellate, motile cells of any kind occur in any of the plants of this group.

Sexual reproduction is so unlike that known among other algae that a special terminology is necessary to describe it. The unique features of these algae are of interest mainly as examples of peculiar outcomes of evolution. A few examples are cited below.

Nemalion

When the tide is out, one may see the gelatinous strands of

the marine summer annual, *Nemalion,* attached to the rocks in the midlittoral zone along coasts in temperate regions. It is a gelatinous short-branched cylindrical plant with a reddish-brown color.

Compared with some other red algae its life history is simple, but it is more complex than the life histories of other algae described in this chapter. It will be described briefly.

The female sex organs are apical cells of special short branches. The apical cell *(carpogonium),* which contains the egg protoplast and resembles an oogonium, terminates in a slender outgrowth *(trichogyne).* There are also numerous small antheridia, each of which contains a nonflagellate male cell *(spermatium)* which is borne by water currents to the trichogyne.

After the male cell becomes attached to the trichogyne, its nucleus divides and one of the resulting nuclei fuses with the egg. After the egg is fertilized, numerous short branches develop from it. Each of these branches is terminated by a spore *(carpospore).*

Branches may also develop from cells adjacent to the fertilized egg. The whole mass of branches and carpospores, which superficially resembles a fruiting body, is called a *cystocarp.* When a carpospore becomes free and germinates, a new *Nemalion* plant develops from it.

Reduction division occurs during the formation of the carpospores. The ordinary *Nemalion* plant, therefore, is the gametophyte phase with the monoploid number of chromosomes. The short branches of the cystocarp that developed from the fertilized egg have the diploid number of chromosomes and constitute the sporophyte *(carposporophyte)* phase in the life cycle of *Nemalion.*

Batrachospermum and Lemanea

The fresh-water *Batrachospermum* grows on the rocks in riffles and waterfalls in streams and in the wavedisturbed margins of lakes of the temperate zone. It has whorls of short branches at the nodes of a central axis, all enclosed in a heavy mucilaginous sheath.

The color varies from bluish green to violet. Its life cycle is similar to that of *Nemalion.* Another common relative in rapidly flowing streams is *Lemanea.* The filaments of some species when magnified look like bamboo rods.

The life cycles of these plants are more complicated than that of *Nemalion,* but they are not as complex as those of many other red algae.

CHAPTER 14 Organization and Life Cycle of Algae

As noted in the preceding chapter, the term "Algae" has been abandoned as a formal taxon or category in modern classifications of the plant kingdom. However, the word is still useful in grouping informally the series of algal divisions, which, in spite of marked diversity, have certain attributes in common that distinguish them from other chlorophyllous plants.

It is necessary to cite several technical aspects of the reproduction of algae if we are to delimit them reliably from the other chlorophyllous plants. Algae differ from the latter in that (1) the organisms themselves (as in some unicellular algae) may function directly as sex cells, or *gametes*, and unite in pairs to form *zygotes*; (2) the gametes may be produced within specialized, unicellular *gametangia*; (3) the gametes may develop in multicellular gametangia, every cell of which is fertile (that is, every cell produces a gamete); (4) the spores develop either within unicellular containers called *sporangia* or in multicellular ones in which every cell is fertile.

What of those organisms that are algal in organization but either lack sexual reproduction or have a different method of genetic interchange from those referred to in defining algae? The large group of blue-green algae belongs to this category, and because of their cellular organization, they are by some biologists considered not to be algae but rather bacteria.

However, there remain many other eukaryotic algae, mostly green algae, in which sexuality has not been demonstrated or in which it does not occur. Inasmuch as sexuality may be present in

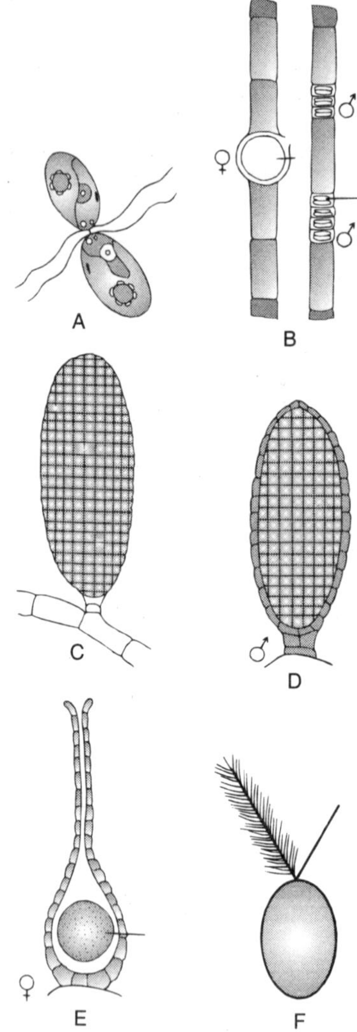

Figure 14.1: Sexual reproduction in algae and nonalgae, diagrammatic. A. Uniting gametes (individual organisms) of a unicellular motile alga. B. Alga with unicellular male (d) and female (Y) sex organs. C. Multicellular sex organ of an alga, every cell of which is fertile. D. Male and, E. female sex organs of nonalgae. F. Whiplash and tinsel flagella, diagrammatic. Note sterile cells; in D and E. e., egg; s., sperm.

some species and absent in other species of a single genus (e.g., *Chlamydomonas*), those that lack it are classified as algae on the basis of their similar morpho-logy. Algal reproduction will be discussed more fully in the chapters that follow.

HABITAT

Algae are largely aquatic in habitat, occurring in waters of a wide range of salinity, in fresh, brackish, and marine waters, and in brines so concentrated that their solutes are crystallizing.

Some algae (certain unicellular types and *Entermorpha*, for example) can tolerate diversified salinities, while others (desmids, *Spirogyra*, and *Oedogonium*, for example) are restricted to fresh waters.

An increasingly large number of algae (especially green algae and diatoms) have been found to be regular inhabitants of the soil surface and considerable depths below it, while many others occur on moist pebbles and rocks, tree bark, woodwork, crushed-stone roofs, and even on rocks that are subject to prolonged desiccation.

Investigation of atmospheric dusts has revealed that these carry a rich algal flora, derived largely, of course, from soil. There is some indication that algae (and other microorganisms) may multiply in clouds. A number of algae, the so-called cryoflora, live on and within long-persistent patches of snow.

Several species live within and among the cells of other plants and animals; special instances of these are described later in this and in other chapters, as are other algae of more bizarre habitats.

Aquatic algae may be attached to rocks, wood, or other aquatic vegetation or may be free-floating. Attached algae in marine habitats often exhibit orderly zonation when their substrates are exposed at low tides.

A number of genera, such as *Porphyra*, *Enteromorpha*, *Fucus*, and *Ascophyllum*, grow in the intertidal zone; they are thus subject to, and able to withstand, periods of desiccation. In contrast, other attached algae, the kelps and *Polysiphonia*, for example, are usually sublittoral.

A vast array of unicellular, colonial, and delicate filamentous algae occur permanently suspended in water, where they may be associated with bacteria, fungi, protozoa, and other minute animals to form a community known as the *plankton* (Gr. *planetis*, wanderer).

Planktonic algae, under unusually favorable conditions, may multiply rapidly and become strikingly abundant as *water blooms*, of which "red tides" are an example.

A variety of algae may be present in blooms, or only a single organism may predominate. Certain blue-green algae and dinoflagellates, when concentrated in blooms, are toxic. Planktonic algae are of tremendous importance as the basis of the food chain for larger animals in aquatic environments.

Thus, it has become routine practice to add commercial fertilizer to tanks and ponds stocked with fish; this enhances the growth of algae, which, in turn, augments the basic food supply for the smaller animals on which the fish feed. Other aspects of the economic importance of algae are discussed in other chapter of this book.

ORGANIZATION OF THE PLANT BODY

As a group, algae are paradoxical in that they include both minute organisms and probably the largest chlorophyllose plants. Thus, certain species of *Chlorella* approach the larger bacteria in size (2-5μm),[2] while the smallest known alga, *Micromonas pusilla*, a golden-brown organism, is 1 × 1.5 μm.

By contrast, certain species of kelp may attain a length of 65m., a length equal to that of larger forest trees. Between 19,000 and 25,000 species of algae are known, and these exemplify a wide range in size and complexity of form. Several types of organization occur. The simplest algae morphologically are unicellular, the cells cohering in groups only temporarily after cell division, after which they separate.

In another series the cells undergo divisions to form incipient tissue complexes. A slightly more complex level of organization is the colonial type, which probably arose through the failure of cells to separate at the conclusion of cell division.

Colonies may be undifferentiated, or they may contain more than one kind of cell, exemplifying differentiation, specialization, and division of labor. Occurrence of cell division predominantly in one direction results in chains of cells called *filaments*. Division of certain cells of a filament in a new direction produces branching.

In a number of algae that are filamentous in their juvenile stages, abundant cell divisions in two or more planes result in a leaflike or membranous structure one or several layers of cells thick, the cells forming *parenchyma* tissue.

Finally, in a large number of green (and a few yellow-green) algae, the plant body is composed of a vesicle, or tube, with few, if any, septations. In these, a large central vacuole is surrounded by a thin layer of multinucleate protoplasm.

These vesicles and tubes may be measured in terms of inches and feet, respectively, and are known as *coenocytes* (Gr. *coenos*, common, + Gr. kystos, bladder; hence, cell). Thus, among algae, five major types of body form have developed: unicellular, colonial, filamentous, membranous, and tubular, or coenocytic.

CLASSIFICATION OF ALGAE

The system of classification of the algae varies with the classifier. Current systems of classifications recognize between four and nine divisions. This variation is occasioned, in part, by the niche assigned to the bluegreen algae.

Although historically and traditionally the blue-green algae have been considered a series of the algae and thus long classified with them, as was done in the first three editions of this book, the overwhelming evidence from electron microscopy and biochemistry now indicates that their affinities are with the bacteria.

Accordingly, the prokaryotic organisms (blue-green "algae" and bacteria) have been classified together in the Superkingdom Prokaryonta and described in other chapter of this book. Recently, Lewin has discovered and described a remarkable organism, *Prochloron didemni*.

This alga is prokaryotic like blue-green algae but, like the green algae, has both chlorophylls a and b and lacks the phycobilin pigments. For this unique organism he has proposed a new division of algae, the Prochlorophyta. Lewin's proposal, however, has met with criticism. Another example of divergent opinion occasioning differences in number of algal divisions is the treatment accorded the stoneworts.

In this text they are classified in a division of their own (Charophyta), but in many others they are included as a special class (Charophyceae) of the green algae.

The divisions of algae have been organized with respect to differences in pigmentation, nature of the stored food reserves, chemical nature of the cell wall, and presence or absence of flagella, and when the latter are present, with respect to their number, length, and site of insertion.

Two basic types of flagella occur in algal (and fungal) cells, the whiplash and the tinsel types. In the latter the flagellar sheath bears one or more rows of appendages.

Table elsewhere in this chapter summarizes the algal divisions, as recognized in this text, and their characteristics.

It should be emphasized that the characteristics ascribed to the several algal divisions have in many cases been extrapolated from results of studies of relatively few genera.

Furthermore, new data are continually being made available regarding the chemistry of algal cell walls, algal pigments, and algal reserve products. Accordingly, as these new data become available, Table elsewhere in this chapter will require modification.

Klein and Cronquist (1967) and Ragan and Chapman (1978) have discussed the evolutionary significance of some of these characteristics. One further point is relevant here.

In a number of books and in an earlier edition of the present one, the combining form *phyco* is not included in the names of the algal divisions-for example, Chlorophyta rather than Chlorophycophyta as in the present text.

Phyco has been incorporated by the writers in accordance with the recommendation of Papenfuss (1946), who noted that use of "*Chlorophyta*"-literally, "green plants"for the green algae was awkward, because it preempted a name that was more appropriate for all chlorophyllose organisms. Of the algal divisions and classes cited in Table elsewhere in this chapter, the major ones are Chlorophycophyta, Phaeophyc-ophyta, and Rhodophyc-ophyta and the Bacillariophyceae of the Chrysophycophyta.

The Chlorophycophyta will be discussed in the remainder of this chapter, while the others form the subject matter in other chapters of this book.

DIVISION CHLOROPHYCOPHYTA

General Features

The division Chlorophycophyta (Gr. *chloros*, green, + Gr. *phykos*, seaweed, hence alga, + Gr. *phyton*, plant), as presented here, includes a single class of algae, the Chlorophyceae (Gr. *chloros* + Gr. *phykos*, seaweed).

The Chlorophycophyta include all plants usually designated as "green algae" with the exception of the stoneworts-Chara, *Nitella*, and related genera-which in this text are grouped in a separate division, the Charophyta.

The green algae are widespread, occurring in both fresh and marine waters, on moist wood and rocks, and on the surface of and within soil.

Many green algae have been recovered from airborne dusts. More than 450 genera and 7500 species of Chlorophycophyta have been described. They are well represented in the plankton and may occur in bodies of water ranging in size from small temporary pools to oceans.

A number of species are epiphytic on other algae, on aquatic flowering plants, and on animals, and still others *(Chlorella*, for example) are endophytic in the cells of certain protozoa, coelenterates, and sponges.

Marine species are frequently attached to rocks, pilings, or larger algae, or grow on the sandy bottoms of quiet estuaries, often on shells. Planktonic species occasionally form water blooms.

The Chlorophycophyta are usually grassgreen during their vegetative stages, except for a few species with tannin-containing, purple vacuolar pigments or orange carotenoid pigments, which mask their green color. The cells contain both chlorophylls a and b as well as α- and β-carotenes and certain xanthophylls.

The predominance of chlorophyll pigments accounts for the typical green color of members of the division. The pigments of the Chlorophycophyta are restricted to cytoplasmic organelles called *chloroplasts*, which are delimited by double membranes. Each chloroplast encloses a number of flattened, saclike *thylakoids* associated in groups of two to six. The chloroplasts exhibit a great range of form, varying from large, urnlike structures to planar or twisted ribbons, to minute, lens-shaped bodies.

As noted earlier, a number of investigators have suggested that chloroplasts originated as symbiotic blue-green algae within originally colorless, eukaryotic cells.

Pyrenoids (Gr. *pyren*, fruit stone) are present in the chloroplasts of most Chlorophycophyta. They may well be centers of formation of the enzyme amylose synthetase, which combines glucose molecules into starch.

Holdsworth has isolated the pyrenoids of *Eremosphaera* and analyzed their protein. Golgi apparatus, mitochondria, and endoplasmic reticulum are present in the cells of Chlorophycophyta and all other plants.

Of all the algae, the Chlorophycophyta are the most like land plants in that their excess carbon compounds are stored within the plastids as starch. The nuclei of Chlorophycophyta are similar in organization to those organisms other than Cyanochloronta and bacteria in having two-layered, perforate nuclear membranes and one or more nucleoli in addition to DNA.

Mitotic nuclear division has been observed in many species. In some, the nuclear membrane remains essentially intact during mitosis, and paired centrioles are present at the apices of the spindles. The nuclei are embedded in colorless cytoplasm and are always centripetal to the chloroplasts.

Cell walls, although absent in a few flagellate green algae, are present in a majority of Chlorophycophyta. Many have somewhat rigid cell walls containing cellulose, and external to this an amorphous, mucilaginous layer.

Cellulose is lacking also from the tubular (siphonous) green algae. Small amounts of silicon may be present *(Pediastrum).* Large central vacuoles occur in the cells of many Chlorophycophyta, and small *contractile vacuoles*, which rid the cells of excess water, are present universally in the motile cells of all freshwater species.

The Chlorophycophyta exhibit a wide range and complexity of structure and reproduction. The details will be discussed in connection with the several illustrative genera.

The latter exemplify five types of organization: (1) motile unicellular and colonial organisms, (2) nonmotile unicellular and colonial organisms, (3) filamentous organisms, (4) membranous organisms, and (5) coenocytic and tubular organisms. The classification of' the illustrative-type organisms is presented on other page of this book.

MOTILE UNICELLULAR AND COLONIAL ORGAISMS

A number of unicellular and colonial green algae are motile throughout their existence by means of flagella. Flagella' are protoplasmic extensions of the cell. In the Chlorophycophyta, the flagella always consist of a sheath surrounding a complex of fibrils.

Electron microscopy has revealed a remarkable uniformity of flagellar organization throughout the plant and animal kingdoms in that the flagellum, in most cases, has been shown to consist of two central fibrils surrounded by nine double ones,' all surrounded by a sheath that is an extension of the cell's plasma membrane.

In having flagella, motile algae resemble certain Protozoa, with which they are sometimes classified. The occurrence of flagellate reproductive cells in the life cycles of many nonmotile algae suggests that the latter may have evolved from motile ancestral precursors. In this connection, two genera, *Chlamydomonas* and *Carteria*, are especially significant.

Unicellular Organisms

Chlamydomonas

Chlamydomonas (Gr. *chlamys*, mantle, + Gr. *moms*, single

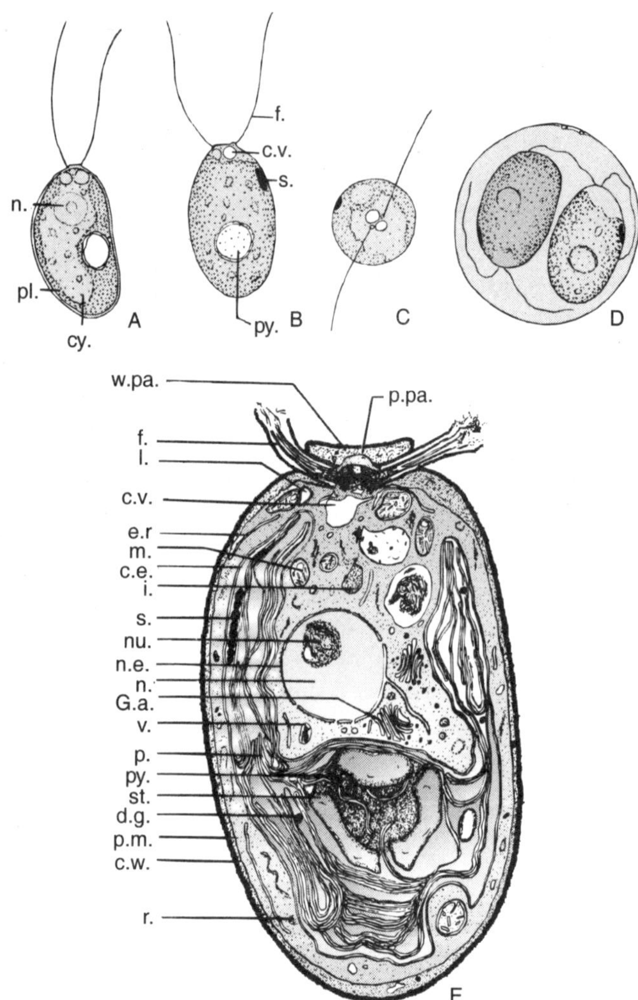

Figure 14.2: Chlamydomonas euganwtos. A-C. Motile individuals. (A. In median optical section. B. In surface view. C. In anterior polar view.) D. Asexual reproduction. E. Diagram of cellular organization as revealed by the electron microscope. ce., chloroplast envelope; c.v., contractile vacuole; c.w., cell wall; cy., cytoplasm; d, g. , dense granule; e, r. , endoplasmic reticulum; f., flagellum; G.a., Golgi apparatus; i., inclusion; 1., lipid body; m., mitochondrion; n., nucleus; n, e. , nuclear envelope; nu., nucleolus; p., plastid; p.pa., plasma papilla; pl., chloroplast; p.m., plasma membrane; py., pyrenoid; r., ribosomes; s., stigma; st., starch; v., vesicle; w, pa. , wall papilla. A-D.

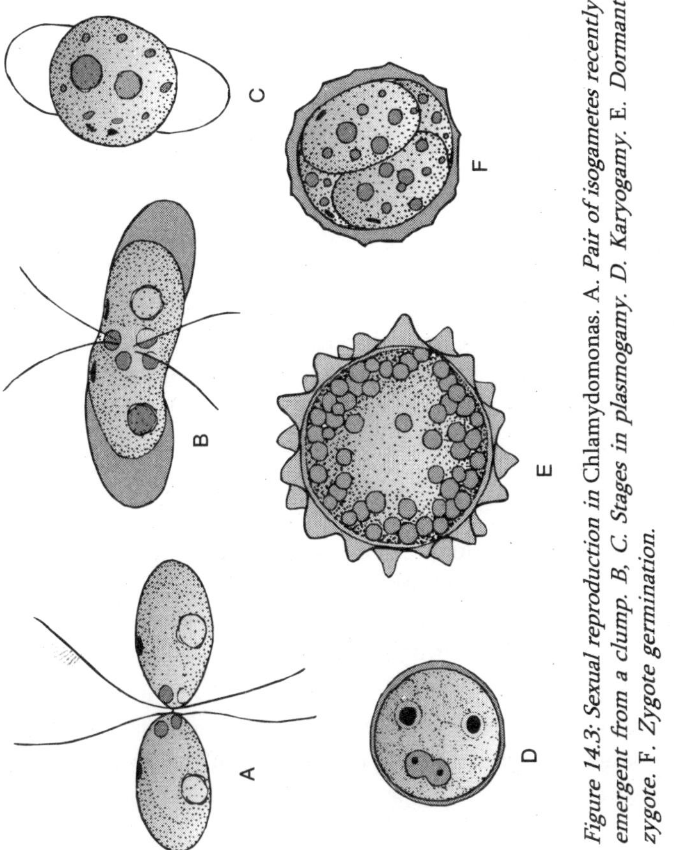

Figure 14.3: Sexual reproduction in Chlamydomonas. A. *Pair of isogametes recently emergent from a clump.* B, C. *Stages in plasmogamy.* D. *Karyogamy.* E. *Dormant zygote.* F. *Zygote germination.*

organism) is widespread in aquatic habitats and soil and has been recovered from airborne dusts. The structure and reproduction of this organism will be described in considerable detail for a number of reasons:

(1) It is readily available in pure cultures for laboratory study;

(2) many of its attributes are shared by other genera of Chlorophycophyta;

(3) the environment can be manipulated so as to evoke asexual or sexual reproduction as one wills;

(4) it is currently the experimental organism in a number of biochemical and genetical investigations.

The cells of most species of *Chlamydomonas* do not exceed 25μm in length. The organisms are surrounded by a wall through which two flagella protrude anteriorly. Motility is effected by the lashing movements of these organelles.

Each cell contains a single massive chloroplast, which may be urn-, cup-band-, or H-shaped or stellate. The chloroplast may contain one or more pyrenoids, as well as a red pigment body often called the *eyespot*, or *stigma* (Gr. *stigma*, mark or brand). With high magnification, one can frequently observe that there is an area of clear cytoplasm subtended by the concave stigma.

It has been suggested that this functions as a primitive lens, and experiments with related organisms containing stigmata indicate that the stigma is indeed a site of light perception. It has been demonstrated that cells of *Chlamydomonas* with stigmata react with greater rapidity to the stimulus of light than those that lack them.

The single nucleus lies in the colorless cytoplasm and often is obscured by teh chloroplast in living cells, but it may be demonstrated by staining. Two or more *contractile vacuoles* are present near the anterior pole of each cell.

There is good evidence that they play a role in the elimination of excess fluids from the cells. Electron microscopy reveals at increased magnification the complexity of the green algal cell as compared with that of prokaryotic cells. Multiplication of the organism is accomplished by cell division involving nuclear and cytoplasmic division.

The process is illustrated in part in figure elsewhere in this chapter. Two or more cellular progeny may arise within a single parent cell by repeated bipartition. The flagella of the parent cell degenerate at the beginning of division.

The young cells emerge, after becoming motile within the parent cell, by the rupture or enzymatic degradation of the parent cell wall. The liberated individuals gradually grow to the size characteristic of the species and then divide again. Under a combination of suitable environmental and protoplasmic conditions, not yet completely understood, certain populations undergo sexual reproduction.

This process is made manifest in many species by the rapid aggregation of a number of individuals in groups, *clumps*, or *clusters*. In *C. moewusii*, the latter arise as the flagella of compatible individuals in crowded cultures become attached at their tips to those of one or more other cells. Careful study reveals that the individuals in a clump become paired because of a chemical attraction between the flagella.

Such pairs are later held together by a delicate protoplasmic thread that connects them at the bases of their flagella; the latter are not entangled, except briefly, after the cells have paired. This connecting strand arises from the union of the plasma papillae of the paired gametes.

As soon as the cells become united by the connecting strand of protoplasm, the paired flagella become free. In *Chlamydomonas moewusii* and in *C. eugametos*, the flagella of only one member of the gametic pair are motile and thus propel the pair in one direction. The cell walls of each member of the pair are ultimately dissolved at the anterior poles, and the protoplasts emerge, gradually uniting to form a single unit; the four flagella gradually shorten and are abscised. Soon after union of the naked protoplasts, a new wall is formed around the fusion product.

The discarded individual cell walls persist for some time in the vicinity of the fusion cell but finally disintegrate. Stained preparations of the uniting cells reveal that the two nuclei, which are thus brought together in one protoplast, unite to form one large nucleus. The chloroplasts also unite subsequently.

Electron and phase-contrast microscopy have provided additional data regarding sexual reproduction in *Chlamydomonas;* in *C. reinhardtii*, a fertilization tube connects the gametes, while none is present in *C. moewusii*. The process just described represents the *sexual reproduction* of *Chlamydomonas*.

It is characterized by the union of two cells, the union of their nuclei, and the association within the fusion nucleus of the chromosome complements (and genes) of the two uniting cells. Each of the uniting cells that undergoes union is called a gamete (Gr. *gamos*, marriage), or sex cell. The product of the sexual union is a zygote (Gr. *zygon*, yoke).

In *Chlamydomonas moewusii* and many other algae, the zygote develops a thick wall, which may be variously ornamented, and undergoes a period of dormancy. It is obvious that the zygote, a product of the union of two cells and their nuclei, will contain in its nucleus two sets of parental chromosomes and the genes they carry.

Whenever this association of two sets of parental chromosomes occurs, there follows inexorably, sooner or later in the life cycle, a phase in which the chromosomes and their genes are redistributed and segregated in different nuclei.

The type of nuclear division that accomplishes this is known as meiosis (Gr. *meiosis*, diminution). Meiosis involves not only a quantitative reduction of the chromosome number by one-half but a qualitative segregation of genes as well. That meiosis has taken place may often be tentatively inferred from the occurrence of two rapidly successive nuclear divisions and cytokineses in which four daughter cells are produced from a single cell.

Cytological and genetical studies of *Chlamydomonas* have demonstrated that meiosis occurs at the time the dormant zygote germinates. Meiosis in this case, therefore, is said to be *zygotic* with reference to its site of occurrence in the life cycle. The germinating zygote of *Chlamydomonas* gives rise to four' motile cells, which are liberated by rupture and/or dissolution of the zygote wall.

These cells are *haploid* as to chromosome constitution, since they have received only a single basic set of chromosomes in meiosis. The zygote itself, having both sets of parental chromosomes before its meiosis, is said to be *diploid*. Accordingly, in the life cycle of *Chlamydomonas*, only the zygote is diploid; all other cells are haploid.

The phenomenon of sexual reproduction is relatively uniform in its essentials at the cellular level in most living organisms. It seems imperative, therefore, to emphasize certain of its significant features.

Cytological investigation has demonstrated that the process usually involves four components:

(1) the union of two cells (gametes) to form a zygote, a

process known as *plasmogamy;*

(2) the union of their nuclei, or the process of karyogamy;

(3) the association of parental chromosomes within the zygote nucleus; and

(4) their segregation in *meiosis.*

Primitive organisms such as *Chlamydomonas* have been receiving intensive study with respect to their sexual reproduction, inasmuch as the process in unicellular organisms is not obscured or complicated by secondary morphological features.

Although the origin of sexual reproduction remains unknown, it is clear that the process is not as indispensable to the maintenance of the species as it is in land plants and in animals, because most unicellular organisms also multiply indefinitely by asexual means.

Figures elsewhere in this chapter illustrate pairs of uniting gametes of *C. eugametos.* In this and other species of sexually reproducing algae, the members of the pair are similar in size' and in other morphological attributes and are, therefore, said to be *isogamous* (Gr. *isos,* equal, + Gr. *gamos,* marriage).

That isogamy is more apparent than real is indicated by three facts, among others. (1) In clonal cultures of isogamous species of *Chlamydomonas,* sexual reproduction may not occur. A *clonal culture* is one in which all the individuals of the population are genetically homogeneous, all being derived from a single cell.

When some clonal cultures are mixed with other appropriate clonal cultures of compatible mating type, sexual reproduction occurs. Such clones are *heterothallic,* that is, selfincompatible: although they are similar in appearance, the gametes are, in fact, different. Extracts of one of such compatible clonal cultures or of their flagella will cause agglutination or clump formation of the opposite mating type.

This is a crude but incontrovertible manifestation of the fact that the isogametes differ chemically. It is evidence, furthermore, that gametic attraction resides, at least in part, in the complementary chemical nature of the flagella.

In *C. eugametos* and in *C. moewusii,* as stated earlier, the flagella of only one pair of gametes beat after their union;

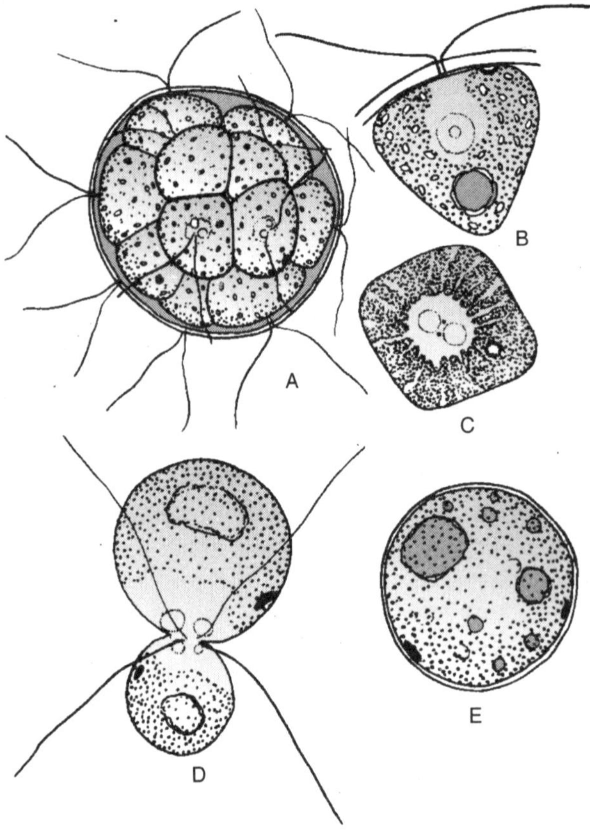

Figure 14.4: Pandorina sp. A. Mature colony, surface view. B. Vegetative cell, median optical longisection. C. Vegetative cell, anterior polar view (flagella omitted). D. Gamete union (isogamy but gametes illustrated of different age). E. Zygote.

accordingly, the gametic pair moves in one direction; this also is a manifestation of difference between the gametes.

In still other species of *Chlamydomonas* and in other algae the uniting gametes are always different in size. This results, in part, from a difference in the number of nuclear divisions and cytokineses in the gamete-producing cells. Such gametes are known as *anisogametes* (Gr. *anisos*, unequal, + Gr. *gamos);* their union is called anisogamy.

Probably on the basis of analogy with sexual reproduction in

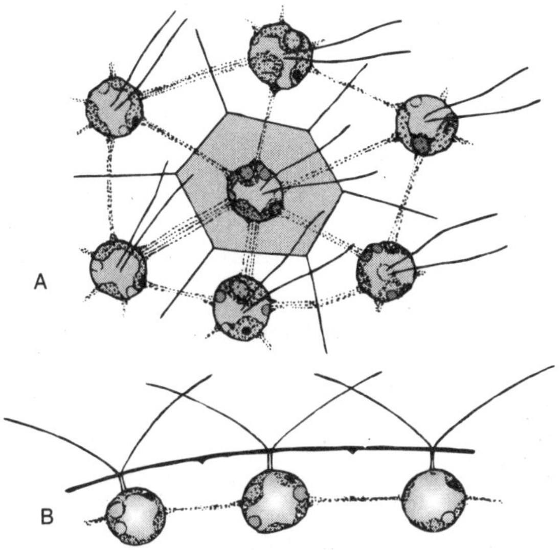

Figure 14.5: Volvox aureus. *Vegetative cells. A. In surface view. B. In vertical section.*

animals, the smaller of the gametes in anisogamy is referred to as male and the larger as female. Finally, in other species of *Chlamydomonas*, and in other algae, the differences in the pairing gametes are more pronounced, one being small and motile and the other large and nonmotile; this condition is called *oogamy* (Gr. *oon*, egg, + Gr. *gamos*), and the smaller gamete is designated the *sperm*, or *antherozoid*, and the larger one, the egg.

Within the single genus *Chlamydomonas*, therefore, there occur among the numerous species isogamy, anisogamy, and oogamy. Reference was made above to the fact that in clonal cultures of certain *Chlamydomonas* species, sexual reproduction would not occur unless the clonal culture were mixed with one of a compatible mating type.

Such species are composed of individuals of two different types, often designated + and –. In other species of *Chlamydomonas*, and in other algae, sexual reproduction does take place within single clonal cultures. This indicates that compatible mating types are present in a single clonal population; the clone, accordingly, is *homothallic*.

In summary, the gametes may be *morphologically* similar, as in isogamy, or differentiated, as in anisogamy and oogamy. In the algae, when compatible gametes occur in a single clone, such a clone is said to be homothallic.

When they occur in separate clones, the condition is called *heterothallism*. When both male and female gametes occur on the same individual, the latter is said to be *monoecious* (or hermaphroditic); if they are on different male and female individuals, the organism is said to be *dioecious*.

The foregoing account of sexuality in *Chlamydomonas* is somewhat protracted and detailed, not only because it is designed to present specific information about a single alga but also because the biological principles and terminology involved are of general application to other groups of plants and animals.

A number of factors affect the sexual process in *Chlamydomonas* (and other algae). Thus, in several species (e.g., *C. eugametos)*, light, adequate CO_2, temperatures below 25°, and depleted nitrogen content of the medium enhance the sexual process.

However, in at least one species, gametic union will occur in darkness if the cells are nitrogen-starved.

Carteria

The genus *Carteria* differs from *Chlamydomonas* in certain ultrastructural details in the wall, chloroplast, pyrenoid, and stigma and in that its cells are quadriflagel late. It is less frequently encountered in nature but occurs in both soil and water.

The structure and asexual and sexual reproduction of *Carteria* are fundamentally similar to those of *Chlamydomonas.* Sexual reproduction in *Carteria* is illustrated in Figure elsewhere in this chapter.

Colonial Organisms

The origin of the colonial type of algal organization probably resides in the tendency for recently divided cells of unicellular organisms to remain associated after cell division. Examples of this are abundantly evident in populations of *Chlamydomonas* and *Carteria*, among others.

Pandorina (mythology, reproduction like the opening of

Pandora's box) and *Volvox (L. volvere,* to roll) are two widely distributed genera that illustrate the motile colonial type of plant body. Both are sometimes present in water blooms.

The individual cells, which are included in a common matrix, show many morphological features reminiscent of *Chlamydomonas,* such as massive chloroplasts, stigmata, and contractile vacuoles.

Multiplication in all these genera is effected by repeated division of cells of the parent colony into miniature daughter colonies, which are liberated ultimately by dissolution of the matrix of the parent colony.

The young colonies increase in cell size, but not in cell number, until the dimensions characteristic of the species have been attained. Such a colony in which the cell number is fixed is called a coenobium.

Pandorina

The mature colonies of *Pandorina* usually consist of 16 cells arranged in an almost solid, ovoidal colony. Each cell is flattened at its anterior pole and narrowed posteriorly. The chloroplast is massive and contains a prominent stigma and basal pyrenoid.

In anterior view, two alternately pulsating contractile vacuoles are visible in the opening of the plastid at the base of the two flagella. The single nucleus lies in the colorless central cytoplasm. Although all the cells of the colony are similar in size, a definite polarity is present, as evidenced by the fact that the stigmata of the more anterior cells are larger than those in the posterior part of the colony.

After attaining the maximum size characteristic of the species, the colonies sink to the bottom of the pond or culture vessel and initiate autocolony formation.

An *autocolony* is a miniature of a parental colony. In autocolony formation, each of the parental cells undergoes repeated nuclear and cytoplasmic division until miniature 16celled colonies are produced. The minute cells of the autocolonies then develop flagella, and the colonies begin to move slowly within the matrix of the parent colony until liberated by its dissolution.

Under certain conditions, colonies of *Pandorina morum* exhibit isogamous sexual reproduction. It has been demonstrated that both homothallic and heterothallic clones of *P. morum* occur in nature. Meiosis is zygotic.

Volvox

Volvox is perhaps the most spectacular of the motile colonial Chlorophyceae, since its slightly ovoidal colonies may contain thousands of cells arranged at the periphery of a matrix.

The plant is readily visible to the unaided eye and has been known for several hundred years. In a number of species of *Volvox*, the protoplasts of the individual cells are connected by delicate protoplasmic extensions.

In ontogeny, the young colonies turn themselves inside out. In *V. aureus*, the cells are entirely similar to one another during the early stages.

However, a dimorphism soon becomes apparent in that certain cells enlarge and become slightly depressed beneath the surface. As the colonies move, it becomes evident that these larger cells lie in the posterior hemisphere.

As in *Pandorina*, the stigmata of the posterior vegetative cells are smaller than those in the anterior hemisphere. The enlarged cells, the gonidia, alone are capable of dividing into daughter colonies; the remaining cells are purely vegetative and disintegrate when the adult colony liberates its daughter colonies.

Sexual reproduction in *Volvox* is oogamous. In some species-for example, *V. rousseletii-the* individual colonies are dioecious; that is, they produce either sperms or eggs.

In other species *(V. globator)* the individual colonies produce both sperm and eggs; that is, they are monoecious. In species such as *V. rousseletii*, special cells enlarge and give rise to gametes as the colonies become sexually mature.

The sperms are borne in compressed spherical packets, each of which may contain as many as 512 male cells. As in *V. aureus*, the intact sperm packets are liberated from the male parent colony and swim to female colonies. There the sperm packets dissolve a hole in the female colony.

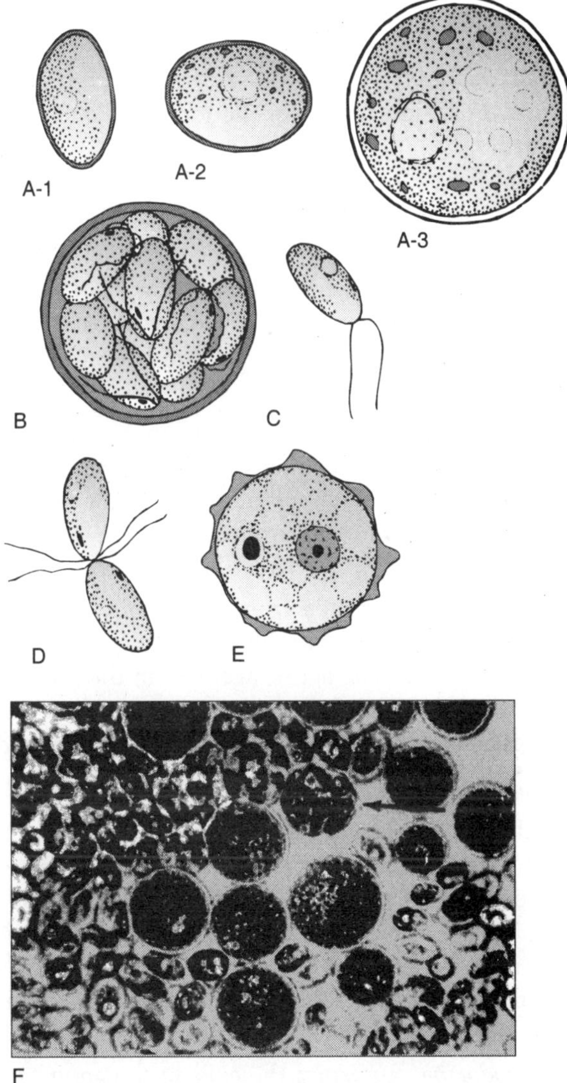

Figure 14.6: Chlorococcum echinozygotum. Increasingly older vegetative cells. B. Zoospore formation. C. Zoospore. D. Isogamy. E. Dormant zygote (stained). F. Photograph of portion of a population: note vegetative cells of various ages and zoosporangium.

The many bifiagellate sperm cells dissociate and penetrate to the vicinity of the eggs so that *fertilization* (oogamous gametic union) takes place within the female colony. The zygotes develop thick walls and undergo a period of dormancy, during which they are set free by disintegration of the female colony in which they are formed.

Darden (1966, 1970), Kochert (1968, 1975), McCracken and Starr (1970), Starr (1969, 1971), and Starr and Jaenicke (1974) have been investigating the control of sexual reproduction in various species of *Volvox*. In a population of *V. aureus*, Darden *(1966)* found that the gonidia of young asexual colonies may function as eggs and may be fertilized by sperm to form smooth-walled zygotes.

Furthermore, Darden demonstrated in *V. aureus* that filtrates from cultures with male colonies would induce the formation of male colonies in other populations in which asexual colonies would otherwise have been formed.

In *V. carteri*, Kochert *(1968)* and Starr *(1969)* have shown that an inducing substance from male populations evokes the formation of male colonies in the male strain and female colonies in the female strain. The active agent from the male populations is glycoprotein, and in the strain studied by Starr and Jaenicke (1974) it is 100% effective at concentrations less than 3×10^{-15}M.

Other Colonial Organisms

In addition to *Pandorina* and *Volvox*, there are other types of motile coenobia that vary in form and arrangement of the cells in the coenobia. Thus, in *Gonium* the organism is a slightly curved, platelike colony. In *Eudorina*, *Pleodorina*, and *Platydorina* the cells are arranged in alternating superficial rings within the colonial matrix, but in *Platydorina* the spherical colony becomes flattened (luring ontogeny.

In *Pleodorina californica* the cells in the anterior half of the coenobium are smaller than those in the posterior half, and only the latter are usually capable of functioning as gonidia. In sexual reproduction, *Gonium is* isogamous, while *Platydorina*, *Eudorina*, and *Pleodorina* are anisogamous. All apparently undergo zygotic meiosis.

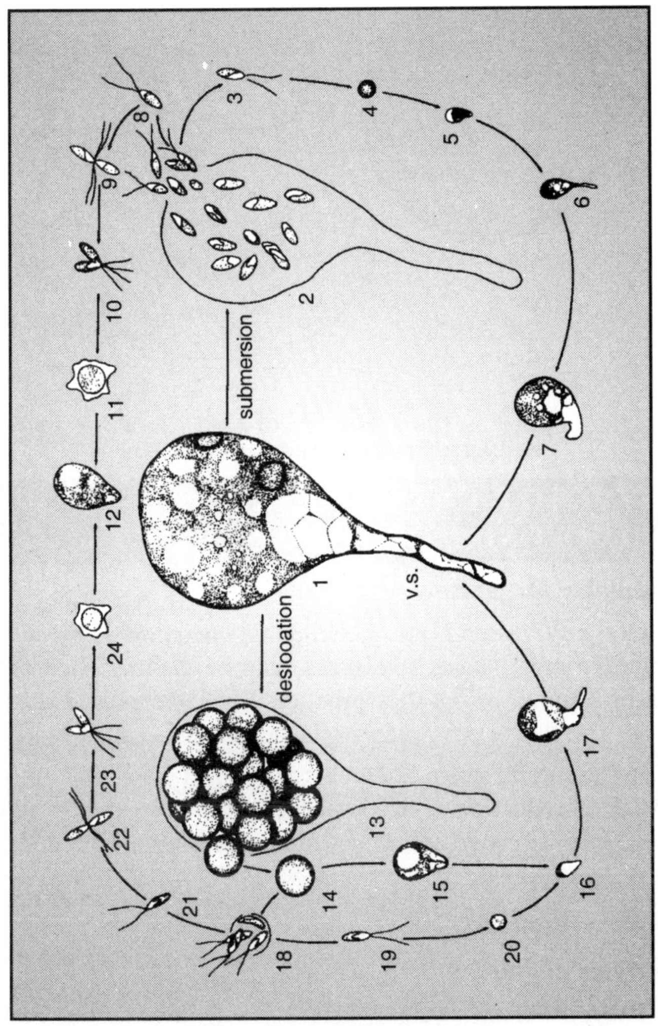

Figure 14.7: The life cycle of Protosiphon botryoides 1. Vegetative cell or sac. 2. Zoospore/gamete formation and release. 3-7. Stages in asexual development of sacs from zoospores. 8-12. Sexual cycle including gamete union (9, 10). 11, 12. Zygote and its germination. 13. Coenocyst formation. 14-17. Direct development of coenocysts into vegetative sac. 18-20. Asexual cycle of zoospores formed by coenocysts. 18-24. Sexual cycle of gametes from coenocysts. v, s., vegetative sac.

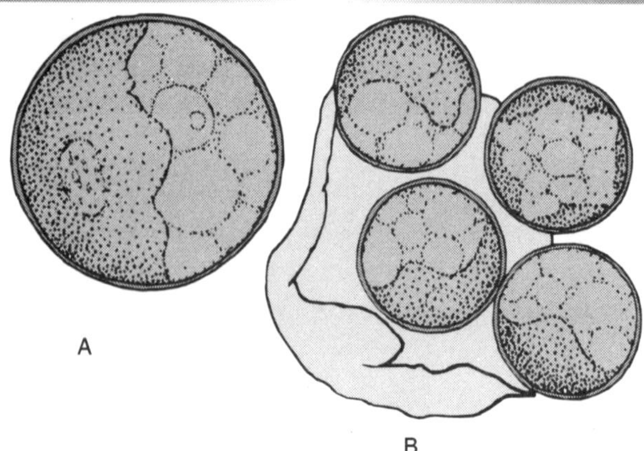

Figure 14.8: Chlorella sp.
A. Vegetative cell. B. Autospore liberation.

NONMOTILE UNICELLULAR AND COLONIAL ORGANISMS

Unicellular Organisms

Of the vast assemblage of commonly encountered unicellular, nonmotile green algae, two series may be distinguished on the basis of whether or not they produce flagellated cells in their life cycles. The first series produces flagellated cells called *zoospores.*

In the second series, zoospores are not produced, but, instead, asexual reproduction is accomplished by autospores or autocolonies. In this second series, flagellated gametes are produced by a very few species.

Zoospore Producers

Tetracystis

The soil-inhabiting alga *Tetracystis* is significant in its combination of seemingly primitive and advanced" attributes. *Tetracystis* produces biflagellate zoospores; the structure of the latter corresponds in all respects to that of *Chlamydomonas.*

After motility, the zoospores lose their flagella, and the cells enlarge and sooner or later become partitioned so that two or four nonmotile daughter cells are formed.

This cell partitioning is similar to that in multicellular plants in that the parental cell walls persist after the daughter cell walls have formed. The component cells of the tetrads enlarge and may again divide into tetrads, and this process may continue, thus giving rise to tissuelike complexes of cells.

We see in this unicellular green alga, accordingly, the potentiality of forming parenchymatous" aggregations of cells such as occur in membranous green algae and in the nonalgal groups of chlorophyllous plants. Incipient tissue formation was a highly significant evolutionary modification. These cellular complexes of *Tetracystis* may dissociate into smaller cell clusters or even to the unicellular level by degradation and/or splitting of old cell walls.

The individual cells of the complex may form zoospores either before or after dissociation. In some species of *Tetracystis*, the zoo-spores may function as isogamous gametes that unite to form zygotes. This occurs in many algae.

Whether we consider such zoospores to be facultative gametes or to be gametes that may develop parthenogenetically if they fail to unite with another gamete seems immaterial. Sexuality in many algae such as *Tetracystis* seems to be incipient or sporadic rather than obligate.

Chlorococcum

Chlorococcum (Gr. *chloros*, green, + Gr. *kokkos*, berry) also is an inhabitant of fresh water and soils (both undisturbed and cultivated). Thirty-six species are known and available in culture."

Chlorococcum is difficult to distinguish from other nonmotile, spherical unicellular Chlorophycophyta, unless one cultivates it in unialgal cultures. The mature cells of *Chlorococcum* are spherical, unless they have become polyhedral by mutual compression.

Each has a cell wall and a protoplast containing a hollow, spherical chloroplast, usually with one aperture. One or more pyrenoids are embedded in the chloroplast, opposite the aperture. Division of one cell into two or four nonmotile daughter cells, as in *Tetracystis*, is absent in *Chlorococcum*.

Instead, the vegetative cells divide and form a number of biflagellate zoospores, which, again, are almost identical with cells of *Chlamydomonas.* A nonmotile cell that produces zoospores is called a *zoosporangium.*

After a period of motility, the duration of which is affected by such environmental factors as light intensity, temperature, and composition and concentration of the culture medium, the zoospores aggregate in the most brightly illuminated portion of the culture vessel, lose their flagella, and grow into new vegetative cells.

Movements by organisms to or away from stimuli are *taxes;* the movement of the zoospores of *Chlorococcum* in the present instance exemplifies *positive phototaxis.* When the zoospores settle, the stigma disappears, but in some species the contractile vacuoles persist.

Under certain conditions, potential zoospores are not freed from the parental cells but develop within directly into young,

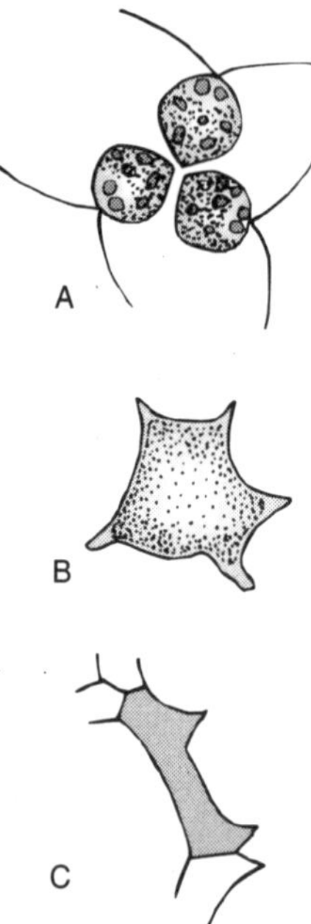

Figure 14.9: Hydrodictyon reticulatum. A. Motile zoospores. B. Polyeder. C. Marginal cell of juvenile net; note Pediastrum-like protuberances. A, C.

nonmotile vegetative cells, or *aplanospores*. The latter rupture the parental wall as they grow and thus are freed.

In *Chlorococcum*, *Tetracystis*, and other algae, production of zoospores by nonmotile vegetative cells is interpreted as a reversion to a primitively motile condition. This could be cited as an example of the biogenetic law that states that ontogeny recapitulates phylogeny.

In some species of *Chlorococcum-C. echinozygotum*, for example-the zoospores may function as isogametes and unite to form spiny-walled dormant zygotes. These give rise upon

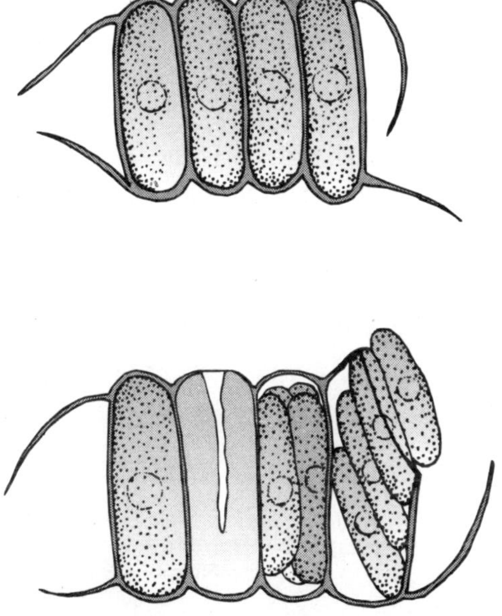

Figure 14.10: Scenedesmus sp. A. Immature vegetative colony. B. Autocolony formation and liberation. C. Coenobia from unialgal culture.

germination to four zoospores, which, upon liberation, develop into vegetative cells. Meiosis is thought to be zygotic.

The capacity of the motile cells of *Chlamydomonas*, *Tetracystis*, and *Chlorococcum* to function either sexually or asexually suggests a primitive grade of development, perhaps incipient sexuality, in contrast to those algae in which gametes and zoospores differ morphologically.

Protosiphon

Protosiphon botryoides, a widespread soil alga, is included here because of its interesting morphology and life cycle and the marked modifications thereof evoked by environmental stimuli. *Protosiphon is* a terrestrial alga of cultivated soils (where it often grows intermingled with *Botrydium*).

After rain, it forms dark-green patches, which become orangered as the soil dries. The mature plants are saclike, with a single basal, rhizoidal protuberance that penetrates the substrate. The upper, bulblike portion contains alveolar cytoplasm with a diffuse chloroplast containing many pyrenoids; the sacs are multinucleate (coenocytic) and, when adequate nitrogen is available, may exceed 1 mm in length.

When it rains, or when agar cultures are submerged, the sacs form numerous biflagellate zoospores, which, here again, may function as gametes. These zoospores, as in *Tetracystis* and *Chlorococcum*, may be transformed into aplanospores if the moisture level falls.

On the other hand, sacs on drying soil or agar become

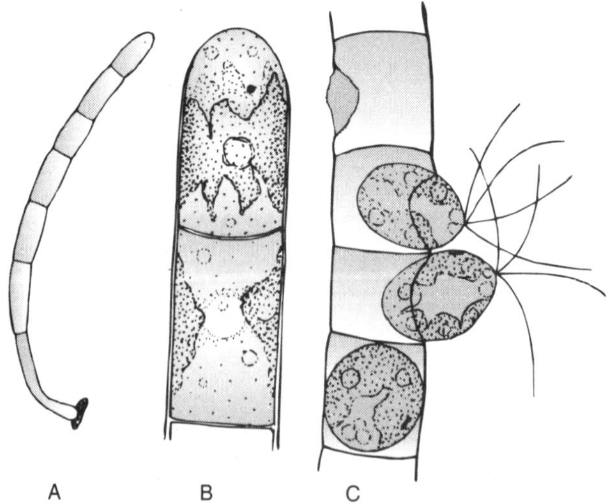

Figure 14.11: Ulothrix fimbriata. A. Young plant attached to particle of debris by a holdfast. B. Cellular organization at apex of filament; apical cell, three-dimensional, second cell in optical section. C. Zoospore formation.

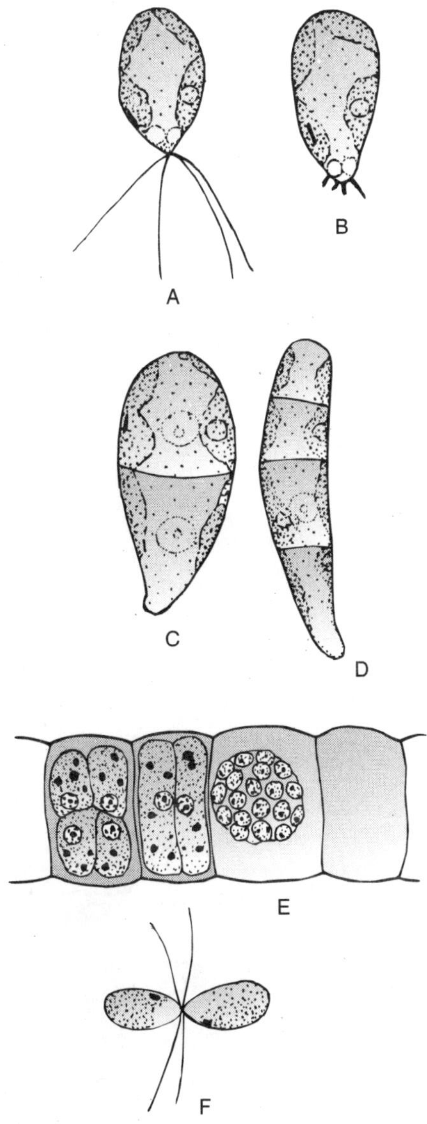

Figure 14.12: Ulothrix. A-D. Development of zoospores of U. fimbriata into a young plant. E, F. U. zonata. E. Gametogenesis. F. Isogamy.

subdivided into a small number of large, multinucleate cells called *coenocysts.* The walls of these thicken as the moisture level falls, and the chlorophyll is replaced or masked by an orange-red carotenoid pigment, the chemical nature of which has not been determined.

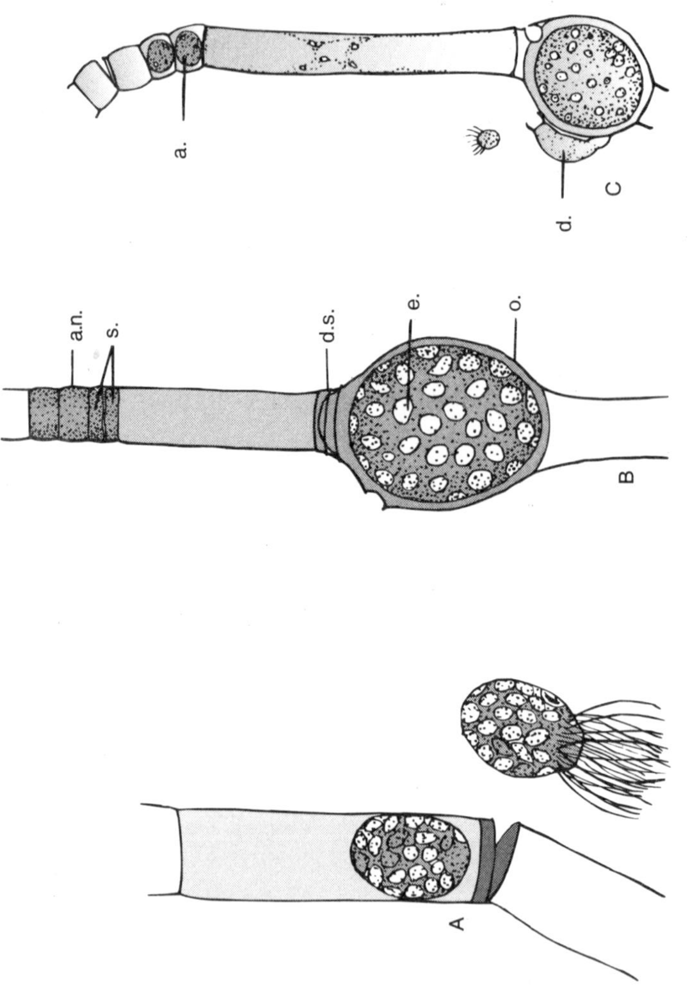

Figure 14.13: Oedogonium intermedium. A. Oe. cardiacum, zoospore formation and single, free-swimming zoospore. B. Oe. foveolatum, a bisexual species; C. Oedogonium sp., a gynandrosporous form.

The coenocysts (and thick-walled zygotes) retain their viability during long periods of desiccation. When moisture again becomes available, they may become green and develop directly into new sacs, or the coenocysts may form zoospores or gametes. The complicated life cycle, as it is determined by availability of moisture, is summarized in figure elsewhere in this chapter.

Azoosporic Organisms

Chlorella

Chlorella (Gr. *chloros*, green, + *L. ella*, dimunitive) is widespread in fresh and salt water and also in soil. It appears often with surprising rapidity in laboratory vessels in which distilled water or inorganic salt solutions are stored. Like *Chlorococcum*, *Chlorella is* most successfully studied in unialgal cultures.

Chlorella was the first alga to be isolated and grown in axenic culture; this was accomplished in 1890 by the Dutch microbiologist Beijerinck. The cells of most species of *Chlorella* are minute green spheres in which the details of cell structure are seen best under high magnification.

The protoplast is composed of a cuplike chloroplast, which may or may not contain a pyrenoid, and of colorless central cytoplasm in which the minute nucleus is embedded. A series of bipartitions may occur, forming four or eight protoplasts endogenously.

These develop delicate cell walls, and after they have begun to enlarge, they are liberated by rupture of the mother cell wall. Such asexual reproductive cells, which have no capacity for motility, are known as *autospores*, because they resemble, in miniature, the mother cells that produce them.

Sexual reproduction has not been observed in *Chlorella*. A number of species of *Chlorella* have been grown in pure culture and have provided the material for experimental studies of photosynthesis.

Eremosphaera (Gr. *eremos*, solitary, + Gr. *sphaira*, ball) is one of the largest and most spectacular unicellular green algae known.

It occurs on the bottoms of swamps and quiet ponds in which the water is at least slightly acid. It grows readily in laboratory culture. The individual cells of *E. viridis* are large enough to be visible to the unaided eye.

Each contains many small, pyrenoid-bearing chloroplasts and a prominent, central nucleus suspended by threads of streaming colorless cytoplasm.

Reproduction is by the division of the parent cell into two, four, or eight (rarely) nonmotile daughter cells (autospores) or by union of biflagellate, almost colorless sperms and autosporelike cells that function as eggs.

Colonial Types

The nonmotile colonial Chlorophycophyta parallel the nonmotile unicellular forms in that two series of genera are known. In one, represented here by *Pediastrum* and *Hydrodictyon*, flagellate

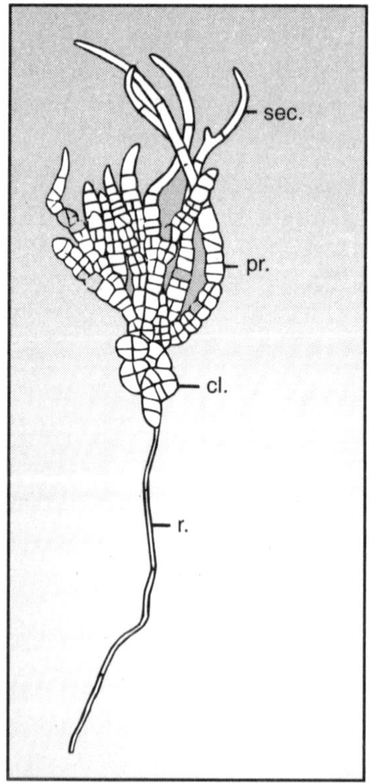

Figure 14.14: Fritschiella tuberosa. Small, but mature, plant.

reproductive cells (zoospores and/or gametes) occur, while in the other, illustrated here by *Scenedesmus* and *Coelastrum*, motile cells are *usually* absent.

Zoospore Producers

Pediastrum and Hydrodictyon

The coenobic colonies of *Pediastrum* (Gr. *pedion*, plane, + Gr. *astron*, star) grow on the bottoms of quiet pools and lakes as well as in their plankton and may readily be grown in laboratory culture. The coenobia of *Pediastrum* are flat plates.

Pediastrum reproduces by zoospores, which form daughter colonies within a vesicle released from the parent cell. It also undergoes isogamous sexual reproduction. *Hydrodictyon reticulatum* (Gr. *hydor*, water, + Gr. *dictyon*, net), commonly known as the "water net," often appears in great abundance in pools, lakes, and quiet streams.

The mature colonies are composed of large cylindrical cells joined together in polygonal configurations, the whole colony being cylindrical. The young cells are uninucleate and delicate green. They ultimately enlarge many times and develop numerous nuclei and large central vacuoles, which force the cytoplasm into a peripheral position.

In asexual reproduction, studied electronmicroscopically by Marchant and PickettHeaps (1970, 1971, 1972) and Hawkins and Leedale (1971), the mature cells cleave into smaller and smaller portions until uninucleate segments result. Each of these functions as a zoospore.

As motility abates, the zoospores are arranged in groups of four to nine, typically six, within the cylindrical parent cell, which serves as a mold for the young net of the next generation. After the flagella have disappeared, the cells begin to enlarge and assume a cylindrical form.

By continuous increase in cell size and rupture of the parent wall, nets more than 75cm in length may develop under uncrowded conditions. Sexual reproduction is isogamous. Unlike the zoospores, which they resemble morphologically, the gametes are liberated from the parent cells.

Meiosis is zygotic, and the germinating zygotes develop four zoospores, which grow into nonmotile, polyhedral cells known as *polyeders.* These enlarge, undergo cleavage and zoosporogenesis, and liberate a number of actively swimming zoospores within a gelatinous vesicle. These zoospores arrange themselves as a hollow sphere (which may be flattened), or as a flat plate, lose their flagella, and grow into cylindrical cells typical

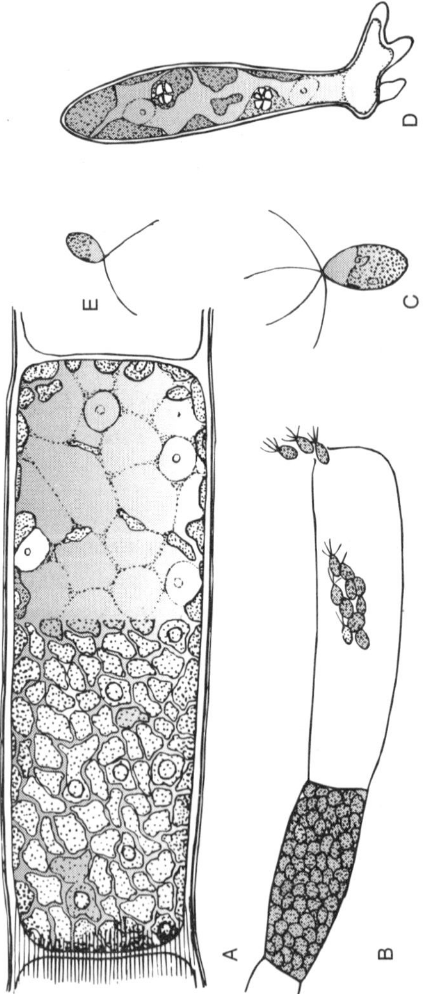

Figure 14.15: Cladophora. A. Cellular organization; surface view at s., median optical section at m.o.s. B. Zoospore formation and liberation in a marine species. C. Zoospore. D. Germling from zoospore.

of the adult plant. This juvenile colony is not cylindrical as in the adult, although its component cells are cylindrical.

Of great interest is the fact that its marginal cells may each bear two *Pediastrum-like* protuberances. These phenomena often are interpreted as evidence of a common ancestry for *Hydrodictyon* and *Pediastrum*.

In this connection, it is of interest that two other species of *Hydrodictyon* have adult colonies that are flattened rather than cylindrical, probably because they lack asexual reproduction.

Azoosporic Organisms

Scenedesmus

With respect to zoospores, *Scenedesmus* stands in relation to *Pediastrum* and *Hydrodictyon* as *Eremosphaera* and *Chlorella* do to *Chlorococcum*. As in *Chlorella*, zoospores are not produced in *Scenedesmus*. This coenobic alga is ubiquitous, occurring abundantly in almost every freshwater habitat and occasionally in soil.

It consists of a colony comprising four or more elongate cells united laterally. In some species the terminal cells have spinelike processes.

The uninucleate cells have a parietal chloroplast containing a single pyrenoid. Reproduction, which in many species is entirely asexual, is by the formation of *autocolonies* within each cell of the adult.

These are liberated by the rupture of the parent cell wall and then gradually achieve the size and ornamentation characteristic of the species. It has been demonstrated that isogamous sexual reproduction occurs under certain conditions in *S. obliquus*.

Clonal cultures are heterothallic, and the two compatible mating types must be mixed before clump formation and gamete union occur.

The zygotes enlarge and later germinate to form 40 or more cells. When these are taken into clonal culture, the clones are unisexual; this is genetic evidence of zygotic meiosis.

In light of these observations, it has been suggested that *S. obliquus* and other species that produce motile cells should be classified with coenobic algae such as *Hydrodictyon* and *Pediastrum*.

Coelastrum

The coenobia of *Coelastrum* (Gr. *kollos*, hollow, + Gr. *astron*, star) are hollow spheres of up to 128 cells, the latter contiguous or united by protuberances of the wall. The sole method of reproduction is by autocolony formation, in which the individual cells divide into miniature colonies, which are liberated by the breaking of the parent cell wall.

FILAMENTOUS ORGANISMS

Restriction of cell division to one direction and coherence of the daughter cells result in filamentous organisms among the green algae; division of certain cells in the filament in a plane at 90° or less, with reference to the prevailing direction, initiates branching.

The genera to be discussed in this section may be grouped into two categories according to the criterion of whether or not they produce flagellate cells or zoospores.

Zoospore Producers

The illustrative genera in this group include both unbranched *(Ulothrix* and *Oedogonium)* and branched *(Stigeoclonium* and *Cladophora)* plants.

Ulothrix

The unbranched filaments of *Ulothrix* grow attached to stones and other submerged objects in cold-water streams and lakes; several species are marine. In *Ulothrix* (Gr. *oulos*, woolly, + Gr. *thrix*, hair), the cells of each filament are similar to one another except that the basal cell is modified as an attaching structure, the *holdfast*.

The cells contain partial or complete band-shaped chloroplasts with more than one pyrenoid and are uninucleate. Cytokinesis is by cell-plate formation in some species, as in *Fritschiella*, liverworts, hornworts, mosses, and vascular plants.

In most other algae, cytokinesis is accomplished by furrowing or constriction of the cytoplasm. After a period of vegetative growth by cell division and elongation, asexual reproduction by zoospores may occur. Zoospores may be produced singly or in multiples of two from each vegetative cell.

The liberated zoospores exhibit the usual attributes of motile cells, such as stigmata, contractile vacuoles, and four flagella, in which respect they resemble *Carteria*. After a period of activity, the zoospores settle on submerged objects with their flagellate poles foremost, lose their flagella, and attach themselves.

Elongation and division of the original zoospore produce a vegetative filament. Sexual reproduction by a union of biflagellate isogametes also occurs. There is evidence that the sexual filaments are heterothallic in some species.

Meiosis, as in all other genera considered so far, occurs just prior to germination of the zygote. The latter gives rise to four zoospores, each of which grows into a new filament.

Oedogonium

Oedogonium (Gr. *oedos*, swelling, + Gr. *gonos*, reproductive structure) differs from *Ulothrix* in that its zoospores possess a crown of about 120 flagella. Furthermore, although the quadriflagellate and biflagellate cells of nonmotile algae suggest, respectively, the unicellular motile genera, *Carteria* and *Chlamydomonas*, no multiflagellate unicellular genus corresponding to the motile cells of *Oedogonium* is known.

Because of its multiflagellate motile cells, *Oedogonium* and its relatives are sometimes grouped in a distinct class of green algae. However, both biflagellate and multiflagellate motile cells may be produced in the life cycle of another green alga *(Derbesia)*; there thus seems to be no reason to create a special class.

Oedogonium grows frequently as an epiphyte on other algae and aquatic angiosperms. It may also be attached to stones or freefloating. Growth is intercalary and localized in certain cells, on which annular scars indicate the number of cell divisions that have occurred.

The cells contain segmented, netlike chloroplasts with pyrenoids. The life cycle of *Oedogonium* is like that of *Ulothrix*. Asexual reproduction is effected by the formation and liberation of single zoospores from vegetative cells. Pickett-Heaps (1971, 1972) has described zoosporog-enesis on the basis of electron microscopy. Sexual reproduction in *Oedogonium is* oogamous. The egg is produced in an enlarged gametangium, the *oogonium*, which opens by a pore or fissure just before fertilization.

The sperms arise in pairs in short, boxlike cells, the *antheridia*. The sperms also are multiflagellate. After fertilization, the zygote develops a wall composed of two or more layers, often becomes reddish, and enters a period of dormancy.

It is liberated by the disintegration of the oogonial wall. The germination of the zygote into four zoospores is preceded by meiosis. Considerable variation occurs among the numerous species of *Oedogonium* with respect to the location of the sex organs.

Both antheridia and oogonia may occur on the same filament, in which case, of course, the species is monoecious. In species with unisexual filaments, a plant that develops from a single zoospore produces either antheridia or oogonia, never both.

The male filaments may be slightly narrower than the female but are almost the same diameter, that is, *macrandrous*. It has been demonstrated that in species with unisexual filaments, the mature oogonia produce a substance that chemically attracts free-swimming sperm; this substance is an example of an *erotactin*, a substance that attracts sperm.

In a number of *nannandrous Oedogonium* species, the male filaments are epiphytic, dwarf filaments; they develop from special *androspores* that attach themselves to the cell, which divides to form the oogonium and its supporting cell. The flagellate androspores are attracted to this site by a substance, also an erotactin, secreted by the oogonial mother cell.

The androspores may arise in the female filament *(gynandrospory)* as in a special, androspore-forming filament *(idioandrospory)*. The direction of growth of the dwarf males, in turn, is determined by a hormone from the oogonium and its supporting cell only after the dwarf males probably produce a chemical that evokes division of the oogonial mother cell.

Stigeoclonium

Occasional cell division in a second direction produces a branching filamentous plant body in *Stigeoclonium* and *Cladop-*

hora. Stigeoclonium (L. stigens, sharp, + *L. clonium*, branch) is a plant widely distributed in lakes and streams, where it grows attached to stones and vegetation.

In most species the plant consists of two portions: a prostrate, and probably perennial, system of irregularly branched filaments or a disc is attached to the substratum; from one or another of these prostrate phases, elongate branching filaments grow out into the water.

These are attenuated and may end in hairlike branches. Because they have two branch systems, the plants are said to be *heterotrichous*. The cells of *Stigeclonium* are uninucleate and contain single chloroplasts with one or several pyrenoids.

In asexual reproduction, quadriflagellate zoospores are liberated singly from the cells of the plant body. After a period of activity, these become attached to the substratum by the formerly flagellate pole, secrete a wall, and develop into new plant bodies.

Union of biflagellate gametes has been described for some species; in others the gametes are reported to be quadriflagellate. The life cycle of *Stigeoclonium* has not been satisfactorily elucidated.

Apparently, meiosis is zygotic in most species. As in *Ulothrix*, the zygote germinates to form four zoospores, which ultimately grow into new plants.

Fritschiella

A rather remarkable alga, *Fritschiella tuberosa*, somewhat like *Stigeoclonium* and originally described from several locations in India, occurs on moist soil in several places in the United States.

The branching, filamentous plants consist of subterranean rhizoids, a prostrate system at, or just beneath, the soil surface, and erect branches of two orders; they are thus more differentiated than other green algae.

The life cycle is probably the D, h + d type; quadriflagellate zoospores are produced on some plants and biflagellate gametes on others. The zygotes develop without dormancy directly into new plants. The subter ranean rhizoids, prostrate system, and erect branches suggest the organization of land plants, as does the parenchymatous construction, but the reproduction is clearly algal. Of special significance is the fact that cytokinesis in *Fritschiella* is by centrifugal cell-plate formation, as in land plants, rather than by furrowing, as in most other green algae.

Cladophora

Cladophora (Gr. *klados*, branch, + Gr. *phoros*, bearer) differs from *Stigeoclonium* in a number of respects, including larger size, multinucleate cells, and, especially, life cycle. Species of *Cladophora* are widespread in both fresh and marine waters, where they may be free-floating or attached to rocks or vegetation.

The plants often are anchored to the substratum by rhizoidal branches. The latter are perennial and persist through adverse conditions. Growth of the branching filaments is localized near the apices of the filaments, in contrast with the generalized growth of *Ulothrix* and the intercalary growth of *Oedogonium*.

In many species the branches arise as eversions from the upper portions of the lateral walls of relatively young cells. When they have achieved a certain length, they are delimited from the parent cell by an annular ingrowth of the wall.

The cylindrical cells of *Cladophora* are much larger than those of *Stigeoclonium*, and their cell walls are thicker and stratified. The structure of the chloroplast varies with the age of the cell. In younger cells it is a continuous network, but in older ones it is largely peripheral and composed of irregular segments, in some of which pyrenoids are embedded.

Segments of the chloroplast may extend toward the center of the cell. Frothy cytoplasm, with numerous nuclei suspended in its meshes, fills the center of the cell. Mitosis and cytokinesis are entirely independent processes in *Cladophora*, in contrast with their rather close relationship in most plants and animals with uninucleate cells.

Asexual reproduction is accomplished by uninucleate, quadriflagellate zoospores. These arise by the cleavage of the protoplasts of terminal and nearterminal cells into uninucleate segments.

Each segment develops four flagella, and the mature zoospores are liberated through a pore in the zoosporangial wall. After a

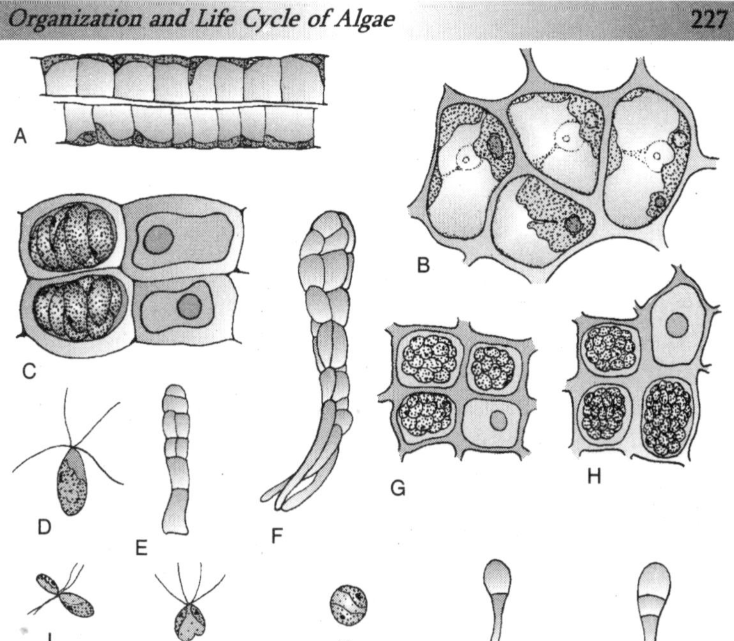

Figure 14.16: Ova lactuca. A. Transection of plant. B. Cellular organization. C. Zoosporogenesis; note liberation pores for zoospores. D. Zoospore. E, F. Germling from zoospores. G. Female gametangia and gametes. H. Male gametangia and gametes. I-K. Stages in anisogamous gamete union. L, M. Germlings from zygote. A, E, F, L, M.

period of motility, the zoospores grow into new plants. The young germlings are uninucleate, but the *coenocytic* (multinu-cleate) condition is soon initiated by continuation of mitosis without ensuing cytokinesis.

Cladophora plants also produce biflagellate isogametes in sexual reproduction. These also are formed in the terminal and near-terminal cells.

The zygotes germinate without a period of dormancy and grow directly into new plants. Cytological studies of plants in nature and in culture indicate that a somewhat complicated cycle occurs in *Cladophora*. In *C. suhriana* and other marine species, it has been shown that two types of plant occur in nature.

These are morphologically indistinguishable but differ in chromosome complement and the nature of their reproductive cells. One type of plant is diploid and produces only zoospores from cells in which meiosis precedes the cleavage into zoospores.

The latter, accordingly, are haploid and develop into haploid plants, morphologically similar to the diploid ones. However, the haploid plants, which are probably heterothallic, produce only biflagellate gametes at maturity. The gametes unite in pairs to form zygotes, which develop without meiosis into diploid filaments.

Meiosis in *Cladophora*, therefore, is sporic-rather than zygotic as in all the other green algae discussed so far. Two final points regarding the life cycle of *Cladophora* are relevant. (1) Gametes that fail to unite with other gametes under suitable environmental conditions develop asexually into new haploid, gametophytic plants of the same type as those that produced the gametes. This

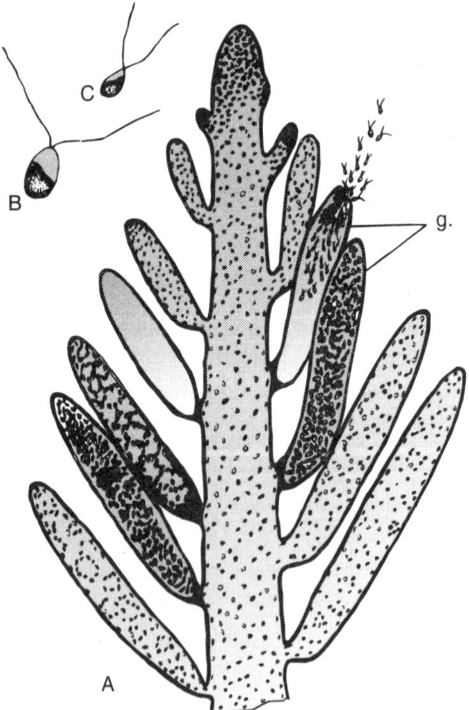

Figure 14.17: Bryopsis corticulans. A. Shoot with gametangia (g.). B, C. Anisogamous gametes.

is an example of *parthenogenesis*, development of a gamete into a new organism without sexual union. (2) Although *Chlamydomonas* and *Carteria* are classified as being different solely on the criterion of having two and four flagella, respectively, both quadriflagellate and biflagellate motile cells occur in *Cladophora*. This is an example of the subjective nature of many schemes of biological classification.

Organisms such as *Cladophora* with two distinct, free-living plants in the life cycle are *diplobiontic* (Gr. *diploos*, double, + Gr. *bion*, living); *Cladophora*, therefore, is diplobiontic. Other genera, in which only one free-living organism occurs in the life cycle, are *haplobiontic* (Gr. *haploos*, single, + Gr. *bion)*, as are all the green algae discussed prior to *Cladophora*.

Diplobiontic life cycles are but one manifestation of the larger phenomenon of *alternation of generations*. They are a specialized example of the latter in which the alternates are freeliving individuals. In contrast, alternation of generations of another type, in which the alternates are physically connected, occurs in the liverworts, mosses, and some vascular plants.

Haplobiontic life cycles may be thought of as exhibiting only alternation of nuclear (haploid and diploid) phases, one alternate, either the zygote or the gametes, consisting merely of a single cell and not of a free-living plant. This condition occurs in *Chlamydo-monas* and *Ulothrix*, among others.

In these genera the entire life cycle consists of haploid individuals, with the exception of the diploid zygotes. It should be noted that the terms "haploid" and "diploid" are used with reference to chromosome constitution. Haploid organisms contain a single basic complement of chromosomes in their nuclei; diploid individuals have nuclei with two such sets.

Quite the reverse type of haplobiontic life cycle is present in coenocytic green algae such as *Codium* and *Caulerpa*. In these the diploid plant body is dominant, and the haploid phase is represented only by the gametes.

Diplobiontic life cycles often are said to exhibit *alternation of morphological generations* (as well as cytological), since in this type both the diploid and haploid phases occur as morphologically

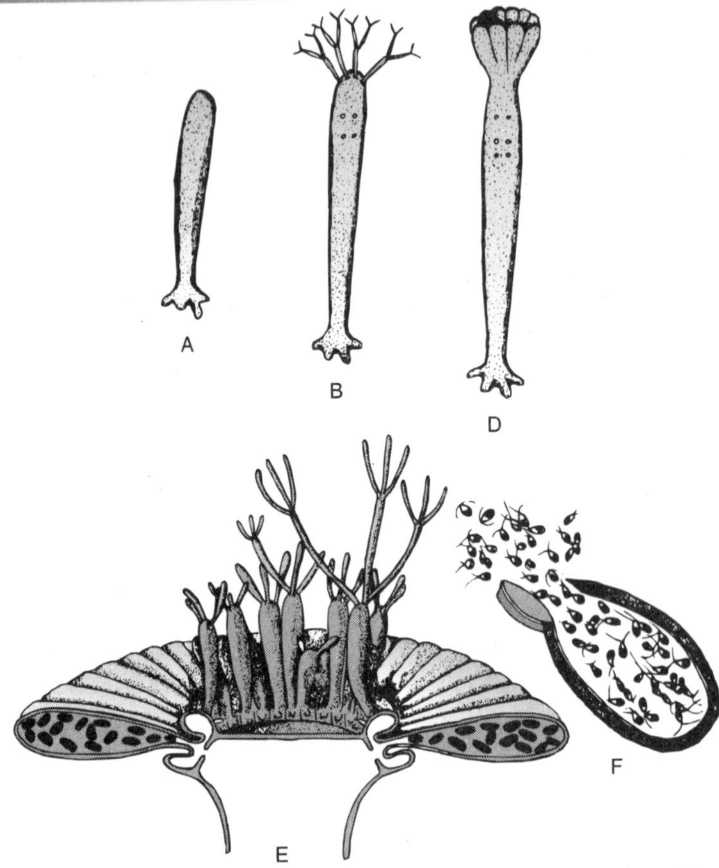

Figure 14.18: Acetabularia. A-C. Successive stages in maturation of the plant, diagrammatic. D. Organization of mature cap; note cysts. E. Liberation of gametes by germinating cysts.

recognizable plants. The alternates may be equal in stature and morphologically similar, as in *Cladophora.*

In this case alternation is said to be *isomorphic.* When the alternating phases are dissimilar morphologically (as in *Bryopsis halymeniae,* in *Laminaria,* a brown alga, and in the fern, for example), the alternation is called *heteromorphic.*

Alternation of generations itself is a sequence in which a diploid phase gives rise by meiosis to haploid spores, which initiate a haploid, gamete-producing phase. The zygote produced in sexual reproduction of the latter reinitiates the diploid phase.

One can compare the two alternating generations of *Cladophora* with the sporophytic and gametophytic phases of the land plants, since in origin, function, and position in the life cycle they seem to be fundamentally similar.

The significance of these facts has sometimes not been appreciated as widely as it should have been by those interested in the problems of evolution and phylogeny of plants.

While an alternation of generations like that described as type D, h + d has long been known in the land plants, some students of these groups, in speculating about their origin, have not considered the significance of the occurrence of a similar type of life cycle in the Chlorophycophyta. This problem will be discussed again in our consideration of the land plants.

Azoosporic Organisms

Finally, among the filamentous algae, representative of two groups that lack flagellate cells will be considered. In one of these groups, as exemplified by *Spirogyra* and *Zygnema*, the plants are unbranched filaments, which under certain conditions may, in some species, dissociate into the unicellular condition.

Spirogyra and Zygnema

Spirogyra (Gr. *speira*, a coil, + Gr. *gyros*, curved) and *Zygnema* (Gr. *zygon*, yoke, + Gr. *nema*, thread), but especially *Spirogyra*, usually are familiar to everyone who has studied biology. These genera often form floating, bright-green, frothy, and/or slimy masses in small bodies of water in the spring of the year and are frequently referred to as "pond scums" by laymen.

The unbranched filaments, generally unattached, grow by generalized cell division and cell elongation. Masses of the plants are slimy to the touch, because the filaments are surrounded by pectic sheaths, demonstrable by India ink and methylene blue dye.

Secretion of pectin by the filaments is involved in the movement of some species. The cell structure of *Spirogyra* is familiar to many, at least superficially, because of the spiral arrangement of the ribbonlike chloroplast or chloroplasts. However, this familiarity and ability to recognize the plant readily often result in a failure to appreciate the many details of cellular organization clearly observable by those determined to see them. A careful study of the cell structure of *Spirogyra* in the living condition, as revealed by an oilimmersion objective, is not only a good test of one's power of perception but also affords an opportunity for observation of detail in three-dimensional relations, which can be transferred, with profit to the observer, to the study of all cells.

Species containing one or a few chloroplasts in each cell are especially favorable for study of the cellular organization, which is illustrated in Figures elsewhere in this chapter. The living cells of *Spirogyra* are excellent for observation of protoplasmic streaming, or cyclosis.

Zygnema differs from *Spirogyra* in having two stellate chloroplasts in each of its cells. Aside from fragmentation of the filaments, no method of asexual reproduction occurs in *Spirogyra* and *Zygnema*. In *Spirogyra*, after a period of vegetative development, the filaments tend to become apposed.

Adjacent cells of contiguous filaments produce papillate protuber-ances, which meet and elongate, thus forcing the filaments apart. Ultimately, the terminal walls of the contiguous papillae are dissolved, and one of the protoplasts of the pair of connected cells, both of which have lost much of the cell sap from their large vacuoles, initiates movement through the tubular connection.

Contractile vacuoles, usually present only in flagellate cells, appear in the protoplasts during dehydration and play an important role in that process. The two protoplasts and their nuclei unite, and the resultant zygote develops a thick wall and enters a period of dormancy.

There is evidence that the chloroplast of the migrant cell subsequently disintegrates. Sexual reproduction of this type is interpreted as morphological isogamy with physiological anisogamy, the migrant protoplast being considered a male gamete.

Grote succeeded in obtaining the complete sexual cycle of *Spirogyra majuscula* in defined inorganic medium in laboratory culture; pH was seemingly the controlling factor. At the conclu-sion of dormancy, the zygote, which has previously been liberated from the cell wall of the vegetative cell, germinates into a new filament.

Meiosis precedes germination, but only one filament emerges from each zygote, because three of the four products of meiosis disintegrate before germination. In one species, meiosis occurs soon after karyogamy in the zygote and before its dormancy is initiated; Tatuno and Liyama (1971) have also reported zygotic meiosis and chromosome numbers of n = 2 in three species, n = 4 in two species, and n = 24 in one species.

In some species of *Spirogyra*, papillae from adjacent cells of the same filament establish contact, and the protoplasts of alternate cells function as male gametes with respect to the next cell of the filament so that zygotes occur in alternate cells.

This is known as *terminal conjugation*, in contrast with the previously described *scalariform*, or ladderlike, pattern. With respect to the life cycle, *Spirogyra* belongs to the H, h type.

Desmids: Closterium, Cosmarium, and Micrasterias

Although they are represented by both unicellular and filamentous genera, the desmids are similar to *Spirogyra* and its relatives because of their structure and sexual reproduction. They differ markedly, however, in their cell division.

The name *desmid* (Gr. *desmos*, bond) is ascribable to the fact that the cells of a majority of these plants are organized as two semicells that are mirror images of each other; the connecting region is known as the *isthmus*.

As in *Spirogyra*, flagellate motile cells are absent. *Micrasterias* (Gr. *micros*, little, + Gr. *asterias*, star), *Closterium* (Gr. *kloster*, spindle), and *Cosmarium* (Gr. *kosmos*, an ornament) are widely distributed genera representative of the unicellular desmids, although *Micrasterias* cells sometimes are connected in chains.

The two semicells of *Micrasterias* are separated by a deep incision, or *sinus*. The nucleus lies in the isthmus. The cell wall of a desmid is composed of several layers, the outermost of which is a rather diffluent pectin. It has been shown in some species that localized secretion of pectin through pores in the wall layers results in movement of the cells.

Asexual reproduction of unicellular genera is by cell division preceded by mitosis. In *Micrasterias* and *Cosmarium*, the two products of cytokinesis, the semicells, each containing a nucleus, regenerate new matching semicells.

Cosmarium and *Closterium* are ubiquitous desmids that have been receiving intensive genetic and cytological analysis. Both homothallic and heterothallic strains are known in *Closterium and Cosmarium.* When abundant sexually compatible individuals are mixed in laboratory cultures provided with adequate carbon dioxide, the cells pair within about 48 hours. This is accomplished through slow movements affected by secretion of pectin at one pole of the cell. The cells lie in a common mass of pectin after they have paired.

This is followed by opening of the cell walls at the isthmus and liberation of the protoplasts, which unite to form a spiny zygote. After a period of dormancy, the zygote germinates, producing two daughter cells. Meiosis occurs during germination, but two of the four products of meiosis disintegrate. A similar mode of gamete union occurs in *Closterium.*

Memberanous Organisms

Ulva

The plant body of a membranous green alga such as *Ulva (L.* Ova, marsh plant), since its life cycle is diplobiontic, may be initiated either by a haploid zoospore or by a zygote. In either case the initial cell develops at first as an unbranched *Ulothrix* like filament, from which longitudinal divisions later form in a flat blade.

In addition, all the cells undergo one division parallel to the blade surface; thus, the plant body becomes two-layered. Ova, the sea lettuce, is a familiar alga of marine and brackish waters. It is a widely distributed alga that grows attached to rocks, woodwork, and larger marine algae in quiet estuaries.

In *U. lactuca* the plant body is bladelike, often lobed and undulate; in some varieties it may exceed 1 m in length. Each plant is anchored to the substratum by a small multicellular holdfast composed of cells with rhizoidal protuberances.

The cell walls of *Ulva* are rather thick, a probable correlative of the fact that the plants can withstand some desiccation when exposed at low tide. Each cell contains a single laminate chloroplast with one or more pyrenoids.

The cells of the blade are uninucleate, but those of the holdfast may have several nuclei in their rhizoidal processes. Growth of the plant is generalized. Ova reproduces by zoospores and anisogametes. If one gathers Ova plants of sufficient maturity, permits them to dry slightly, and then immerses them individually in dishes of seawater under strong unilateral illumination, such dishes soon become green with liberated motile cells.

The latter manifest strong positive phototaxis. Careful microscopic examination of the motile cells of the several dishes reveals that three types are produced, each by different plants. Some of them liberate large zoospores, which are quadriflagellate; a second group of plants shed biflagellate gametes of two distinct sizes. The small male gametes arise from plants other than those that produce the female ones, so that *U. lactuca* is dioecious.

Thus, three types of plants, one zoosporic and two gametic, constitute a population of Ova *lactuca*. The zoospores grow directly into new plants. These plants are the male and female gametophytes, which liberate the anisogametes at maturity. The zygotes develop into diploid, zoospore-producing plants.

Meiosis occurs in the first two nuclear divisions in the cells that produce the zoospores, which accordingly are haploid; half of the zoospores of a given zoosporangium develop into male and the other half into female plants; the gametophytes, of course, are haploid.

Gametes that fail to unite may grow parthenogenetically into new plants. The life cycle of *Ova* is entirely similar to that of *Cladophora*, being diplobiontic and isomorphic; it clearly belongs to the D, h + d type.

COENOCYTIC AND TUBULAR ORGANISMS

In addition to the unicellular, colonial, filamentous, and membranous types of plant bodies of Chlorophycophyta already described, brief mention must be made of one additional type, the coenocytic, tubular, or siphonous. These green algae are marine, with but a single exception.

They may be simple, bilaterally symmetrical, tubular, pinnately branching plants such as *Bryopsis* or radially symmetrical as in *Acetabularia.* In all these plants the unit of structure is a coenocytic tubular "cell," the multinucleate protoplasm of which is peripherally disposed around a large central vacuole.

Transverse septa usually occur only at sites of injury or when reproductive organs are delimited from the vegetative branches.

Bryopsis

Bryopsis (Gr. *bryon,* a moss, + Gr. opsis, appearance) grows attached to rocks in shallow marine waters. Growth is apical. At maturity, certain of the branches of *Bryopsis* become segregated from the main axis by the formation of septa and become transformed into gametangia. Burr and West (1970) have described the important role of certain protein bodies in forming these septa and in healing wounds.

The plants are dioecious and produce either male or female gametes." Gametes that do not unite to form zygotes do not develop further.

Two kinds of life cycle have been found to occur in *B. plunwsa,* depending on where the plants are growing. In northern European waters (Holland) the zygotes develop directly into new diploid plants; in this case the life cycle is probably of the H, d type.

On the coast of France, by contrast, the zygotes develop into branched tubular structures 4-6 mm long, which produce lateral zoosporangia. The latter form zoospores with a crown of flagella, as in *Oedogonium,* and these grow into *Bryopsis* plants. This type of life cycle is diplobiontic and heteromorphic; that is, the alternating plants differ in morphology.

Both types of life cycle occur in the same populations of *B. plumosa* from Naples. The postzygotic tubular phase suggests the branching siphonous alga *Derbesia.* In the case of *B. halymeniae,* the sporophytic alternate in life cycle is *D. neglecta.*

The site of meiosis in these species of *Bryopsis* is not known with certainty; it was reported long ago to take place during gametogenesis, but this requires substantiation. For a further discussion of life cycles in *Bryopsis* see Bold and Wynne (1978).

Caulerpa

In *Caulerpa* (Gr. *kaulos*, a stem, + Gr. *herpo*, to creep), also haplobiontic and diploid, the coenocytic plant bodies are composed of large-diameter, sometimes flattened tubes, the vacuoles of which are traversed by supporting ingrowths of the wall.

These tubes may colonize extensive areas and simulate the vascular plants with their stemlike, rootlike, and leaflike branches. As the plants mature sexually, the protoplasm of the "leaf" or "stem" cleaves into biflagellate gametes.

These are released through extrusion papillae on the plant surface and are clearly anisogamous. The plants may be monoecious or dioecious, depending on the species. The zygotes develop directly into the branching plant.

Codium

In *Codium* (Gr. *codion*, a fleece), the branched, ropelike plants are composed of a longitudinal axis of smalldiameter tubes that bear vesicular branches (utricles) all over their surface. At the bases of these, gametangia are delimited by walls as in *Bryopsis.*

The reproduction of the Pacific *C. fragile* has been studied by Borden and Stein (1969). Individual plants of *C. fragile* are dioecious, and the gametes are anisogamous. The female gametangia are dark green, and the male gametangia are bright yellow.

The zygotes develop into small plants with utricles, but a new generation of sexually mature plants with utricles has not yet been grown in culture, so the life cycle is incompletely known. *Codium* can rapidly colonize new areas from which it had been absent (i.e., the New England coast) and is highly destructive of oysters, clams, and scallops.

Acetabularia

Finally, among the marine, coenocytic algae, mention must be made of *Acetabularia* (L. *acetabulum*, vinegar cup), the "mermaid's wine goblet," or "mermaid's parasol," a calcified organism widely distributed in subtropical and tropical waters.

The radially symmetrical plants arise from zygotes that

become attached to calcareous substrates and differentiate slowly into a rhizoidal portion, an erect axis, and, ultimately, a disclike cap. Throughout the major portion of this development, the zygote nucleus, although it enlarges, remains undivided in the rhizoidal portion.

As the cap and its branching appendages mature, the zygote nucleus divides meiotically or dissociates into numerous secondary nuclei, which become distributed, presumably by cytoplasmic streaming, throughout the plant.

Microspectrophotometric analysis indicated that all the nuclei except the primary zygote nucleus are haploid; accordingly, meiosis seemingly occurs as the zygote nucleus forms secondary nuclei. Koop (1975a,b) has most recently investigated the life cycle of *A. mediterranea*. In the chambers of the cap, each nucleus becomes a center about which cytokineses delimit a number of cysts.

These become multinucleate later in development. Subsequent disintegration of the old plants liberates the cysts, in which numerous biflagellate gametes arise after cytokinesis. The zygotes formed by the union of the gametes from different cysts again initiate a new generation of plants. *Acetabularia*, of which there are a number of species, has been intensively investigated with respect to morphogenesis and metabolism.

Graft hybrids between different species and nuclear-transplant studies have been made successfully and have provided basic information regarding the role of nuclei and cytoplasm in morphogenesis and in inheritance.

The existence of large and complex bodies composed of coenocytic tubes from which transverse septa are lacking, except during reproduction, has led to speculation regarding the relation of such plants to other types of plant body. To some, the extensive growths represent single giant multinucleate cells.

According to others, they are to be interpreted as acellular plant bodies, the individual nuclei and their surrounding cytoplasm being considered as representing cellular units not delimited by cell walls. More extensive accounts of *Acetabularia* have been published by Brachet (1965), Gibor (1966), and Puiseux-Dao (1970).

CHAPTER 15 Mosses & Liverworts (Bryophytes)

Mosses and liverworts grow throughout the world, from the high mountains of Antarctica to northernmost Greenland. Species of moss occur in nearly every habitat, from 180 feet under water in a Swiss lake to the driest deserts of Arizona.

Liverworts grow in less extreme situations but in a surprising variety of them. Neither the mosses nor the liverworts live in sea water. Bryophytes are common in the vegetation on the arctic and alpine tundra.

They are most abundant in moist and wet situations. Bryophytes are also abundant in the north woods and in the moist forested regions of the Pacific coast. There they and the lichens not only live on the soil and on the trunks and branches of living trees, but they soon cover the fallen trees with a living green spongy mantle, beneath which the relentless processes of disintegration proceed.

Mosses form the primary mats of the floating and semi-solid substrates of bogs and "muskegs." Held together by the tangled fibrous roots of sedges, ferns, and shrubs, they grow above and die below, thus contributing to the gradual filling of depressions and lake basins with peat.

Clearing of the forests and cultivation of the land by man have destroyed numerous habitats of many kinds of bryophytes in agricultural regions. But these species may still be found in rock gorges, swamp woods, and other forest remnants where they have survived and are often locally abundant. On the other hand, some species are more abundant in partially cleared forests, and a few may be found in cultivated fields. The grasses of old shaded lawns are often replaced by several species of mosses and liverworts.

Examination of clover fields and pastures will reveal a surprising carpet of these little plants growing with the soil algae. When farms are abandoned, bryophytes are among the pioneer invaders of "worn-out" soils.

Years later, when young woodland has occupied the farm site, it is often amazing to see the extent to which the species of bryophytes that formerly lived in the forests of the region have reappeared.

In tropical and subtropical forests, 'where rainfall is ample, mosses and liverworts grow profusely in glades and on stream banks. Many grow as epiphytes, forming spongy cushions on tree trunks and branches in the forest canopy. Some even grow on the surfaces of leaves.

Certain aquatic species live attached to rocks in swift clear streams, and even in waterfalls. Most species of bryophytes are land plants, in contrast to the algae, most of which are aquatics.

Locally, the occurrence of some species is limited by the acidity or alkalinity of the habitat. The pigeon-wheat moss *(Polytrichum),* the wind-blown moss *(Dicranum),* and the white-cushion moss *(Leucobryum)* grow almost wholly in acid situations.

The cord moss *(Funaria)* and the silvery *Bryum* are largely limited to alkaline or neutral areas. Other mosses, such as *Climacium* and *Mnium,* grow equally well in both acid and alkaline habitats. Some species of bryophytes survive in very acid, and others in extremely alkaline, substrates.

Many mosses withstand freezing temperatures at any stage of development, and in subarctic lands live under snow and ice for the longer part of every year. Whenever the snow disappears, food-making, growth, and reproduction proceed from the stage at which they stopped the previous season.

In rock crevices on the mountains of the Antarctic the Byrd Expedition found living mosses and lichens, where temperatures are seldom above freezing, and in winter often 75° F. below zero. Mosses also occur in the water of hot springs.

Their endurance of cold and drought is not dependent upon any special anatomical structures. Owing to their habit of growth as compact cushions or as sponge-like mats, water accumulates during rains and fogs by capillarity and remains available for much longer periods. When the plants become dry, their processes are largely suspended; but in nature recovery is possible even after prolonged droughts.

Moss plants dried for several days in the laboratory fail to recover, but the same species endure droughts of several weeks out-of-doors. Apparently they obtain enough water from the atmosphere at night to survive.

The spores of certain mosses, however, have germinated after being kept for 14 years in the dry air of a herbarium. Adequate light, a moist atmosphere, a rather constant water supply, and suitable temperatures are all essential to the abundant growth of most bryophytes.

Some grow in the entrances to caves and below rock ledges, where the light is as low as 1/500 of full sunlight. Moss plants have been found living in complete darkness. Obviously these plants were living as saprophytes similar to the subterranean green algae.

The species of moss that lives at a depth of 180 feet in the water of Lake Geneva, Switzerland, survives at an extremely low light intensity, and must have a very low compensation point. The so-called "luminous moss" *(Schistostega)* found under rock ledges and in dark recesses in woods is probably the material basis of the fairy tales of "goblin gold."

The cobwebby threads of the green plant are easily overlooked among the rock particles. From certain angles, however, the refracted and reflected light rays from the lens-like cells of the plant are seen as a goldengreen glow. None of the bryophytes is more than a few inches tall.

They are simple in structure, although many of them have organs that superficially resemble leaves, stems, and rootlets. No conducting system is present and the cell walls are not lignified. Mosses imbibe water rapidly, even from moist air.

The cells of the green parts of the plants have welldeveloped round chloroplasts. No true parasites are known among bryophytes, but many species are probably partial saprophytes. Moss communities frequently become the substrates of lichens and die in their shade.

Their remains accumulate as humus on bare rock surfaces, and become the substrate in which the roots of ferns and other plants may grow. The remains of these plants in turn contribute further to the humus, and the roots of the living plants bind the material together and anchor it still more securely.

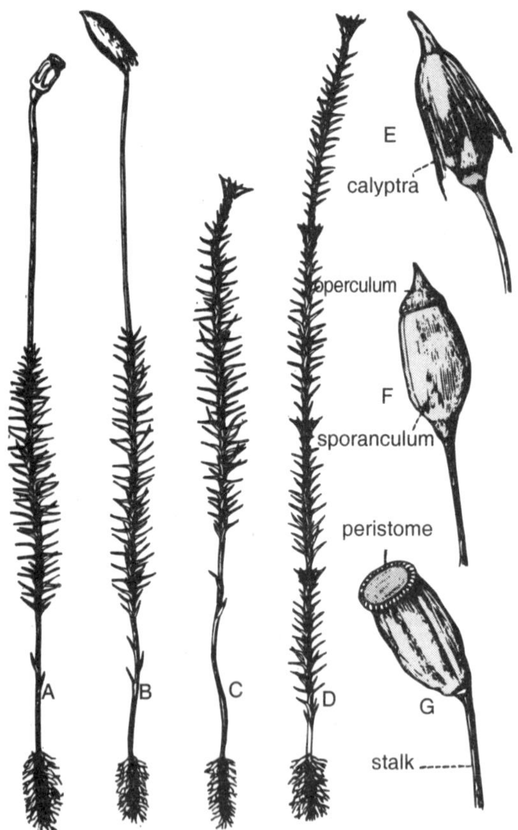

Figure 15.1: Polytrichum. Annual stem segments and terms applied to parts of the capsule. A and B, gametophyte and sporophyte phases; C and D, male gametophytes. E, the calyptra develops from the archegonium.

These are the pioneer stages of soil development, and of vegetation on exposed rocks. Owing to their rapid and compact horizontal spreading, bryophytes soon form patch-like communities in many kinds of situations. On the basis of their habitat relations, they are conveniently classified (1) as suspended, attached, and floating species in quiet water, (2) as species anchored in running water, (3) as plants on wet or dry fallen logs, soils, and rocks, (4) as epiphytes on bark and leaves, (5) as bog species, and (6) as pioneers on calcareous and non-calcareous rock surfaces.

Bryophytes are either annuals or perennials. It is difficult to estimate the age of the perennials, since they have no annual rings or bud scars. Annual stem segments are recognizable, however, in some moss plants, such as *Polytrichum*, in which a characteristic rosette of permanent leaves surrounds the terminal male reproductive structures.

Each year a new stem segment grows from near the center of the terminal rosette of the previous stem segment. *Polytrichum* plants have been found in bogs, with 1 to 3 upper live segments and 4 to 8 dead ones below.

In most species the lower and older parts disintegrate about as fast as new growths appear terminally. The bog mosses grow in poorly aerated habitats, and as they die below they accumulate as peat deposits, several to many feet in thickness.

Mosses that grow in springs heavily charged with calcium bicarbonate become incrusted below with lime and build up layers of porous hard tufa many feet thick. The tufa deposits later recrystallize and form solid masses of limestone.

The moss *Gymnostomum,* important in tufa formation, is known to elongate a little over an inch in four years. In a thousand years these processes would form a layer of tufa and rock some 20 feet in thickness. Living cells occur only in the uppermost segments.

In moist, shaded habitats various small salamanders, insects, snails, worms, fungi, bacteria, and algae live with the bryophytes as a miniature microcosm.

From the plants, both living and dead, the animals obtain

food, cover, and a more continuous water supply. The saprophytic fungi simply grow through the mass of liverworts and mosses and become interlaced with them.

Some of the fungi, however, are wholly or partially parasitic, and live on and within the bryophyte cells. Certain species of aerial and terrestrial algae as well as various soil bacteria are also sure to be found in the community. The commonest example of an alga living within liverworts is the blue-green *Nostoc* in cavities of such liverworts as *Anthoceros* and *Blasia.*

The economic and biological importance of the bryophytes is much less than that of either the algae or the fungi. They have been contributory factors in the formation of peat, muck, and brown coal through the centuries, and they contribute annually to the organic matter of the soil.

They hold the soil against wind and water erosion, and decrease run-off of water by their spongy texture. They are the food of many small animals. Some species are important pioneers, sharing with the lichens the initial development of soil on bare rocks, volcanic deposits, and newly exposed land.

During the World War certain bog mosses of the genus *Sphagnum* were collected, sterilized, and used as wound dressings because of their superior absorptive quality.

Peat formed by *Sphagnum, Calliergon,* and other mosses is prized by gardeners as a means of increasing the organic content and porosity of soils in gardens and in lawns. A bale, or about 8 bushels, of peat moss absorbs nearly 200 gallons of water.

Florists and nurserymen use these mosses as packing around the roots of shrubs and trees that are being transported and replanted. Approximately 23,000 species of bryophytes have been described and classified. Of these, nearly 9000 are liverworts *(Hepaticae),* and 14,000 are mosses *(Musci).*

The moss plant. Some of the mosses and liverworts look much alike, but most of the common mosses are easily recognized. They usually have leafy erect or creeping stems, which develop from a much-branched filamentous or thallose green structure growing on the surface of the soil, and known as the *protonenaa* (Gr. *first thread).*

A clone of numerous upright leafy stems may grow from each protonema. A leafless stalk may eventually develop from the apex or from the side of the leafy stem, ending terminally in a spore-bearing capsule.

At the basal end of the leafy stem, many-celled branching rhizoids, seldom more than a few millimeters long, penetrate the soil or other substrate. Mosses multiply freely by vegetative

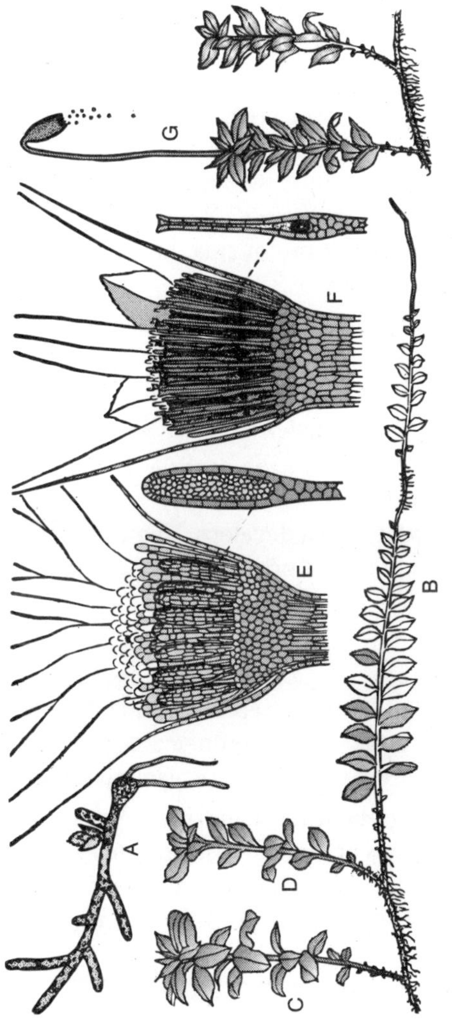

Figure 15.2: Structures in the life cycle of a moss (Mnium) : A, the protonema which develops from a spore; B, a horizontal vegetative shoot from a bud of the protonema; C, a female branch; D, a male branch; E, antheridia at the tip of a male branch; F, archegonia at the tip of a female branch; G, the leafless stalk (sporophyte) which develops from a zygote in an archegonium and bears a terminal sporangium containing numerous spores.

propagation. On culture media new individuals may develop from nearly any fragment of the plant.

In many species small buds occur on stems, and when they become detached new individuals develop from each of them. More specialized propagative buds, called "brood bodies," occur abundantly on leaves, stems, and even rhizoids of some species.

Vegetative multiplication by fragmentation of the protonema appears almost limitless, especially if the protonema is perennial. Adventitious protonemata may develop from almost any part of the plant.

The filaments of the protonema, except for their small roundish chloroplasts, are difficult to distinguish from branching filamentous algae. They continue to branch, and soon form a thin green mat over the surface of the soil. Numerous buds, or bulbils, form on the branches of the protonema, and rhizoids and leafy branches develop from them.

If the buds are numerous, the upright branches develop close together and form dense clusters or cushions. Some species have an extensive perennial felt-like protonema that completely covers the soil surface, but the upright shoots are small and scattered.

When the spores formed in the capsule of the leafless stalk fall upon soil or other moist substrates, they germinate, and from each of them a new protonema develops. These spores constitute a definite stage in the life cycle of a moss plant, which consists of two distinct phases.

One phase ends with the development of spores; the other, with the development of gametes, and fertilization. The gametophyte phase and sexual reproduction. The commonly observed moss plant composed of protonema, leafy branches, and rhizoids is the gamete-bearing phase, or gametophyte.

At the apex of the green leafy stems there appear tufted heads of leaves enclosing groups of slender flask-shaped egg cases, called *archegonia* (sing. *archegonium).* An archegonium ordinarily contains one egg cell and is analogous to the oogonium of the algae, but differs from it in being a multicellular structure.

Antheridia also develop at the apex of leafy stems, sometimes in the same head with the archegonia, and sometimes alone on other stem tips. They may also develop singly or in pairs in the axils of leaves. They are multicellular, and many sperms develop in each of them. Scattered among the antheridia and archegonia may be numerous sterile filaments. When the entrance of water causes a mature antheridium to swell and burst, the sperms are set free. Since they are motile they swim about in the film of water on top of the plant or mass of plants, and some of them eventually swim near the tips of archegonia.

As the egg matures, the interior row of cells (neck-canal cells) of each archegonium disintegrates into a mucilaginous mass from which sugars diffuse into the surrounding water. When the sperms come in contact with the diffusing sugar they may swim toward the archegonium where the sugar is most concentrated.

A few eventually pass into the neck of the archegonium, and one may finally move all the way to the egg and fuse with it. The fertilized egg, or zygote, is the beginning of the sporophyte phase of the moss plant.

The Sporophyte and Asexual Reproduction

The zygote germinates while still within the archegonium at the apex of the leafy stem, and from it develops a slender, stalk-like, leafless structure terminating in a capsule, or sporangium. In some mosses the stalk, or seta, is very short; in others two to four inches in length.

The capsule is usually simple, but in some of the common mosses it is quite complex. In most species the main body or *urn* of the sporangium is surmounted by an easily separable lid, or *operculum,* and the whole structure, or at least a part of it, is covered by a hood or *calyptra.*

Extending partly across the mouth of the urn is a *peristome* composed of from 4 to 64 variously ornamented and radially disposed teeth. Large numbers of spores develop in the sporangium; and when they are released, new protonemata develop from them.

Thus the life cycle of a moss from spore to spore consists of two alternating phases: the gamete-bearing phase (the gametophyte) and the spore-bearing phase (the sporophyte).

Reduction division takes place at the time of the formation

of the spores within the sporangium. The spores and each of the cells of the gametophyte ordinarily have the monoploid number of chromosomes, and those of the sporophyte the diploid number.

The leafless stalk with its sporangium is the sporophyte. Since it is not a continuation of the stem of the gametophyte usually only a slight pull is necessary to separate them. The sporophyte is green when young; at most it is only a partial parasite on the green leafy gametophyte.

Owing to the location of the archegonium and the germination of the zygote within it, the position of the sporophyte in some mosses is apical on the main stem, and in others on minute lateral branches.

The sporophytes of most species develop at a definite season of the year. This fact may often be helpful in distinguishing one species from another. In a few mosses, notably *Tetraphis,* the sporophyte persists for a year or more.

In others the sporangia mature in autumn and remain until spring. In still other species the sporophytes mature in the spring and early summer and soon disappear. There are a few species of mosses on which sporophytes have never been found.

The gametophyte phase of the moss begins with the formation of spores in the sporangium of the sporophyte, and ends with the development of gametes, and fertilization. The sporophyte phase begins with the fertilized egg, or zygote, and ends with the formation of spores.

Among flowering plants the plant that bears the flowers is the sporophyte phase. The gametophyte phase consists of the embryo sac in the ovule, and of the pollen grain and pollen tube: a female and a male gametophyte.

Among the mosses, the gametophyte (protonema and leafy branches) may be male or female, or it may be bisexual (monoecious), bearing both antheridia and archegonia with their sperms and eggs.

Of all the plants in the world, the bryophytes have the largest gametophytes, and the seed plants have the largest sporophytes.

Chromosomes and the life cycle of mosses. Since reduction division occurs during the formation of spores in the sporophyte,

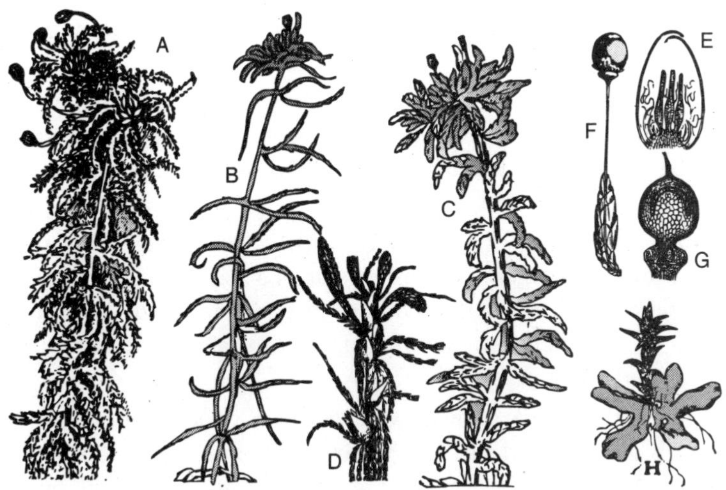

Figure 15.3: Three species of Sphagnum (A-C), reproductive structures (D-G), and thalloid protonema with young leafy shoot (H). G represents the sporophyte stage, which consists of a sporangium and a very short stalk. The small urn-shaped bodies on A, B, and C are sporophytes.

these spores and all cells of the gametophyte have the *n,* or monoploid, number of chromosomes; while the cells of the sporophyte, which develops from the fertilized egg, have the *2n,* or diploid number.

Moreover, all the cells of the gametophyte, including the protonema with all of its leafy branches and all of their sperms and eggs, have the same chromosome complement. Consequently if self-fertilization occurs, each of the fertilized eggs and resulting sporophytes will have two sets of like chromosomes.

They will be completely homozygous. If reduction division is regular, all the spores formed in these sporophytes will have the same chromosome complement, and so will all of the subsequent gametophytes that develop from them. Similar chromosome phenomena may occur in bisexual liverworts and ferns also.

Classification of Mosses

The foregoing description of a moss life cycle refers especially to the group sometimes called the "true mosses" *(Bryales). Two* other groups or orders of mosses are generally recognized: the peat or bog mosses *(Sphagnales)* and the rock or granite mosses *(Andreaeales).*

These differ from the *Bryales* in various structural details of both gametophytes and sporophytes. Descriptions of these orders may be readily found in books on the mosses, some of which are listed at the end of this chapter.

The peat mosses, *Sphagnales,* differ from other mosses in several characteristics. The protonema is a flat thallus similar in appearance to a small liverwort or the prothallus of a fern. It begins as a filament, but soon becomes a flat plate one-cell thick and irregularly lobed.

The visible stalk (*pseudopodium*) upon which the capsule is borne is an outgrowth of the gametophyte and is not the lower part of the sporophyte. The sporophyte consists of a globular capsule, a very short and slender stalk, and a foot.

The spore-bearing part of the capsule is domeshaped, overarc-hing a region of sterile tissue. The leaves are a single cell laver in

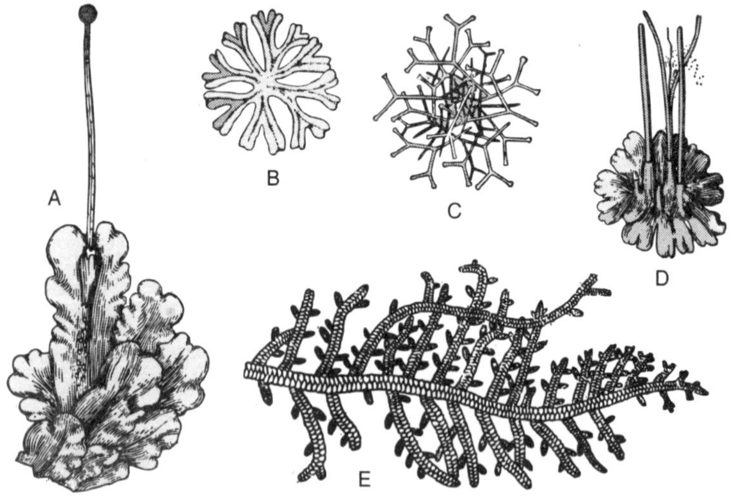

Figure 15.4: Some widely distributed liverworts: A, Pellia thallus with antheridia (dots on surface) and a sporophyte; B and C, land and water forms of Riccia; D, archegonial thallus of Anthoceros with sporophytes; E, a portion of the thallus of Porella, a leafy liverwort.

thickness, have no midrib, and contain both living and dead cells. In young leaves all the cells look alike; but later, differentiation results in slender living cells, which possess chloroplasts and form a network enclosing larger, short-lived, non-green cells.

The peat mosses are of more commercial value than any others. These plants often form floating masses on the surface of lakes and ponds. Continued growth of the plants upward forces lower layers downward, and the dead and decaying parts accumulate, disintegrate but little in the absence of oxygen, and

Figure 15.5: Vegetative and reproductive structures of Marchantia: A, *vegetative propagules, or gemmae, in cupules on a portion of a thallus; B, part of a male thallus with upright antheridial branches terminating in disk-like structures in which antheridia and sperms develop; C, a female thallus with upright archegonial branches terminating in radially branched structures in which archegonia and eggs develop; D, diagram of a vertical section of the apex of an archegonial branch to show location of the pendant archegonia; E, diagram of a vertical section of the apex of an antheridial branch to show location of antheridia; F, form of sperms; G, isolated sporophytes that have developed from fertilized eggs within archegonia represented in D. Elongation of the sporophyte stalk pushes the sporangium out of the archegonium, but the base of the stalk remains attached to the gametophyte as it does in mosses.*

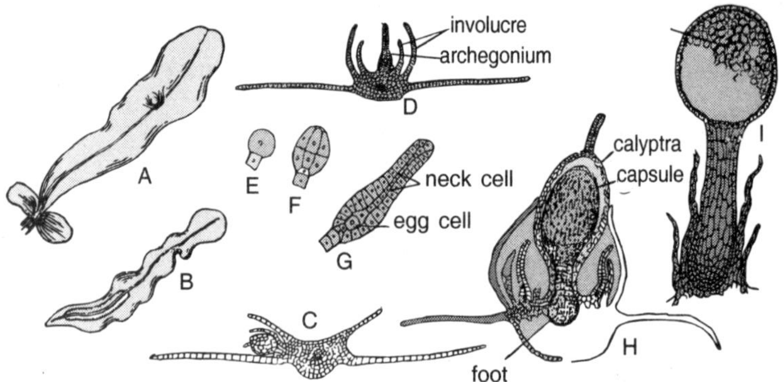

Figure 15.6: Antheridial and archegonial thalli of Pallavicinia (A-B); *stages in the development of the sporophyte (C-1).*

become peat.

These mosses may also become established on the shore of a lake and gradually encroach on the water, forming a quaking bog. Creeping bogs may develop in very moist climates. The sphagnum mat grows out of the depression, invades forested land, and kills the trees by raising the water table and excluding oxygen from the tree roots.

The characteristic genus of peat mosses is *Sphagnum,* more than 300 species of which have been described. Mature peat mosses have no rhizoids, and absorption of water is direct. The upward movement of water is largely effected by capillarity through the closely adhering lateral branches and the compactness of the plant mass.

The rock mosses, *Andreaeales,* grow principally in arctic and alpine regions upon granite or slate. They are dark or almost black in appearance, have very brittle leaves densely aggregated, and are rarely more than an inch or two long. The gametophytes resemble the true mosses, while the sporophyte is supported by a pseudopodium as in the peat mosses.

The capsule is unique among mosses in its longitudinal dehiscence by four valves when mature. There are approximately 120 species of rock mosses. The true mosses, or *Bryales,* consist of about 13,500 species classified among 80 families and 655 genera. This is the largest group of the mosses.

The Liverwort Plant

Two groups of liverworts are easily recognizable: the thalloid and the leafy forms. The thalloid species are easily distinguished from mosses by their irregular, leaf-like, much-branched vegetative body.

The *thalli* (sing. *thallus)* may be from one to several cell layers in thickness, and are sometimes dichotomously branched at short intervals. The middle line of the thallus is a groove in some species and has the appearance of a midrib, but no veins are present.

The leafy liverworts have flat shoots and the conspicuous leaves grow in two ranks. There is a third row of smaller leaves on the under side of the stem in many species. The leaves are entire, lobed, folded, or dissected.

Many of the thalloid liverworts, such as *Marchantia*, have distinctly differentiated tissues. Above is an epidermis with open pores beneath which are cavities, or air chambers, containing tufts of erect green filaments. Photosynthesis occurs in these upper cell layers.

Below are large, compactly arranged cells containing water; and extending from the lower epidermis are scales and one-celled rhizoids. As an example of the foliose liverworts, *Porella may* be studied. It is common on tree trunks, on rocks, and even on walls of buildings.

The novice often mistakes it for a moss. Its curved reclining stems bear three rows of flattened leaves, two on the dorsal side and one on the ventral side.

Vegetative propagation occurs in liverworts by fragmentation, by "brood bodies," and by gemmae formed in variously shaped gemmaecups. These are small cup-shaped outgrowths from the upper epidermis of the thallus.

From the bottom of the cup numerous upright fiddleshaped green thalli develop. They germinate immediately when transported to the soil by rain or wind. The parts of *Marchantia* and *Porella* just described are the gametophyte phases of these two liverworts.

They bear archegonia and antheridia in which eggs and sperms are formed much as in the mosses. The sporophyte phase develops from the fertilized egg and is similar to the sporophytes of certain mosses.

Reduction division occurs when the spores are formed in the sporangium. When a spore germinates, a new thallus develops from it. Elongated, spindle-shaped, and often spirally thickened cells known as *elaters may* develop within the sporangia along with the spores.

This is one of the characteristics of liverworts. Some of the features by which mosses can be distinguished from liverworts may be summarized as follows:

Mosses	*Liverworts*
Stems leafy, never thalloid	Stems leafy or thalloid
Protonema present	No protonema
Many-celled branching rhizoids	One-celled rhizoids
Elaters absent from sporangia	Elaters present in sporangia

The Hornworts

Some thalloid bryophytes, such as *Anthoceros*, have unique characteristics which distinguish them from other liverworts. They are known as *hornworts,* because of the horn-like appearance of the sporophytes.

Cells of the structurally simple gametophytes usually contain a single large chloroplast, within which is an evident pyrenoid. The cells of the capsule of the sporophyte do not all mature simultaneously, and the basal portion continues to grow after the apical portion has matured.

Some 320 species of thalloid bryophytes comprise the hornworts, which are considered by some botanists as a third group of bryophytes: the *Anthocerotae.*

CHAPTER 16

Ferns, Club Mosses and Equisetums (Pteridophyes)

Superficially the ferns, club mosses, equisetums, and quillworts may appear much too diverse in form to be classified within one group, known as the *Pteridophytes* (Gr. *pteris,* fern, and *phyton,* plant). The fundamental features of their life cycles, however, are quite similar, and are sufficiently unlike those of other groups of plants to warrant the consideration of them as a single group.

Altogether about 10,000 species of Pteridophytes have been described and named, of which more than 9000 are ferns.The Carboniferous forests 300 million years ago were dominated by hundreds of tree species of primitive Pteridophytes and Gymnosperms now extinct.

The coal deposits of Pennsylvania were formed primarily from the wood of these trees. These species have all become extinct, and only a few of the modem ferns are trees. Most of the modern Pteridophytes are small and comparatively inconspicuous except when they grow in masses.

In the forests of today they are understory plants, and are usually most abundant along stream banks, in open glades, in clearings made by man, or where the forests have been destroyed by storm and fire. In such areas some of the species reproduce so rapidly and grow in such dense masses that reforestation is greatly delayed. Some of these species also become troublesome weeds in pastures in moist climates.

A few species are prized as decorative plants, and others are used in medicine.

THE FERNS

Ferns grow in a great diversity of habitats. We usually associate them with shade, ample water supply, and warm temperatures. While in general this is true, particularly for those of very rapid growth, ferns are not necessarily so restricted.

Some species thrive in open fields and on dry hillsides, others on dry exposed rocks, still others in marshes not especially shaded, and many in the forests of the tropics and semi-tropics as epiphytes; a few are strictly aquatic. They are reported from the frigid zone; but the number of species there, as well as of individuals, is small.

As one goes from cool temperate regions toward the equator the number of species increases rapidly. Ferns attain their greatest size and variety in the moist tropics, where some of the species are trees. In warm temperate regions the largest and most striking ferns occur in swamps and in rich soil along streams.

Most species of ferns grow in acid soils, but many of them grow on both acid and alkaline soils. Geologically ferns are very old. Fossil remains of ferns are reported from the Devonian rocks, but their greatest abundance occurred during Carboniferous times.

Some of the early ferns were trees, and some fernlike plants reproduced by seeds.Aside from their use as decorative plants, the commercial value of ferns is almost negligible. Certain species that grow in masses and invade bare soil areas contribute to soil development and the protection of soil from wind and water erosion.

The young rhizomes of a few species are sometimes used as a source of food by animals and man; and the leaves have been used in the making of tea and liquors. The aquatic species are eaten by ducks, some fish, and by other water animals.

The greatest common interest in ferns, however, is undoubtedly esthetic. They are cultivated for ornamental purposes, and the supply and sale of cut ferns have become an important industry.

The Fern Plant

Ferns are generally recognized by their leaves. They are the most conspicuous and characteristic parts of the plant and bear characteristic reproductive structures. They vary in length from an inch, or less, in the smallest species to 100 feet in species of climbing ferns. The spirally twisting petiole (rachis) of the climbing fern of the Eastern States seldom exceeds 3 feet in length. Some of the common ferns of temperate zones have a blade a yard or more in length supported by a prominent petiole often mistaken for a stem by the novice.

Sessile leaves are rare among ferns. The leaves may be simple, but they are more often compound. The leaflets of compound leaves may be ftirther divided and dissected, resulting in a very complex frond.' The leaf develops from a primordium near the

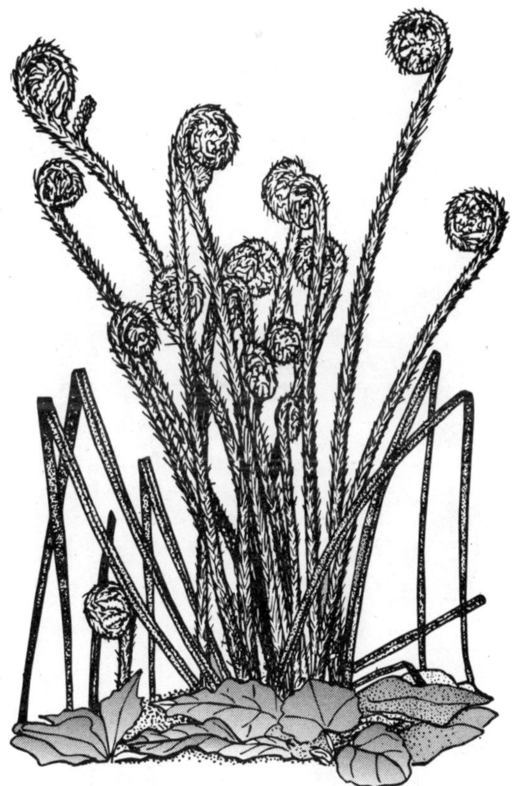

Figure 16.1: Uncoiling of young leaves of cinnamon fern (Osmunda cinnamomea).

apex of the stem and, owing to slightly more rapid enlargements on the outer side, becomes coiled.

As development proceeds, growth on the inner side catches up with the outer, and the apex uncoils. Leaves usually mature in one season, though in some species they grow for a period of three or more years.

The characteristic venation of ferns is dichotomous, but there are all gradations from dichotomy to a very complex net arrangement that is better termed reticulate. The leaves of a few species are somewhat succulent and the venation is not easily seen.

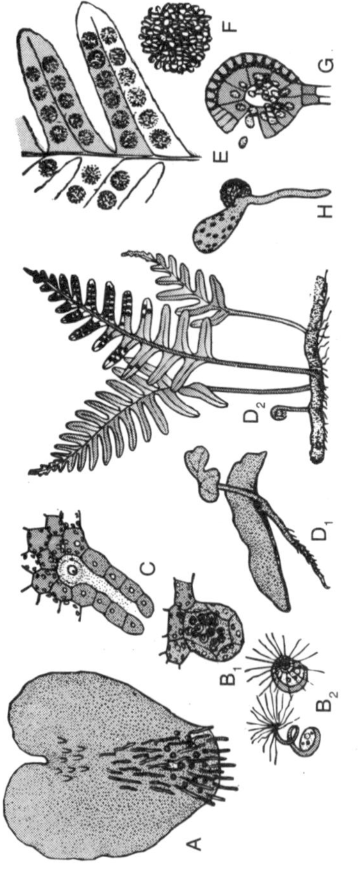

Figure 16.2: The life cycle of a fern. The gametophyte (A) bears egg cells and sperms in archegonia and antheridia. When one of the sperms (B_2) from an antheridium (B1) unites with an egg cell in an archegonium (C) a zygote is formed. From this zygote the sporophyte (D_1 and D_2) develops and bears spores in groups of sporangia (E and F) on the lower side of the leaves. By the bursting of a sporangium (G) the spores are set free. When these spores germinate (H) on moist substrates a new gametophyte, like the one represented by A, develops from each of them.

Most of our common ferns may be readily recognized, however, by their *dichotomous venation* and the uncoiling of their young leaves, known as *circinate vernation.* The fern leaf is similar in structure to that of the seed plant.

The epidermis is a definite layer with stomates usually on the under side of the leaf. Green plastids occur in the guard cells. The mesophyll is often not differentiated into palisade and spongy tissues.

The leaflets of some of the filmy ferns are but a single cell layer in thickness. Structurally, the veins are quite like those of seed plants, and they are branches of the vein tissues of the stem and roots. The stems of most ferns are horizontal branched rhizomes.

They may grow on the surface of the soil or below. The life duration of any part of a horizontal stem is relatively short, for the rhizome continues to elongate at the growing tip and die at the other end.

A few of our common ferns, such as the cinnamon fern, have erect stems, sometimes extending a foot or more above the soil in swamps. The upright stems of tree ferns in the tropics may be 20 to 30 feet high. Some ferns are epiphytes.

The ferns, in marked contrast to all bryophytes and thallophytes, have highly differentiated conducting systems with both phloem and xylem tissues. Special elongated cells known as tracheids are the fundamental structures of the xylem.

Xylem tubes, or vessels, occur rarely. The phloem is composed of sieve tubes and phloem parenchyma. Cambium, though common in the fossil ancestors, is very rare in living ferns, having been found in only two genera. The "bundles" of xylem and phloem may be few and scattered, or sometimes numerous and arranged in a cylinder.

Pith is absent in stems of some species and conspicuous in that of others. The cortex is usually prominent and may have several outer layers of thick-walled cells. The roots of ferns in comparison to leaf surface are smaller, shorter, and less branched than the roots of seed plants.

In the herbaceous ferns they originate adventitiously at the

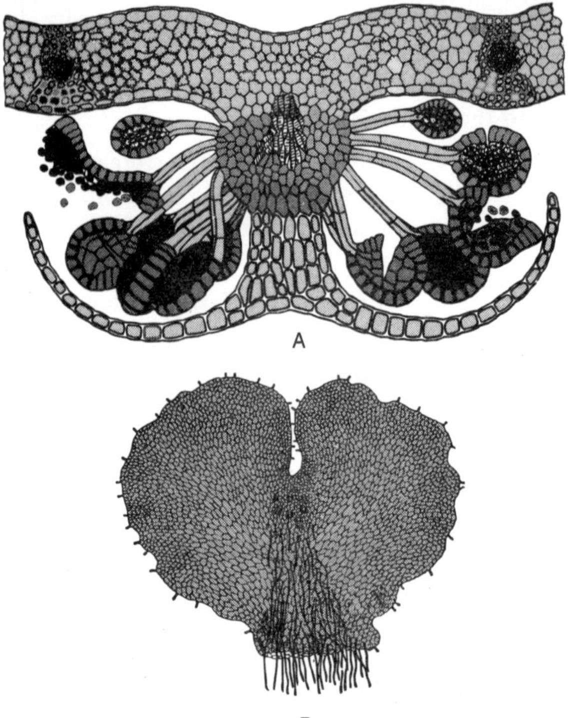

Figure 16.3: Reproductive structures of a fern: A, section through part of a leaf and a sorus composed of a stalked shield, or indusium, which covers a cluster of sporangia in which numerous spores have developed; B, ventral surface of a bisexual gametophyte; the antheridia are near the bases of the rhizoids, the archegonia are just below the central sinus.

nodes and along the internodes of the rhizome. In the tree ferns the root systems are more complex, but they do not attain the size and spread of the root systems of seed plants.

Their internal structure is quite similar to that of the roots of seed plants. Roots may be lacking in some aquatic species, and in the filmy ferns only rhizoids develop. Ferns multiply vegetatively by means of their branching rhizomes, from which a succession of new leaves develops each season.

New individuals may also develop vegetatively from adventitious buds (bulbils) on the surface or in the axils of the leaves of certain species. New plants of the walking fern develop from buds formed at the tips of the leaves in contact with the soil. Some tropical species multiply vegetatively from the swollen leaf bases.

The Sporophyte

The conspicuous fern plants described above are all sporophytes. They are much larger and far more complex than the sporophytes of the mosses and liverworts. Among the bryophytes the conspicuous phase in the life history is the gametophyte; among the ferns it is the sporophyte phase. The sporophyte of ferns has definite leaves, stems, and roots with a well-developed vascular system and other tissues comparable to those of seed plants.

Sporangia may develop on the under side of a green fern leaf. They may occur in irregular lines or areas, or cover nearly the whole under surface of the leaf. The sporangia are often grouped in distinct clusters known as *sori* (sing. *sorus).* The sori may be located along the veins, at the ends of veins, or along the margin of the leaf.

The shape, arrangement, and general appearance of the sori are commonly used in distinguishing different genera and species of ferns.They are usually covered by a delicate shield-like structure known as the *indusium.* Species such as the cinnamon fern and sensitive fern have two kinds of leaves: the usual foliage leaf, and a smaller one on which sporangia and spores develop.

Such special spore-bearing leaves have been called *sporophylls;* and this term is applied to any spore-bearing leaf, whether of fern or of seed plant. Stamens and carpels of ordinary flowers and the scales of pine cones are often referred to as sporophylls.

The cinnamon fern has cinnamon-colored sporophylls. Fern sporangia develop at the ends of short stalks. The epidermis of the sporangium is composed of two kinds of cells: a single row of cells with walls greatly thickened inwardly (the annulus), and several larger thin-walled cells forming the remainder of the sporangium wall.

Upon losing water the cells of the annulus contract, and the maturing sporangium splits open at the side. The number of spores in a sporangium ordinarily ranges from 32 to 64, but it may be higher in a few genera: 400-500 in *Osmunda,* the royal ferns; 1500-2000 in *Botrychium,* the grape ferns; and 12,500-15,000 in *Ophioglossum,* the adder's-tongue ferns.

Many millions of spores may develop on one fern plant in a single season. The spores develop in tetrads following reduction division of the spore mother cells. Familiar ferns include, besides the ones referred to above, the walking fern, *Camptosorus;* the common polypody, *Poly podium;* the maidenhair fern, *Adiantum;* the bracken fern, *Pteris;* the Christmas fern, *Polystichum;* and the sensitive fern, *Onoclea.*

The Gametophyte

Under appropriate conditions the spores germinate either directly or after a short period of dormancy, and from each spore there develops a small heart-shaped thallus that superficially resembles a very simple liverwort.

The first few cells form a filament that resembles an alga or a moss protonema; in a few species of fern the filamentous form is permanent. In most species, however, subsequent cell divisions result in a thallose structure. This structure, unnecessarily termed a *prothallus, is* the gametophyte of the fern.

Thalli of ferns may be found growing naturally on moist rocks, on soil, and on decaying logs near the sporophytes. They grow readily from spores sown on culture media or on the surface of flower pots after the pots have been filled with sphagnum moss and inverted in a pan of water.

In two genera of ferns (the grape fern, *Botrychium* and the adder'stongue, *Ophioglossum)* the gametophyte is quite unique. In *Botrychium* it is entirely subterranean and without chlorophyll; in *Ophioglossum* it is subterranean with green parts extending above the soil surface. In both, a fungus lives in the non-green part of the gametophyte and extends into the surrounding humus.

As the flat expanse of cells forming the fern gametophyte grows, rhizoids develop on the lower side; and soon afterward antheridia develop near them. The antheridia are comparatively simple structures, with an external layer of several cells enclosing the sperm mother cells, in each of which one sperm develops.

The sperms have a spirally twisted body with 40 or 50 long

cilia. The archegonia develop as the gametophyte matures, and are also located on the under side near the notch or youngest part of the thallus.

Fertilization

The sperms are released by the swelling and bursting of the mature antheridium when water collects under the gametophyte. Under similar conditions the archegonium opens, and the products of the disintegration of the neck canal cells diffuse into the water.

The sperms swim toward the regions of greatest concentration of these diffusing substances, and one of the sperms after entering the archegonium fuses with the egg cell, forming a zygote. When fertilization has taken place in one or two of the archegonia, the further development of the remaining archegonia of the gametophyte ceases.

Consequently one sporophyte ordinarily develops from a zygote in each fern gametophyte, rarely two of them. If the young embryos of the sporophytes are removed as rapidly as they begin to develop, the fern gametophytes continue to grow vegetatively for years.

Apparently a hormonelike substance formed in the young sporophyte inhibits not only the further development of other embryos, but also the further growth of the prothallus, or gametophyte.

Embryo of the **Sporophyte**

The zygote germinates directly after fertilization. Cell division soon results in an embryo with four distinct regions:

(1) the foot, or holdfast, by which the embryo is attached for a short time to the gametophyte;

(2) a root tip, which rapidly elongates and penetrates the soil;

(3) a leaf primordium, from which the first leaf of the sporophyte develops; and

(4) a stem tip, which elongates slowly, and from which successive leaves and adventitious roots develop. The sporophyte is thus at first dependent on the gametophyte, but it soon becomes green and develops rapidly; and the

thallus disintegrates. From the embryo the mature sporophyte grows.

Chromosome Numbers

The cells of the sporophyte all have the diploid number of chromosomes. Reduction division occurs in the spore mother cells during the formation of spores in the sporangia on the leaves. These spores, the cells of the subsequent gametophytes, and the sperms and eggs have the monoploid number of chromosomes.

All the eggs and sperms formed in the same gametophyte have the same chromosome complement. If self-fertilization occurs, the resultant zygote and sporophyte will be completely homozygous. If reduction division is regular, all of the spores formed in this sporophyte will have the same chromosome complement; and so will all of the cells of all of the gametophytes that develop from these spores.

Mutation, hybridization, and parthenogenesis occur in ferns as in flowering plants. Changes in chromosome number in ferns, however, may also occur in another peculiar way. Gametophytes sometimes originate vegetatively from the diploid cells of the sporophyte; and sporophytes sometimes originate vegetatively from monoploid cells of the gametophyte.

Alternating phases in the life cycle of plants. In the life cycle of many algae, and of all bryophytes, pteridophytes, and seed plants, a diploid spore-bearing phase, the sporophyte, ordinarily alternates with a monoploid gamete-bearing phase, the gametophyte.

In the ferns and brown algae either phase may continue to multiply vegetatively. In the bryophytes and such algae as *Oedogoniuni,* vegetative multiplication is limited largely to the gametophyte, while in the seed plants it usually occurs only in the sporophyte.

There are no alternating phases in the bluegreen algae. The sporophyte phase of seed plants, pteridophytes, and brown algae is the conspicuous one. The gametophyte phase (pollen and embryo sac) of the seed plants and of some of the pteridophytes is very small.

The gametophyte phase of the bryophytes is the conspicuous

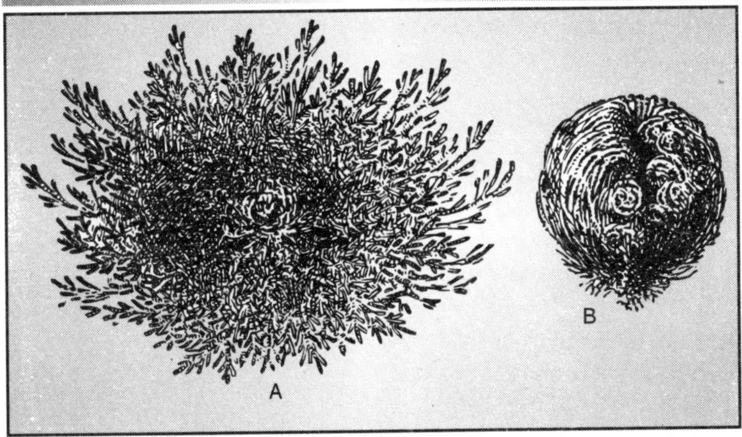

Figure 16.4: Resurrection plant (Selaginella) of Texas and New Mexico. During the rainy season the plant spreads out and grows as a rosette. When drought comes, it dries out and curls up into a ball, as indicated at the right.

one, and the smaller sporophyte phase is wholly or partially dependent upon it as a source of food.

The gametophyte phase of the seed plants develops within the megasporangium (ovule), whereas that of non-seed plants develops on the soil or in water.

The first step in the formation of seeds is the germination of the spores within the sporangia of the sporophyte. If these spores fall upon the soil, no seeds are formed. Some of the ancient ferns had seeds, and some of the modern pteridophytes occasionally have seeds or structures closely resembling seeds.

The Aquatic Ferns

The water ferns constitute a small group consisting of four genera that are considerably unlike the plants so far described in this chapter. *Salvinia* and *Azolla* are floating, while *Marsilia* and *Pilularia* are rooted at the bottom of small ponds or sluggish streams. *Salvinia* has a whorl of three leaves at each node, two of which are floating, hairy, entire leaves; the third leaf looks much like a branched root.

Stems and roots are more conspicuous in *Azolla*. The other two genera are larger plants with prominent leaves from rhizomes

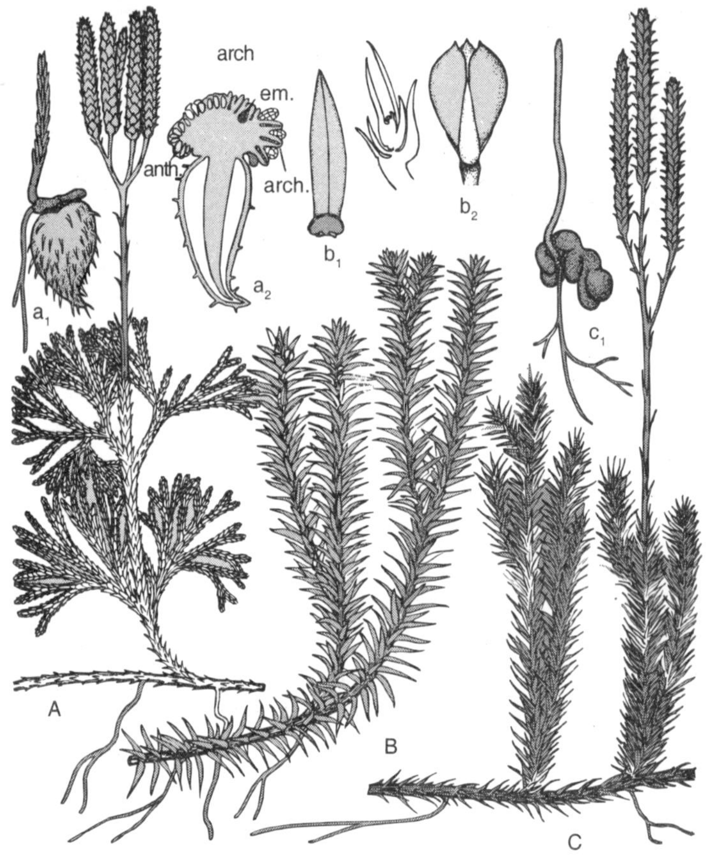

Figure 16.5: Three species of Lycopodium: A, L. complanatum with gametophyte (after Bruchmann); B, L. lucidulum with sporangium (b) and vegetative propagules (b-..); C, L. clavatum with garnetophyte (c.).

rooted in the mud below the water. Superficially the leaves of *Marsilia* resemble a four-leaved clover; those of *Pilularia* resemble leaves of grasses.

Two kinds of spores develop in the water ferns: microspores and megaspores. Male gametophytes develop from the microspores, and female gametophytes from the megaspores. Plants that bear both microspores and megaspores are said to be *heterosporous* (different spores), in contrast to *homosporous* plants in which the spores are all alike and the gametophytes that develop from them are bisexual.

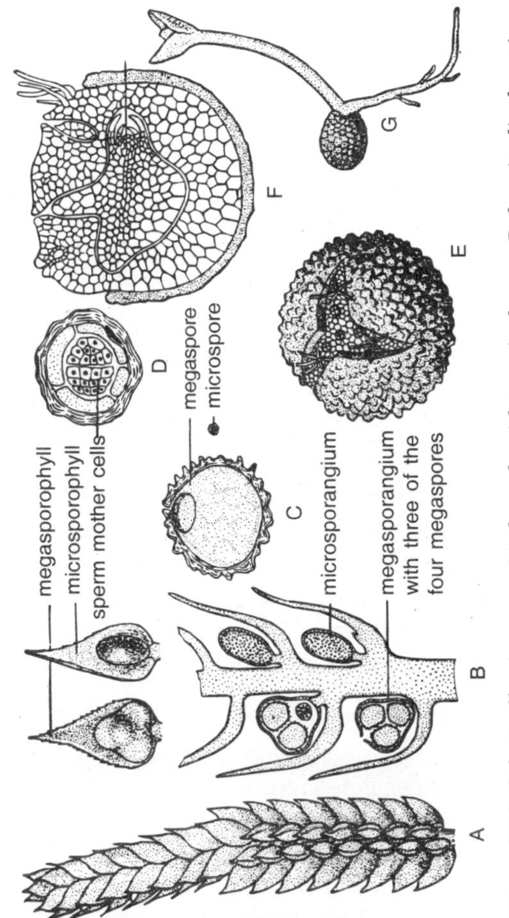

Figure 16.6: Selaginella: A, vegetative branch with terminal cone; B, longitudinal section of a cone with megasporangia and microsporangia; C, relative sizes of megaspores and microspores; D, male gametophyte with sperm mother cells seen in section; E, female gametophyte with apical cells of 4 archegonia and 3 groups of rhizoids partly enclosed by spore wall; F, section of E with two sporophyte embryos; G, young sporophyte, the beginning of a leafy plant with branches similar to A. C and D after F. M. Lyon, E and F after H. Bruchmann.

The Lycopods or Club Mosses

The club mosses are relatively small in size, frequently evergreen, and flourish especially in the tropics. The common name refers to their moss-like leaves and club-shaped cones. The upright appearance of some species is that of a small pine tree; hence the name "ground pine." Species of the two genera, *Lycopodium* and *Selaginella*, also grow in temperate climates, and as far north as Newfoundland and Labrador. They are much more abundant in the northern conifer forests than in the deciduous forest of the Central States.

The tropical species are frequently epiphytic. Many of the species have long creeping stems; in others the stems are erect. The stems usually branch dichotomously. Most of the species are perennials, but a few of the smaller ones are annuals.

Some species of *Selaginella* grow in dry climates. During the rainy seasons the numerous stems are spread out in the form of a dense rosette. During dry weather the stems curve upward and inroll toward the center of the plant, with the result that the whole plant has the form of a ball and may be blown about.

When moisture is again available, the stems unroll and new roots grow. Such plants are the so-called "resurrection plants." The plant rolls and unrolls even when dead. Fossil records of the ancestors of the lycopods are very abundant in Carboniferous rocks.

From them it is evident that during this period hundreds of species of club mosses were dichotomously branched trees up to several feet in diameter and a hundred or more feet in height. The leaves were somewhat scale-like, arranged in spirals or in whorls, and often a half-foot long. The number of species of present-day lycopods, all of which are small plants, is estimated at about 600.

The Sporophyte

Both *Lycopodium* and *Selaginella* consist of a muchbranched, creeping or erect stem, practically covered by small scale-like leaves attached by a broad base. The adventitious roots are filiform and develop from the under side of the stem in contact with the soil or in moist air. Both the stems and leaves have a fundamental structure similar to that of seed plants.

The more primitive species have rather large sporangia in the axils of leaves; in the more specialized types the sporophylls are small, often non-green, and arranged in compact cones at the ends of upright branches.

In *Lycopodium* four spores develop in each of the mother cells in the sporangium, and all the spores are alike morphologically and physiologically. Consequently *Lycopodium* is said to be homosporous. In *Selaginella* the spores are of two kinds formed in different sporangia.

The small spores (microspores) develop by the hundreds in small sporangia (microsporangia), and four large spores (megaspores) develop in each large sporangium (megasporangium). *Selaginella* is thus heterosporous.

The relative size of the two kinds of spores is perhaps insignificant, for in equisetums the spores are indistinguishable, and in some seed plants the microspores are larger than the megaspores. The significant fact is that in *Selaginella* the gametophytes resulting from the germination of the spores bear either archegonia or antheridia, but not both.

A thallus bearing only one kind of gamete is *unisexual;* one bearing both kinds is *bisexual.* The gametophyte. From the germinating spore of *Lycopodium* cylindrical, tuberous, or fleshy thalloid gametophytes develop, either underground and without chlorophyll, or partly aboveground and green.

They are thus partly saprophytic or parasitic on fungi. These gametophytes are very minute, rarely more than a few millimeter in length. The antheridia and archegonia are borne at the apex of the gametophytes. The sperms are straight, uncoiled, and biciliate.

Fertilization of the egg by the sperm occurs in the same manner as in ferns. As noted above, two kinds of gametophytes develop from the spores of *Selaginella.*

Male gametophytes develop within microspores, and female gametophytes develop within the megaspores. Both the male and the female gametophytes are small and are largely contained within the old spore walls. The male gametophyte consists of a vegetative cell and a single antheridium.

The sperms formed are few in number and are similar to those of *Lycopodium.* The female gametophyte is multicellular and at first is contained within the megaspore. Subsequent growth bursts the spore wall, and part of the gametophyte protrudes. The archegonia develop on the apical segments that extend beyond the spore wall. Fertilization takes place as in ferns.

Germination of the zygote begins at once. The early stages of the developing embryo occur within the walls of the megaspore. Later the partly formed embryo continues growth on the soil or other substrate. These gametophytes are among the smallest found

Figure 16.7: Three widely distributed species of Equisetum: A, silvaticum; B, hiemale; and C, arvense; D and E, underground tubers; F, spores with appendages; G, prothallus with four young sporophytes.

in pteridophytes, and are somewhat similar in size to those of seed plants.

Seeds

Occasionally a megaspore of *Selaginella* germinates within the megasporangium, in contrast to others that fall out of the sporangium and germinate on the soil. Consequently the female gametophyte with its archegonium and egg is inside the megaspore wall within the megasporangium. Fertilization may take place, followed by the development of an embryo sporophyte within these structures.

These phenomena occur rarely in *Selaginella,* but when they do occur a seed is the result. *The seeds of pine and all other gymnosperms are formed in this same manner.*

A seed is merely the result of the germination of the megaspore within the megasporangium or ovule, and the formation of the gametophyte and of a new sporophyte within the megasporangium. If the spores fall out of the sporangium and germinate on the soil as they ordinarily do in mosses and ferns, no seeds are formed.

The Quillworts

This group of unique plants is quite unlike any other pteridophytes. Approximately 60 species of quillworts have been described and named, and all of them belong to the genus *Isoetes.* They have the general appearance of a small tufted rush and grow on muddy flats or in the water. They are perennial, and native to north temperate regions.

The plant has a bulb-like axis consisting of an upper leafbearing part and a lower part from which lateral roots grow. The leaves are narrow and grass-like, with a bulbous clasping base, rarely more than a few inches long. *Isoetes* and the grape fern, *Botrychium,* are the only modern pteridophytes in which the stem uniformly has a cambium. Each leaf of *Isoetes* is a potential sporophyll.

The plants are heterosporous, and as many as 300 megaspores or 300,000 microspores may be formed within a single sporangium. The sperms are multiciliate, but the other reproductive structures are similar to those of *Selaginella.*

THE EQUISETUMS

The equisetums constitute another small group of about 25 living species that superficially bear little resemblance to the ferns. Their life cycles, however, are very similar. Like the ferns and lycopods, they are the modern descendants of an ancient phylum of plants.

During the Carboniferous period equisetum-like plants with trunks 90 feet in height and 3 feet in diameter formed extensive forests. Fossil equisetumrelatives have been found also in rocks of the Devonian age.

The modern species are usually less than 3 feet high, although there are two tropical species that may grow to a height of 10 or 15 feet, and a South American species that is said to attain a height of 40 feet when partly supported by trees.

Equisetums occur today in the tropics and semi-tropics, and in the temperate and arctic zones. None has as yet been reported from Australia or New Zealand, from the islands of the Indian Ocean, or from Antarctica. The plants grow best in mildly acid habitats; in the north they are likely to be found in peat bogs.

Elsewhere they are found generally in sandy areas, particularly along streams and rivers, or where there is an underground source of water. One species, *Equisetum kansanum*, is found in prairie patches and the more moist situations of the plains.

The horsetails-or scouring rushes, as they are often popularly called -have columnar, upright, jointed stems, externally fluted and internally characterized by long, tubular air cavities. The central axis of the young stem is pith, but this soon disappears, and the older stem is hollow.

Laterally fused colorless scales occur in whorls at the nodes. Photosynthesis takes place in the chlorenchyma of the stem. Some of the ancient fossil species had true foliage leaves. Stomates occur regularly in the furrows of the stems, and their arrangement is used in the classification of the various species.

The name horsetail is probably suggested by the brush-like character of the numerous slender whorled branches occurring on the upright stems of a few species.

The name scouring rush refers to the accumulation of silica in the walls of the stem tissues. In pioneer days these were gathered and used for scouring metal utensils. The roots are small and adventitious, and arise along the perennial rhizomes, mostly at the nodes.

The Sporophyte

The plant described above is the sporophyte phase of *Equisetum.* It is perennial, although the erect aerial branches may be annual. The peculiar shield-shaped sporophylls are arranged in whorls within a terminal cone and each bears five to ten sporangia.

Within the sporangia are numerous spores which are peculiar in having four long appendages that coil around the spore when moist and uncoil when dry. The spores contain chlorophyll, are short-lived, and cannot withstand desiccation. Consequently, they survive longest and germinate best on shaded moist banks.

The Gametophyte

The gametophytes of equisetums are irregularly lobed, thalloid structures growing on moist substrates near streams or in bogs. The spores from the sporangia are essentially alike in appearance, and the gametophytes of most species, if not all, are potentially bisexual.

But the expression of sex in bisexual gametophytes is influenced by environmental factors, and may be controlled by experimental conditions. Some species such as *E. arvense,* which may be bisexual under certain conditions, are usually unisexual.

Archegonia usually develop on the larger gametophytes, and antheridia on the smaller ones. Fertilization takes place when a motile sperm fuses with an egg. The resulting zygote germinates at once, and an embryo sporophyte is formed.

CHAPTER 17 Euglenophycophyta and Charophyta

In addition to the Chlorophycophyta, two other groups of organisms, often considered to be algae, have chloroplasts that contain chlorophylls *a* and *b* as well as a largely similar array of carotenes and xanthophylls. These two groups, the divisions Euglenophycophyta and Charophyta, clearly not closely related to each other, will be discussed in this chapter.

DIVISION EUGLENOPHYCOPHYTA

The Euglenophycophyta contain approximately 11 chlorophyllous genera and 25 colorless ones, seemingly with a number of characteristics in common.

More than 800 species have been described, but the number will certainly be revised downward when the organisms have been studied critically in culture. The green genera contain chlorophylls *a* and *b,* s-carotene, antheraxanthin, neoxanthin, and several other carotenoids and quinones in their plastids.

Euglena, Trachelomonas, and *Phacus,* all chlorophyllous, are included in the following discussion, which emphasizes *Euglena. Euglena* (Gr. *eu,* good, + Gr. *glene,* eyeball), *Phacus* (Gr. *phakos,* lentil), and *Trachelomonas* (Gr. *trachelos,* neck, + Gr. *moms,* single organism) are widely distributed in freshwater pools, often in such abundance as to form water blooms.

A comprehensive summary of the biology of *Euglena* has been published by Buetow *(1968).* At first glance, one would be inclined to classify *Euglena* and *Phacus* as members of the Chlorophycophyta, but closer study reveals a number of respects in which they differ. In the first place, the protoplast in these genera is unwalled and is bounded externally by the plasma membrane. Just beneath this, a specialized series of ridged and grooved strips forms a structure that together with the plasma membrane is called the periplast.

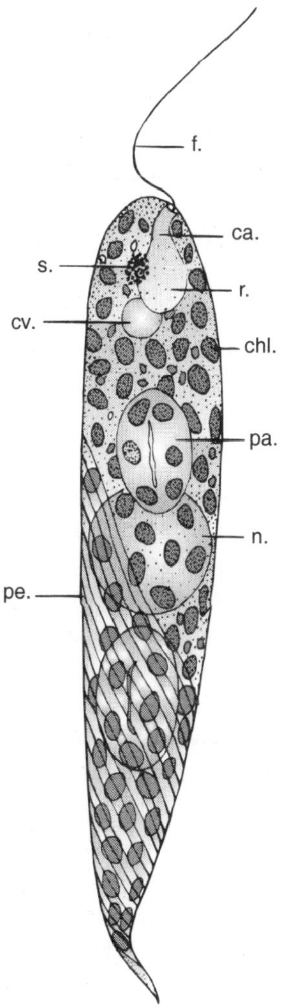

Figure 17.1: Euglena sp. Living individual. ca., canal; chl., chloroplast; c.v., contractile vacuole; f., flagellum; n., nucleus; pa., paramylum; pe., periplast; r., reservoir; s., stigma.

The latter is largely proteinaceous but contains a small amount (ca. 6-17%) of lipids and/or carbohydrates. The periplast is apparently elastic, and cellulose is entirely absent. The strips of periplast are arranged in a helix in most species.

A row of mucilage-producing bodies, each connected by a canal to a strip of periplast, is present along each of the latter. The strips may be ornamented with warts or lumps. In a number of species of *Euglena* the periplast is nonrigid, and the organisms undergo marked changes in body form, sometimes called *metaboly.*

The anterior portion of a *Euglena* cell contains a slightly excentric opening, which leads through a canal to a reservoir. Attached separately to the base of the latter are two flagella, one long and emergent and one much shorter and nonemergent.

The long flagellum bears many very fine hairs, sometimes in a single row; the hairs are usually not visible with ordinary light microscopy. The emergent flagellum has a lateral swelling at about the level of the eyespot.

At one side, or slightly posterior to the reservoir, occurs a large contractile vacuole, which discharges into the reservoir usually once every 15-60 sec. Chloroplasts of varying form (discoid, elongate, platelike, according to the species) are present in *Euglena,* and these, except for the small discoid type, contain pyrenoids.

Mitochondria, Golgi apparatus, and endoplasmic reticulum also are present. The large nucleus is usually central. Unlike the stigma of the Chlorophycophyta, that of *Euglena is* not included in a plastid but lies free in the cytoplasm in the vicinity of the *flagellar swelling* (parabasal body).

The stigma, or eyespot, is composed of 20-60 orange-red droplets, each one of which, or groups of which, is bounded by a membrane. The pigments ascribed to the eyespot include echinenone along with at least two other carotenoids and possibly others.

Investigations of and speculations regarding the function of the stigma of *Euglena* and related genera have been numerous and contradictory. It seems clear that the positive movement of euglenoid cells toward light of moderate intensity (positive phototaxis) and their movement away from intense light (negative phototaxis) are connected with the eyespot, directly or indirectly. According to one hypothesis, the eyespot is the primary site of light perception, and this is supported by the fact that the action and absorption spectra of the eyespot pigments (ca. 485 nm) coincide; on the other hand, it has been postulated that the true site of reception of light stimuli is the flagellar swelling and that the eyespot serves merely as a shield or shade for the organelle.

The reserve polysaccharide of euglenoid cells is a β-1 : 3-linked glucan called *paramylon*, which does not stain with iodine. It will be recalled that most Chlorophycophyta form starch, an α-1 : 4-linked glucan.

Unlike the starch of green algae, paramylon forms in the colorless cytoplasm outside the chloroplast, although in some cases it may arise in close association with pyrenoids but outside the chloroplast membrane. In some species the cells may contain two large paramylon grains, one anterior to and one posterior to the nucleus.

Reproduction in *Euglena* is by cell division, which is preceded by nuclear division (mitosis). The latter differs from that in many other organisms in the persistence and division of the nucleolus, the persistence of the nuclear membrane during mitosis, and the absence of a highly differentiated mitotic spindle, so that the replicated chromosomes seem to separate and to migrate autonomously to the poles during the anaphases.

There is no incontrovertible evidence of sexual reproduction in the Euglenophycophyta. With respect to nutrition, *Euglena* and the related green species show some variation, although none has been proved to be completely photoautotrophic or phagotrophic.

Photoautotrophic organisms can synthesize their protoplasm *entirely* from inorganic substrates using light energy. Phagotrophy is the animallike ingestion of food particles. Almost all euglenoids *require* vitamins B_1 and B_{12}, and they need reduced nitrogen compounds, not nitrates. A number can use, but seemingly do not require, amino acids and proteins as nitrogen sources.

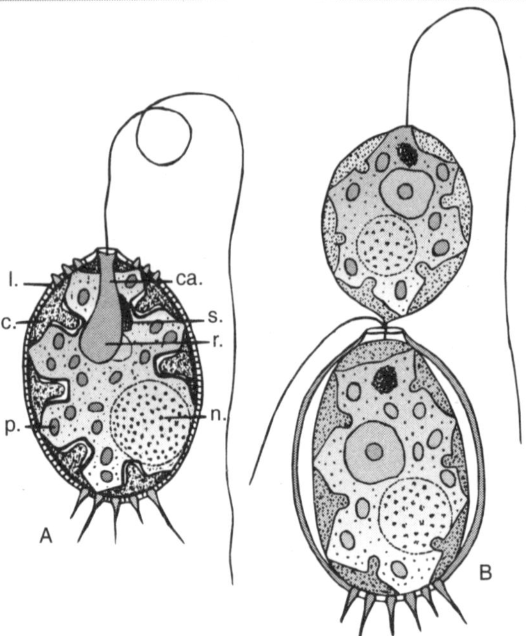

Figure 17.2: Trachelomonas armata. A. Longisection of a single individual. B. Reproduction. c., chloroplast; ca., canal; I., lorica; n., nucleus; P., paramylum; r., reservoir; s., stigma.

Chlorophyllous euglenids may be facultatively heterotrophic in darkness, using organic compounds such as acetate, organic acids, and alcohol, and their growth rate may be increased by addition of organic compounds to light-green cultures.

In relation to nutrition and also to phylogeny, it is of interest that certain strains of *Euglena (E. gracilis)* can be transformed experimentally into colorless organisms by cultivating them at high temperatures (35° C), or by subjecting them to ultraviolet radiation or to antibiotics (streptomycin, etc.).

In such a regime the division of the chloroplast is retarded, while cell division continues, so that some of the cellular division products ultimately lack chloroplasts.

From such individuals, colorless races may be developed and maintained, of course, in media with organic carbon sources. These colorless races of *Euglena* correspond to the colorless genera *Khawkinea* and *Astasia,* which are clearly protozoa.

Similarly, both *Phacus*, a flattened, rigid euglenoid, and *Trachelomonas*, a euglenid living in a pectic shell, or *lorica*, have colorless counterparts *(Hyalophacus* and *Hyalotrachelomonas*, respectively).

The division Euglenophycophyta contains the single class Euglenop-hyceae, which in turn contains six orders, distinguished largely in flagellation. The genera discussed above, except *Khawkinea* and *Astasia*, all belong to the class Euglenophyceae, order Euglenales, and family Euglenaceae.

DIVISION CHAROPHYTA

It should be noted that the root *phyco*, although traditionally classified with the algae, has been omitted from our divisional

Figure 17.3: Chara sejuncta. Portion of axis.

designation. This is to emphasize the important differences, to be summarized below, between members of this division and algae.

The *stoneworts* and *brittleworts*, represented here by the genera *Chara* (Latin name) and *Nitella (L. nitella,* splendor), are sometimes classified in the division Chlorophycophyta as a class coordinate with the Chlorophyceae. This reflects the point of view that their morphological deviations from the Chlorophyceae are of insufficient magnitude to warrant their removal to a separate division.

In this text, however, for reasons to be enumerated below, the stoneworts are considered to represent a group of divisional rank coordinate with the Chlorophycophyta.

The division Charophyta contains the single class Charophyceae, order Charales, and family Characeae. *Chara* and *Nitella* grow in the muddy or sandy bottoms of clear lakes and ponds, or in limestone streams and quarry basins.

In the latter habitats, certain species have the capacity of precipitating calcium carbonate from the water and covering themselves with calcareous surface layers. This last attribute has suggested the names stoneworts and brittleworts.

Calcareous casts of the oogonial and vegetative branches of stoneworts have been preserved abundantly as fossils. Unlike most freshwater algae, the Charophyta are plants with macroscopically distinctive features.

The markedly whorled branching, the organization of the plant body into regular nodes and inter nodes, and its regular pattern of ontogeny from the single apical cell are all features that suggest the Arthrophyta and/or *Ephedra* among the vascular plants.

The plant consists of a branching axis on which arise whorls or smaller branches of limited growth, often called "leaves." The lower portions of the axes are anchored to the substratum by branching filaments, the *rhizoids*.

The rhizoids serve as organs of vegetative propagation, giving rise to erect green shoots. Branches arise at the nodes among the leaf bases. Median longitudinal sections through the apex of the axis reveal the very regular manner of development that occurs in the stoneworts. All the cells have their origin from the descendants of a prominent, dome-shaped apical cell that cuts off derivatives in a transverse direction, parallel to its basal wall. Each of these segments divides again transversely into a nodal and an internodal cell.

The internodal cells elongate tremendously and may remain uncovered, as in *Nitella;* or, as in most species of *Chara,* the internodal cells become clothed with corticating cells that arise from the node above and below a given internode.

Nuclear division in the internodal cells is amitotic, and more than 2000 nuclei may occur within a single cell. The protoplasm of the internodal cells streams rapidly in a direction parallel to the long axis of the cell; the minute peripheral chloroplasts are embedded in stationary cytoplasm.

A prominent vacuole occupies the central portion of the elongate internodal cells, which are multinucleate. The nodal initials divide in such fashion as to form two central cells surrounded by one or more rings of cells.

The outermost of these are the precursors of the whorled lateral branches of "leaves." The latter develop nodes, internodes, and cortications like those of the main axes in *Chara;* in *Nitella* the leaves are uncorticated.

Reproduction in the Charophyta is strictly oogamous, and

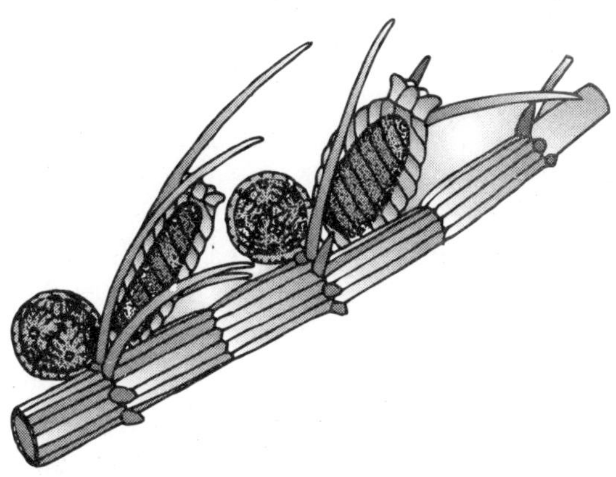

Figure 17.4: Chara contraria. Portion of axis with sex organs.

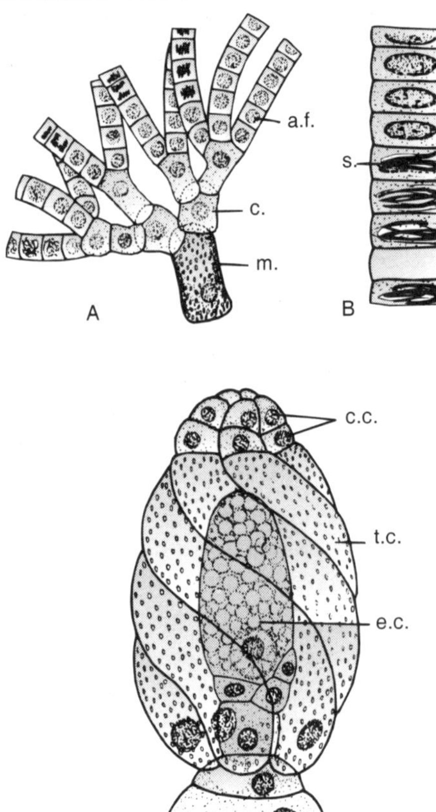

Figure 17.5: Nitella opaca. A. Manubrium with capitula and antheridial filaments. B. Segment of antheridial filament enlarged; note empty cell, which has released its sperm. C. Living, immature oogonium. a.£, antheridial filament; c., capitulum; c.c., crown cells; e, c. , egg cell; M., manubrium; S., sperm; t. c., tube cell.

the gametes are produced in specialized complex structures usually called antheridia and oogonia, but sometimes designated the *globule* and *nucule*, respectively.

Some species are dioecious, while others are monoecious. The reproductive structures are borne on the leaves. A mature plant furnishes a rather complete series in the ontogeny of the sex organs, if one examines leaves of successively older nodes.

The younger sex organs are green, but as development

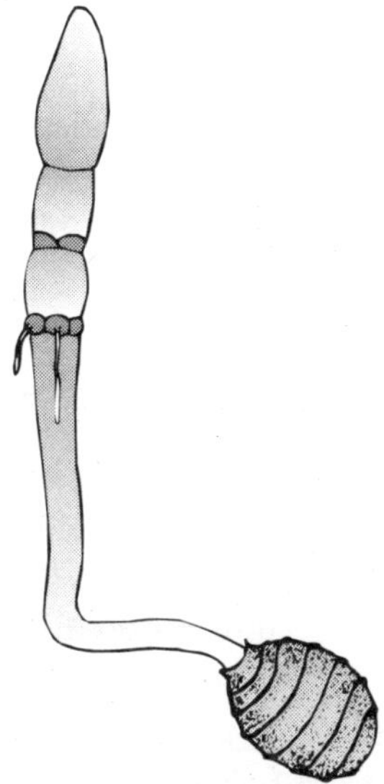

Figure 17.6: Nitella sp. Germination of the oospore (zygote).

proceeds, the antheridia become orange-red and the oogonia rather blackish brown (after fertilization) in many species. The mature male reproductive organ consists of chains of colorless cells, each of which produces a single sperm, surrounded by several types of sterile accessory cells; the whole structure is stalked.

Its surface is composed of eight large, epidermislike *shield cells*, which are orange-red at maturity and contain incomplete, anticlinal' septa. To the inner tangential surface of each of these is attached a prismatic cell, the *manubrium* (*L. manus,* hand), to which, in turn, are attached one or more isodiametric cells, the *primary capitulum* (*L. ca put,* head).

The primary capitula are all contiguous at the center and give rise to secondary and, in some cases, tertiary capitular cells, which generate the colorless *antheridial filaments*. These are composed of boxlike cells coiled up within the cavities formed in the male organ by the enlargement of the developing shield cells.

A single biflagellate sperm emerges through a pore in the wall of each antheridial cell at maturity. The sperms are liberated by the partial separation of contiguous shield cells. The sperms of Charophyta are quite complex.

They consist of a "head," an intermediate portion, and a "tail." The anterior "head" consists of the flagella, their basal bodies, and a row of mitochondria; the slightly unequal flagella emerge at the base of the "head."

The intermediate region consists largely of the elongate, conde-nsed nucleus. The posterior "tail" contains plastids, mitochondria, and possibly residual cytoplasm. The female reproductive organ of the Charophyta is less complicated.

It, too, consists of a fertile cell, the *oogonium* proper, surrounded by spirally elongate sterile cells, the *tube cells.* The apices of these are delimited to form the five cells *(Chara)* of the *corona* or *crown*; there are two tiers or ten crown cells in *Nitella.*

The female reproductive organ also is pedicellate. At maturity, the tube cells separate from one another immediately under the corona, thus providing pathways for the entrance of sperms. The single large egg is uninucleate and contains abundant starch grains.

After fertilization, the zygote develops a thickened wall, and the oogonium is abscised from the leaf. The inner walls of the tube cells also thicken and persist as spiral markings on the dormant zygote (oospore) surface. After a period of dormancy, which is probably followed by meiosis, the zygote germinates into a juvenile plantlet, all the nuclei of which are the descendants of one of the products of meiosis, as in *Spirogyra.*

Comparison of the morphology of *Chara, Nitella,* and other genera of Charophyta with that of the Chlorophycophyta provides few points of similarity. The complexity of the plant body in the Charophyta is unparalleled among the Chlorophycophyta, except, perhaps, in certain marine, siphonous genera.

Furthermore, such features as division into nodes and intern-odes, cortication of the axes and leaves, and the occurrence of special cellular sheaths around the sexual organs are absent among Chlorophycophyta.

For these reasons, among others, it is thought that the stoneworts represent a distinct phyletic line and that, as such, they should be placed in a division separate from the Chlorophycophyta. It is argued by some that their sex organs suggest affinity with the Hepatophyta, or Bryophyta.

This claim is denied by others on the ground that the sex organs of the Charophyta are really unicellular, while those of the Hepatophyta and Bryophyta are multicellular.

It is not clear to the writers, however, why the egg protoplast enclosed in a cell wall and surrounded by tube cells in the Charophyta should all together be considered "unicellular," while the egg protoplast of a liverwort or moss, enclosed in its cell wall, surrounded by the venter, and associated with neck canal and neck cells, should be considered "multicellular."

Even if they are not homologous, both are apparently multicellular organs. If the term "antheridium" is applied in the Charophyta to one of the colorless cells of the antheridial filament, because it produces one sperm, by those who wish to reserve the older terms "globule" and "nucule," application of similar reasoning would restrict the use of the term "antheridium" to what is now called a spermatogenous cell or, possibly, an androcyte, in liverworts, mosses, and other plants.

Is this not, perhaps, an eloquent example of the statement that "nature mocks at human categories"? Once again, it should be emphas-ized that the divisional name Charophyta (rather than Charophycophyta) emphasizes the authors' uncertainty that these plants are algae.

CHAPTER 18

Phaeophycophyta

The division Phaeophycophyta (Gr. *phaios,* dusky, + Gr. *phykos,* seaweed, + Gr. *phyton,* plant), the brown algae, includes a single class, the Phaeophyceae (Gr. *phaios* + Gr. *phykos).* The Phaeophycophyta are marine in habitat, with the exception of about four genera. They occur in the open ocean as well as in quiet estuaries, and may be abundant on the muddy bottoms of salt marshes.

Many grow attached to rocks, shells, or coarser algae such as the kelps. Approximately 250 genera and 1500 species of Phaeophycophyta have been described. In general, brown algae flourish in colder ocean waters and on rocky coasts, where many grow attached in relatively shallow water in the intertidal and sublittoral zones.

A number of genera are able to withstand exposure to the atmosphere during low tide, whereas others are sublittoral and continuously subme-rged. Some of the large genera live in shoal waters, and most thrive in waters with considerable current. Few brown algae occur at great depths. Both annual and perennial genera are known.

The brownish shades of the plant reflect the abundant presence in the plastids of the xanthophyll, *fucoxanthin*, which is dominant over chlorophylls *a* and c, the other xanthophylls, and β-carotene. The *plastids* are single, few, or numerous in each cell, and may be elaborate in form. No starch occurs in *Phaeophycophyta*; instead, the excess photosynthate accumulates as a carbohydrate, *laminarin* (a mixture of polysaccharides with

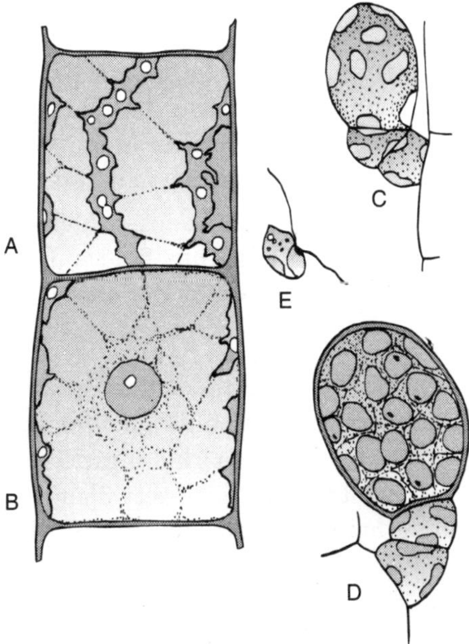

Figure 18.1: Ectocarpus siliculosus. A. Surface and B. Median optical view of vegetative cell. C, D. Stages in development of unilocular zoosporangia. E. Motile cell from plurilocular organ.

1 : 3 and 1 : 6 linkages), as mannitol, or in the form of fat droplets. The nuclei of Phaeophyc-ophyta are prominent structures. In many genera, centrosomes and astral radiations appear during mitosis, as viewed by light microscopy, as in many animal cells.

The protoplast is bounded by a primary wall and middle lamella composed of a gummy substance, alginic acid. This may represent 10-25% of the dry weight. Alginic acid is a polymer of Dmannuronic and L-guluronic acids. Alginic acid has considerable commercial importance as a stabilizer, emulsifier, and coating for paper.

The motile cells of brown algae are distinctive and differ from those of the Chlorophycophyta in that they are laterally or subapically biflagellate. The longer, usually anterior, flagellum is of the tinsel type, and the shorter, posterior one is whiplash. Although it has been suggested that the Phaeophycophyta originated from unicellular motile organisms with similar lateral or subapical flagellation, no such organisms have yet been discovered.

The simplest type of plant body in the group is the branched filament. Many Phaeophycophyta have considerable complexity of structure, as manifested in their leaflike, stemlike, and rootlike organs, which exhibit obvious histological differentiation.

Certain brown algae, the giant kelps, which may attain a length of 50m, rival forest trees in stature. Bold and Wynne (1978) include a more extensive discussion of the brown algae.

Ectocarpus

Ectocarpus (Gr. ektos, outside, + Gr. karpos, fruit) is a relatively simple brown alga commonly growing on stones and shells or epiphytically on larger marine algae. *Ectocarpus* is a branching filamentous plant in which erect filaments arise from an attached prostrate branch system, much as in the green alga *Stigeoclonium.*

Its growth is diffuse or generalized. The mature cells contain band-shaped plastids with pyrenoidlike bodies; the function of the latter is not known. The life cycle and reproduction of *Ectocarpus* are fundamentally similar to those in Ova and *Cladophora-namely,* type D, h + d—in that meiosis is sporic during an alternation of isomorphic generations.

In the diploid sporophytic plants, the terminal cells of lateral branchlets enlarge, and their protoplasts segment into approximately 32-64 zoospores, each of which becomes pearshaped and laterally biflagellate. These are discharged through an apical pore, and after a period of motility they begin to develop into new filaments.

The organs producing these zoospores are called *unilocular zoosporangia,* inasmuch as the zoospores lie within a single cavity. It has been shown that meiosis occurs during the first two nuclear divisions in the unilocular zoosporangium, so that the zoospores produced from these structures are haploid.

These zoospores grow into plants morphologically similar to the zoospore-producing sporophytes, but these produce multicellular gametangia on lateral branches. Every cell of these plurilocular gametangia produces a laterally biflagellate gamete. Although

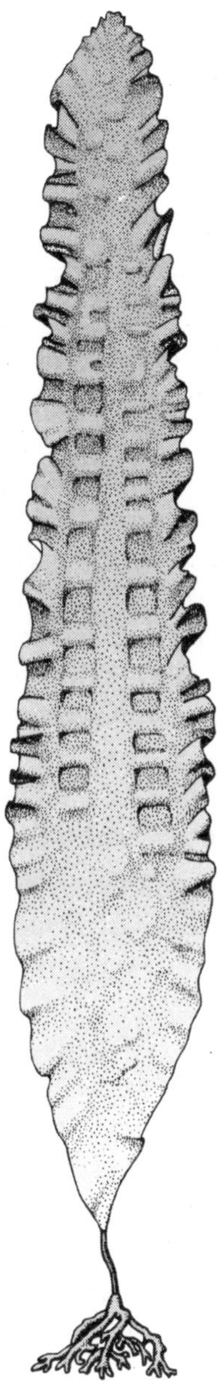

Figure 18.2: Laminaria agardhii (young specimen). Note blade, stipe, and attaching organs.

morphologi-cally isogamous, the compatible gametes of *E. siliculosus*, which develop on different plants (heterothallism), are functionally anisogamous, since some gametes (the female) settle on a substrate and attract other motile gametes (the male).

The male gametes become attached to the female by the tip of their long flagellum. The attractant produced by the female gametes is volatile and is known as *Ectocarpene* (All-cis-1[cycloheptadien-2',5'-yl]butene-1). Its chemical structure was elucidated in 1971 by Muller, Jaenicke, Donike, and Akintobi. Its action and that of other sex hormones in brown algae are discussed by Jaenicke (1977). After plasmogamy has occurred between the female gamete and one male, the female gamete no longer attracts males.

The life cycle (type D, h + d) of *Ectocarpus* is summarized in other chapter of this book. The life cycle here described occurs in E. *siliculosus.* Few other species have received adequate study. There is some indication that the life cycle of *E. siliculosus* varies with geographical location, being different in Naples and England from that reported above for the coast of Massachusetts.

For example, Muller (1966, 1967) has reported an exceedingly complex life cycle for *E. siliculosus* on the basis of field studies and laboratory cultures of material from Naples.

According to him, in addition to the D, h + d type of life cycle, several additional alternatives occur. These include the occurrence of haploid, diploid, and tetraploid sporophytes, all of which produce unilocular zoosporangia, although meiosis occurs only in those of diploid and tetraploid plants.

The haploid sporophytes arise from gametes that develop parthenoge-netically. Gametophytes develop only from zoospores released by unilocular zoosporangia.

That sporophytes may be morphologically sporophytes and yet haploid, diploid, or tetraploid is evidence (more of which will be cited and discussed later) that chromosome constitution *per se* does not determine whether gametophyte or sporophyte develops.

The Kelps

The kelps are of interest not only because of the complexity of their vegetative structure but also because their life cycle is

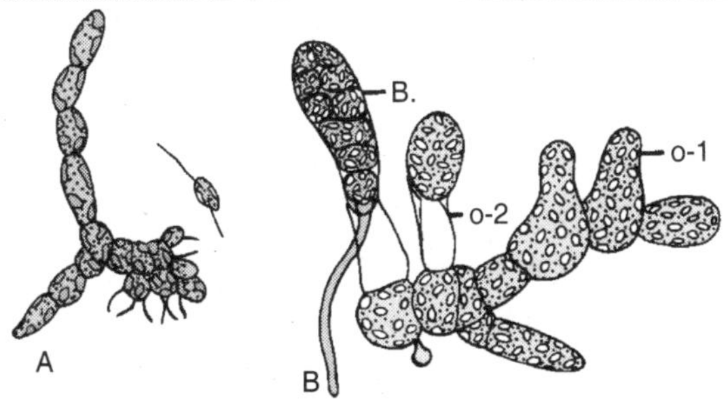

Figure 18.3: Laminaria japonica. A. Male gametophyte; note cluster of antheridia and sperm. B. Female gametophyte; o-1, immature oogonium; o-2, oogonium with extruded egg; s., young sporophyte at mouth of oogonium.

representative of a type that occurs in few Chlorophycophyta but is similar in many respects to that of ferns and other vascular plants.

Laminaria

Laminaria (L. lamina, blade) occurs attached to rocks that are usually submerged, even at extreme low tide. The plant consists of a branching *holdfast*, a *stipe*, and an expanded *blade*. Growth occurs at the junction of the stipe and is, therefore, *intercalary*.

The oldest portion of the blade is the apex. Both blade and stipe are quite complex histologically. Only the more superficial cells of both stipe and blade are photosynthetic, other cells having very few plastids. The central part of the blade is composed of elongate, colorless, filamentous cells constituting the medulla.

Some of these, the *trumpet hyphae*, have flaring ends and function as sieve elements. Late in the growing season, during the winter and spring on the eastern coast of North America, certain superficial cells of the blade elongate and become transformed into unilocular zoosporangia.

These occur in extensive groups, or *sori*. Between the zoosporangia occur sterile filaments called *paraphyses*. Paraphyses may occur among sex organs or sporangia. Meiosis is sporic and occurs in the unilocular zoosporangia, as in *Ectocarpus*.

Sex chromosomes of the X-Y type have been described in

Laminaria and other kelps, so that sexuality of the gametophytes is under genetic control and determined at meiosis. Each zoosporangium produces 32-64 zoospores, which are liberated and develop asexually into prostrate, *Ectocarpus-like* branching filaments that ultimately produce gametangia.

The *Laminaria* plant is diploid and sporophytic. The prostrate, branching filaments that develop from the haploid zoospores are gametophytic, haploid, dioecious, and oogamous. The male gametophytic filaments are of smaller diameter than the female and often grow intertwined with them.

The antheridia are produced as lateral cells on the male gametophyte; each antheridium produces a minute, laterally biflagellate sperm. The oogonia produce single eggs, which are released from but remain attached to a tubular protuberance of the oogonium, so that fertilization and the development of the embryonic sporophyte occur *in situ.*

Without undergoing a dormant period, the zygote grows into a new sporophyte, which ultimately develops the form typical of the species. The life cycle' of *Laminaria* is summarized elsewhere in this chapter. In laboratory culture at 10°C, gametophytes of *L. saccharina* produced antheridia before oogonia matured; antheridia matured within 23 days, and oogonia within 28 days, after the cultures had been started from zoospores.

A photoperiod of 18 hours daily was most favorable for evoking sexual reproduction. The life cycle of *Laminaria* and other kelps is instructive in a number of respects. It is fundamentally similar to that of Ova, the marine species of *Cladophora* and *Ectocarpus*, all of which have sporic meiosis and alternation of free-living, sporophytic and haploid, gametophytic generations (type D, h + d).

However, in *Laminaria* and other kelps, the sporophyte and gametophyte differ markedly in size, structure, and longevity; alternation here is *heteromorphic*, as in some species of *Bryopsis.* The sporophyte of *Laminaria* and other kelps is a large, complex, perennial plant, dominant in the life cycle, whereas the gametophytes are microscopic, few-celled, branching filaments, and relatively ephemeral.

It should be noted that both generations are free-living plants and presumably photoautotropic. In balance of the two generations, the life cycle of *Laminaria* and other kelps is practically identical with that of ferns and related vascular plants.

As a basis for theoretical discussions of the origin and relation of the alternating generations, it must be borne in mind that various genera of algae in the same aquatic environment illustrate alternation of both similar and dissimilar generations.

Among the land plants, the alternating generations always are markedly dissimilar morphologically. The partial retention of the egg, and consequently the zygote, within the oogonium, which occurs in *Laminaria* and other kelps, represents an intermediate condition between their expulsion in many other algae and their

Figure 18.4: Macrocystis intergrifolia. A. Portion of plant showing holdfasts and branching stipes with air bladders and blades. B. Single segment enlarged.

permanent retention in the land plants. The significance of these features will be referred to later in our discussion of the land plants.

Other Kelps

Plants of *Macrocystis* (Gr. *makros,* long, + *kystis,* bladder), the giant kelp, are among the largest of the brown algae, specimens 45m in length being common on the Pacific coast of North America.

The large plants are attached in deep water, and the branching stipes bear leafy blades, at the base of each of which is a gas-filled bulb, the *pneumatocyst. Macrocystis, Nereocystis,* and *Pelagophycus,* among other kelps, are of interest in that they have specialized series of cells, called sieve tubes, in their stipes.

These are very similar to the sieve tubes of the phloem of the vascular plants. The word "sieve" refers to the pores present in the terminal walls of the adjacent cellular components of the sieve tube.

The sieve tubes here, as in vascular plants, lack nuclei at maturity. Although conduction by the sieve tubes themselves has not been demonstrated, it has been shown that ^{14}C-labeled products of photosynthesis do move through the stipes of *Macrocystis* at rates comparable to movement of substances in the phloem of vascular plants.

Nicholson and Briggs (1972) have demonstrated movement of ^{14}C-labeled photosynthate through the medulla (containing sieve tubes) of *Nereocystis* at an average rate of 37cm/hour.

In *Nereocystis* (Gr. *Nereus,* god of the sea, + Gr. *kystis,* bladder), a large kelp of the North Pacific, the stipe is usually unbranched and terminates in a large pneumatocyst that bears a profusion of blades. *Postelsia* (after A. Postels, German naturalist), the sea palm of the Pacific coast of the United States and Canada, grows in the intertidal zone.

The stout and fleshy unbranched stipes are anchored to the rocky substrate and may be 60cm tall. Each bears distally a number of leaflike blades. In *Macrocystis, Pelagophycus, Nereocystis,* and *Postelsia,* as in *Laminaria* and other kelps, the diploid plants become fertile and by meiosis produce haploid zoospores,

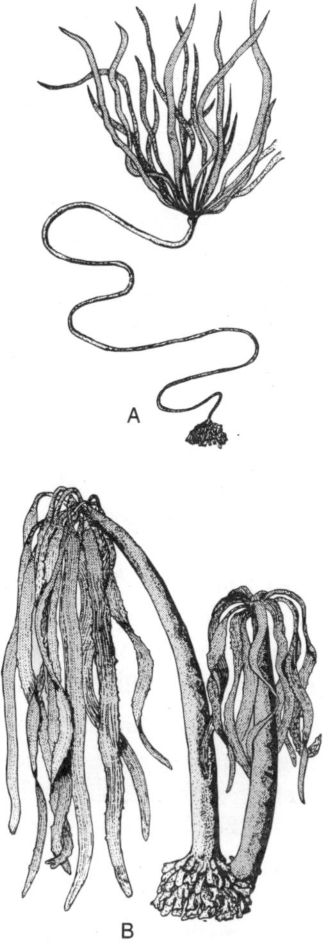

Figure 18.5: A. Nereocystis luetkeana. B. Postelsia palmaeformis.

which grow into microscopic, oogamous gametophytes; some of the latter bear eggs and others bear sperms.

In all the kelps, accordingly, the life cycle is diplobiontic and heteromorphic. A comprehensive account of the kelp beds of California has been published by North (1971).

Dictyota* and *Padina

In contrast to the other genera of Phaeophycophyta discussed in this chapter, which live in cold ocean waters, *Dictyota* and

Figure 18.6: Padina vickersiae, growth habit.

Padina grow in tropical and subtropical latitudes. Both are lithophilic and continuously submerged. Growth in the blades of *Dictyota* is geometric in precision and may be traced to a prominent, dome-shaped apical cell. The derivatives of this cell divide twice in a plane parallel to the surface of the blade so as to form two cortical layers of small, plastid-rich cells and, between these, a medullary layer of larger cells with fewer plastids.

The life cycle of *Dictyota* was long ago shown to be D, h + d and isomorphic. The gametophytes are dioecious and oogamous and the sperms uniflagellate with a tinsel flagellum. Both oogonia and antheridia, the latter like plurilocular gametangia, are borne in groups, or sori, on the surface of the plants.

The zygote grows rapidly into the sporophytic phase, which, except for chromosome constitution and reproductive cells, is identical with the gametophytes. The unilocular sporangia develop on the surfaces of the sporophyte and after meiosis produce four

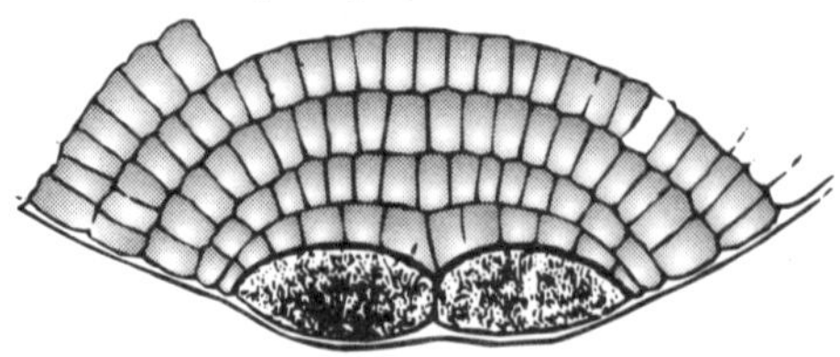

Figure 18.7: Dictyota sp. Origin of dichotomy by equal division of apical cell, diagrammatic.

nonflagellate spores, which develop into gametophytes. The life cycle of *Padina,* the "sea fan," is like that of *Dictyota.*

The Rockweeds: *Fucus* and *Sargassum*

The widely distributed genera *Fucus (L. fucus,* from Gr. *phykos,* seaweed) (the rockweed) and *Sargassum* (Sp. *sargazo,* seaweed) represent still a third type of life cycle that occurs among the Phaeophycophyta. While four species of *Fucus* have been grown from zygotes in the laboratory, only one, *F. distichus,* attained sexual maturity .

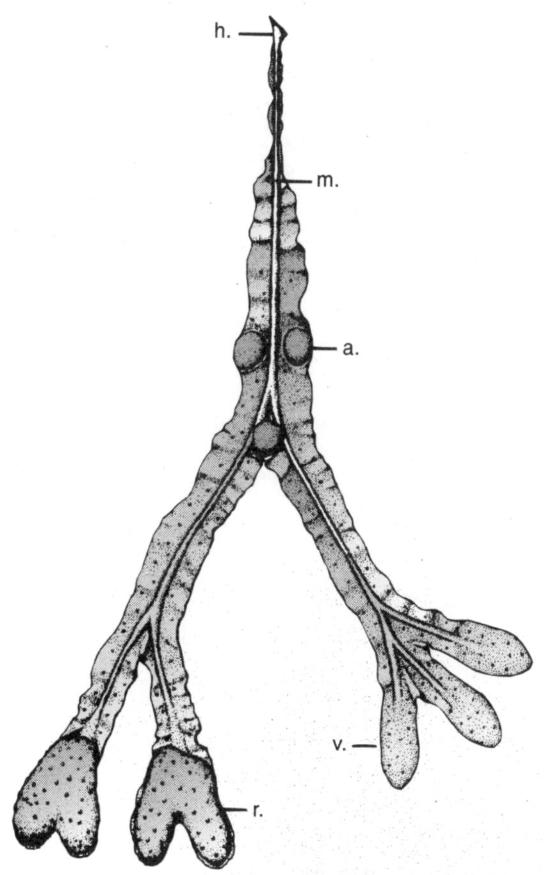

Figure 18.8: Fucus vesiculosus.a., air vesicle; h., holdfast; m., midrib; r., receptacle with conceptacles; V., vegetative apex.

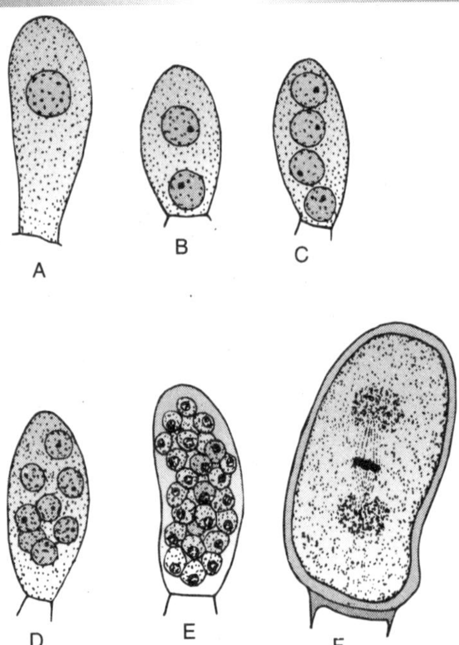

Figure 18.9: Fucus vesiculosus. A-E. Stages in development of an antheridium. F. Young oogonium, first meiotic metaphase; note polar asters.

Fucus commonly grows attached to rocks in the intertidal zone, where the plants are exposed at low tide. The plant body, which may attain a length of 2 m in certain species, is leathery, flattened, and dichotomously branched.

Growth is initiated by the divisions of several clearly differentiated apical cells, derivatives of which, by subsequent division, enlargement, and differentiation, build up a rather complex plant body.

The plants are attached by multicellular holdfast discs. Prominent midribs, *cryptoblasts* (probably sterile conceptacles, the latter described below), and *air bladders* occur in some species.

The plant body of *Fucus* and other rock-weeds is quite complex histologically. The derivatives of the apical cells differentiate into an epidermis, a cortex, and a central region of branching filaments and fibers, the last two embedded in a slimy, polysaccharide matrix.

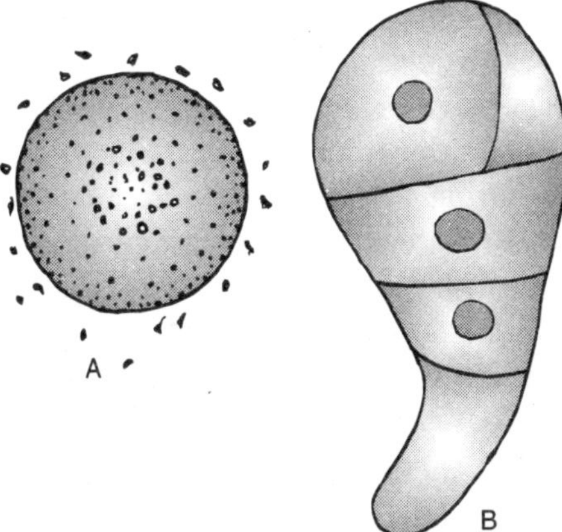

Figure 18.10: A. Fucus serratus. Egg surrounded by sperm. B. Fucus vesiculosus. Young plant from germinating zygote.

The walls of all the cells are thick and fibrillar and are composed of alginic acid, while the amorphous matrix seems to be fucoidin, a sulphated polysaccharide. The latter is produced within the cells, as is the alginic acid, and the fucoidin is secreted through the fibrillar (alginic acid walls) into the intercellular spaces.

The production of reproductive cells is localized at the tips of the branches in fertile areas called *receptacles*, which become enlarged and distended because of the internal secretion of large quantities of hydrophilic compounds.

The receptacles bear scattered, pustulelike cavities, the *concept-acles*, which communicate with the surrounding water through narrow ostioles, through which tufts of colorless filaments protrude.

At maturity, the conceptacles bear eggs and sperms; either these may be in the same conceptacle (monoecism), or those that produce the eggs may be on different plants (dioecism) from those producing sperms, depending on the species. Thus, plants of *F. vesiculosus* are usually unisexual; certain other species found along the Atlantic coast of North America, *F. spiralis* and *F. distichus*, are monoecious.

The sperms are laterally biflagellate and produced in groups of 64 from antheridia developed on branching filaments from the wall of the conceptacle. In *Fucus,* each oogonium, also an outgrowth from the conceptacle wall, produces eight eggs.

The conceptacles contain colorless paraphyses, which undergo basal growth. Young oogonia and antheridia are uninucleate. Meiosis occurs during the first two nuclear divisions in these structures, the plants themselves being diploid.

Large amounts of alginic acid and fucoidin are synthesized, especially within the oogonia, and contribute to the development of the three-layered oogonial wall. Liberation of gametes is closely connected with tidal conditions in some species.

At low tide, when the plants are exposed to the drying action of the air, shrinkage of the plant body may be accompanied by extrusion of ripe oogonia and antheridia in slimy masses through the ostioles to the surface of the plant.

The incoming tide, in submerging these droplets containing the sex organs, effects swelling and dissolution of their walls, so that the individual gametes are set free in the water. However, in other species, extrusion of gametes occurs in continuously submerged plants.

The eggs are large, spherical, and nonmotile and are penetrated by individual sperms, which swarm about the eggs in great numbers. The sperms of Fucus are unusual in that the posterior flagellum is longer than the anterior.

Fertilization in *F. distichus* has been studied by Pollock (1970), whose illustrations are produced as Figure elsewhere in this chapter and explained in its caption. The outermost layer of the threelayered oogonium ruptures so that the eggs are enclosed by two layers when they leave the conceptacles.

In *F. distichus*, about 20 min elapse before the sperms emerge from the freed antheridia and before the eggs are liberated from the remaining oogonial wall layers.

The eggs of Fucus serratus also produce a volatile sperm attractant designated Fucoserratene. Chemically this is 1,3-trans-5-cisoctatriene. Nuclear union follows plasmogamy, and the resulting zygote secretes a thin wall and germinates, without a period of dormancy, into a new Fucus plant. The life cycle' of Fucus may be summarized elsewhere in this chapter.

Figure 18.11: Sargassum filipendula. Portion of plant. a., air vesicle; r., immature receptacles; v., leaf-like vegetative branch.

It seems clear from this summary that the life cycle of Fucus, like that of some species of Bryopsis, Codium, Caulerpa, and other siphonous green algae, falls into type H, d, in which a diploid organism undergoes gametic meiosis and the zygote grows directly into the new plant.

Sargassum, unlike Fucus, is, with the exception of one or two species, largely a plant of warm marine waters. Sargassum is complex in having leaflike organs, stalked air bladders, and much-modified receptacles. In *Sargassum,* seven of the eight nuclei disintegrate, so that each oogonium gives rise to only a single egg. *Sargassum natans,* the "Gulf weed," is abundant in the Gulf of Mexico, and tremendous quantities of it are often washed onto Gulf beaches after tropical storms.

CHAPTER 19

Chrysophycophyta and Pyrrhophycophyta

The division Chrysophycophyta includes three classes of algae in the plastids, of which carotenes and xanthophylls are prominent in relation to the chlorophylls; in this respect (and others) they resemble the brown algae (Phaeophycophyta).

The cells, accordingly, are varying shades of yellow-green and brown. Their excess photosynthate is never stored as starch but in the form of another carbohydrate or oil. The cell walls are silicified in some and may be composed of two articulated portions.

The Chrysophycophyta, as here discussed, may be subdivided as follows:

Class 1. Xanthophyceae, the yellow-green algae

Class 2. Chrysophyceae, the golden-brown algae

Class 3. Bacillariophyceae, the diatoms

A brief account of representatives of these three classes is given in the present chapter. More than 325 genera and 6000 species of Chrysophycophyta have been described.

CLASS 1. XANTHOPHYCEAE

General features. The Xanthophyceae (Gr. *xanthos,* yellow, + Gr. *phykos*), with about 80 genera and 450 species, are called the "yellow-green algae" because their color is distinctly that hue, especially if they are compared directly with members of the Chlorophycophyta. They were classified formerly among the Chlorophyceae until it was recognized that several of their attributes differ markedly from those of that group.

They are sometimes assigned to divisional rank as the Xanthophyc-ophyta. The yellow-green color results from a combination of pigments, among them chlorophyll α and ε, β-carotene, and several xanthophyll pigments.

The pigments are localized in plastids that are usually lens- or disc-shaped. Droplets of oil and granules of a substance called *leucosin*, or *chrysolaminarin*, related chemically to phaeophycean laminarin, are frequently observable in cells of Xanthophyceae.

In many *genera-Tribonema,* for example-the cell wall is not homogeneous but is composed of overlapping segments. This attribute is not demonstrable in all Xanthophyceae, however, except by special chemical treatment. The cell wall is silicified in some genera.

The flagella of Xanthophyceae are of unequal length, the longer tinsel and the shorter whiplash in organization, as in the Phaeophycophyta. The Xanthophyceae are predominantly freshwater organisms, but they may be aerial (moist rocks and other vegetation) or terrestrial in habitat.

A few are marine. A number of species have been isolated into culture from subterranean soil samples. The genera of Xanthophyceae, now grouped in a separate class, formerly were distributed among the orders and families of Chlorophyceae, the members of which they resemble in body structure.

Removal of these xanthophycean genera into a separate class revealed that they comprise a series of body types largely parallel to those described in the Chlorophyceae. Space does not permit

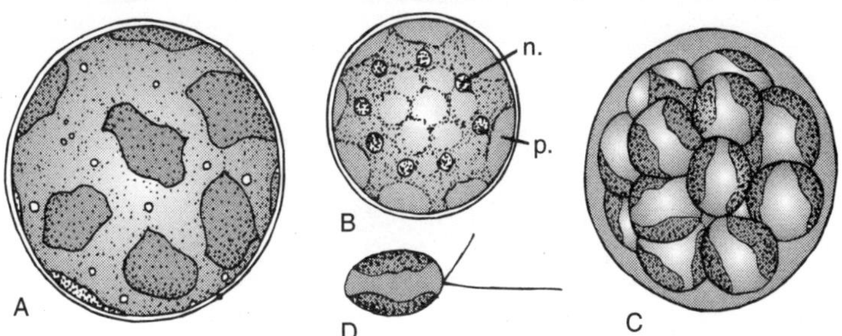

Figure 19.1: Botrydiopsis arhiza. A. Vegetative cell, surface view. B. Stained cell. C. Zoospore formation. D. Single liberated zoospore. E. Photomicrograph of living vegetative cells. n„ nucleus; p., plastid.

discussion of a complete array of parallel genera, but four commonly occurring and readily available xanthophycean organisms will be described.

Botrydiopsis

Botrydiopsis (Gr. *botrydion,* in clusters, + Gr. *opsis,* resemblance), the simplest of these, is unicellular. *Botrydiopsis* occurs on and in soil, from which it may be readily isolated into unialgal culture. The spherical cells are thin-walled and contain an increasingly large number of lenticular plastids as the cells grow older and larger.

The cells are multinucleate. As in *Chlorococcum,* each cell undergoes cleavage to form a number of zoospores, the number varying with the size of the cell. The zoospores lack walls and have two flagella of unequal length; the longer of these bears two rows of stiff hairs.

After a short period of motility, they become spherical, develop walls, and grow. Sexual reproduction has not been observed in *Botrydiopsis.*

Tribonema

Tribonema (Gr. *tribein,* to rub, + Gr. *nema,* thread) is representative of the unbranched, filamentous Xanthophyceae. *Tribonema is* cosmopolitan and occurs as floating masses and as overgrowth on submerged sticks and aquatic vegetation during the cooler months of the year. The uniseriate cells are often shaped

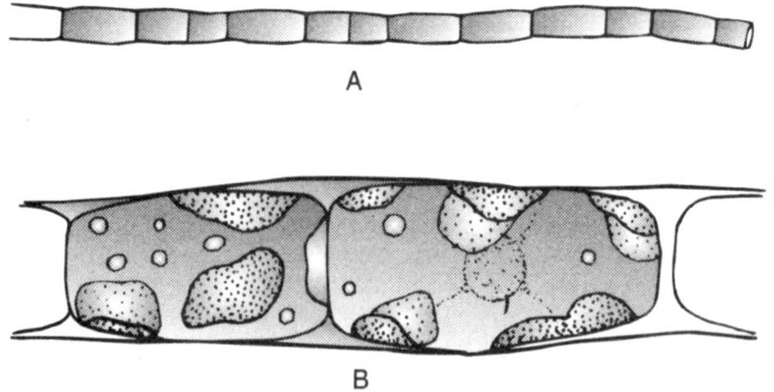

Figure 19.2: Tribonema sp. A. Outline drawing of a segment of a filament. B. Two vegetative cells, the one at the left in surface view, the other in median optical section.

like slightly inflated cylinders. Each contains a single nucleus and several discrete, discoidal, decidedly yellow-green plastids. *Tribonema* clearly illustrates the fact that certain Xanthophyceae have walls composed of overlapping halves. These are reported to contain cellulose.

When the filaments break apart or dissociate, the wall sections may readily be observed to consist of H-shaped segments, as viewed in optical section. They actually consist of segments of cylinders joined together by a planar, disclike wall.

At the conclusion of cytokinesis in a given vegetative cell, the two daughter protoplasts form such a wall segment within the original wall of the parent cell. As in *Ulothrix* among the Chlorophyceae, *Tribonema* reproduces by forming zoospores, which arise within the vegetative cells; *Tribonema* zoospores have

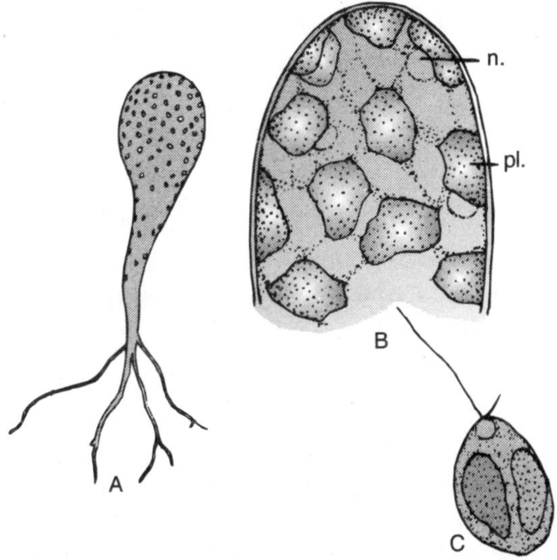

Figure 19.3: Botrydium granulatum. A. Small vegetative plant. B. Apex of young sac. C. Zoospore; n., nucleus; pl., plastid.

flagella of unequal length, the longer with two rows of appendages.

The longer flagellum is forward during motion, and the shorter is directed posteriorly or laterally. The germling produced by a zoospore has a holdfast, but the mature filaments are rarely encountered in an attached condition. Union of isogamous

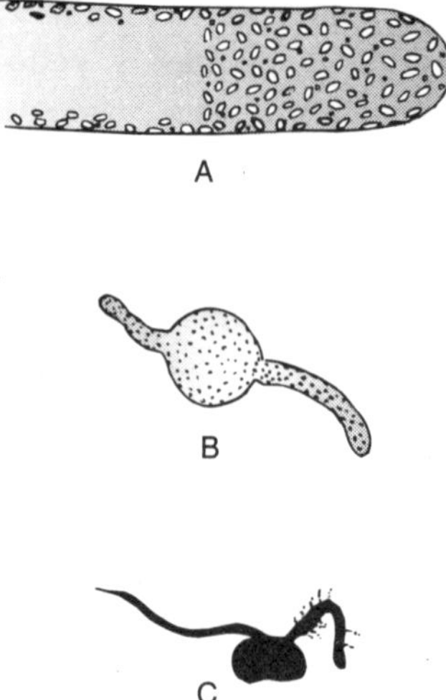

Figure 19.4: Vaucheria sp. A. Apex of plant; the tip in surface view, the remainder in optical section. B. Germinating zoospore. C. Stained sperm of V. pachyderma. D, E. V. sescuplicaria.

gametes has also been reported in *Tribonema.*

Botrydium

The terrestrial genus *Botrydium* (Gr. *botrydion,* in clusters), of widespread occurrence on damp soil, often grows in association with *Protosiphon,* its Chlorophycophytan counterpart, with which it was long confused.

The cells of *Botrydium* consist of an inflated, epiterranean vesicle and a rhizoidal system; the latter is usually richly branched. Under appropriate conditions of laboratory cultur the vesicular portion of the plant is prominent, and in nature it may attain a size of 2 mm; it is frequently ornamented with granules of calcium carbonate.

Mature plants of *Botrydium* contain a thin peripheral layer of protoplasm surrounding an extensive central vacuole. The protoplasm is composed of a superficial layer of chloroplasts, and slightly centripetal to these are numerous minute nuclei embedded in colorless cytoplasm. The rhizoidal portion of the plant contains few, if any, plastids and is filled with highly vacuolate protoplasm.

Botrydium reproduces by zoospore and aplanospore forma-

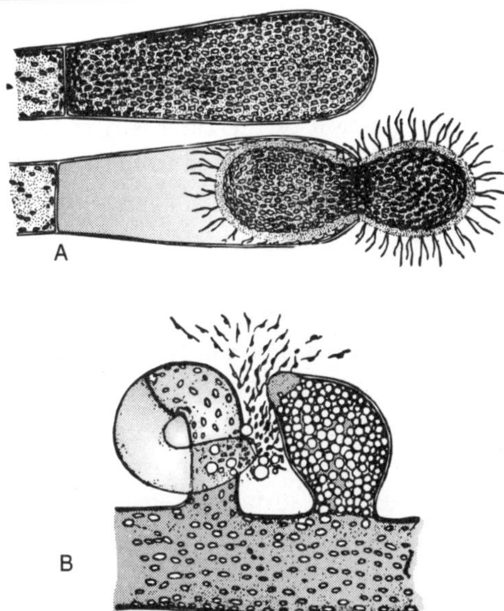

Figure 19.5: A. Vaucheria sp. Zoospore formation. B. V. sessilis. Mature antheridium (left) and oogonium.

tion. The zoospores arise by cleavage of the protoplast when the vesicles are submerged in water during rains. The zoospores are facultative, isogamous gametes, which may unite in pairs to form zygotes.

Zoospores may also develop into new plants without union. Meiosis in *Botrydium is* probably zygotic, but it has not been demonstrated unequivocally.

Vaucheria

Vaucheria (in honor of Vaucher, a Swiss phycologist), the "water felt", is a widely distributed member of the Xanthophyceae; the genus was formerly included among Chlorophycophyta. Careful examination of its pigments, of its photosynthetic storage products, and of the flagellation of its motile cells has demonstrated that the affinities of *Vaucheria* are probably with the Xanthophyceae.

Species of *Vaucheria* may be amphibious, like certain liverworts. Some flourish as darkgreen mats in running water or floating or submerged in quiet pools or on moist, undisturbed soil like that in greenhouse flowerpots. The plant body consists of an elongate, sparingly branched tube from which septations are absent except in the reproductive stages or as a response to injury. The central portion of the tube is occu-pied by a large, continuous vacuole, which is separated from the wall by a delicate peripheral layer of protoplasm.

Numerous discoidal plastids, which overlie the minute nuclei, occur in this layer. Growth of the siphonlike tubes is apical. Asexual reproduction in the coenocytic *Vaucheria* plant is effected by the formation of large zoospores at the tips of the tubes, which are delimited by septa as *zoosporangia.*

The protoplast in the sporangium contracts, and an interchange of position between nuclei and plastids occurs, so that the nuclei are now nearer the surface. A pair of slightly unequal flagella is then generated from the surface of the protoplast in the region of each beak-shaped nucleus.

The large compound zoospore is liberated from the terminal zoosporangium and undergoes rather slow, narrowly circumscribed movements. It soon loses its flagella and germinates, frequently from both poles, to form a new *Vaucheria* siphon.

Sexual reproduction, which is oogamous, is rather striking in *Vaucheria* because of the large size of the sex organs. These may be sessile on the main siphons, or they may occur in groups on special reproductive branches. Both sex organs arise as protuberances, into which the streaming protoplasm carries numerous nuclei and plastids.

They become segregated from the subtending branch relatively late in their ontogeny. The oogonium is at first multinucleate, but prior to formation of the delimiting septum, all the nuclei except one migrate back into the subtending siphon.

At maturity, each oogonium contains a single uninucleate egg cell. The sperms enter through a pore in the oogonial wall in a special receptive region. The antheridium, which is multinucleate when it is delimited by a septum from its subtending branch, produces a large number of minute, almost colorless, unequally flagellate sperms.

The flagellation of the sperms is lateral, much as in *Fucus*

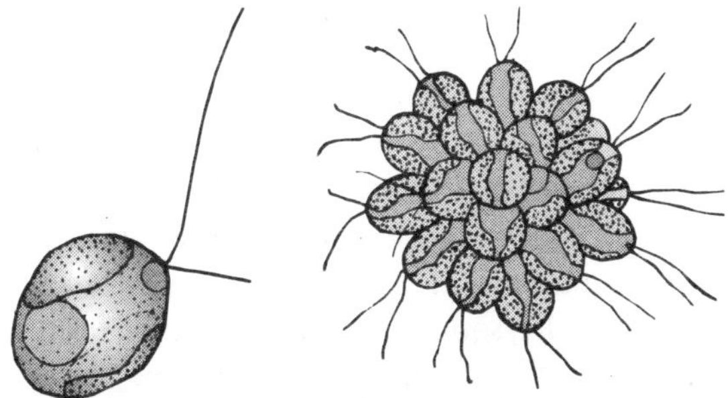

Figure 19.6: A. Ochromonas sp. Single vegetative cell.
B. Synura uvella. Single colony.

and its relatives, the short anterior flagellum having two rows of appendages and the longer posterior one being without appendages. Furthermore, the sperms have a proboscis, as in *Fucus*.

In nature, the sperms are liberated early in the morning. The zygote develops a thick wall soon after fertilization and loses its green pigment. The oogonium containing the zygote often is abscised from the parent branch. Germination into a few filaments after a period of dormancy probably involves zygotic meiosis.

CLASS 2. CHRYSOPHYCEAE

General Features

The Chrysophyceae (Gr. *chrysos,* gold, + Gr. *phykos),* or golden-brown algae, consisting of about 70 genera and 325 species, are widely distributed in fresh and salt water, but with the exception of a few genera they are rarely encountered in any great number. Many of the species are planktonic and flourish in bodies of cold water or only in the colder months of the year.

The golden-brown color is the result of a combination of pigments, including chlorophylls *a* and *c*, β-carotenes, and several xanthophylls; the abundance of β-carotene and of the xanthophylls masks the chlorophyll in most species.

The excess photosynthate is stored in the form of oil droplets or as rather large granules of chrysolaminarin. In a great majority of genera the cells contain one or two parietal plastids and are uninucleate.

The surface of the protoplast is often ornamented with small siliceous scales, or an internal siliceous skeleton may be present. The Chrysophyceae, like the Xanthophyceae, represent a series in which types of plant body have developed in a manner parallel to that observed in the Chlorophyceae.

In addition, in spite of the fact that the cells contain pigmented plastids, a number of motile genera carry on phagotrophic nutrition. Many Chrysophyceae are capable of forming siliceous cysts, which are often ornamented in various ways.

Although a considerable number of genera and species of Chrysophyceae have been found in this country and abroad, with few exceptions they do not seem to be organisms that appear with frequency in collectors' jars.

Furthermore, few of them have been grown in culture in the laboratory. For these reasons, only a few, relatively widely distributed genera *Ochromonas* (Gr. *ochros,* pale yellow, + Gr. *monas,* single organism), *Synura* (Gr. *syn,* together, + Gr. *oura,* tail), and *Dinobryon* (Gr. *dins,* whirling, + Gr. *brown,* moss)will be described.

Ochromonas

Ochromonas is a unicellular motile organism that varies from a spherical to a somewhat irregular shape. The naked cells contain

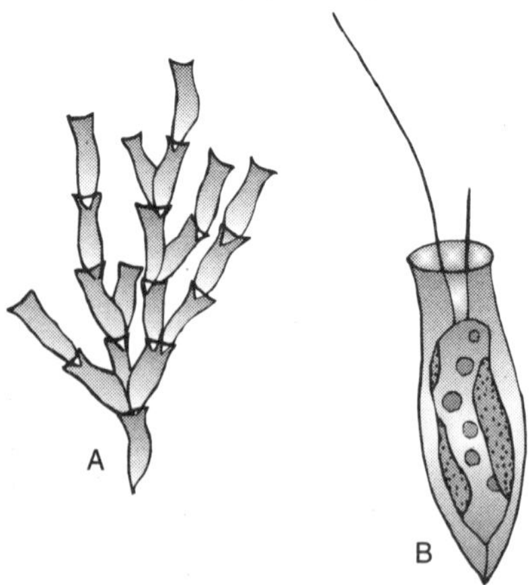

Figure 19.7: Dinobryon setularia. A. Arborescent colony. B. Single lorica with protoplast enclosed.

one or two pale-yellow plastids, which are curved and parietal. Two very unequal flagella, the longer tinsel and the shorter whiplash, emerge from the anterior portion of the protoplast. Each cell contains a single nucleus; contractile vacuoles and a stigma are present in the cells of certain species.

Actively photosynthetic cells usually contain a single, large, posterior grain of excess photosynthate, called chrysolaminarin. Reproduction is by cell division. The cells may form siliceous cysts with prominent pores. Various species of *O. chromonas* differ physiologically.

In two species of *O. chromonas, O. danica* and O. *malhamensis,* distinct metabolic differences occur, which are directly reflected in the relative amounts of growth. Growth of *O. danica* is fairly rapid in inorganic medium, while *O. malham-ensis* will not grow well unless organic carbon sources (sugars, etc.), amino acids, and vitamins are added to the growth medium.

The mode of nutrition also varies between the above species, because *O. malhamensis* and *O. danica* have the capacity to ingest particulate food materials, like protozoa. Aaronson, De Angelis, Frank, and Baker (1971) have shown that O. *danica* secretes carbohydrates, nucleic acidlike molecules, proteins, and lipids into its environment.

Synura

Synura is a motile colonial organism in which the individual cells are stipitate and united into spherical clusters. The cells are ovoid to elongate, and the anterior pole is broader than the stipitate posterior pole. Each is biflagellate and covered with delicate siliceous scales.

The protoplast contains two parietal, concave plastids, a single nucleus, and contractile vacuoles. Cell division augments the number of individuals in a colony. Multiplication is accomplished by fragmentation of the colony and continued growth of the fragments.

Dinobryon

The colonies of *Dinobryon* are branching and composed of a series of urn- or bell-like loricas, usually widely separated from their contained protoplasts except at the base. Each protoplast has two apical flagella (one of which, a tinsel flagellum, is markedly longer than the other, which is of the whiplash type), usually two plastids, a single nucleus, contractile vacuoles, and a stigma.

After longitudinal division, one of the daughter cells moves to the mouth of the lorica, becomes fixed there, and forms a new lorica. Continuation of this process through a number of divisions results in the formation of dendroid colonies.

These fragment readily, and the fragments continue to grow as individual colonies. Isogamous union of two vegetative individuals has been reported in *D. borgei.*

CLASS 3. BACILLARIOPHYCEAE

General features. The diatoms, Bacillariophyceae, are at once the best known, the most numerous (in number of genera, species, and individuals, about 200 genera, 5000 species), and, economically, the most important members of the division Chrysophycophyta.

Diatoms are the despair of the amateur and the joy of the professional microscopist because of their structural complexity. Their great beauty and perfection of design rival those of the desmids, but the beauty of diatoms is perhaps more subtle, since it is mostly confined to their cell walls.

To appreciate this beauty in full measure, it is usually necessary to dissolve the protoplast with acid and to mount the cells in a highly refractive medium, a process known as "*cleaning*" the diatoms.

Although some diatoms are bottom dwellers and epiphytes in salt and fresh water, a great number occur in the plankton, where they are of inestimable and basic value in the nutritional cycle of aquatic animals.

They have been extant at least since the Jurassic period (inside front cover). The abundance of diatoms in earlier geological periods is attested by the finding of great deposits of their cell walls-"*shells*," or *frustules*, as they are often called.

As individual diatoms died in certain bodies of water, they

sank to the bottom; there the protoplasts disintegrated, leaving the siliceous cell walls. In this way there were built up great deposits, which were exposed in later geological periods and which are now mined as *diatomaceous earth* for use in industrial and technical processes.

The economic importance of this substance is tremendous, and its uses are many. At the present time, living diatoms are ubiquitous and important components of algal vegetation. In bodies of fresh water they seem to be more abundant when the temperature is low.

In marine habitats they often cover other algae with a heavy epiphytic growth. In running water they often form a brownish coating on submerged rocks and other vegetation. Diatoms may be strictly unicellular, colonial, or filamentous.

They are divided into two types on the basis of symmetry. In the first, the *pennate diatoms*, exemplified by such genera as *Navicula (L. navicula,* small ship) and *Pinnularia (L. pinnula,* small feather), the symmetry is bilateral. The second group, the *centric diatoms*, to which many marine genera belong, is characterized by radial symmetry.

Melosira (Gr. *melos,* jointed, + Gr. *seira,* rope), a common genus in both fresh and salt water, and *Coscinodiscus* (Gr. *koskinon,* sieve, + NL. *discus,* disc), *Arachnodiscus,* and *Stictodiscus*, usually marine, illustrate this type.

The taxonomy of diatoms is based almost exclusively on differences in the structure and ornamentation of the cell walls, or frustules, rather than on attributes of the living protoplasts. The wall is impregnated with polymerized, opaline silica ($SiO_2 \cdot nH_2O$), which is assimilated at the surface of the cell from the silicic acid of the environment.

In several diatoms (e.g., *Navicula pelliculosa)* the silicon is deposited within a very delicate, flattened surface sac, the *silicolemma*, as are the plates of "armored" dinoflagellates. The diverse types of marking represent ridges, thin places, or minute pores in the walls; these are rather constant in arrangement and form the basis for delimitation of species.

The transverse lines seen on the valves of many pennate

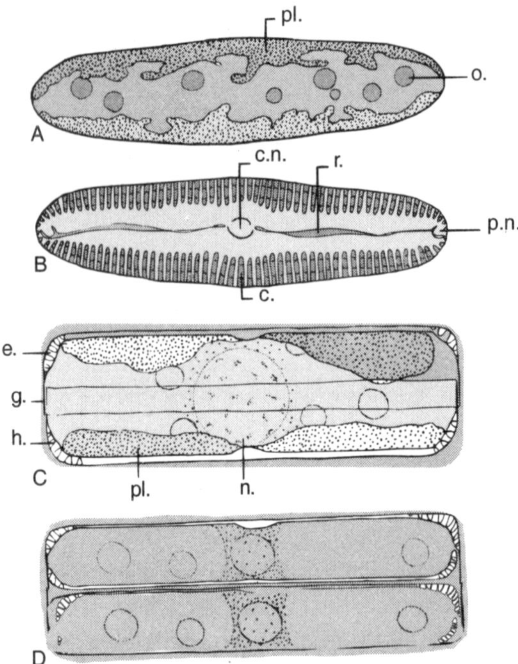

Figure 19.8: Pinnularia streptoraphe. Organization of living cells. A. *Valve view.* B. *Valve view, protoplast omitted. C. Girdle view.* D. *Recently divided cells. c., costae; c, n. , central nodule; e., epitheca; g., girdle band; h., hypotheca; n., nucleus; o., oil droplet; pl., plastid; p.n., polar nodule.*

diatoms represent lines of pores, which can be resolved as such with good oil-immersion lenses as well as with the electron microscope. The cell wall in all diatoms is composed of two overlapping portions, the *valves*; one is usually slightly larger than the other, much like the bottom and cover of a box.

The larger, coverlike portion is called the *epitheca* (Gr. *epi,* over, + Gr. *theke,* case); the smaller is known as the *hypotheca* (Gr. *hypo,* under, + Gr. *theke).* The two valves, instead of overlapping each other directly, frequently are attached to *girdle bands*; these are composed of two overlapping portions.

Supernumerary bands may be intercalated between the valves and girdle-band segments; hence, the epitheca and hypotheca may be quite widely separated in certain species. The cells are shaped like elongate boxes in *Navicula* and *Pinnularia.* When viewed from either above or below (valve view), *Pinnularia* cells usually have parallel sides and rounded polar portions.

A prominent line, the *raphe* (Gr. *raphe,* seam) traverses each valve. When observed in lateral aspect (girdle view), the same cells appear rectangular.

Each valve of *Pinnularia* is marked by two series of prominent riblike lines, the *costae.* In *Navicula,* rows of pores, or punctae, extend from the margin toward the central region of the wall, which, as in *Pinnularia, is* traversed by the raphe.

The raphe is connected to a *central nodule* and to two *polar nodules,* all of which open to the external aqueous medium. The raphe is wedgeshaped or ridge-and-valleylike, as viewed in transverse section. It has been reported that the secretion of an adhesive from the raphe and its subsequent hydration account for movement of diatoms with raphes.

The most conspicuous structures of the diatom protoplasts are the brownish plastids, which are reported to contain, in addition to chlorophylls *a* and c, β-carotene and a number of xanthophylls, including fucoxanthin, which is largely responsible for the color of diatoms; the latter is also present in Phaeophycophyta.

The plastids may be few in number and massive, as in the

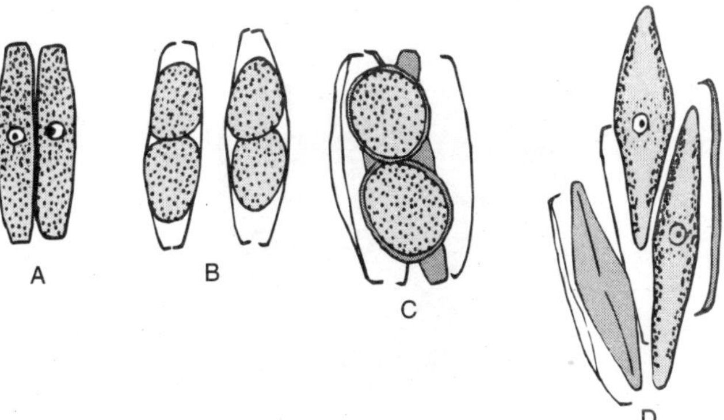

Figure 19.9: Navicula halophila. Stages in sexual reproduction. A. Pairing of cells. B. Formation of two gametes in each cell. C. Two auxospores (zygotes) formed. D. Elongation of auxospores.

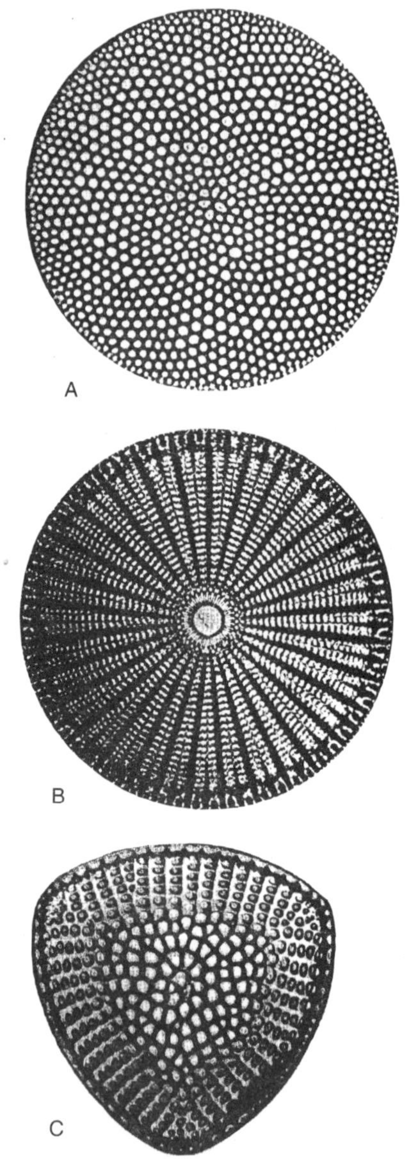

Figure 19.10: Frustules of marine, centric diatoms. A. *Coscinodiscus radiatus. B. Arachnodiscus indiscus. C. Strictodiscus johnsonianus.*

pennate diatoms, or numerous and discoidal, as in the centric types. The excess photosynthate is stored in the form of oil or chrysolaminarin, which is frequently conspicuous in the living cells. The single nucleus is usually readily observable in the center of the cells in pennate genera.

In addition to the nucleus, which lies in a bridge of colorless cytoplasm, the central portion of the cell is occupied by a large central vacuole. Asexual reproduction in unicellular diatoms is effected by nuclear and cell division.

Immediately after cytokinesis, the original wall contains two protoplasts, each approximately half the volume of the parental one. As the filial protoplasts enlarge, each develops a new wall, using the half-wall of the parent cell as the epitheca.

It is obvious, therefore, that one of the filial cells thus formed will be slightly smaller than the parent cell, and that if this process were to continue, some of the progeny would become progressively smaller. While there is evidence that this may occur, there is apparently a compensating ability of the girdle band and valve to increase slightly in size in some species.

Furthermore, in several marine diatoms it has been demonstrated that cell enlargement can he achieved by partial or complete extrusion of the protoplast from its frustule (its enlargement) and finally by the formation of a new and larger frustule around the extruded protoplast.

The problem of size reduction in the progeny of asexually reproducing diatoms has been discussed by Rao and Desikachary (1970). Sexual reproduction in pennate diatoms results in the formation of *auxospores* (Gr. *auxo,* increase, + Gr. *spora,* spore).

These are so called because they are naked protoplasts that increase markedly in size after their formation. Sexuality is superficially similar to that in certain desmids, because the protoplasts of two cells may escape from their walls and unite directly to form a zygote.

It differs, however, in that the pennate diatoms are diploid during their vegetative stages and sexual reproduction is immediately preceded by meiosis. In some species-Navicula *halophila,* for exampleeach member of the pair of vegetative cells forms two gametes, so that two zygotes are formed.

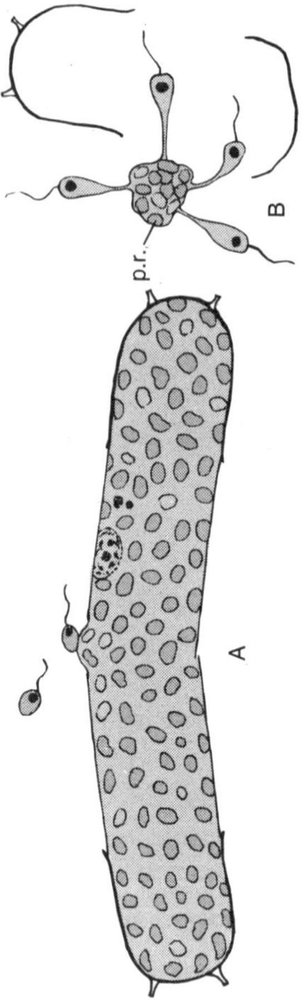

Figure 19.11: Sexual reproduction in Stephanopyxis turris a centric diatom. A. Protoplast of vegetative cell functioning as an oogonium, sperm making contact. B. Liberation of sperm. p. r., plastid remnant. Diagrammatic.

In others, each cell forms only one gamete. The zygotes increase rapidly in size and become auxospores that are larger than the parent cells whose protoplasts functioned as gametes. In this way, when the auxospore has formed new cell walls, it again achieves the maximum size characteristic of the species and functions as a vegetative cell. Granetti (1968) has demonstrated a similar cycle in clonal cultures of N. *minima.*

Sexual reproduction has been observed to occur abundantly when leaves of aquatic plants on which the epiphytic *Cocconeis placentula* is growing are transferred to petri dishes containing water from the natural habitat enriched with inorganic culture medium and/or soil extract. The diatoms move from the host in great numbers and attach to the bottom of the petri dish, where they multiply rapidly. Within several days, many of the cells pair, their frustules open, and their protoplasts unite to form zygotes.

These enlarge rapidly as auxospores and within 48-72 hours secrete a new frustule and initiate cell division. Parthenoge-netic auxospores also are formed.

The centric diatoms are largely marine, but a few also occur in fresh water. Of the latter, the filamentous genus *Melosira*, with marine and freshwater species, is by far the most widely distributed. It is frequently present in the plankton in sufficient abundance to color the water, but benthic species are also common.

The elongate cells, when joined together, are observed in girdle view. The cells contain many small, brownish plastids and are uninucleate. The epitheca and hypotheca are joined by connecting bands that seem scarcely to overlap. The valve view of *Melosira* cells, which is circular, becomes apparent when the filaments dissociate into individual cells.

Coscinodiscus (Gr. *koskinon,* sieve, + *L. discus,* disc), *Arachnodiscus* (Gr. *arkys,* net, + *discus),* and *Stictodiscus* (Gr. *stiktos,* spotted, + *discus*) are representative of numerous marine species of centric diatoms. Their cells are markedly flattened in the manner of extremely shallow petri dishes.

Sexual reproduction has been reported to be oogamous for a number of centric forms. Our knowledge of sexual reproduction in centric diatoms has been greatly augmented by investigations of certain marine species, such as *Stephanopyxis* (Gr. *stephanos,* crown, + M. L. *pyxis,* box) *turris* in laboratory culture.

In this organism the large eggs, which are little-modified vegetative cells, are fertilized by uniflagellate sperms. Both eggs and sperms arise as a result of (gametic) meiosis. Only one of the nuclear products of meiosis survives in the oogonium.

After fertilization, the zygotes (auxospores) increase greatly in size and form two new valves. Figure elsewhere in this chapter and its caption illustrate and explain sexual reproduction in *Stephanopyxis palnwniana,* also a marine species.

As a group, diatoms are perhaps economically the most important of the algae because of their role in the food cycle of aquatic animals and because of the many uses of diatomaceous earth. While diatoms have received considerable taxonomic study, many other aspects require further investigation.

The Bacillariophyceae are clearly delimited from other Chrysophyc-ophyta by their specialized wall structure, method of wall formation, and sexual reproduction. For more comprehensive discussions of diatoms.

Classification of Diatoms

The genera of diatoms discussed in the preceding account may be classified as follows:

Division Chrysophycophyta

Class 3. Bacillariophyceae

Order 1. Centrales

Family 1. Coscinodiscaceae

Genera: *Melosira, Coscinodiscus,*

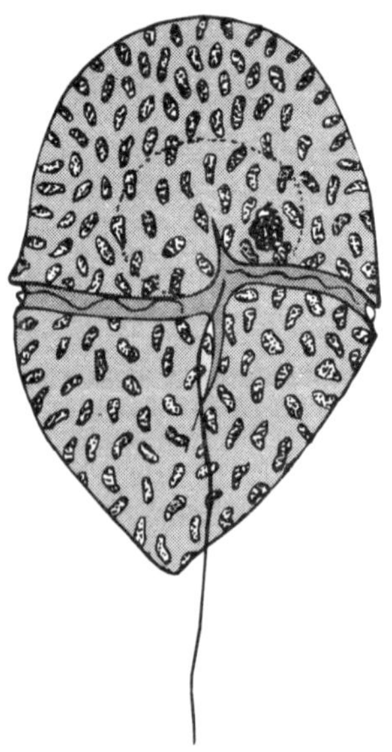

Figure 19.12: Gymnodinium sp. Single individual from freshwater plankton.

Arachnodiscus, Stictodiscus, Stephanopyxis

Order 2. Pennales

Family 1. Naviculaceae

Genera: *Navicula, Pinnularia*

Family 2. Achnanthaceae

Genus: *Cocconeis*

DIVISION PYRRHOPHYCOPHYTA

General features. Like the Euglenophycophyta, the division Pyrrhophycophyta (Gr. *pyr,* fire, + Gr. *phykos,* dusky, + Gr. *phyton,* plant), contains both chlorophyllous and colorless organisms.

The Pyrrhophycophyta, as represented in this account by the single class Dinophyceae (Gr. *dinein,* to whirl, + Gr. *phykos),* the *dinoflagellates*, are often considered to be members of the Protozoa; they are still so classified by many protozoologists.

However, nonmotile unicellular and filamentous genera have been discovered that produce motile stages in which the cells are dinoflagellate in character; this indicates an affinity with plantlike organisms.

The carotenoid pigments in the dinoflagellates are present in sufficient abundance (as in the Bacillariophyceae, Chrysophyceae, and Phaeophyco-phyta) to mask the chlorophylls *a* and c. In addition to β-carotene, several xanthophylls are present, including peridinin and dinoxanthin, which are peculiar to the group.

Starch accumulates both within the chloroplast and colorless cytoplasm, and oils may also be stored. Dinoflagellates are abundant in both fresh and marine waters, where they frequently form an important constituent of the plankton.

Marine water blooms of the genera *Gonyaulax* and *Gymnodinium* in the Gulf of Mexico and elsewhere may form "red tides" and cause widespread destruction of fish. *Gonyaulax catenella* produces a toxin that paralyzes shellfish, while species of *Gymnodinium* produce other types of toxin, Steidinger (1975) has distinguished three aspects common to all toxic red tides as:

(1) increase in population size or initiation;

(2) support (i.e., proper salinity, temperature and growth factors); and

(3) maintenance and transport of blooms by hydrologic and meteorologic factors.

The motile genera as well as the motile cells of nonmotile genera are characterized by the arrangement of their flagella. One flagellum is elongate, usually extending posteriorly with reference to the direction of motion.

The second flagellum, which emerges from the same point as the first, is ribbonlike and lies in a transverse groove in which it undergoes undulating movement. Both flagella are of the tinsel type. The furrow divides the cell into anterior and posterior portions, which may be unequal in size in some genera.

A few dinoflagellates, such as *Gymnodinium* (Gr. *gymnos,* naked, + Gr. *dinein,* to whirl), lack cell-wall material, but in others the wall is prominent and composed of regular platelike segments. The plates that form the wall are in vesicles inside the plasma membrane and not outside it, as are the cell walls of most algae.

Genera with walls of the latter types are often said to be "armored." The walls probably contain cellulose; the empty walls persist for some time after the death of the protoplasts. The nuclei of dinofiagellates are highly interesting in a number of respects.

Unlike those of eukaryotic organisms, the chromosomes remain condensed and clearly recognizable individually throughout the cell cycle. Furthermore, they contain no RNA or histone, or any other protein component, in which respect they are similar to prokaryotic organisms.

The chromosomes of a number of species are clearly fibrillar in organization. For these reasons they are sometimes called Mesokaryotes. Dodge has reviewed the fine structure of the Pyrrhophycophyta. *Ceratium* (Gr. *keration,* little horn), *Gymnodinium,* and *Peridinium* (Gr. *peridines,* whirled around) are representatives of the motile type of dinoflagellates of common occurrence in the plankton in bodies of cold water or during the colder seasons of the year.

The protoplasts contain discoid plastids, which are yellow

brown to dark brown. The excess photosynthate is stored as starch or oil. Each cell has a single prominent nucleus, and most genera have prominent stigmata as well. Small, noncontractile vacuoles are frequently visible.

There is some evidence that certain species of dinoflagellates, although photosynthetic, may undergo phagotrophic nutrition and ingest solid foods, but the exact mechanism of ingestion is not clearly understood.

Asexual reproduction is by cell division, frequently of cells in a motile condition. The nuclear membrane persists during mitosis, and a spindle is absent. In plate-walled genera, each daughter cell receives a portion of the original cell wall.

Sexual reproduction has been observed in several species of dinoflagellates. In the genus *Ceratium* it has been reported that small individuals function as male gametes. In *C. horridum,* a marine species, fusion of male and female gametes, the latter similar in size to normal vegetative cells, has been observed.

The zygote in this species remains motile. In *C. cornutum, a* freshwater species, the zygote becomes dormant and enclosed in a cyst. At its germination, meiosis occurs. Pfiester has been able to induce sexual reproduction of *Peridinium* in a nitrogendeficient medium.

In this process small, naked individuals unite in pairs. Here, too, meiosis is zygotic. It should be noted that some dinoflagellates apparently are diploid. In a colorless, luminescent marine dinoflagellate, *Noctiluca miliaris,* Zingmark has also reported that uniflagellate isogamous gametes unite to form zygotes.

Classification of Pyrrhophycophyta

The chlorophyllous genera of dinoflagellates included in this brief discussion may be classified as follows:

Division Pyrrhophycophyta

Class 1. Dinophyceae

Order 1. Gymnodiniales

Family 1. Gymnodiniaceae

Genus: *Gymnodinium*

Order 2. Peridiniales

Family 1. Gonyaulacaceae

Genus: *Gonyaulax*

Family 2. Peridiniaceae

Genus: *Peridinium*

Family 3. Ceratiaceae

Genus: *Ceratium*

CHAPTER 20

Rhodophycophyta

The division Rhodophycophyta (Gr. *rhodon,* rose, + Gr. *phykos,* seaweed, + Gr. *phyton,* plant) contains a single class, the Rhodophyceae (Gr. *rhodon* + Gr. *phykos),* commonly called the red algae. About 400 genera and 3900 species are known.

The Rhodophyceae, like the Phaeophyceae, are predominantly marine organisms; however, several genera, such as *Batrochospermum* (Gr. *batrachos,* frog, + Gr. *sperma,* semen), are widely distributed in freshwater streams, lakes and springs. Marine Rhodophyceae flourish in both littoral and sublittoral zones.

Rhodophyceae are very abundant in tropical seas, where they often grow at great depths in clear waters. A number of red algae precipitate calcium carbonate on their cell surfaces and become calcareous. These are important in reef formation.

Many of the marine Rhodophyceae are strikingly beautiful, both in living condition and when mounted on herbarium sheets. In most genera, chlorophylls *a* and *d* (when present) and the carotenoids are largely concealed by a red pigment, *phycoerythrin,* and sometimes by the blue pigments *phycocyanin* and *allophycocyanin.*

These pigments absorb light energy, which they transfer to chlorophyll *a.* There is also evidence that, in addition, the accessory pigments may have a more direct role in the photosynthetic process. They are apparently associated with the surfaces of the plastid lamellae.

The numerous genera exhibit a range of color; various shades of red are common, and some plants are almost black. Some species of *Batrachospermum*, on the other hand, are markedly blue-green. The pigments are localized in plastids, which may be massive, with a single plastid in each cell, or the plastids may be numerous and discoid.

The excess photosynthate is stored as a complex carbohydrate, called *Floridean starch*, composed of approximately 15 glucose units; grains of this substance stain slightly red with iodine-potassium iodide solution. They usually occur in the colorless cytoplasm at the surface of plastids rather than within them.

The accumulated carbohydrate is often associated with the nucleus rather than with the pyrenoid when the latter is present. Floridean starch is similar to the amylopectin fraction of green algal and other green-plant starches but differs in requiring prolonged boiling for gelatination; glycogen may also be present.

The vegetative cells of Rhodophyceae may be uninucleate (as in *Nemalion* and *Batrachospermum)* or multinucleate (as in *Polysiphonia, Callithamnion, and Griffithsia).* The vacuole of large, multinucleate cells is more prominent than in the uninucleate cells of genera such as *Nemalion.*

The cellulose cell wall is often surrounded by a slimy layer. Other components such as xylans are present in the walls of some red algae. In a number of genera, such as *Nemalion,* the filaments are covered, in addition, by copious gelatinous material of rather firm consistency. The hydrocolloids of red algae have been classified as agars, carrageenans, and gelans.

Agars are of prime importance in biology as relatively inert agents for solidification of culture media. The walls between two adjoining cells in most of the Rhodophycophyta contain structures known as *pit connections*. The nature and function of these structures remain in doubt.

They have been interpreted by some as evidence of protoplasmic continuity between contiguous cells. Although a few unicellular and colonial rhodophycean genera have been described, the vast majority are filamentous or membranous and foliaceous plants. The basic pattern, however, is filamentous, and this can be demonstrated even in many membranous types.

The development of the plant body is initiated by the activity of one or more apical cells. The membranous Rhodophyceae are less complex internally than similar types of Phaeophyceae. Most red algae have diplobiontic life cycles, with sporic meiosis occurring in the sporangia of a special alternate, the *tetrasporophyte*. The details of the reproductive process are discussed with the illustrative genera.

The Rhodophycophyta, with the single class Rhodophyceae, are usually further classified into the subclasses Bangiophycidae and Florideophycidae; the latter contains the majority of red algae.

Class 1. Rhodophyceae

Subclass 1. Bangiophycidae

The Bangiophycidae take their name from the genus *Bangia* and include unicellular, filamentous, and foliose plants. In some of the last two types, pit connections are absent between cells, and the female sex organs, if present, are not highly differentiated. Only a few genera are known to have sexual reproduction.

Porphyridium

The unicellular red alga *Porphyridium* (Gr. *porphyra,* purple, + Gr. *idion,* similarity) is an inhabitant of moist soils, on which it forms shiny patches, and also occurs in fresh, brackish, and marine waters. The wall-less, spherical, uninucleate cells of *Porphyridium* contain a stellate plastid with a central pyrenoid.

The cells in mass may be blood-red or bluish green, depending on the relative amounts of phycocyanin and phycoerythrin present, and these occur as minute particles, the phycobilosomes, on the surface of the thylakoids.

The cells have colloidal sheaths, which under some circumstances may have stalklike protuberances. Reproduction is by cell division into two or more cells. Certain isolates of *Porphyridium* apparently move by means of unipolar secretion of a slime exudate.

Bangia

Bangia is an unbranched, firmly sheathed filamentous genus, which may become pluriseriate as the filaments age. Here again, each uninucleate cell contains a massive, stellate plastid with central pyrenoid. *Bangia fuscopurpurea* grows on rocks and woodwork, is often exposed at low tide, and hence is periodically wet by both fresh and salt water.

Another species, *B. atropurpurea,* seems to be restricted entirely to fresh water and is increasingly common in the Great Lakes. In asexual reproduction, the protoplasts of cells in both uniseriate and pluriseriate filaments are liberated from their enclosing walls as *monospores*, which may be amoeboid.

Cells that produce monospores are called *monosporangia*. The monospores germinate and grow into new plants. Two phases occur in the life cycle of *B. fuscopurpurea,* the macroscopic, filamentous phase (uniseriate and pluriseriate) and a microscopic, branching filamentous state most frequently growing on animal shells in nature.

The microscopic phase was originally described as a free-living alga, *Conchocelis* (Gr. *conche,* conch, + Gr. *kele,* tumor). The development of each phase in the life cycle is markedly affected by the duration of light during each 24-hour period.

If the cultures are illuminated for less than 12 hours, the *Bangia* phase develops; longer periods of illumination evoke the development of the *Conchocelis* phase. Both phases can reproduce by monospores, and the nature of the product of monosporic germination is determined by the duration of illumination.

The *Conchocelis* phase can be maintained under a regime of 16 hours of light followed by 8 hours of dark, and its monospores duplicate the *Conchocelis* phase. The Bangia-filament stage prevailed and reproduced by monospores under less than 12 hours of light diurnally.

In addition to monospores, the *Bangia* phase forms more than one spore per cell. These are of two types, which differ in size. The smaller, lighter-colored spores arise in groups of more than 16 per parent cell. In *B. fuscopurpurea* they are seemingly functionless and do not germinate.

The larger spores, formed 16 or fewer per cell, develop into the *Bangia* or *Conchocelis* phase, depending on the photoperiod. Sexual reproduction has not been demonstrated unequivocably in *Bangia,* and the chromosome numbers in both the *Bangia* phase and *Conchocelis* phase have been reported to be n = 3, so that if sexual reproduction does occur, it must be followed by zygotic meiosis in *B.fuscopurpurea*; Richardson (1970), however, reports a chromosome number of 10 in both the *Bangia* and *Conchocelis* phases. The life cycle of these algae may be summarized elsewhere in this chapter.

Porphyra

Porphyra (Gr. *porphyra,* purple) also is representative of a group of algae that are considered to be primitive Rhodophyceae. The brown-purple or rose-tinted, Ulva-like plant bodies of *Porphyra* grow attached to rocks or to larger marine algae. They are often inhabitants of the intertidal zone.

The fronds may become more than a foot in length. They are composed of one or two layers (depending on the species) of cells, which are surrounded by thick, colloidal cell walls. The plants are attached to the substratum by rhizoidal holdfasts.

The uninucleate cells of *Porphyra* contain one or two prominent, stellate chloroplasts, which are central. The cells of *P. leucosticta* have pit connections in the *Conchocelis* phase characteristic of so many Floridean Rhodophyceae. Growth in *Porphyra* is generalized; that is, cell division is not restricted to a certain region of the maturing plant body.

A number of careful and intensive investigations in field and laboratory have added a great deal to our knowledge of the life cycle of *Porphyra.* It is known with certainty that in several species spores shed from membranous plants germinate into branching filaments, long ago described, from examples growing on discarded mollusk shells, as a distinct genus, *Conchocelis.*

Spores ("Conchospores") of the latter, in culture, have given rise, in turn, to the membranous *Porphyra* phase. *Conchocelis* grows on rocks as well as on shells. The reproductive cycle of *Porphyra,* then, is much like that in *Bangia* in that there is an alternate *Conchocelis* phase.

The spores from the latter develop into *Porphyra* plants. In some species, it has been shown that the *Porphyra* plants are haploid, while the *Conchocelis* filaments are diploid. Meiosis occurs in the fertile cells of *Conchocelis* which give rise to the spores destined to form the *Porphyra* plants (gametophytes). The occurrence of meiosis is evidence that sexual union has preceded it.

The *Porphyra* plants produce minute, almost colorless cells, the spermatia and also groups of 8-16 larger spores, often called carpospores, an implication that they are products of a zygote, although conclusive evidence of sexual union has until recently rarely been presented.

The diploid carpospores develop into the *Conchocelis* phase. In addition, the *Porphyra* plantlets can arise directly from the *Conchocelis* filaments, and both phases may perennate. Chen, Edelstein, Ogata, and McLachlan have investigated the life cycle of *P. miniata* in culture.

As in *P. purpureaviolacea*, the bladelike plants are haploid, while the *Conchocelis* phase is diploid. Kito, Ogata, and McLachlan (1971) report chromosome numbers of $n = 3,4$ and 5 in three different Atlantic species of *Porphyra*. For one species, *P. gardneri*, a thoroughly convincing report of sexual reproduction has been published.

This report includes micrographs showing spermatia attached to, and contributing nuclei to, carpogonia. It also provides evidence that the *Conchocelis* phase is diploid.

Subclass 2. Florideophycidae

The distinctions cited between the Bangiophycidae and Florideoph-ycidae are increasingly less impressive. Most of the latter have apical growth, pit connections, and, except for *Nemalion* and related forms, discoid plastids. Furthermore, the sex organs are highly differentiated.

The greater number of genera and species of red algae are classified in the Florideophycidae, and space permits the discussion of just a few representatives, namely, *Nemalion, Batrachospermum, Griffithsia, Callithamnion,* and *Polysiphonia.*

In the Florideophycidae prominent female gametangia, called *carpogonia*, are developed on branches, usually recognizable because of their pale color, which is occasioned by the arrested development of their plastids. In the great majority, the life cycle is a slightly modified D, h + d type, which may be isomorphic or heteromorphic.

The "modification" is the occurrence, between the zygote and sporophytic plant, of a group of diploid carpospores epiphytically on the gametophyte, primarily at the site where the zygote is formed. This intercalated, diploid phase is often called the *carposporophyte*.

Nemalion

Nemalion (Gr. *nema,* thread) differs from *Porphyra* in a number of important respects. In *Nemalion* growth is strictly apical and traceable to several apical cells. Prominent pit connections are present.

Nemalion helminthoides is a marine organism that grows attached to rocks that may be exposed at low tide; the living plants have the appearance and texture of gelatinous wormlike branching strands; they are anchored to rocks by discoidal bases, which may perennate.

In median longitudinal sections or in crushed preparations of apices, it is apparent that the plant body is composed of a number of colorless, central, longitudinal filaments, the tips of which elongate through the activity of apical cells. From the central filaments, tufts of lateral photosynthetic filaments arise in dense whorls.

The axial and photosynthetic systems are both embedded in a rather firm colloidal material. The uninucleate photosynthetic cells are beadlike, each with a single starlike chloroplast in which a single pyrenoid is embedded. The function of the latter and its relation, if any, to Floridean starch have not yet been ascertained.

The apices of the photosynthetic filaments may terminate in hairlike cells. The reproductive organs of *Nemalion* and those of most Rhodophycophyta are unlike those of other algae. In some respects, however, they resemble those of certain ascomycetous and basidiomy-cetous fungi. *Nemalion* is monoecious.

The female reproductive organ, here called the *carpogonium*, is an oogonium with a more or less well-developed protuberance, the *trichogyne* (Gr. *thrix,* hair, + Gr. *gyne,* female). The carpogonia are borne on almost colorless lateral branches, which arise near the center of a tuft of photosynthetic filaments.

Other branches on the same plant, by successive divisions,

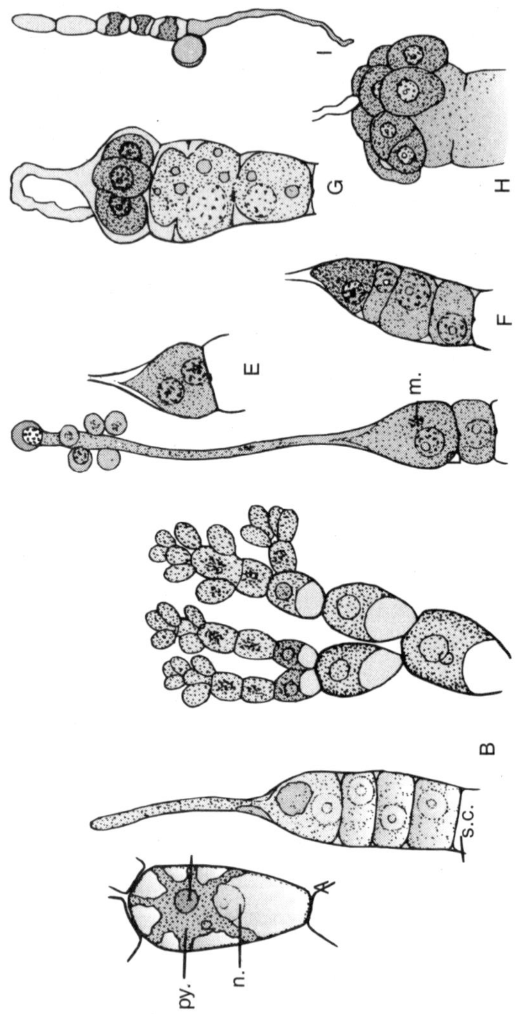

Figure 20.1: Nemalion helminthoides. A. Organization of a cell of photosynthetic filament. B. Mature carpogonial branch; note rudimentary plastid in carpogonium. C. Branch with spermatangia. D. Fertilization. E. End of first division in zygote. F. Completion of first cytokinesis of zygote. G, H. Early stages in development of carposporangia. I. Germinating carpospore. A-C. Living; the remainder from acetocarmine preparations. m., spermatial nucleus; n., nucleus; p., plastid; py., pyrenoid; s.c., supporting cell.

produce male sex organs, the *spermatangia*, which are analogous to the unicellular antheridia of other algae. Each spermatangium produces a single *spermatium*, a male gamete, which is discharged at maturity.

The spermatia, which are produced and liberated in large numbers, are transported by water currents; they may be slightly amoeboid. When a spermatium makes contact with the trichogyne, its nucleus divides. The walls then dissolve at the point of contact, and one of the spermatial nuclei enters the trichogyne, migrating to the base of the carpogonium, where union of a spermatial nucleus with the carpogonial nucleus ensues.

Union of the sperm and egg in oogamous reproduction is called *fertilization.* Soon after fertilization, the trichogyne withers. A series of mitoses and cell divisions follow, which result in the production of a tuft of short filaments, the cells of which become naked *carpospores.* Until recently it was agreed that the life cycle in *Nemalion* is of the H, h type with zygotic meiosis. However, the parpospores of *N. helminthoides,* upon germinating in laboratory culture, give rise to branching filaments, putatively the *tetrasporophyte,* which so far have not developed into characteristic *Nemalion* plants.

It has been reported that the carpospores of *N. helminthoides* are diploid, so that meiosis probably is not zygotic. In a Japanese species, *N. vermiculare,* it has been demonstrated that the carpospores germinate into uniseriate, microscopic filaments, which produce *tetrasporangia,* each of which produces four *tetraspores.*

These are released and germinate to form prostrate, branching filaments from which the typical, multiaxial erect branches of *Nemalion* arise. The tetraspore-bearing phase of red algae is called the *tetraspor-ophyte.* The tetrasporophyte of *Nemalion* may duplicate itself through the agency of monospores.

The life cycle of *Nemalion,* accordingly, is diplobiontic and

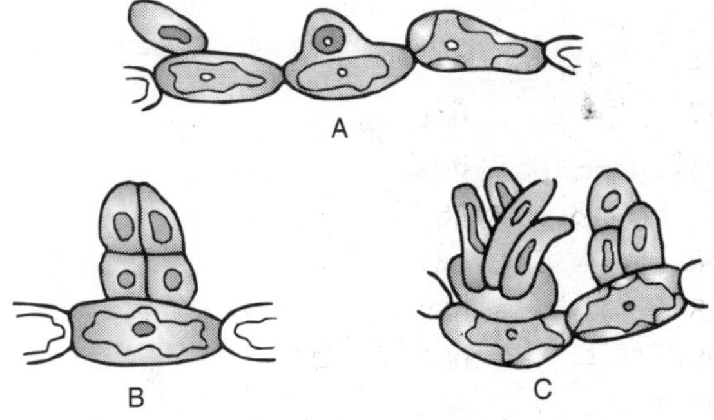

Figure 20.2: Nemalion vermiculare. A. Portion of filament. B. Tetrasporangium. C. Tetraspores germinating in situ.

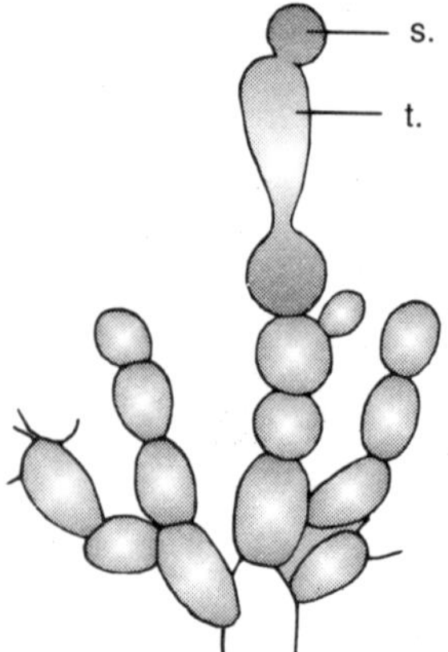

Figure 20.3: Batrachospermum sp. Outline drawing of carpogonial branch at fertilization. s., spermatium; t., trichogyne.

heteromorphic, inasmuch as the large *Nemalion* plants (gametophytes) alternate with minute, filamentous tetrasporophytes. Although meiosis may be presumed to occur in the tetrasporangia, as it does in many other red algae, it remains to be demonstrated in *Nemalion.*

Batrachospermum

Batrachospermum, a freshwater red alga, differs from *Nemalion* in vegetative structure. Instead of the numerous axial filaments and apical cells of the latter, *Batrachospermum* develops from a single apical cell; derivatives of the latter form an axial filament and tufts of photosynthetic filaments that are loosely verticilate and embedded in slime. Plants of *Batrachospermum* may be blue-green or deep wine red, depending on the ratios between phycocyanin and phycoerythrin. The carpogonial branches of *Batrachospermum* occur near the base of photosynthetic filaments.

The spermatia are larger than those of *Nemalion.* Huge masses of carpospores develop after fertilization. These germinate, developing into prostrate branching filaments, which, in turn, produce the erect plants. The complete life cycle and site of meiosis in *Batrachosp-ermum* have not yet been elucidated.

Callithamnion

Alternation of generations in *Bangia, Porphyra,* and *Nemalion*

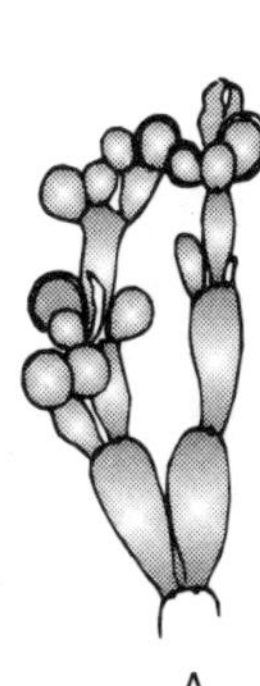

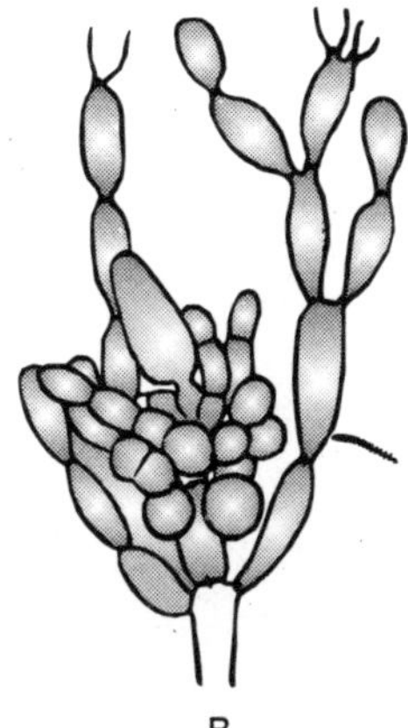

Figure 20.4: Batrachospermum A. B. moniliforme, branch with spermatangia. B. B. anatinum, early stages in development of the carpospores.

is diplobiontic and heteromorphic. By contrast, isomorphic diplobiontic life cycles occur in a majority of Florideophycidae, here exemplified by *Callithamnion, Griffithsia,* and *Polysiphonia.*

Callithamnion (Gr. *kallos,* beauty, + Gr. *thamnion,* little shrub) is widespread in marine waters and often grows epiphytically on other, larger algae. The plants consist of delicate, branching filaments with pronounced apical growth. The cells are multinucleate at maturity and contain numerous lenticular plastids.

As populations of *Callithamnion* mature in the field or in laboratory cultures, male and female sexual plants and morphologically similar tetrasporophytes develop. The tetraspores germinate into equal numbers of male and female gametophytes, which at maturity produce spermatangia and carpogonia on separate individuals.

The spermatangia develop near the distal terminal walls of the branch cells, and the carpogonia arise at a corresponding location on the main axes of the female gametophytes; the carpogonia are readily recognizable because of their extremely elongate trichogynes.

In cultures containing male and female plants, fertilization, development of the carposporophyte, and release of carpospores

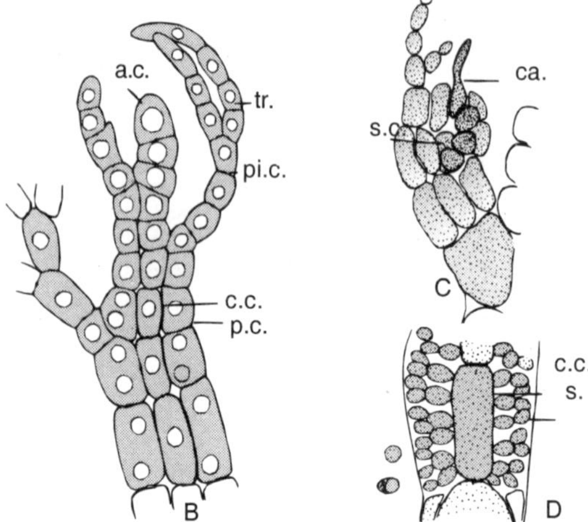

Figure 20.5: Polysiphonia. A. Habit of growth of a vegetative plant. B-D. P. harveyi. B. Apex, showing ontogeny. C. Carpogonial branch (densely stippled). D. Median longisection of spermatangial branch. a.c., apical cell; ca., carpogonium; c.c., central or axial cell; p.c., pericentral cell; pi.c., pit connection; s., spermatangium; s.c., supporting cell; tr., trichoblast.

require 5 days. The carpospores develop into tetrasporophytes; in the tetraspor-angia of the latter meiosis is inferred to occur on the basis of the segregation and tetraspores into male- or female-producing types. The entire life cycle in laboratory culture requires one month for completion.

Polysiphonia

Polysiphonia (Gr. *polys,* many, + Gr. *siphon,* tube) is also widely distributed in marine waters, where it grows both epiphytically on larger algae and aquatic flowering plants and also on rocks and woodwork. The life cycle of *P. boldii* has been elucidated in laboratory cultures from tetraspore to tetraspore.

Polysiphonia is a branching filamentous plant. Growth is strictly apical, and the derivatives of the apical cell segment in a regular pattern, thus forming the multiseriate axis, which in some species achieves considerable complexity through superficial cortication.

Pit connections are clearly visible between contiguous cells of *Polysiphonia,* and delicate, hairlike branches, the *trichoblasts,* may be present in some species. *Polysiphonia* is diplobiontic in life cycle.

The gametophytes are dioecious, spermatia and carpogonia being produced on different individuals. The sex organs arise from derivatives of the apical cell near the tips of the branches.

The curved carpogonial branch of *Polysiphonia* at fertilization consists of four almost colorless cells, the most distal one of which develops a trichogyne. This branch arises from a pericentral cell known as the *supporting cell.*

Certain cells at the base and above the carpogonial branch grow up around it, forming an urn-shaped envelope, the *pericarp* (Gr. per!, around, + Gr. *karpon,* fruit). The spermatangia and spermatia are borne on lateral branches, the pericentral cells of which produce spermatangial mother cells, which give rise to large numbers of colorless spermatangia that are abscised and function directly as spermatias.

As in all Rhodophycophyta, the spermatia are borne passively in the trichogyne by water currents. After attachment of spermatia to the trichogyne, their contents flow into the latter. The spermatial nucleus migrates down through the trichogyne and ultimately unites with the carpogonial nucleus, as in *Nemalion.*

Postfertilization development is rather complicated in detail.

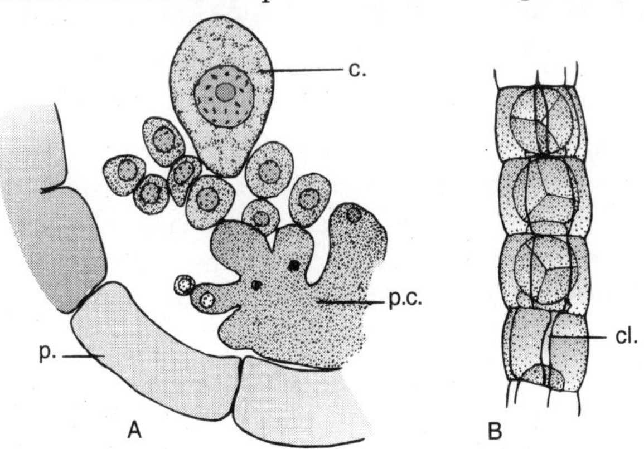

Figure 20.6: Polysiphonia harveyi. A. Portion of cystocarp with placental cell and developing carposporangia. B. Portion of tetrasporic plant. c., carposporangium; cl., cleft through which tetraspores were liberated; p., pericarp cell; p.c., placental cell.

It involves extensive cell fusions, degeneration of the carpogonial branch, and migration of the zygote nucleus into an *auxiliary cell*, which arises after fertilization.

Mitotic divisions of the zygote nucleus give rise to a number of diploid nuclei, which are present in a large fusion cell, the *placental cell*. Carpospores, each with a diploid nucleus, are abstricted from this cell and develop in a series. The mature carpospores are liberated through the terminal opening of the urnlike pericarp and germinate into diploid plants under suitable conditions.

The carpospores surrounded by the pericarp are called the *cystocarp*. These plants, the tetrasporophytes, are similar in size and general appearance to the male and female gametophytes, but at maturity they produce tetrasporangia, which arise on short stalk cells.

Cytological investigation has demonstrated that the two successive nuclear divisions in the tetrasporangium accomplish meiosis, so the four spores produced are haploid. The tetrasporangial wall breaks open, and the tetraspores are shed through clefts between the pericentral cells.

It has been shown by culture methods that tetraspores develop into gametophytic plants. This rather complicated life cycle of *Polysiphonia* (and of *Callithamnion* and *Griffithsia)* is summarized elsewhere in this chapter.

Griffithsia

Griffithsia (after Mrs. Amelia Griffiths) is similar in life cycle to *Polysiphonia,* but its vegetative structure is simpler, because the branching filaments are composed of large cells that are not covered by pericentral cells or cortications. *Griffithsia globulifera,* an Atlantic coast species, appears during the summer, when the water temperature is relatively high.

The bushy growths are attached to stones and pilings in sublittoral habitats and are rosy pink in color. The multinucleate cells are very large, those near the base of the branches attaining a length as great as 5 mm. Growth is apical, from a multinucleate cell with dense cytoplasm and without a vacuole.

The apparently dichotomous branching develops because of

the upgrowth of the lateral surface of the cell below an apical cell to form a new growing point. In mature cells the cytoplasm is peripheral; it contains beautiful ribbonlike, segmented plastids, which are arranged in curved mosaics.

The attaching system of *Griffithsia is* weak and restricted, as evidenced by the frequency with which free-floating plants are encountered. Trichoblasts-colorless, branched, hairlike filaments-are present on the axes.

The life history of *Griffithsia* involves three types of free-living plants, as in *Polysiphonia* and *Callithamnion-namely,* male and female gametophytes and tetrasporophytes, the female plants bearing cystocarps at maturity.

The male plants are readily recognizable because of their caplike mantles of spermatangial filaments, which produce spermatia in enormous numbers and because cell size decreases from apex to base. The carpogonial branches arise from special three-celled, short, lateral branches, which originate on the free distal surface of vegetative cells.

The earliest stages in the development of these branches, and of the carpogonial branches they produce, occur near the growing point of each main axis. The supporting cell generates a four-celled carpogonial branch, which is recurved, as in *Polysiphonia.*

After fertilization, the supporting cell gives rise to the auxiliary cell, with which the fertilized carpogonium becomes united. The zygote nucleus passes from the carpogonium into the auxiliary cell, after which the carpogonial branch withers and is abscised. Further development involves extensive cell fusions and the ultimate formation of a placental cell, as well as generation of diploid nuclei within the auxiliary cell and the contiguous regions of the placental cell.

Later, the formation of carpospores is initiated. These are borne in groups. Meanwhile, soon after fertilization, the basal cell of the short lateral axis that bears the carpogonial branch gives rise to a number of curved, elongate, sausage-shaped pericarp cells that partially conceal the developing carpospores.

The latter are shed at maturity and then germinate. There is good evidence that the carpospores germinate into plantlets that

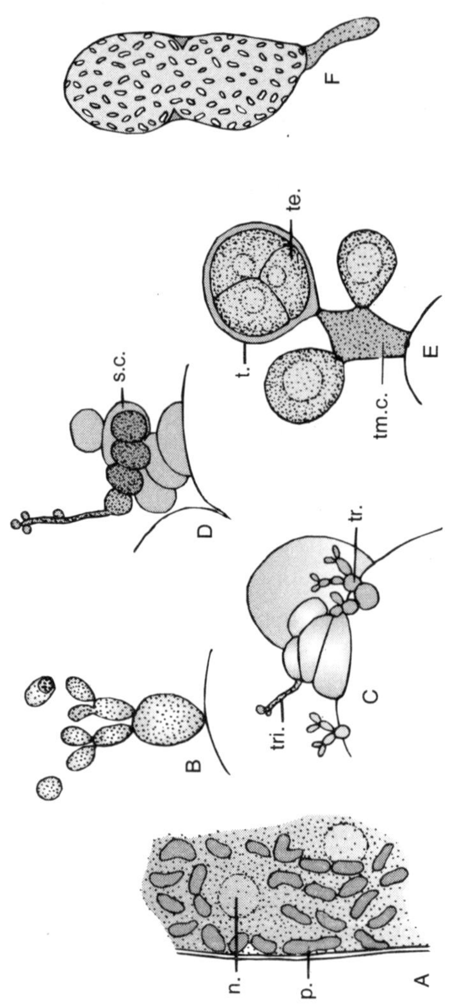

Figure 20.7: Griffithsia globulifera. A. Portion of living vegetative cell, surface view. B. Detail of single spermatangial branch. C, D. Details of reproductive branches and fertilization. E. Tetrasporangium mother cell with three tetrasporangia. F. Germinating carpospore. n., nucleus; p., plastid; s.c., supporting cell; t., tetrasporangium; te., tetraspore; t, m. c. , tetrasporangium mother cell; tr., trichoblast; tri., trichogyne with spermatia attached.

mature as tetrasporophytes. In these, the distal portions of vegetative cells bud off a circle of tetrasporangial mother cells, which give rise to three tetrasporangia each.

Meiosis occurs in these while they are small, and each tetraspora-ngium is finally divided into four tetraspores. When these have been liberated, they germinate, ultimately developing into male and female gametophytes. A circle of involucral cells surrounds each fertile, tetrasporangiumbearing mode.

The *Polysiphonia-Callithamnion-Griffithsia* type of life cycle is most similar to that observed among such Chlorophycophyta as *Cladophora* and in such Phaeophycophyta *as Ectocarpus (D, h* + d, p. 74). It differs, however, in one important respect: In *Polysiphonia, Callithamnion, Griffithsia,* and *Nemalion* there is intercalated between fertilization and the developing tetrasporophyte a series of cell generations consisting of the placental cell and the carpospores.

This phase has been interpreted by some as still a third alternating phase, The *carposporophyte.* According to this point of view, alternation in *Polysiphonia, Callithamnion, Griffithsia,* and *Nemalion* involves the haploid gametophytes, the diploid carposporophyte, and finally the diploid tetrasporophyte. There is no phase similar to the carposporophyte in groups of algae other than Rhodophycophyta, nor does it occur among the land plants; the moss sporophyte is somewhat analogous in its location.

The closest approach to it, perhaps, is found in the postfertilization development in certain ascomycetous fungi. It should be emphasized that interpolation of the diploid carposporophyte makes possible the development of many tetrasporophytes (rather than only one) as a result of a single act of fertilization and from one zygote.

C

c 298
C. cornutum, a 312
C. echinozygotum 201
C. eugametos 189, 191, 194
C. fragile 226
C. horridum, 312
C. moewusii 188, 189, 191
C. suhriana 216
Calliergon 233
Callithamnion 318, 322, 326
Callithamnion, Griffithsia, 322
Callithamnion-namely, 326
calyptra 236
Camptosorus; 250
Cankers 115
Carbon dioxide: 127
carotenoids 25
carpogonia 318
carpogonium 319
carpospores 320
carposporophyte 318, 327
Carteria 185, 194, 212, 216
Caulerpa 218, 225
cause 74
cell differentiation 50
cell division 50
Cell division and reproduction 67
cell enlargement 50
central nodule 303
centric diatoms 302
Ceratium 311
Chara 269
Chara, 270
Chara, Nitella, 273
Chara 270
chemical theory of fermentation 73
chemosynthesis 57
Chlamydomonas 156, 179, 185, 187, 188, 189, 190, 1 91, 192, 193, 194, 198, 201, 202, 212, 216, 217
Chlamydomonas moewusii 189
Chlamydomonas; 189
chlamys 185
Chlorella 180, 204, 207, 209
Chlorella is 204
Chlorococcum 201, 202, 203, 204, 209
Chlorococcum, 293
chlorophylls 25
Chlorophyta 182
chloroplasts 183
chloros 183, 201, 204
chloros + 183
chrysolaminarin 292
chrysos, 298
circinate vernation. 247
Cladonia 106
Cladophora 152, 211, 213, 215, 216, 218, 219, 224, 281, 327
Cladophora-namely, 277
cleaning 301
Climacium 229
clonal culture 191
Closterium 222, 223
Closterium and Cosmarium 223
Clostridium 84
Clostridium. 84
clumps 188

clusters 188
coagulates 41
Cocconeis placentula 306
codion 226
Codium 218, 226
Coelastrum 207, 211
coenocysts 203
coenocytes 181
coenocytic 216
coenos 181
colloids. 39
complete 104
complete leaf 15
compound 17
conceptacles 288
conche, 316
Conchocelis 316, 317, 318
Conchospores 317
conjugation 159
contractile vacuoles 184, 188
corona 273
Coscinodiscus 302, 308
Cosmarium 222, 223
costae 303
crown 273
cryptoblasts 287
cyclic. 18
cystocarp 325
cystocarp. 176
cytoplasm 37

D

d 313
D. borgei. 301
D. neglecta 225
danica 300
deciduous. 29
denitrification. 81, 84
denitrifying bacteria, 79
denitrifying bacteria. 81
Derbesia 212, 225
desmid 222
desmos 222
Destruction of Bacteria by Viruses 67
desulfofication. 85
diatomaceous earth 301
dichotomous venation 247, 17
Dicranum 229
dictyon 207
Dictyota 283, 284
Dictyota and Padina 283
Dictyota. 285
dinein, 310, 311
Dinobryon 299, 300
dinoflagellates 310
dins, 299
dioecious 193
diplobiontic 216
diploid 190
diploos 216
discus, 302
Diversity among the Non-green Plants 56
downy mildews 98
dwarf branches. 16
dwarf males 160

E

E. arvense, 262
E. siliculosus 277, 279
E. viridis 207
Ectocarp 281
Ectocarpene 279
Ectocarpus 171, 277, 279
Ectocarpus-like 280

Ectocarpus 171, 280
egg 160
elaters may 243
energy 150
Entermorpha 179
Enteromorpha 179
entirely 266
Entomoph-thorales, 98
Ephedra 269
epi, 302
epidermis, 50
epiphytes, 54
epitheca 302
Equisetum kansanum 261
Equisetum. 261
eremos 207
Eremosphaera 184, 207, 209
erotactin 213
Eudorina 198
Euglena 148, 263, 265, 266, 267
Euglena, 148, 265
Euglena (E. gracilis) 267
Euglena is 265
evergreen 29
eyespot 187

F

F. distichus 289
F. distichus, 286, 288
F. spiralis 288
F. vesiculosus 288
facultative species. 52
fairy rings 100
fascicles, 16
ferns 4
fertilization 196, 320
filaments 180
first thread 233
flagella 66
flagellar swelling 265
flagellum) 66
Floridean starch 314
flowers 9
forked 17
Fritschiella 211, 215
Fritschiella tuberosa 214
fruits 9
frustules 301
fucoxanthin 275
Fucus 173, 179, 285, 287, 297
Fucus, 288
Fucus (L. fucus, 285
fully formed 71
Funaria 229
fungi 4, 87
Fungi Imperfecti 107
fungus 88

G

gametangia 177
gametes 177
gametes. 159
gamos 189, 191, 192
gel. 41
genera 22
genera-Tribonema, 292
genus 22
girdle bands 302
glene 263
globule 270
Gonium 198
Gonyaulax 310
Gonyaulax catenella 310
Griffithsia 318, 326

Griffithsia globulifera, 326
Griffithsia is 326
Griffithsia) 326
grows. 45
Gymnodinium 310, 311
Gymnodinium, 311
gymnos, 311
Gymnostomum, 232
gynandrospory 213
gyne, 319
gyros 219

H

halophila, 306
haplobiontic 216
haploid 190
haploos 216
Hepaticae 233
herpo 225
heteromorphic 219, 281
heterosporous 254
heterothallic 191
heterothallism 193
heterotrichous 214
holdfast 211, 280
homosporous 254
homothallic 193
hornworts, 243
host. 53
Hyalotrachelomonas, 267
hydor 207
Hydrodictyon 207, 209, 211
Hydrodictyon reticulatum 207
hypha 88
hyphae 88
hypo, 302
hypocotyl 8
hypotheca 302

I

idioandrospory 213
idion, 315
immunity 69
in situ 281
indusium 250
infection. 69
intercalary 280
is alba; 22
is Quercus alba. All 22
Isoetes 260
Isoetes. 260
isogamous 191
isomorphic 219
isos 191
isthmus 222

K

kallos 322
karpon, 324
kaulos 225
kele, 316
keration, 311
key 21
Khawkinea 267, 268
klados 215
kloster 222
kokkos 201
kollos 211
koskinon, 302, 308
kosmos 222
Kram.eria, 55
kystis, 283

L

L. acetabulum 226
L. ca put, 272

L. clonium 213
L. discus 308
L. ella 204
L. manus, 272
L. Ova 223
L. saccharina 281
L. stigens 213
L. volvere 194
lactuca 224
Laminaria
173, 219, 280, 281, 282, 283
Laminaria, 173
LaminariaLaminaria 279
laminarin 275
leaf scar. 53
Leaf scars, 21
Leaf spots 115
Leeuwenhoek and his Microscopes 72
Lemanea. 176
leucosin 292
lichens 4, 106
lichens. 146
Light: 127, 128
limited to certain fundamental features. 5
loose smut of wheat 102
lorica 267
Lycopodium 255, 257
Lycopodium. 258
lysis.Do bacteria cause disease? 67

M

macrandrous 213
Macrocystis 282, 283
Macrocystis, Pelagophycus, Nereocystis, 283
makros, 282
malhamensis, 300
manubrium 272
Marchantia 242
margins. 18
Marsilia 254
medium. 62
meiosis 190
melos, 302
Melosira 302, 307, 308
Melosira, Coscinodiscus, Arachnodiscus, Stictod 309
mesophyll. 52
metaboly 265
Micrasteri 222
Micrasterias 222
Micromonas pusilla 180
Microspectrophotometric 227
midrib. 16
mildews 87
Mnium, 229
mold 4
moms 185, 263
monas, 299
monoecious 193
monosporangia 316
monospores 316
morphologically 193
mosses 4
Mougeotia 162
Musci 233
Mycelia 115
mycelium 88
mycorhizal fungi. 56

N

N. helminthoides 321

N. helminthoides, 321
N. vermiculare 321
Names of Plastids Characteristic Contents 43
nannandrous Oedogonium 213
Navicula 303
Navicula, 303
Navicula (L. navicula, 302
Navicula pelliculosa) 302
nema 219
nema, 293, 319
Nemalion 176, 314, 318, 319, 321, 322, 327, 328
Nemalion, 175, 176, 314, 321
Nemalion helminthoides 319
Nemalion. 176, 314, 322, 325
Nereocystis 283
Nereocystis, 283
Nereus, 283
Neurospora 107
Nitella 183, 269, 270, 273
Nitella (L. nitella, 269
Nitella; 270
nitrification. 84
nitrifying bacteria, 79
Nitrobacter 81
nitrogen bacteria, 79
nitrogen cycle 84
nitrogen-fixation. 82, 84
nitrogen-fixing bacteria. 79
Nitrosococcus; 80
Nitrosomonas 80
nodules 82

O

O. chromonas 300
O. chromonas, O. danica 300
O. danica 300
O. malhamensis 300
obligate parasites. 52
obligate saprophytes. 52
Ochromonas 299
ochros, 299
Oedogonium 160, 179, 211, 212, 213, 215, 225
Oedogoniuni, 253
Onoclea. 251
oogamy 192
oogonia, 95, 160
oogonium 160, 213, 273
operculum, 236
Ophioglossum 251
Ophioglossum, 250
Ophioglossum) 251
opposite 18
opsis, 293
Osmunda, 250
Other Common Filamentous Genera 162
oulos 211
oura, 299
Ova 224
Overgrowths 115
Oxygen: 127, 128

P

P. boldii 323
P. chrysogenum 96
P. gardneri, 318
P. leucosticta 317
P. miniata 318
P. morum 195
P. purpureaviolacea 318
Padina 283

shells 301
shield cells 272
silicolemma 302
siliculosus. 279
sinus 222
siphon 323
smuts 87
smuts, 101
Soil: 127, 128
solutions 39
sori 250, 280
sorus). 250
species 14, 22
species. 22
speira 219
sperm 192
sperma, 313
spermagonia, 103
spermatangia 319
spermatium 319
spermatium. 103
sperms, 160
Sphagnales 238, 239
Sphagnum 233
Sphagnum, 241
sphaira 207
spines. 15
spirally 18
Spirogyra 179, 219, 220, 221, 222
Spirogyra, 162
Spirogyra majuscula 221
Spirogyra. 273
spongy mesophyll, 50
spora, 306
sporangia 177
sporangia, 92
spore. 68
sporophylls; 250
stem rust 102
stems 8
Stephanopyxis 308
Stephanopyxis palnwniana, 308
stephanos, 308
Stictodiscus 302, 308
Stigeclonium 214
Stigeoclonium 211, 213, 214, 215
Stigeoclonium. 277
stigma 187
stiktos, 308
stinking smut of wheat, 101
stipe 280
stipules. 15
stoneworts 268
Streptococcus 63
Subclass 1. Bangiophycidae 315
sulfofication, 85
sulfur bacteria 85
supporting cell 324
susceptible 70
symbiotic. 83
syn, 299
Synura 299, 300

T

taxes; 201
teliospores 103
Temperature: 127, 128
tendrils, 15
terminal conjugation 222
Tetracystis 198, 200, 201, 202, 203
Tetraphis, 237
tetrasporangia 321

tetraspores 321
tetrasporophyte 315, 321
thalli 242
thallus) 242
thamnion 322
The cell as a whole 44
The medium: 127
theke, 302
theke). 302
thermocline. 133
thrix 211
thrix, 319
thylakoids 183
tissues 47
toxins. 69
Trachelomonas 263, 267
trachelos 263
tribein, 293
Tribonema 293, 294
Tribonema is 293
Tribonema. 294
trichoblasts 324
trichogyne 319
trumpet hyphae 280
tube cells 273
turris 308

U

U. lactuca 223, 224
Ulothrix 156, 160, 211, 212, 214, 215, 217, 223, 294
Ulothrix is 156
Ulothrix. 160
Ulva 223
unilocular zoosporangia 277
unisexual; 257
uredospores 103
urn 236

V

V olvox 156
V. aureus 195, 196
V. carteri 196
V. globator 196
V. rousseletii 196
vacuole 37
valves 302
Vaucheria 163, 296, 297
Vaucheria. 152
venation. 16
viruses, 67
Volvox 194, 195, 196, 198

W

water blooms 180
whorled 18
Wilts 115
woody perennials; 31

X

xanthos 291

Y

Yellowing or chlorosis 115

Z

zoosporangia 297
zoosporangium 201
zoospores 198
Zygnema 162, 219, 221
zygon 189
zygote 161
zygote 95